1 MONTH OF
FREE
READING

at

www.ForgottenBooks.com

By purchasing this book you are eligible for one month membership to ForgottenBooks.com, giving you unlimited access to our entire collection of over 1,000,000 titles via our web site and mobile apps.

To claim your free month visit:

www.forgottenbooks.com/free519650

ISBN 978-0-265-41234-3
PIBN 10519650

INLAND MASSACHUSETTS

ILLUSTRATED.

A CONCISE RÉSUMÉ OF THE

NATURAL FEATURES AND PAST HISTORY

52

OF

WORCESTER, BRISTOL AND NORFOLK,

AND ADJACENT COUNTIES,

THEIR TOWNS, VILLAGES, AND CITIES,

TOGETHER WITH A CONDENSED SUMMARY OF

THEIR INDUSTRIAL ADVANTAGES and DEVELOPMENT,

AND A

COMPREHENSIVE SERIES OF SKETCHES

DESCRIPTIVE OF

REPRESENTATIVE BUSINESS HOUSES,

TO WHICH IS PREFIXED

A SHORT CHAPTER ON THE COMMONWEALTH AT LARGE.

WORCESTER, MASS.:

THE ELSTNER PUBLISHING COMPANY.

1891.

SOLDIER'S MONUMENT, WORCESTER.

PREFACE.

SOME keen observer has said that "brevity is the soul of wit." A fitting emendation may be formulated in the words, condensation is the grand secret of conveying instruction. Diffusiveness too often defeats its own object. Prolixity may be justifiable in the case of those annalists who have at their command unlimited time and space in which to review and particularize unimportant facts—a condition which does not apply to the compiler of such a work as this, necessarily confined to generalization, the crowding of great events into a line and the history of centuries into a paragraph.

The labor of preparing for the press the present little volume has been much greater than is apparent upon the surface, and consisted not so much in the actual amount of writing done as in the comparison of authorities, the securing of data, and the winnowing of the chaff from the grain. This task has been conscientiously performed, and the narrative part of INLAND MASSACHUSETTS ILLUSTRATED will be found clear and concise, suited to popular reading and to the purpose in view—that of describing in the fewest possible words the country, the villages and cities, the public institutions, the industries and attractions presented to those who seek advantageous opportunities for the investment of capital in productive enterprises as well as the topographical and climatic beauties sought by the tourist for pleasure or instruction. Incidentally our pages bear witness to the energy and indomitable public spirit of a people who have by sheer force of genius and hard work made this portion of Massachusetts the fairest and in some respects the most prosperous region of New England.

We have spared no exertion to render our work complete and acceptable. If any individual or community has been slighted, the blame rests not with us.

In conclusion, we desire to return thanks for the encouragement and patronage extended us by many prominent gentlemen, firms, and companies, a few of whom may be mentioned, viz : The Washburn & Moen Manufacturing Company, the Knowles Loom Works, the Crompton Loom Works, the Worcester National Bank, the State Safe Deposit Company, and the State Mutual Life Assurance Company of Worcester; Isaac Prouty & Co., of Spencer; the Fitchburg Steam Engine Company and others of Fitchburg; the Bigelow Carpet Company of Clinton; Geo. Draper & Sons of Hopedale; J. G. and J. P. Ray of Franklin; Reed & Barton, and P. H. Carr of Taunton; Kilburn, Lincoln & Co., the Osborn Mills and others of Fall River, and the enterprising jewelry manufacturers of the Attleboroughs.

WORCESTER ARMORY BUILDING.

CONTENTS.

MASSACHUSETTS	7–16
WORCESTER COUNTY	17–19
THE TOWN OF WORCESTER	20–24
WORCESTER AS A CITY	24–33
THE PRESS	33–35
WORCESTER REPRESENTATIVE HOUSES	36–116
SPENCER	117–120–168
FITCHBURG	121–136
CLINTON	137–139
MILFORD	139–144
HOPEDALE	144–147
WINCHENDON	147–152
LEOMINSTER	152–154
WESTBOROUGH	154–155
MILLBURY	155–156
OAKHAM	156–157
WEBSTER	157–158
ATHOL	158–159
EAST BROOKFIELD	200
NORFOLK COUNTY	160
FRANKLIN	160–165
FOXBOROUGH	165–166
WRENTHAM	166–167
MEDWAY	167–168
PLAINVILLE	227
BRISTOL COUNTY	169
FALL RIVER	169–179
TAUNTON	179–198
DIGHTON	198–200
ATTLEBOROUGH	201–212
NORTH ATTLEBOROUGH	212–221
ATTLEBOROUGH FALLS	221–225
MANSFIELD	226
INDEX	230

WORCESTER LUNATIC HOSPITAL.

MASSACHUSETTS.

THE STATE AT LARGE—TOPOGRAPHY AND CLIMATE—A BRIEF HISTORICAL SYNOPSIS.

THE eastern coast line of Massachusetts is about 300 miles in length, one-half of which belongs to Cape Cod; but the actual breadth of the State from the southeast to the northeast corners in a direct line is only ninety-five miles. Extending forty miles almost due northwest from near the entrance to Buzzard's bay to the vicinity of Shepardsville in Norfolk county runs the boundary line of Rhode Island, extending thence due west twenty-one miles to the Connecticut line near East Thompson. From thence eighty-seven miles to the town of Mount Washington, Berkshire county, Connecticut forms the southern boundary. Thence the line extends forty-seven miles a little east of north along the eastern boundary of New York to the Vermont State line, which it follows in a direction slightly south of east to the Connecticut river and the boundary of New Hampshire, forty miles. For sixty miles further, to within three miles of the Merrimac river, it follows the same general course, thence running in an irregular northeasterly course to the sea at the southeast corner of New Hampshire. The average width of the State west of a line drawn through the towns of Wrentham in Norfolk and Dracut in Essex is forty-seven and a half miles, while the distance from Rhode Island along the line of Norfolk on the north and Plymouth and Bristol counties on the south to the sea is thirty-five or forty miles—the State having somewhat the shape of a boot, Cape Cod and the island counties of Dukes and Nantucket forming the broken and dilapidated toe, Bristol and Plymouth the instep, Norfolk and Middlesex the ankle, Essex the heel, and Worcester, Hampden, Hampshire, Franklin, and Berkshire the leg.

The soil of Massachusetts is not as a general thing fertile, though in some portions of the State excellent crops of maize, rye, potatoes, and market vegetables are produced. The surface is more or less hilly and rocky everywhere, save along the water courses, and in the west the elevations approach the dignity of mountains, the loftiest eminence being Greylock mountain in northern Berkshire, the top of which is more than 3,500 feet above the sea. The rough country west of the Connecticut river is a continuation of the Green and White mountains. Among their most prominent features are Mounts Tom, Holyoke, and Nonotuck, in the vicinity of Holyoke, and the Berkshire hills, the latter bordering the Hudson river valley on the east and forming the connecting link between the Green mountains and the Catskills. Wachusett mountain in Worcester county, an outlying sentinel of the White mountains, rises to a height of 2,018 feet. The hills to the eastward diminish in magnitude as we approach the coast, and though numerous are of small consequence except in the case of the Blue hills of Norfolk and the country near Cape Ann in Essex. Much of the land of Middlesex, Essex, and Norfolk, and nearly all of Bristol, Plymouth, Barnstable, Dukes, and Nantucket counties, and Martha's Vineyard are quite level, sandy, and sterile, as are the Elizabeth islands.

The coast abounds with inlets, harbors, and bays, alternating with rocky headlands. Massachusetts bay (from which is taken the *soubriquet* "Old Bay State") embraces Cape Cod bay—lying between the mainland and Cape Cod—and covers nearly the whole eastern front. Boston harbor, deep and commodious, is one of the safest on the Atlantic coast, sheltered as it is by promontories and islands. Of the other capacious and desirable harbors the most prominent and famous are those of Gloucester, Salem, Marblehead, Lynn, Plymouth, Barnstable, and Provincetown. Cape Cod—the "great right arm of Massachusetts"—bears in outline a striking resemblance to that member of the human body with bent elbow and clenched hand. It is forty miles from shoulder (where it joins the mainland) to elbow, eastward, and thirty miles northward to Race Point light at the extremity. The Elizabeth islands, sixteen in number, comprise a chain about eighteen miles in length lying between Buzzard's bay and Vineyard sound, and are known as the town of Gosnold, Barnstable county. To the east, across the sound and distant five or six miles, is Martha's Vineyard (Dukes county), and ten miles east of that is Nantucket island and county, containing fifty square miles of land (or sand) and possessed of a fine harbor—Holmes' Hole. Monomoy island is a mere sand-spit just off Cape Cod elbow. Buzzard's bay, thirty miles long and of an average width of ten miles, lies between the counties of Bristol and Plymouth on the north and Barnstable and the Elizabeth islands on the south. The famous old whaling port of New Bedford and its fine harbor are situated on the northern shore in the county of Bristol.

The Connecticut, taking its rise in northern New Hampshire, enters Massachusetts forty miles east of the New York State line, forming at that point the boundary between New Hampshire and Vermont, and runs nearly due south through Franklin, Hampshire, and Hampden counties, crossing the State line into Connecticut about five miles south of Springfield. This noble stream, emptying into Long Island sound, is more than 400 miles in length, is navigable for small craft to Holyoke, and is the largest and most important river that enters the State. The scenery along its course is celebrated for variety, beauty, and grandeur, and immense dams for the utilization of the water power exist at numerous points. Those at Turner's Falls and Holyoke are the most extensive, and are described at length in the chapters devoted to the industries of those flourishing manufacturing centers. The average fall of the river in this State is about two and a half feet to the mile. This river and its Massachusetts affluents—the Deerfield, Miller's, Chicopee, and Westfield rivers —all abound with favorable mill-sites, which are gradually being utilized, though there is yet plenty of room for new-comers. Franklin, Hampshire, Hampden, and portions of Worcester and Berkshire counties are drained by the Connecticut and its tributaries. The Merrimac comes next to the Connecticut in point of volume ; is 110 miles in length, forty of which are in Massachusetts, and furnishes vast power. It drains portions of Worcester and Middlesex counties, receives the flow of the Concord and Nashua rivers, and drives the busy mill-wheels of Lowell and

Lawrence. The Watuppa ponds furnish power for the Fall River mills. The Taunton empties into Narragansett bay. The Ipswich rises in Essex county, the Mystic in Middlesex, the Charles in Middlesex and Norfolk counties, and all flow into Massachusetts bay. The Blackstone and Quinnebaug drain portions of Worcester and Hampden counties, and by the exercise of engineering skill and the construction of reservoirs have been made extremely valuable for manufacturing purposes. Lake Chaubunagungamauy, a natural lake improved by man, is noted for its extent, its value as a reservoir, its beautiful scenery, and its name, which, it is popularly believed, has never been pronounced since the last of the Pequots, disgusted with the white man's soap and whisky,

"Folded his tent like the Arab, and silently stole away."

The Housatonic and the Hoosick, wild, rapid, and lined with valuable sites for mills, drain portions of Berkshire county, and the Ware, rising near Rutland, Vt., is dammed at various points and put to use at Ware and elsewhere.

The district of Maine was erected into a State in 1820. Since then the territory of Massachusetts comprises about 7,800 square miles, divided into fourteen counties, which contain about 340 towns and cities.

THE CLIMATE.

The climate of Massachusetts, says Lorin Blodgett, the eminent climatologist, may be generally described as one representing very nearly the average of temperate latitudes on this hemisphere, though more severe than the average of temperate latitudes in Europe—a difference due to the fact that a portion on the eastern side of the continent is greatly modified by the circulation of the atmosphere across the land surface in its general movement eastward, thus increasing its heat in summer and its cold in winter, while the same circulation, moderated by its passage over the sea, brings to the west of Europe much milder and more uniform temperatures. The New England climate, called severe, partakes of the character of that of continental rather than of maritime Europe. As compared with the southern and western states it is severe, and still more so in contrast with the west and south of Europe. . . . This comparatively extreme and severe climate is, however, highly favorable to mental and physical activity. In all the results of energy and industry, which make the State a model in development and eminent above almost any other in wealth, prosperity, and intelligence, the influence of climate must be recognized as leading and decisive. Locally there are marked modifications of this general character, as on the southeastern coast and islands, the Gulf stream coming near enough to be felt quite sensibly, in addition to the general modifications caused by the apparent extension of these districts into the sea. Though violent storms are not uncommon off Cape Cod and the circuit southward to Nantucket, the temperature is still so much modified as to register for the mean of the winter months 7° warmer at Nantucket than at Cambridge, and nearly 5° warmer at New Bedford. Williamstown, in the northwest corner of Berkshire county, is 10° colder than Nantucket, and 7° colder than New Bedford, in winter, though the difference in summer is hardly perceptible, the mean for the whole State being from 68 to 70°. In the elevated parts of Berkshire, Franklin, and Hampshire counties the winters are quite severe and the spring and summer often late and cold; even Williamstown, at an elevation of 900 feet above the sea, has a mean winter average of 23°, while at Princeton in Worcester county, 1,150 feet above, it falls to 22°; but the valleys and level country at a distance from the mountains enjoy a temperature that seldom falls below 25° in winter and ranges from 67 to 70° in summer. Taking the whole State together the range of temperature is very great for any single day, the minimum being 20° below in the northwest and 10° below at New Bedford, while in summer it may rise to 90° on the mountains, 98° in the valleys, and in some localities to 100°, though the atmosphere is much more dry, and consequently more healthful, than further south. As regards rain, snow, and atmospheric moisture, the general character of the climate is similar to its temperature—variable and extreme in some details, while the average is that of the best part of the temperate latitudes, the annual humidity, including rain and melted snow, varying from 39 inches at Nantucket to 45 inches in the hill country near Worcester, the profuse summer showers inland sensibly decreasing from the sea exposure along the coast. The same conditions obtain in winter, the rainfall averaging 41 inches at New Bedford, 34 to 40 inches in the western counties, and 46 inches at Worcester. There is no rainy or dry season, properly so called, and the rainfall is pretty evenly distributed among the seasons. The snowfall averages 60 inches in the mountains of the western and central divisions, 50 inches in the valleys, and 30 inches in the eastern and southeastern counties. There are occasional snows of two feet in the central portion of the State, decreasing in depth nearer the coast and turned to rain or sleet by the warmer easterly winds. Fogs and continuous light rains are common all along the New England coast, and there is an almost constant precipitation of moisture, caused by easterly winds, apparently return currents from the northeast supplying the exhaustion of the lower stratum resulting from storms on the continent. Northeast winds are the bane of the New England climate in spring and late autumn. The weather in summer and fall is usually fine and sometimes peculiarly beautiful, with a pure, elastic atmosphere, singularly cool, comparatively dry and healthful, and more than compensates for the cold of winter and the northeast storms of early spring and advanced fall.

GEOLOGICAL AND MINERALOGICAL.

Nothing short of an extended scientific paper, for which we have not space, would give an adequate idea of the geological and mineral wealth of Massachusetts, the development of which is still in its infancy. Of building and decorative stones there is no lack—granite, porphyry, marbles, limestone, sandstone, syenite, slate, mica, etc.—while numerous deposits of the finest emery and corundum have been found. The coal measures of Plymouth and Bristol counties, extending into Rhode Island, cover about 750 square miles, but have never been fully developed for the reason that the coal, an extremely hard anthracite, is unsuited to the generation of steam and domestic use, though it is employed to some extent in the smelting of iron, which is found in considerable quantities at various places. The hematite ore-beds of Berkshire county are famous.

HISTORICAL SUMMARY.

The historic annals of Massachusetts and New England really begin with the arrival of the Mayflower in Cape Cod bay November 11, 1620, with one hundred and two Puritan pilgrims on board. These people, dissenters from the state church of England, persecuted for opinion's sake, retired first to Amsterdam and later to Leyden, Holland, in 1607-8, where they enjoyed unrestricted liberty of conscience for some years; but becoming dissatisfied with their surroundings, secured from the Virginia Company of England a charter authorizing them to settle upon the northern part of the company's American possessions. Peculiar to themselves, they had clung together as a congregation in Holland, and it was determined upon due consideration that a part only should cross the ocean at first and thus prepare the way for the remainder. Arrived in England, two small vessels were bought or chartered, but one proved unseaworthy, and only the Mayflower with her complement of passengers stretched away upon what proved a tedious and stormy voyage across an unknown sea upon the grandest mission in which men ever embarked—a mission of which they themselves had no conception—the founding in the New World of the greatest and strongest and freest nation men ever saw. They builded better than they knew or designed, for in declaring the object of the voyage they simply said they "thought they might on these shores more glorify God, do more good to their country, better provide for their posterity, and live to be better refreshed by their labors than ever they could do in Holland." Their original destination was some point not far from the present site of New York, but for reasons not necessary to particularize they decided to attempt a settlement where they first landed and which they subsequently named Plymouth, now a coast village of Plymouth harbor in the town and county of Plymouth, distant about thirty-five miles south by east in a direct line from Boston. In view of the fact that there was neither law nor government in the country, on the day they cast anchor these stern men met in the cabin of the Mayflower and signed the first compact ever drawn up between civilized men on this continent, and which may be fairly pronounced the first stone in the glorious fabric of civil and religious liberty in which all true Americans rejoice. The document, quaint in terms and orthography, is worthy of preservation, and reads:—

"In ye name of God, Amen. We, whose names are vnderwritten, the loyall svbjects of our dread Soueraigne Lord, King James, by ye grace of God of Great Britain, France and Ireland King, defender of ye faith, &c., haueing vndertaken, for ye glorie of God and aduancement of ye Christian faith, and honovr of ovr King and Countrie, a uoyage to plant ye first Colonie in ye northerne parts of Virginia, doe, by these presents, solemnly and mvtvally, in ye presence of God, and of one another, couenant and combine ovrselues togeather into a ciuill body politick, for ovr better ordering and preseruation and fvrtherance of ye ends aforesaid; and by uirtve hereof do enact, constitvte and frame svch jvst and eqvall lawes, ordinances, acts, constitvtions, and officers, from time to time, as shall be thovght most meet and conuenient for ye generall good of ye Colonie, vnto which we promise all dve svbmission and obedience. In vvitness vvhereof, vve haue herevnder svbscribed ovr names, at Cape Cod, ye 11 of Nouember, in ye year of ye raigne of ovr Soueraigne Lord, King James, of England, France and Ireland ye eighteenth, and of Scotland ye fiftie-fovrth, Ano Dom. 1620."

A small party of adventurous explorers entered the snug harbor and landed on the present site of Plymouth just a month later, December 11, and on the 16th of the same month the Mayflower arrived from Cape Cod. The actual debarkation and settlement dates from Christmas day, 1620. This handful of zealous colonists had brought with them a spiritual director in the person of the pious and discreet Elder William Brewster, and previous to establishing themselves on land they chose proper civil officers with John Carver at their head as governor. The colony suffered terrible hardships and privations the first winter, and ere the summer of 1621 arrived forty-three of the original one hundred and two had found rest in the waters of the harbor or under the sands of the coast. The sturdy spirit of the survivors was undismayed, however, and they continued to labor at building homes, clearing the forest, tilling the soil, and perfecting their government, making treaties with the Indians that were rigidly observed on both sides, and prospering as they deserved, increasing in numbers and wealth as the years went by, and maintaining a distinct and separate governmental existence until 1692, when Plymouth became incorporated as a part of the great colony of Massachusetts Bay, established by "The Council at Plymouth in the county of Devon (England) for the planting, ordering, ruling, and governing of New England in America," under a patent granted to certain noblemen and others in the same month that witnessed the arrival of the Pilgrims in Cape Cod bay. That neither king nor council, nor for that matter the recipients, had any conception of the extent of North America is shown by the terms of the patent, which guaranteed to the grantees all that territory on this continent from the fortieth to the forty-eighth degrees of north latitude, which includes all the territory lying between lines running due east and west from the Atlantic to the Pacific and extending in width from the New Jersey coast on the south to the Gulf of St. Lawrence on the north. The charter was vacated in 1635, after the company had disposed of most of its lands to the various companies and individuals interested in colonization. Plantations or settlements were begun in 1622 at Weymouth, in 1624 at Cape Ann, and in 1625 at Mount Wollaston, but bad management and Indian difficulties led to their early abandonment. A patent was granted March 19, 1628, by the Plymouth Company to Sir Henry Rosewell and associates, conveying to them a strip of land which in width extended from three miles south of Charles river to three miles north of the Merrimac and in length "from the Atlantic to the South sea," and the ensuing summer the Cape Ann colony, which had removed to Salem, came under the control of a new company organized under that grant, of which John Endicott was governor. The royal charter to the territory thus acquired was granted March 4, 1629, creating Rosewell and his associates a corporation under the title of the Governor and Company of the Massachusetts Bay in New England. Seventeen ship-loads of colonists, among them many people of consequence, arrived from England in 1630. Of these John Winthrop, the new governor of the company and subsequently governor of the colony, was the most prominent figure. New settlements were soon afterward established at various points, of which the most important were those of Charlestown, Newtown (now Cambridge), Matapan (now Dorchester), Roxbury, Shawmut (now Boston), Nantasket (now Hull), Mystic (now Medford), Lynn, and Winisimmet (now Chelsea).

At the first general court, held at Boston, October 19, 1630, the freemen were empowered to choose from their own number the assistants provided for in the charter, and the latter to choose from among themselves the governor, deputy governor, and assistants, who should make the laws and appoint the other officers. This was the first attempt ever made in this country to establish representative government, and though, like all new experiments, the system was crude and required much subsequent amendment, it is substantially the same that supplied a foundation for the governmental fabric of the State and nation in later times. The Puritans, refugees from their own country because of religious persecution, stern, uncompromising, fanatical in upholding liberty of conscience for themselves, came to America for the purpose of founding a state the corner-stone of which should be absolute adhesion to their peculiar tenets, the creed in which they sincerely believed, and they had no tolerance for any other form of worship. Honest, earnest, hardy, yet narrow, they determined that no interloper should share with them in the work to which they devoted themselves, and consequently made communion in their church the first test for all who would aid them in the construction of a civilization dependent for its very existence, as they imagined, upon the fashioning of each individual conscience upon an unvarying model. It must not be forgotten, however, that these men lived and many of them were notable actors in an age when civil and religious liberty was neither known nor practiced, when men's minds were just emerging from the gloom of the middle ages, when might made right, when the sword was the universal arbiter, when the thunderings of the prophets rather than the teachings and example of the Redeemer formed the staple texts of pulpit disquisition, and they unquestionably acted for the best according to their light. Members of their own church only were permitted to exercise political functions, and they banished from their borders with rigorous severity any and all who refused to accept their interpretation of the Scriptures or otherwise proved obnoxious. Among those thus banished were Roger Williams, excluded in 1634, subsequently one of the founders of Rhode Island ; Rev. John Wheelwright, banished in 1637 ; Mrs. Anne Hutchinson and her followers, and the Quakers, expelled in 1656 and following years.

The emigration from England to the colony increased rapidly in the years 1632-3, many eminent men coming over. The general court—the germ of the House of Representatives—became an established institution in 1634. The Pequot war, brought on by acts of bad faith on the part of certain whites and growing jealousy of their power on the part of the natives, broke out in 1636, resulting in the humiliation of the red men, after a struggle of more than a year, during which many colonists lost their lives, others their dwellings and live stock, and all suffered severely, but for forty years thereafter peace reigned between the races in New England. A change of government in the mother country by which the Puritans and their allies obtained power caused emigration to cease by 1640, and not a few of the 21,000 who had come over returned.

The famous colonial federation, by which Massachusetts Bay, Plymouth, Connecticut, and New Haven joined hands for mutual protection against the Indians, the French, and the Dutch of New Amsterdam, was formed at a conference in Boston, and continued until 1684, when the Massachusetts charter was revoked by royal authority and the government was vested in the Council of New England.

The first compilation of laws for Massachusetts Bay was made by Rev. Nathaniel Ward and adopted in 1641, was styled the "Body of Liberties," and reduced the number of capital offenses from one hundred and fifty in England to twelve in the colony—a long step in the direction of reason and mercy. The colony began the issue of silver coins in denominations of threepence, sixpence, and a shilling in 1652.

But while the whites were thus planting and reaping, building and trading, preaching and praying, a terrible storm was gathering. The Indians had gradually obtained and perfected themselves in the use of fire-arms and otherwise prepared themselves for a renewal of the struggle of 1636-7. The most capable of their leaders was Philip, king of the

Pequots, through whose influence and statesmanship the various New England tribes were united, and in 1675, all being prepared, the long-expected outbreak occurred and a bloody war of a year's duration ensued which ended only with Philip's death at the hands of an assassin. Six hundred whites fell in this war, thirteen towns were destroyed, and 600 houses were burned. The fiercest engagements occurred at Swanzey, Brookfield, Hadley, Deerfield, Northampton, Lancaster, Medfield, Wey-mouth, Groton, Springfield, Sudbury, and Marlborough, Mass., and War-wick and Providence, R. I.

We have already referred to the abrogation of the Massachusetts Bay charter in 1684. Joseph Dudley, president of the Council of New England, took possession of the government in May, 1686, and in the following December arrived Sir Edmund Andros, commissioned by the king governor of all New England save Connecticut. The people, however, complained of his unjust harshness and oppressions, and on the accession of William and Mary to the throne in 1689 he was removed. A year later, in retaliation for outrages perpetrated by the French and Indians along the northern frontier, the New England colonies dispatched an army and a fleet against the Canadian French—an expedition that accomplished nothing. The consolidation of Plymouth with Massachusetts Bay was the principal event of 1692, and the same year witnessed the outbreak at Salem of that peculiar phase of mental delusion, a belief in witchcraft, the cruelties and follies incident to which, extending over many months, have formed the basis for many a gruesome tale. Twenty alleged witches were put to death that year, and a few before and afterward; but, after all, the sin and shame bore no comparison to that of England, where 30,000 miserable wretches were hanged, burned, and drowned.

Indian depredations were resumed in 1704, when Deerfield was surprised, forty men, women, and children slain, and one hundred carried away as prisoners. This outrage was known to have been instigated by the French, then at war with England, and in 1707 the colonies of Massachusetts, New Hampshire, and Rhode Island sent an armed expedition against Port Royal, Nova Scotia, but nothing was accomplished. Three years afterward—in 1710—another attempt was made, backed by an English fleet, and the fortress capitulated after a stout resistance. The next year an attempted capture of Quebec failed, and in 1713 peace was declared.

Colonel Samuel Shute was made royal governor of Massachusetts and New Hampshire, and remained in office for six years. Peace and prosperity reigned for a period of thirty-one·years—1713 to 1744—when England and France again became involved in hostilities, in which the Canadians took an active part, fitting out privateers at Louisburg to prey upon the colonial fisheries. It was determined to stop these depredations if possible, and a small army of 4,000, raised in New Hampshire, Massachusetts, and Connecticut, assisted by a fleet of English ships, besieged Louisburg in May, 1745, forcing the garrison to capitulate June 11. Peace followed in 1748, only to be again broken in 1754, when a war of eight years' duration ensued, ending in the conquest of Nova Scotia and Canada by troops principally from Massachusetts. The territory thus acquired is still held by England.

In 1765 commenced the series of annoyances and tyrannies that culminated in American independence. The arbitrary acts of certain royal governors had already engendered a widespread feeling of dissatisfaction, when, March 22 of that year, the infamous Stamp Act passed· the

British parliament, the object being to force a tax from Americans upon all paper, vellum, and parchment used in the colonies. The opposition was instant and general; all classes were united in antagonism to this and similar attempted oppressions, and the measure was repealed the next year. A second act was passed in 1767 designed to lay an import tariff on numerous articles brought from abroad, but this also met the same opposition, in which Massachusetts led, and the duty was reluctantly removed from all commodities but one—tea. This temporizing policy only added fuel to the flames of resistance, and the famous Boston tea party was the result, followed by the quartering of British troops in the town and the suspension of civil authority. Things went steadily from bad to worse until in 1774 the port was closed and the government transferred to Salem. General Gage took control in May as provincial governor and commander of the royal forces, and perpetrated so many outrages in the name of the king that popular sentiment not only in Massachusetts but in all her sister colonies was wrought up to a white heat and only awaited concert of purpose to inaugurate a conflict. The various legislative assemblies adopted resolutions of sympathy and support, and a conference called together at Philadelphia, September 5, attended by eminent representatives from all the colonies, organized as the Continental Congress, resolved against the importation or exportation of merchandise from or to Great Britain, and took measures to enforce them. Events followed each other rapidly, and the fires of rebellion smouldered everywhere, ready to burst forth at any moment. The people associated themselves together, formed militia companies, provided munitions of war, subscribed money, and urged their leaders to organized resistance. Independence was as yet scarcely thought of, but there was a fixed purpose to maintain their rights as free-born subjects of the crown, and for the restoration of all their privileges. The first actual collision occurred in April, 1775, when British troops sent from Boston to destroy certain military supplies belonging to the colonists were met by militia and citizens, and on the 19th a series of skirmishes ensued at Concord and Lexington in which several were killed and wounded on both sides. The British retired to Boston, but the country was now thoroughly aroused, and reinforcements were rapidly collected in the vicinity of Boston with the object of driving the royal troops from that city. Charlestown was occupied, Breed's hill fortified, and on the 17th of June occurred the ever-memorable assault by the British troops and men-of-war in the harbor, in which the Americans, though forced to withdraw, proved their willingness and ability to cope with the much-vaunted British regular. The battle of Bunker Hill had been fought and lost, but the raw militia had gained an experience that proved on many subsequent occasions of more value than an easy victory in their first engagement could have done.

Washington arrived in July and took command; reinforcements were brought up from every direction; fortifications were erected, and the siege began in good earnest. The British sailed away to Halifax in March, 1776, and the scene of war shifted further south. The part played by Massachusetts in the seven years' war that made the United States a free nation forms a brilliant part of the history of those times.

The State government, founded upon a written constitution, was organized in 1780, while the revolution was still in progress. Shays' ridiculous little rebellion, involving Worcester and Hampshire parties, started in resistance to the forcible collection of debts contracted between 1776 and

1783, occurred in 1786. One man was killed in its suppression. The war of 1812 was a serious blow to Massachusetts interests, and was not very generally indorsed. The civil war, 1861-5, gave her an opportunity to retrieve her reputation for patriotism, and she contributed liberally with men, money, and brains to its successful prosecution, sending to the front no less than 160,000 effectives out of a population of 1,250,000.

Agriculture, fisheries, the mechanic arts, manufactures, and commerce engage the attention of the masses, while the educational institutions of the State rank with the best in the world. Public works of every kind are liberally supported, as are the public schools, from which the ranks of intelligent citizens are constantly recruited. Nor are the mental and physical training of her young men and women monopolized to her own exclusive advantage, since the statistics show that many hundred thousands of her brightest sons and daughters have emigrated and continue to remove annually to the newer and less crowded commonwealths and territories south and west, where their acute minds and skillful hands are employed in the building up of local and national wealth and power. The influence of the Old Bay State thus exerted is beyond computation and increases year by year. The following table is compiled from the census returns of 1885, and presents the totals of capital (including credit capital), product, and hands employed for all industries, and for each of the fifteen leading manufacturing industries of the State:—

INDUSTRIES.	CAPITAL.	PRODUCT.	HANDS.
All industries................	$500,594,000	$674,634,000	379,398
Boots and shoes.............	34,313,000	114,729,000	64,858
Building...................	11,292,000	39,801,000	27,873
Clothing...................	12,399,000	32,659,000	18,395
Cotton goods..............	118,947,000	61,425,000	60,132
Food preparations..........	20,832,000	80,488,000	11,518
Furniture	9,313,000	12,716,000	8,190
Leather.	12,258,000	28,008,000	9,228
Machinery.................	24,743,000	20,365,000	14,644
Metallic goods.............	33,194,000	41,332,000	24,233
Paper......................	21,979,000	21,223,000	8,620
Printing, book-binding, etc...	10,554,000	16,552,000	9,950
Dyeing, bleaching, etc.......	16,191,000	15,880,000	8,601
Rubber, elastic goods........	10,893,000	12,638,000	6,469
Woolen goods..............	29,995,000	31,748,000	18,970
Worsted goods.............	10,706,000	11,198,000	7,963
Other industries............	122,977,000	133,864,000	79,754

The subjoined figures, from the census of 1885, exhibit the increase of capital invested in manufactures since 1865, value of product, and comparative product during each period of five years:—

Year.	Capital invested.	Value of product.	Proportional product to $1 of capital.
1865	$93,385,849	$271,959,122	$2.91
1870	201,634,345	482,082,305	2.39
1875	252,396,177	528,867,823	2.10
1880	303,806,185	631,135,284	2.08
1885	407,581,920	674,634,269	1.66

Population of State, census 1890, 2,238,943; increase in ten years, 455,858—25.57 per cent.

WORCESTER COUNTY.

THE county of Worcester was incorporated by act of the General Court, of date April 2, 1731, which became a law and went into effect july 10 ensuing. By the same act Worcester was made the shire town. The territory originally embraced in the county comprised the towns of Worcester, Lancaster, Westborough, Shrewsbury, Southborough, Leicester, Rutland, and Lunenburg (taken from Middlesex county); Mendon, Woodstock, Oxford, Sutton—including Hassanamisco—Uxbridge, and certain lands granted to residents of Medfield (taken from Suffolk county); Brookfield (taken from Hampshire county); a district spoken of as "the South town, laid out to the Narragansett soldiers," and all other lands and the inhabitants of said townships. The same act provided for county government, the levying of taxes, the establishment of courts, etc. The Hassanamisco tract, at first included in the town of Sutton, was reserved by the chief or sachem, John Wampus, when he sold the adjacent territory to the whites; it was about four miles square, and is now the town of Grafton. The Narragansett soldiers' tract, called the "South town," was a part of seven townships granted in 1828 by the General Court to survivors and heirs of soldiers of the Narragansett war. It is now the town of Westminster. There are now fifty-nine towns in the county, which is the largest in the State, central in position, borders upon Rhode Island and Connecticut at the south, upon New Hampshire and Vermont at the north, and is about 1,500 square miles in area. The surface is uneven, and for the most part rocky, yet the soil compares favorably with any in New England save that in the river valleys, and, owing to improved methods of cultivation, the growing of special crops, the rearing of poultry and the ready sale found in the various manufacturing cities and villages for dairy products and small fruits, farming is profitable and lands are held at high prices. The progress of the county, from a material standpoint, must be gratifying to those identified therewith, and is best shown here by the increase in population during the past decade, taking as a guide the United States census of 1880 and 1890:

CLARK UNIVERSITY.

	1890	1880	Gain	Loss
Ashburnham, . . .	2,076	1,666	410	. . .
Athol, ...	6,318	4,307	2,011	. . .
Auburn, ...	1,543	1,317	226	. . .
Barre, ...	2,249	2,419	. , .	170
Berlin, ...	880	977	, . .	97
Blackstone, ...	6,095	4,907	1,188	. . .
Bolton, ...	835	903	. . .	68
Boylston, ...	790	854	. . .	64
Brookfield, ...	3,352	2,820	532	. . .
Charlton, ...	1,841	1,900	. . .	59
Clinton, ...	10,185	8,029	2,156	. . .
Dana, ...	700	736	. . .	36
Douglas, ...	1,940	2,241	. . .	301
Dudley, ...	2,926	2,803	123	. . .
Fitchburg, ...	21,856	12,429	9,427	. . .
Gardner, ...	8,386	4,988	3,398	. . .
Grafton, ...	4,989	4,030	959	. . .
Hardwick, ...	2,922	2,233	709	. . .
Harvard, ...	1,096	1,253	. . .	157
Holden, ...	2,637	2,499	138	. . .
Hopedale, ...	1,176	(Established 1886)		
Hubbardston, . .	1,343	1,386	. . .	43
Lancaster, ...	2,331	2,008	323	. . .
Leicester, ...	3,114	2,779	335	. . .
Leominster, . . .	7,266	5,772	1,494	. . .
Lunenburg, ...	1,138	1,101	37	. . .
Mendon, ...	919	1,094	. . .	175
Milford, ...	8,769	9,310	. . .	541
Millbury, ...	4,427	4,741	. . .	314
New Braintree, .	573	610	. . .	37
Northboro, ...	1,952	1,676	276	. . .
Northbridge, . . .	4,595	4,053	542	. . .
North Brookfield,	3,868	4,459	. . .	591
Oakham, ...	738	869	. . .	131
Oxford, ...	2,644	2,604	40	. . .
Paxton, ...	449	592	. . .	143
Petersham, ...	1,051	1,109	. . .	58
Phillipston, ...	502	621	. . .	119
Princeton, ...	974	1,100	. . .	126
Royalston, ...	1,030	1,192	. . .	162
Rutland, ...	986	1,059	. . .	63
Shrewsbury, . . .	1,438	1,500	. . .	62
Southboro, ...	2,088	2,142	. . .	54
Southbridge, . . .	7,649	6,464	1,185	. . .
Spencer, ...	8,696	7,466	1,230	. . .
Sterling, ...	1,246	1,414	. . .	168
Sturbridge, ...	2,075	2,062	13	. . .
Sutton, ...	3,180	3,105	75	. . .
Templeton, ...	2,984	2,789	195	. . .
Upton, ...	1,881	2,023	. . .	142
Uxbridge, ...	3,386	3,111	275	. . .
Warren, ...	4,676	3,889	787	. . .
Webster, ...	7,015	5,696	1,319	. . .
Westboro, ...	5,263	5,214	49	. . .
West Boylston, .	3,019	2,994	25	. . .
West Brookfield,	1,588	1,917	. . .	329
Westminster, . . .	1,684	1,652	32	. . .
Winchendon, . . .	4,379	3,722	657	. . .
Worcester, ...	84,536	58,291	25,109	. . .
Totals,	281,723	226,885	56,531	4,410

Receipts and expenditures of Worcester County for 1890.

RECEIPTS.

Balance in the Treasury Jan. 1st, 1890, ...	$78,921	91
County Tax, 1890, ...	125,000	00
Clerk of Courts' Fees, ...	4,145	70
District Attorney Forfeitures, . .	'636	91
Sheriff Fines and Costs, ...	6,812	78
Master House of Correction (Worcester) Fines and Costs, . . .	6,624	75
Master House of Correction (Fitchburg) Fines and Costs, ...	2,520	56
District and Police Courts Fines and Costs, ...	18,753	59
Trial Justices, Fines and Costs, .	2,957	20
Clerk of Court, Naturalization Fees,	454	00
District and Police Courts, Naturalization Fees, ...	1,453	00
Labor House Correction $2,359 55		
Board of Prisoners . . . 76 20		
Sundries sold Prisoners, 180 24		
	2,615	99
Labor House Correction, Fitchburg, $4,553 69		
Sundries sold, 1,062 61		
	5,616	30
Interest on Deposits, ...	1,298	46
Peddlers' Licenses, ...	516	00
Miscellaneous Items, ...	69	60
Total Receipts, ...	$258,396	75

EXPENDITURES.

Expense Worcester Jail and House of Correction, ...	$26,777	08
Expense Fitchburg Jail and House of Correction, ...	16,945	42
County Commissioner's Orders— Miscellaneous Pay roll, ...	18,854	37
County Commissioners' Orders— Commitment of Insane Persons,	2,089	74
Court Orders—Paid Auditors, Masters, etc., ...	2,574	80
Court Orders Paid—Expenses Superior Court, Civil Term, . . .	4,609	52
Court Orders Paid— Expenses Superior Court, Criminal Term, . .	4,548	36
Costs of Criminal Prosecutions, .	36,835	15
Jurors for Service and Travel, . .	18,407	32
Constables for Serving Venires, .	703	35
Salaries of County Officers, . . .	16,466	66
Salaries of Justices of District and Police Courts, ...	13,406	96
Salaries of Clerks of District and Police Courts, ...	5,465	95
County Law Library, ...	3,907	00
Board of Examiners, ...	6	00
Total Expenditures, ...	$171,597	68
	86,799	07
Balance carried to new acc't,	$258,396	75

THE TOWN OF WORCESTER.

EARLY SETTLEMENT — INDIAN TROUBLES — DEVELOPMENT — INCORPORATION OF THE
TOWN AND CITY — PRESENT POPULATION — FINANCIAL CONDITION — EDUCA-
TIONAL ADVANTAGES — BANKS AND BANKING — THE PRESS.

May 6, 1657, the General Court granted to the widow and son of Increase
Nowell, of Charlestown, 3,200 acres of land. May 6, 1662, 1,000 acres were
appropriated to the church at Malden, and October 19, 1664, 250 acres were
similarly ceded to Ensign Thomas Noyes of Sudbury, in recognition of his
military services. These were the first grants of lands in the present town of
Worcester. The Nowell grant, situated along the west shore of Lake Quinsigamond, was soon afterward sold to other parties. A committee appointed
May 15, 1667, to view the land, reported to the General Court in favor of opening a plantation eight miles square, but it was not until 1673 that an actual
settlement occurred, thirty families undertaking the work under the direction of
Captain Daniel Gookin, Thomas Prentice, Richard Beeres and Daniel Hench-
man. One Ephraim Curtis, however, had in the meantime purchased the
Noyes grant of 250 acres in the very centre of the town, and declined to come
to terms, whereupon the matter was carried to the General Court, which adjudged
that he should retain fifty acres adjacent to his house, with the privilege of
taking up 250 acres "without the bounds of the town, but adjoining thereto."
July 13, 1674, the Indian title was extinguished for and in consideration of the
sum of £12 in goods. A block-house fort had already been built, highways, a
church and school provided for, and the community, "only a day's journey
from Boston," containing thirty house lots and a number of houses, seemed
fairly prosperous for the time. But a good many became discouraged and
abandoned the enterprise within a year, leaving the remainder to continue the
struggle, which they did so effectually that, according to a contemporaneous
chronicler, by the summer of 1675 the deserters had been more than replaced,
and the inhabitants had so improved their surroundings that the settlement re-
sembled a village. All travel from the bay to the Connecticut passed through
over the famous "Bay path," and the outlook was full of promise. The neighboring Indians, influenced by Captain Gookin and the celebrated missionary,
Eliot, had been brought into friendly intercourse with the whites, and all seemed
safe and peaceful, when, suddenly, King Philip's war burst forth in Plymouth
colony, and rapidly spread to that of Massachusetts Bay. Utter ruin resulted
to the "Plantation at Quinsigamond." Captain Richard Beeres, of the Quinsigamond committee, was slain, with most of his men, in an attempt to rescue
the Northfield garrison, September 3, 1675.

Efforts were made in 1678 to reoccupy the plantation, but it was not until the General Court, in October, 1682, notified the committee that unless re-peopled the grant would be forfeited, that Gookin and his associates induced a few of the original settlers to return. These were soon joined by others; a new apportionment of lands was made, and once more the axe was heard in the wilderness, the plow seen upon the hillsides, and the vocations of peace were re-sumed. The General Court passed an act, September 10, 1684, conferring upon the town the name of Worcester, in honor of the ancient English-city. Dissensions soon after arose among the inhabitants from various causes, many removed to other localities, and finally, on the application of the remainder to the General Court for aid in 1699, that body refused and struck Worcester from the list of frontier towns. This cruel blow once more depopulated the town, all leaving save Digory Serjent and his family, who remained at Sagatabscot hill, where the bold pioneer perished at last in a desperate fight with the savages, and his wife and children were carried into captivity. This occurred either 1702, 1703 or 1704. Political troubles and French and Indian depredations pre-vented a third settlement of Worcester until 1713, when, October 13, a petition was presented to the General Court by Colonel Adam Winthrop, Gershom Rice and Jonas Rice, former residents, setting forth their desire and that of others to re-establish themselves at Quinsigamond. Their appeal was favorably received, and Hon. William Taylor, Colonel Winthrop, Hon. William Dudley, Lieutenant-Colonel John Ballentine and Captain Thomas Howe were appointed a committee to manage the enterprise. Jonas Rice was the first to return, Oc-tober 21, 1713, made his home on Sagatabscot hill, and here remained, the sole inhabitant, until the spring of 1715, when his brother Gershom arrived and took up his residence. Others soon followed; block-houses, grain and saw mills and roads were built, and as early as 1714 a meeting-house was erected, the popula-tion having increased to some 200. About this time a body of Scotch Presby-terians made their appearance here, began the erection of a place of worship, which was destroyed by a mob, and were so persecuted by their brother Chris-tians that most of them fled to Hampshire county, settling in the town of Pelham.

At a meeting of the proprietors and freeholders, June 14, 1712, it was resolved :

"That the inhabitants of Worcester be vested with the power and privileges of other towns within this province, and that it be earnestly recommended to that council only of the seven churches which did meet at Worcester in Sep-tember, 1721, to whom the contending parties submitted their differences re-lating to the Rev. Mr. Andrew Gardner, that the said council proceed and go to Worcester on or before the first Wednesday in September next, to finish what is further necessary to be done for the procuring and establishing of peace in said town, according to the submission of the parties; and that the freehold-ers and inhabitants of Worcester be assembled on the last Wednesday in Sep-tember next, at 10 o'clock in the forenoon, to choose all town officers as by law as accustomed for towns to do at their annual meeting in March; and that, at the opening of the meeting, they first proceed to the choice of a moderator by written votes."

The above is the original act of incorporation of Worcester, ratified by the State Constitution, adopted fifty-eight years later (1780), which provided that all towns under the government are bodies politic and corporate. The first regular town meeting occurred September 28, 1722, at which officers were chosen and immediately assumed the performance of their duties. At that

STATE NORMAL SCHOOL.

time Worcester was a part of Middlesex county. On the second of April, 1731, Worcester county was organized by act of the General Court, as detailed elsewhere. The village of Worcester, perhaps because of its importance and ease of access, was made the seat of · justice of the new county. The town of Holden (long known as North Worcester) was set apart in 1740, by popular consent and act of the Great and General Court. The history of Worcester, in public matters, is from that time to the present identical with that of the State, but her growth in population, manufactures, wealth and influence, while comparatively slow, has been solid and enduring. In the revolution she did her full duty, and in every great exigency since has earned the plaudits of the country. She took no part in Shay's rebellion, but furnished troops to aid in its suppression. At the close of the revolution the population of the town was about 2,000.

The first important public work attempted was the construction of the Blackstone canal, opened in 1828; the second, the building of the Boston & Worcester railroad, subsequently extended to Springfield and Albany, and succeeded, at varying intervals, by the opening of the many other iron highways that radiate to all points of the compass, facilitating travel and the transportation of the manufactured commodities for which "the heart of the Commonwealth" is famous.

A fire engine was purchased in 1793, and in January of the same year the Worcester Fire Society (still in existence) was organized, composed of leading citizens. Daniel Goulding was authorized to construct water works on a limited scale—that is, "to conduct water in subterraneous pipes from a certain spring in his own land, within the town of Worcester, for the accommodation of himself and some other inhabitants of said town"—March 2, 1798. Washington passed through, enroute to Boston, October 23 of the same year. The next year the town appropriated $2,500 for school houses and $1,000 for the maintenance of schools. Ten school-houses were erected in 1800. The Worcester Bank was incorporated March 7, 1804. A poor-house was built in 1806, at a cost of $2,000. The Antiquarian Society, founded by Isaiah Thomas, was incorporated October 24, 1812. On February 11, 1823, was incorporated the Worcester Mutual Fire Insurance Company; in 1844 the State Mutual Life; in 1846 the Merchants and Farmers; in 1846 the People's Mutual Fire. Lafayette visited Worcester September 4, 1824. A modest town hall was dedicated May 2, 1825. The Worcester Institution for Savings was incorporated in 1828; the Central Bank in 1829; the Quinsigamond Bank in 1833; the Citizens' in 1836; the Mechanics' in 1848.

The construction of the Blackstone canal began at Providence in 1824, and at Worcester in 1826, and the first boat arrived here October 6, 1828. The result was to greatly stimulate trade with Providence and to infuse renewed activity into local manufactures, while building up the Blackstone valley; but Boston was a severe loser thereby, and this led to the incorporation, June 23, 1831, of the Boston & Worcester Railroad Company, which constructed the first railroad of considerable importance in the State, the opening of which was celebrated July 6, 1835, though trains had passed over its entire length two days previously. The next step was the building of the Western railroad to Springfield, opened October 1, 1839. The line through to Albany was completed in 1841. The Norwich & Worcester railroad was opened for traffic April 1, 1840, and the Providence & Worcester (now the New York, Providence & Boston) October 25, 1847. From that period, probably, dates the favorite Worcester *soubriquet*, "Heart of the Commonwealth." The growth of the place was both rapid and substantial, as is shown by the census figures for 1840-48 : Population, 1840, 7,497 ; 1848, 15,000.   Valuation, 1840, $4,288,950 ; 1848, $8,721,100.

The streets were first lighted by oil lamps in 1833 ; the Manual Labor High School was incorporated 1834, and the Worcester Fire Department was established in 1835.   In 1837 there were twelve school districts in the town. Between 1831 and 1834 the Mount St. James Seminary was established and the State Lunatic Hospital located here.   (The first-named is now Holy Cross College, and the latter, entirely rebuilt, vastly enlarged and handsomely embellished, is illustrated elsewhere in these pages.)   The Worcester Aqueduct Company was incorporated in 1845, for the purpose of "supplying water for the extinguishment of fires and for other purposes," the same to be obtained from Bladder pond.   Previous to 1845 the nearest daily newspapers were published at Boston, but on the 9th of June of that year Julius L. Clarke issued the first number of the *Daily Transcript*.   The *Spy*, established as a weekly long before the revolution, was not slow to imitate its young rival, and on the first of July ensuing issued its first daily edition.

WORCESTER AS A CITY.

The act for the incorporation of the city of Worcester was approved by Governor Briggs February 29, 1848, and the city government was inaugurated April 17, 1848, Hon. Levi Lincoln, Mayor; Parley Goddard, Benjamin F. Thomas, John W. Lincoln, James S. Woodworth, William B. Fox, James Estabrook, Isaac Davis and Stephen Salisbury, aldermen.   The names of subsequent mayors and their terms of office are appended, several having been re-elected once or oftener: Henry Chapin, 1849-50 ; Peter C. Bacon, 1851-52 ; John S. C. Newton, 1853-54 ; George W. Richardson, 1855-57 ; Isaac Davis, 1856-58-61 ; Alexander H. Bullock, 1859 ; William W. Rice, 1860 ; P. Emory Aldrich, 1862 ; D. W. Lincoln, 1863-64 ; Phinehas Ball, 1865 ; James P. Blake, 1866-67-68-69-70 ; Edward Earle, 1871 ; George F. Verry, 1872 ; Clark Jillson, 1873-75-76 ; Edward L. Davis, 1874 ; Charles B. Pratt, 1877-78-79 ; Frank H. Kelly, 1880-81 ; E. B. Stoddard, 1882 ; Samuel E. Hildreth, 1883 ; Charles G. Reed, 1884-85 ; Samuel Winslow, 1886-87-88-89 ; Francis A. Harrington, 1890-91.

The career of the city from the first has been one of uniform and remarkable progress and prosperity.   During the first year the Worcester & Nashua railroad was completed, and the Fitchburg & Worcester was added to her lines of railway communication in 1850.   The population that year had increased 128 per cent. over that of 1840, and footed up 17,049.   While the valuation of property had increased 158 per cent. during the decade.   Ten years more brought the population up to 24,973.   In 1880 it had swelled to 58,291, and the census of the present year credits her with 84,655 souls.   Mechanics' Hall was erected in 1857.   The numbering of front doors was begun in 1848.   The original gas-works were erected and telegraph wires introduced in 1849.   The Common, an institution dating from the earliest settlement, was the only public breathing place until Elm Park was opened in 1856.   The Public Library was founded by Dr. John Green in 1859.   The causeway across Lake Quinsigamond was constructed in 1862—a short-sighted ill-advised work that practically divides that beautiful sheet of water into two parts. A spasm of purblind economy seems to have controlled the city Solons about that time, for they rejected an offer of fourteen acres adjoining the lake, made in 1863 by ex-Mayor Isaac Davis, for park purposes. Subsequently the offer was renewed by his son, Hon. Edward L. Davis, and Lake Park is in course of improvement from year to year, with the prospect of ultimately becoming the most delightful and popular resort in this vicinity.

We have not space to enter into a detailed account of Worcester's part in the war; that duty has been well and conscientiously performed by abler pens — among others, that of Captain J. Evarts Green, himself an active participant, whose concise yet comprehensive chapter of military annals forms one of the most interesting features of Lewis & Co.'s *History of Worcester County.* To the first call for troops Worcester instantly responded, and April 17, 1861, the Light Infantry proceeded to Boston, where it was attached to the Sixth Massachusetts Militia. On the 19th the regiment was mobbed in the streets of Baltimore. The Third Battalion of Rifles was next organized, consisting of two militia companies — the City Guards, and the Holden Rifles — and the Emmet Guards, an independent Irish organization, and went to the front. These and the Light Infantry were the three months' men, and were never in battle under their original organization, though most of them re-enlisted in other commands when their first term expired. The Fifteenth Massachusetts Volunteers was the first regiment recruited in this county, contained many Worcester city men, was commanded by Colonel (afterwards Major-General) Charles Devens, recently deceased, took an important part in the disastrous battle of Ball's Bluff, October 21, 1861, lost heavily in killed, wounded and prisoners, was soon filled up by recruits from home, and afterward achieved distinction on many a stubbornly-contested field, losing 310 out of 621 men in action at Antietam. The next regiment organized here was the Twenty-first, composed of men from various parts of the county, from Springfield, Belchertown and Pittsfield. The third was the Worcester regiment *par excellence,* the Twenty-fifth, containing seven companies of city men, the remaining three coming from Fitchburg, Templeton and Milford. These two regiments saw their first service under Burnside at Roanoke Island and Newbern. They afterward performed faithful and arduous service elsewhere. Three more regiments — the Thirty-fourth, Thirty-sixth and Fifty-first — were organized in Worcester during 1862, and all did heroic service. The gallant Fifty-seventh also contained many Worcester men, and hundreds were attached to regiments from other portions of this and from other States.

Worcester shared to the full in the tremendous impetus given to Northern manufactures by the war and the needs of the country resulting therefrom, and still maintains a proud supremacy in many departments of industry.

Private parties had at different times sought and obtained permission to lay pipes and deliver water from springs to private consumers, and in 1854 a survey was made with a view to the erection of municipal water-works, but the proposition was voted down by the citizens, and it was not until ten years later that at another election it was decided to act upon the privilege accorded by the Legislature of 1860 to obtain water from Lynde brook, in the town of Leicester. A reservoir of 228,000,000 gallons' capacity was constructed, conduits laid and water turned on November 14, 1864. The building of a sewer system was inaugurated in 1867, and has been steadily enlarged from year to year. The Lynde brook reservoir, enlarged, is now of 680,000,000 gallons' capacity; in addition, there are two other reservoirs, Tatnuck brook and Bell pond, in all affording storage for 1,080,000,000 gallons. The distribution is accomplished

through nearly 115 miles of mains, and the daily consumption exceeds 4,000,-
000 gallons. The entire cost of the system approximates $2,500,000, and that
of the sewer system about the same. In this connection it should be stated
that the city of Worcester has just completed, under the direction of City

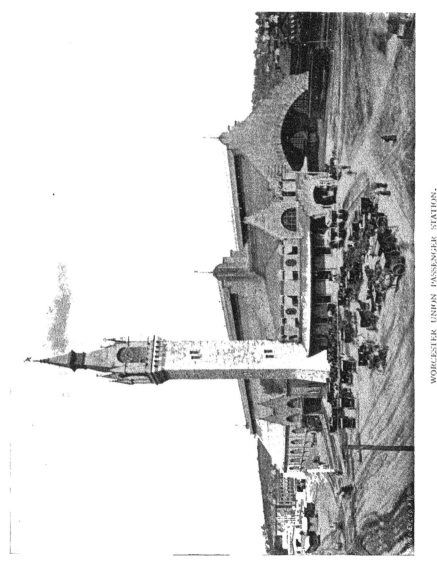

WORCESTER UNION PASSENGER STATION.

Engineer Allen, the most perfect system of sewage purification ever devised.

All departments of the city government are well organized and equipped,
and this applies with especial force to the fire and police service. Extensive
conflagrations are almost unknown, as is proved by the report of Chief Combs

for 1890, showing cost of maintenance, $75,132.51 ; losses, $137,130.60 ; insurance, $56,672.76. The courtesy of the police is proverbial, while the efficiency and watchfulness of the force, and its reliability under all circumstances, cannot be too highly commended. For 1889 there were 4,241 arrests, 3,216 of which were for drunkenness. May 1, 1890, the prohibition of liquor-selling went into effect, and arrests for intoxication fell off more than 50 per cent. for the year.

The annual statement of City Auditor J. F. Howell, for the fiscal year ending November 30, 1890, shows a decrease in the city debt of $21,322.13 compared with 1889. The rate of taxation was reduced 40 cents per $1000, and there was no revenue from liquor licenses. The comparative debt statement is as follows :

	1889	1890
Funded City Loans,	$3,855,700 00	$3,930,700 00
Cash in Treasury,	320,135 07 ·	272,656 38
Sinking Fund,	1,045,773 37	1,189,574 19
Net Debt,	$2,489,791 56	$2,468,469 43

Expenditures and unexpended balances for the year :

	Expended.	Balances Unexpended.
Abatements,	$4,897 42	
Board of Health,	4,033 11	
City Hall,	3,500 70	
City Hospital,	22,442 62	
City Hospital (trust funds),	10,480 34	
Engine and Police Buildings, Waldo Street,	5,337 53	$386 66
Fire Department,	75,132 51	
Fire Patrol,	1,500 00	
Free Public Library,	21,327 27	
Free Public Library (new building account),	52,382 75	20,753 57
Highways, Sidewalks and Paving,	144,227 92	611 65
Incidental Expenses,	36,845 15	
Interest,	104,213 65	
Interest on Sewer Loan,	37,900 00	
Lighting Streets,	71,397 97	3,646 83
Parks Commission,	14,206 60	3,375 52
Parks Commission (order of May, 1888),	32,476 44	16,567 18
Pauper Department (city relief),	15,129 77	1,265 17
Pauper Department (farm),	33,770 70	1,398 65
Pauper Department (farm, new addition),	9,391 05	
Pauper Department (house offal),	15,245 05	1,824 61
Pauper Department (truant school),	3,124 62	
Police Department,	104,599 95	690 38
Salaries,	24,641 66	
School Department,	278,956 69	
School Houses,	82,731 64	32,602 08
Sewers (construction),	71,734 28	28,566 14
Sewers construction (special order, 1888),	51,211 42	30,678 80
Sewers construction (order July 1, 1889),	10,332 59	
Sewers (maintenance),	14,731 38	1,313 62
Sinking Fund (general debt),	23,500 00	
Sinking Funds, per order City Council,	3,000 00	
Street Construction,	26,611 07	22,002 03
Water Works (new supply),		2,658 16
Water Works (construction),	53,982 91	5,161 50
Water Works (maintenance),	59,876 02	}
Interest on Water Loan,	41,988 00	} 37,529 69
Sinking Funds, per order City Council,	900 00	}
Totals,	$1,567,760 78	$211,032 24

Expenditures of 1889, $1,333,410.82, against $1,567,760.78, 1890; balance unexpended 1889, $114,664.75, against $211,032.24 for 1890.

Worcester has three daily newspapers and a prospect óf another in the near future, several weekly journals and two or three monthly publications. In addition, the press of Boston and New York is liberally patronized here. Though not, strictly speaking, a university town, the educational facilities

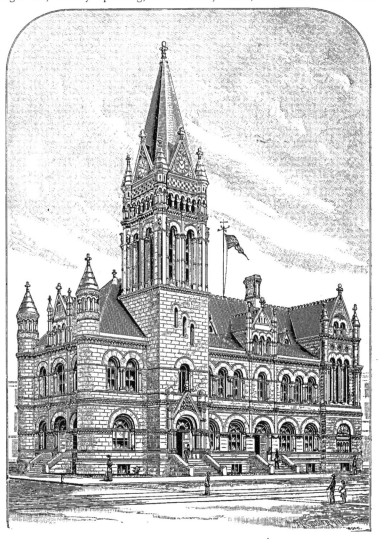

U. S. POST OFFICE AND COURT HOUSE.

afforded by her numerous institutions of learning — independently of her superbly equipped public school system — are surpassed by those of no city of equal population in America. We have room only for mention of these more advanced seats of learning in alphabetical order, and the passing remark that the administration of each is unexceptionable. They are :   Clark University,.

incorporated 1887 ; College of the Holy Cross, founded 1843 ; Massachusetts State Normal School, founded 1874 ; Worcester Academy, incorporated 1834 ; Worcester Polytechnic Institute, founded 1868. Students in all of these have access to all the privileges of the Free Public Library (recently enlarged by the erection of a handsome and commodious new $73,000 building) ; of the American Antiquarian Society ; of the Worcester County Mechanics Association ; of the Worcester Natural History Society ; of the Worcester Society of Antiquity, and many large and valuable private libraries and art collections.

BANKS AND BANKING.

It is stated on good authority that the savings banks of Worcester hold deposits of nearly $23,000,000. Of National banks there are seven, as follows :

BANKS.	CAPITAL STOCK.	ASSETS AND LIABILITIES.
Quinsigamond National, ...	$250,000 00	$1,032,667 28
City National, ...	400,000 00	2,008,984 74
Worcester National, ...	500,000 00	1,855,731 86
Citizens National, ...	150,000 00	578,515 34
Central National, ...	300,000 00	1,492,492 22
Mechanics National, ...	350,000 00	1,282,918 09
First National, ...	300,000 00	2,858,059 23
Totals, ...	$2,250,000 00	$11,109,368 76

Clearing-house transactions for 1890, $60,048,318.

FREE PUBLIC LIBRARY.

Toward the close of the year 1859 the late Dr. John Green and the Lyceum and Library Association offered to give, upon certain conditions, to the city of Worcester libraries containing respectively 7000 and 4500 volumes, to form the nucleus of a public library. The offer was accepted by the city government, and an ordinance establishing the Free Public Library was passed December 23 of the same year. The library was opened to the public in the Worcester Bank block, Foster street, April 30, 1860. In accordance with a stipulation made in the deed by which Dr. Green transferred his books to the city, the latter bought from Hon. Emory Washburn a lot of land on Elm street, at an expense of $5042, and began the erection of a library building. The corner-stone of that building, which is the older of the two buildings now occupied by the library, was laid July 4, 1860 ; it was completed in 1861 at a cost, including the lot, of about $30,000, and thrown open to the public September 4 of that year. That building having become filled with books and having ceased to afford room enough to the readers and students who wished to use it, the city bought in 1889 an estate adjoining the library lot on the east for $35,000, and in the summer of 1888 began to put up a new building. That building was opened to the public April 1, 1891. When a few items of expenditures, contemplated, shall have been made, the building will have cost about $100,000, exclusive of the land and furniture.

At the start the library contained 11,500 volumes. December 1, 1890, the date of the last annual report, it had 81,425 volumes, divided among the different departments as follows : Green, or Reference Library, 22,942 ; Intermediate Department, 21,287 ; Circulating Department, 37,196.

The books have been selected with especial reference to the needs of residents of Worcester, and the library, therefore, while well supplied with works in the different branches of knowledge, is particularly rich in the departments of chemistry, physics, mechanics and the fine and industrial arts. According to the first annual report of the library, 31,454 volumes were used by frequenters in the eight months covered by the report. During the last year, which ended No-

FREE PUBLIC LIBRARY BUILDINGS.

vember 30, 1890, 185,123 volumes were either taken to the homes of residents or used within the library building. The aim in the library is to establish pleasant personal relations between the frequenters of the library and its officers, and all persons having questions to ask, answers to which may be found in books, are cordially welcomed, encouraged to ask questions, and sympathetically aided in getting answers to them. There were used 57,782 volumes during the last year by persons seeking information within the library building. The library has become distinguished for the value and efficiency of the aid which it has rendered to the teachers and scholars of the public and private schools of Worcester. A reading room was founded in connection with the library in 1865. It contains 300 reviews, magazines and papers.

Dr. Green died in 1865, and left by will $30,000 to the library, mainly to endow his department of it. One provision of the bequest is that one-quarter of the income shall be added to the principal every year. The Green Library Fund amounted November 30, 1890, to $44,223. Hon. George F. Hoar raised by subscription $10,000 or $11,000, which constitutes a reading-room fund, the income of which is used in paying annual dues for reviews, magazines and papers. The expenditures of the last library year were $23,951. The income was as follows : City appropriation, $16,496 ; dog license money, $4273 ; income from Green library fund, $1647 ; income from reading room fund, $493 ; receipts from fines, etc., $585. December 8, 1872, the reading-rooms and library for purposes of reference were thrown open to the public on Sunday. The Free Public Library was the first public library in New England to open its doors on Sunday. During the last twelve years 134.77 persons, on an average, have used the library annually on that day of the week.

The librarians have been : Zephaniah Baker, February 17, 1860, to January 14, 1871, and Samuel Swett Green since January 15, 1871. Mr. Green belongs to the progressive school of librarians, and is a prominent member of the American Library Association. He has originated and introduced new methods in library management, and is the author of several treatises upon subjects pertaining to his occupation. The office hours of the librarian are 10 A. M. to 1 P. M., 3 to 6 P. M. ; Sundays, 3 to 5 P. M. The circulating department is open for the delivery and return of books from 9 A. M. to 8 P. M. ; Saturday, open until 9 P. M. The upper reading-room and the Green library room are open from 9 A. M. to 9 P. M. ; the lower reading-room from 8 A. M. to 9.30 P. M. Sunday, both reading-rooms are open from 2 to 9 P. M. The reading-rooms and the library for purposes of reference are open every day in the year. The circulating department is closed Sunday and legal holidays. The books of that department can be taken to their homes freely by residents who have reached the age of fifteen years, and in some cases by younger persons. Books belonging to the intermediate department can be taken out under certain conditions. Books in the reference department which were given to the library by Dr. Green, or which have been bought with the income of the Green library fund, can only be used in the library building. Every facility is afforded there, however, for their use. The books of the Worcester District Medical Society are kept in the Free Public Library building, and may be consulted on the same easy conditions which prevail in regard to the use of the Green library.

The successive presidents of the Board of Directors have been Hon. Alexander H. Bullock, Hon. William W. Rice, Hon. Stephen Salisbury, Hon. George F. Hoar, Hon. Thomas L. Nelson, Hon. Peter C. Bacon, J. Evarts Greene, Esq., Rev. Dr. William R. Huntington, Hon. Francis H. Dewey and Hon. Francis A. Gaskill. Following are the names of the present Board of Directors : john O. Marble, A. George Bullock, Edward B. Glasgow, Edwin T. Marble, Philip L. Moen, Burton W. Potter, Edward I. Comins, Waldo Lincoln, Samuel Winslow, Everett J. Bardwell, Thomas J. Conaty, George M. Woodward. Mr. A. George Bullock is president of the board, and Mr. Edward I. Comins secretary.

Y. M. C. A. BUILDING.

This handsome edifice, constructed of pressed brick and brown stone, was erected in 1887, upon a lot 60 feet front on Pearl and Elm streets and extending through 190 feet from one thoroughfare to the other, with principal entrance adjoining the Public Library on Elm street. Total cost of building and lot, $145,000 ; of furnishings, $10,000, making $155,000 in all, of which $55,000 is secured by mortgage on the property. The building fund was started by a young man named Albert H. Brooks, who, being about to die, left the Association his savings bank book, from which was realized $110.25. To this was added 3100 subscriptions, in amounts from 25 cents to $25,000—the highest, of which there

YOUNG MEN'S CHRISTIAN ASSOCIATION BUILDING.

was but one. There was one $10,000, several $5000, and sixteen of $1000 or over. The fund was known, and deservedly so, as "the popular fund." The building contains a beautiful hall which will seat 1000 persons, a fine gymnasium, with running track, 23 1-2 laps to the mile ; excellent bathing facilities, commodious reading room, attractive parlors, class rooms, social rooms, and everything else calculated to carry on a live, aggressive work. The rentals give an income of $6000, the membership $6000 more, and $3000 is raised by subscription. The attendance averages about 4000 daily, and the gospel meetings have an average attendance of 250 young men, which is an increase of 200 per cent. above that while in rented quarters.

THE PRESS.

THE SPY.

The *Massachusetts Spy* dates as a weekly from 1770, and was published for some years in Boston, but on the outbreak of revolutionary hostilities in 1775 was removed to Worcester as a precaution against suppression or confiscation at the hands of the British. There were at the time many wealthy and influential tories here, but the energetic and fiery patriotism of the *Spy's* editorials, inspired by the subsequently celebrated Isaiah Thomas, the publisher, soon awakened the insurrectionary element, who expelled the loyalists and then turned their attention to aiding in the war for independence, at the close of which Mr. Thomas was made postmaster, while retaining his interest in the paper, which had then become one of the most influential and prosperous in New England. It has during its long career since that period supported in turn as an organ the principles of the Federal, Whig, Native American and Republican parties, has maintained an uniformly consistent attitude of opposition to the democratic idea, and has advocated at all times and under all changes of political nomenclature what it believes to be a correct policy of protection to American industry through high tariff laws. Eminently respectable, conservative and courteous, the *Spy* enjoys the warm support of the wealthy and cultured class, and is a profitable business venture as well as a powerful engine for the advancement of partisan views and the encouragement of certain business interests, the logical calmness with which living questions are discussed attracting and persuading instead of repelling and exasperating opposition. Full Associated Press telegraphic reports are published daily ; proper attention is given to the news of the city, county and State, and the advertising patronage is excellent. The daily *Worcester Spy* is a neat eight-page six-column quarto usually, though occasionally enlarged to ten or twelve pages of seven columns. The weekly edition—the *Massachusetts Spy*—consists of eight, ten or twelve seven-column pages, and circulates all over New England and some middle and western States.

WORCESTER EVENING GAZETTE.

In the year 1801 was established here the *National Ægis*, organ of the Jeffersonian, or, as then called, the Republican party. It was a remarkably influential paper, honest and fearless. Identified with its editorial direction at various times were several of the ablest and most honored of Worcester's citizens, among them Levi Lincoln, who became the first mayor of the city in 1848. When the original Republican party dissolved, and the Whig and Democratic parties were organized, true to its principles, the *Ægis* cast its lot with the latter, but lost some ground by reason of the change in popular sentiment upon the subject of the tariff. A daily edition, the *Transcript*, was started in 1845, which was afterward made a Whig paper, the name changed to *The Gazette*, and the weekly edition rechristened the *Ægis and Gazette*, under which title it is still

TOWER, LAKE VIEW PARK.

issued. Charles H. Doe & Co. have owned and published both daily and weekly since 1869, and it cannot be disputed that as a fireside and home newspaper of temperate tone and decided though moderately expressed views upon all matters in which the community is interested, the *Evening Gazette* in particular has a far-reaching and salutary influence, while its circulation—principally in the quiet homes of the people—is extremely large in proportion to the city's population. Openly and frankly Republican in politics, it is not in any sense an organ, nor does it indulge, upon the one hand, in senseless denunciation of political opponents, nor, upon the other, in concealment or apology for the faults of political friends. In local affairs it is emphatically non-partisan and has the respect and enjoys the patronage of the masses of all shades of opinion. Primarily a newspaper, the *Gazette* owns franchises in both the Associated and United Press, and places an account of the world's occurrences before its readers ordinarily twelve or fourteen hours earlier than do its rivals. Generally it consists of eight six-column pages of telegraphic and local news, interesting general reading, editorials and advertisements, but twelve pages and more are not infrequent. Two or three editions are printed on a fast perfecting press from stereotype plates every afternoon except Sunday.

THE TELEGRAM.

The Worcester *Sunday Telegram* began publication in November, 1884, Austin P. Cristy being its founder and owner. Within a year from its first issue it reached a larger circulation than any other paper in Worcester county. It has many times been increased in size, and its present circulation is claimed to be larger than the combined circulation of all other Worcester papers, the *Daily Telegram* alone excepted.

The *Daily Telegram* is the outgrowth of the progress and prosperity of the *Sunday Telegram*, and issued its first edition in May, 1886. At the end of its first year it had passed all other Worcester dailies in circulation, and it now claims a larger circulation than all other Worcester dailies combined. Both publications have been conspicuously fortunate in avoiding the financial embarrassments that often cripple newspaper ventures, and the steady progress of both has already accumulated an unsurpassed mechanical outfit and a volume of business that is the wonder of the newspaper fraternity. The number of men constantly employed in all departments of the *Telegram* has grown from three, in November, 1884, to between seventy and eighty.

The features of the *Telegram* are its adherence to the principles of the Republican party, its alertness in gathering and distributing news, and its aggressive opposition to the liquor trade. Both papers are now owned by a stock company, of which A. P. Cristy is president and treasurer.

LIGHT.

The New York *Journalist* of April 12, 1890, paid the following warm but deserved tribute to Worcester's recognized literary organ :

"Three years ago Mr. Nathaniel C. Fowler, jr., well known in Massachusetts press circles, started Worcester *Light*, in which were shown unmistakable marks of his originality and newspaper experience. Worcester people were surprised, but they grasped the situation and the new paper instantaneously, and at the end of the month the support was so generous that the the new paper was more than paying expenses, a success unheard of in the history of starting new newspapers in this country. The success of *Light* is due to three things : First, the best family field in the country ; second, the best conducted local paper of its class anywhere ; third, indomitable push and energy, with marked originality. *Light* covers the clean side of Worcester completely, and besides gives its readers many pages of choice literary matter, and other reading especially interesting to the household. It is a home paper, always clean and pure, and ever bright, entertaining and instructive."

Mr. Alfred S. Roe attends to the editorial department. *Light* has as regular contributors the best writers in Worcester. *Light's* staff is one of the strongest, and everything considered, it is easy to believe the statement made by the publishers, that *Light* has a bona fide sale of as many papers as any of the old-established weekly papers of Boston. Worcester people are proud of *Light*."

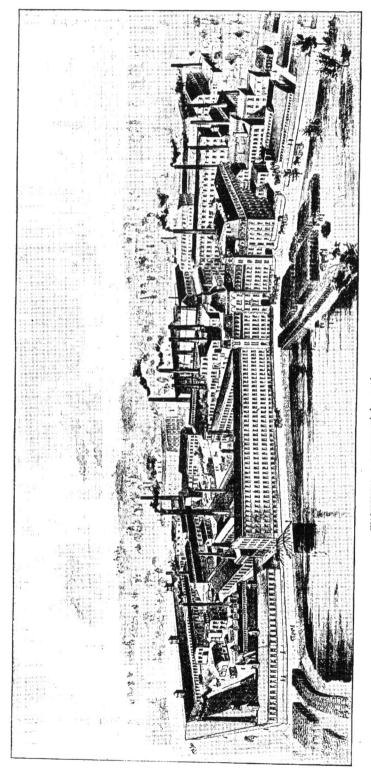

WASHBURN & MOEN M'F'G CO.'S GROVE STREET WORKS.

REPRESENTATIVE HOUSES.

IN the series of descriptive articles that follow we have endeavored to make concise and appropriate mention of every prominent, well-established, and deserving business house in Worcester, for it is to their capital, industry, energy, and enterprise that the city is indebted for its material prosperity and widespread fame. We have made room for those only whose reputation is beyond suspicion, and if any have failed of representation it is not because of bias or neglect upon the part of the editors and publishers.

With the utmost confidence we commend each and all to the good will and patronage of the entire country and of foreign buyers. Progressive, liberal, of sterling business and personal character, this is the kind of men upon whom depends the continued prosperity not only of this community but of the Commonwealth and of the nation at large.

WASHBURN & MOEN MANUFACTURING COMPANY.

Philip L. Moen, President and Treasurer; Charles F. Washburn, Vice-President and
Secretary; P. W. Moen, Assistant Treasurer and General Superintendent;
Charles G. Washburn, Assistant Secretary and Counsel —Manufacturers of Iron,
Steel and Copper Wires of Every Description—Capital $1,500,000—North Works
on Grove Street, and South Works at Quinsigamond.

Prefatory to a sketch of the rise and progress of this great leading concern, a brief glance at the early history of wire manufacturing may not be out of place. It is not known where or by whom the industry was originated, but from reliable records it is learned that as late as 1810 the entire English output did not exceed one four-horse wagon-load—say about three tons—per week, the appliances and machinery being of the most primitive description. Pioneer Worcester hardware dealers imported what wire was needed in small quantities from England. Soon after the Revolution wire-drawing on a limited scale was begun at Walpole, Norfolk county, by Eleazur Smith, and as early as 1809 hand-drawn wire was made at Leicester, this county. In 1813 Joseph White of West Boylston, this county, engaged in the same business, and in 1814 other enterprising men started small wire works at Phillipston and at Barre, on the Ware river. Prior to 1815, stimulated probably by the scarcity growing out of the second war with Great Britain, some one, name unknown, established a factory on what is now Leicester street, New Worcester, where the Coes wrench works stand. From 1815 to 1820 wire was also manufactured at Spencer, Worcester county. Not a vestige of these early enterprises remains.

This brings us to the founding of the Washburn & Moen Manufacturing Company. In 1820 Ichabod Washburn and William H. Howard formed a copartnership for the purpose of manufacturing woolen machinery. Mr. Howard soon afterward retired, Mr. Washburn buying his in-

WASHBURN & MOEN M'F'G CO.'S QUINSIGAMOND WORKS.

terest and forming a new firm with Benjamin Goddard as his associate. The winter of 1830-31 they occupied a wooden building on School street, and experimented with machinery for making wood screws. Later in 1831 they removed to Northville and took possession of a wooden building on Grove street, to which, in conjunction with General Heard, they induced the Reads of North Providence to remove their wooden screw factory. Here they remained until January, 1835, when the firm dissolved, Mr. Goddard remaining and continuing the manufacture of woolen machinery, while Mr. Washburn engaged in the manufacture of wire exclusively, in a three-story brick building, 40x80 feet, erected for him on Mill brook (the site of the present North works) by Stephen Salisbury, senior, the dam constructed at the time forming what is still known as Salisbury pond. The same year—1835—Mr. Washburn's brother Charles, a member of the Maine bar, came to Worcester, and a copartnership was formed that lasted for three years, Charles retiring in 1838. In 1840 Ichabod Washburn, who had prospered in his undertakings, purchased the South Worcester land and water power and erected the present works of the Worcester Wire Company. This mill he placed in charge of his former partner, Mr. Goddard, who managed it up to the time of his death in 1867. Charles Washburn again became a member of the firm.

With 1847 came a new era in the wire manufacturing business. The telegraph had passed from the experimental to the practical stage, and lines were being extended in every direction, causing a vast increase in the demand, which Mr. Washburn was one of the first to provide for. The wire used was No. 9 Stubs' gauge up to 1859, and was not galvanized, painting or boiling in oil being resorted to as a preventive of oxidation. From 1837 to 1847 all of the iron billets used by Mr. Washburn for making wire and rods were purchased in Sweden; they were twelve feet long, one and one-eighth inches square, and were rolled into wires at Troy, N. Y., Fall River, Mass., and Windsor Locks, Conn.

In 1847 the Washburns bought the Lincoln family property at Quinsigamond, now the South works of the company; the firm of Washburn, Moen & Co. (Henry S. Washburn, Chas. Washburn and Philip L. Moen) was organized, a complete new mill was erected, and the business of rod-rolling and wire-drawing was established on a large scale. January 12, 1849, the firm dissolved, Mr. Henry S. Washburn becoming sole proprietor. On the first of the same month the copartnership between I. and C. Washburn was terminated, and in the partition the wire mills fell to Ichabod, Charles accepting the ownership of the Quinsigamond works. April 1, 1850, Mr. Philip L. Moen, who had been one of the firm in the Quinsigamond plant, was admitted to a copartnership with Mr. Ichabod Washburn, and from that day to this has been identified with the house. As above noted, H. S. & Charles F. Washburn were engaged in the rolling mill business at Quinsigamond from the beginning of 1853. In 1856 this firm added to their premises a one-story building, 150 feet front, with two 150-foot wings, between which was a hoop rolling-mill building 30x60 feet. At that time they employed eighty-five hands, three water wheels and steam aggregating 100 horse-power, produced ten tons per day, and transacted a business of $300,000 a year. By mutual agreement the copartnership was dissolved in 1857, and on May 1 of the same year Messrs. Charles and Charles F. Washburn and Charles Washburn & Son assumed proprietorship of the Quinsigamond mill. Henry S. Washburn erected a new wire factory in the rear of the Western (now Boston & Albany) freight-house, and continued business alone.

In 1859 I. Washburn & Co. were making twelve tons per day of rods and wire at the Grove street mill, giving employment to 120 hands. The Quinsigamond mill of C. Washburn & Son was burned November, 1862. In 1863 Messrs. Washburn & Moen erected a cotton mill for the manufacture of crinoline yarns, which was run for ten years, turning out four tons daily. While controlling the rod and wire mills at Grove street and South Worcester in 1864, this firm owned no rolling mill, confining their operations to the working of iron and cast steel of various grades. Bessemer and open-hearth steels were not then known. January 2, 1865, the firm reorganized as a company, under the style of the I. Washburn & Moen Wire Works, for the manufacture of wire and wire rods; capital $500,000. November 27, 1866, the concern was incorporated as the Washburn & Moen Wire Works, for the manufacture of wire and wire rods and cotton goods; capital $600,000. July 7, 1867, the South Worcester mill was burned. Business, however, was prosecuted as usual at the Grove street mill, and in March, 1868, the new mill at South Worcester was occupied.

THE PRESENT COMPANY.

February 24, 1868, was effected a consolidation of the Washburn & Moen Wire Works and the Quinsigamond Iron and Wire Works under one management. The name chosen was the "Washburn & Moen Manufacturing Company." Under the act of incorporation the capital was fixed at one million dollars, with the privilege of increasing the same to one and a-half millions, which increase was assumed May 26, 1869. In the autumn of 1869 they built their first rolling-mill on Grove street—a so-called "continuous" mill of English origin in the essential features with certain American improvements. The culmination of Bessemer's experiments, the

steel that bears his name, perfected in 1876, completely revolutionized the processes and products of wire manufacturers, substituting for iron and the old-fashioned steel a better and cheaper
material for most purposes, and giving a wonderful impetus to the barbed wire fencing industry,
then in its infancy.   Some idea of the stimulus given to this style of fencing by the invention named may be obtained from government statistics, from which it appears that in 1871,
with thirty-seven States, the original cost of the old-fashioned wooden fences had reached
$1,747,549,933, and the annual expense of repairs was $93,963,187. Since then wire has been
substituted generally for new and largely for old fences, and the saving to the farmers aggregates
about $4,500,000 per annum.   Barbed wire possesses many and obvious advantages over all
other materials for this purpose, among which may be specified—1. It takes up no space: 2. It
does not exhaust the soil: 3. It does not shade vegetation: 4. It is proof against all large animals and high winds: 5. It makes no snow drifts: 6. It affords no refuge for noxious weeds,
brush, bushes or wild grass: and 7. It is both cheap and durable, easily and rapidly constructed by any one.
    The attention of the Washburn & Moen Manufacturing Company having been directed to
barbed wire in the spring of 1876, they became impressed with its value and were in the midst
of experiments looking to its economical production when the first furnace for making Bessemer
steel was put into successful operation and the problem of material was solved.   Control of the
barbed wire patents was acquired, automatic machinery devised, constructed and patented, and
in a short time the company was fully enlisted in the new industry.   Improvements succeeded
each other rapidly, and in order to protect itself and its business this company has purchased
and utilized more than two hundred and fifty patents upon barbed wire and barbed wire machinery.   The output of all the mills in this country has grown from five tons in 1874 to probably
150,000 tons, or 850,000 miles, in 1890, of which 18,000 tons—100,000 miles—was made at
these mills, the capacity being 426 miles, or seventy-five tons per day of ten hours.   The cost to
the consumers, by reason of cheaper wire and improvements in processes, has been reduced from
eighteen cents per pound in 1874 to less than five cents in 1890.   It is hardly necessary to state,
in view of the tremendous advance of western development, more especially in farming, that
the increase of the Washburn & Moen Manufacturing Company's business has been most marked
since the introduction of barbed wire for fencing.   This, however, is but one of many specialties to which they devote attention, and their output of iron, steel, copper, brass, electro-plated
and galvanized wires for all purposes, bale ties, wire rope and wire nails, is simply enormous,
the items of telegraph and telephone wires alone aggregating in value millions of dollars annually.   Early in his career Mr. Ichabod Washburn experimented largely and adopted improved
processes for annealing and restoring to wire its softness, ductility and strength when rendered
hard and brittle by repeated drawings.   In 1850 his attention was attracted to the making of
steel wire for piano-fortes, and at the suggestion of Mr. Chickering, the great Boston piano manufacturer, he experimented so successfully that the English music wire was driven out of the
American market, leaving this establishment the only one on this side of the Atlantic that produces this class of wire.
    The plant, comprising a great number of one, two, three, four and five-story buildings, a part
of which are situated on Grove street, and the remainder at Quinsigamond village, two miles
south on the Blackstone river, embraces in all twenty-five acres of land.   A description of the interior arrangements and equipments would simply weary the general reader.   Suffice it to say
that every provision is made for the economizing of time, labor and material, and that further
improvement in that respect seems impossible.   The machinery is driven by numerous steam engines, the aggregate being computed at 7,200 horse-power.   Four thousand men are employed,
and, nearly all being the heads of families, it is safe to state that not less than 16,000 people
draw their support from this establishment, much the largest wire-drawing and rod-rolling
concern in the world, of which Worcester, Massachusetts and the entire country may well
be proud.

GEO. N. NEWHALL & CO.,

Manufacturers of Newhall's Heavy Team Rings, Breeching Loops, Trace Hooks and
Bent Ball Top Hames and Dees—Manufacturers and Jobbers of Saddlery Hardware and Horse Clothing—Silver Plating to Order—No. 30 Exchange Street.

    The above caption gives a very full outline of the business carried on by Mr. Geo. N. Newhall,
under the style of Geo. N. Newhall & Co.   His salesroom, No. 30 Exchange street, is handsomely appointed and completely stocked, 20x100 feet in dimensions, with workshop of like size
in rear, where seven men are constantly employed.   The appliances are of the best, as are the
commodities produced, and sales range from $50,000 to $75,000 per annum.   His trade—a
general jobbing—extends principally over the New England States, Mr. Newhall being widely
known and popular in this community.   He served with honor in the civil war, is a member of
the G. A. R., and has filled every chair in the Knights of Honor.

WORCESTER NATIONAL BANK.

Stephen Salisbury, President; J. P. Hamilton, Cashier; Capital Stock, $500,000; Surplus, $200,000—No. 9 Foster St.

The Worcester National is the direct successor of the Worcester State Bank, incorporated March 7, 1804, and, counting from that event, is one of the oldest financial concerns in the State. The reorganization under the National banking act occurred in 1864, and May 9 of that year the charter was received and the doors reopened under improved auspices. It is almost supererogatory to recount the history of the old Worcester Bank, and with the above glance at the more salient points we proceed to speak of the institution as it is.

The banking house is an appropriate home for the bank itself — square, substantial, devoid of meretricious ornament, suggestive of solid character and unpretentious worth. Our cut gives a tolerably fair idea of its general appearance. The executive officers are named in our ·ption. President Salisbury and Cashier Hamilton rank well among New England financiers, and their services are in constant demand. The former is also president of the Worcester County Institution for Savings, and the latter a member of the board of managers of the People's Savings Bank. The board of directors of the Worcester National is exceptionally strong, and embraces such noted names as those of President Salisbury, Josiah H. Clarke, A. George Bullock, Jonas G. Clark, Charles A. Chase, Lincoln N. Kinnicutt, Edward L. Davis and Cashier Hamilton. A general banking business is transacted, including deposits of corporations, firms and individuals, loans and discounts, foreign and domestic exchange, collections on all accessible points, etc., the bank having as correspondents the National Park and Hanover National of New York and the National Exchange Bank of Boston. Subjoined is the latest official statement to the Comptroller of the Currency, which bears evidence to the flourishing condition of this model institution:

RESOURCES.		LIABILITIES.	
Loans and discounts	$1,358,136 55	Capital stock paid in	$500,000 00
Overdrafts, secured and unsecured	721 67	Surplus fund	200 000 00
U. S. bonds to secure circulation	50 000 00	Undivided profits	55 684 01
U. S. bonds on hand	1,000 00	National bank notes outstanding	45 000 00
Stocks and securities	137,040 00	Dividends unpaid	21 00
Due from approved reserve agents	99,204 39	Individual deposits subject to check	967 285 32
Due from other National banks	36 595 45	Demand certificates of deposit	25 099 32
Banking house, furniture and fixtures	46,000 00	Due to other National banks	62 642 21
Current expenses and taxes paid	2 803 17		
Checks and other cash items	4,930 08		
Exchanges for clearing house	4,190 46		
Bills of other banks	8 648 00		
Fractional paper currency, nickels and cents	309 09		
Specie	56 792 00		
Legal tender notes	26 111 00		
U. S. certificates of deposit for legal tenders	20,000 00		
Redemption fund with U. S. treasurer (5 per cent. of circulation)	2,250 00		
Due from U. S. Treasurer, other than 5 per cent. redemption fund	1 000 00		
Total	$1,855 731 86	Total	$1 855 731 86

THE STATE MUTUAL LIFE ASSURANCE COMPANY, OF WORCESTER, MASS.

A. G. Bullock, President; Thos. H. Gage, M. D., Vice-President; Henry M. Witter, Secretary; J. D. E. Jones, Superintendent of Agencies—Home Office, No. 240 Main Street.

A home institution of which every citizen of Worcester has reason to feel proud is the State Mutual Life Assurance Company, organized in 1846 and granted a perpetual charter by the Legislature, with a provision to the effect that a guarantee capital of $100,000 should be carried. At the expiration of twenty years the plan of operations was made purely mutual, the stock was retired, and the policy-holders, owning the assets, became the company, managing its affairs through officers selected by themselves. The forty-fifth annual report, dated January, 1891, contains some interesting figures, which we transfer to our pages, showing the progress and present condition of the institution:

GROWTH.   ANNUAL INCOME.

Year.	Policies in force.	Ins. in force.	Income.	Premiums.	Interest, Rent, etc.
1881	4,845	$10,819,729	$459,412.55	330 680.65	128 731 90
1882	5,165	12,016,345	501,068.39	382.870 83	118,197.56
1883	5,711	14,162,113	610,887.49	467.136 52	143 750.97
1884	6,242	15,832,144	744,716.91	572.129 55	172,587 36
1885	7,020	18,367,467	914,910.96	694,554 84	220,356.12
1886	7,902	20,968,635	987,879.46	798,339.66	189.539 80
1887	8,797	23,387,840	1,101,240.32	898 116.26	203,124 06
1888	9,826	26,665,185	1,257,684.22	1,033,523 31	224,160.91
1889	11,007	30,476,430	1,444,387.46	1.189.975 28	242 827 38
1890	12,380	35.017,951	1,161,163.13	1,374,276 02	286,887 11

The gain for the year last named is exhibited thus:

	POLICIES.	INSURANCE.
In force December 31, 1890,	12,380	$35,017,951.00
" " 1889,	11,007	30,476,430.00
Gain,	1,373	$4,541,521.00

No better evidence of the conservatism and wisdom that characterizes the administration could be desired than is furnished by these brief but comprehensive tables. Under the non-forfeiture law of Massachusetts every policy issued by this company, on which two or more annual premiums have been paid, is good for a proportionate part of the sum named in the policy. The amount to which the insured is entitled is defined and his right thereto protected by the statute. No action on his part is necessary to secure his rights. He has only to leave his policy to the operation of the law, which law is a pledge of the Commonwealth that his rights shall not be compromised or his property be confiscated. Under this law every policy-holder may know for himself, without inquiring of the company or consulting an actuary, the amount for which he is insured, if at any time he discontinues the payment of premiums. The assets of the company are in excess of its liabilities—$1,165 for every $1,000, under the rigid four per cent. standard of Massachusetts. It issues life policies, payable at death only; endowment policies, payable after a designated term of years, or at death if prior to the end of such term; and life rate endowment policies issued at all insurable ages, and payable between the ages of 75 and 81, or at death if prior, and in each instance affords the holder the option of paying for it in a single lump sum or by equal annual payments, either for a term of years or for life. The largest risk on a male life is $20,000; on a female $2,500; the smallest on any life, $1,000. All death claims are paid on receipt and approval of proofs; endowments on expiration of term, and litigation is avoided when possible.

Hon. John Davis, Governor and United States Senator, was the first president, serving from 1846 to 1853, when he died and was succeeded by Hon. Isaac Davis. The latter died in 1882, after twenty-nine years of service, whereupon ex-Governor Alex. H. Bullock was chosen, but passed away within ten days. Hon. P. L. Moen acted in the capacity of president in the interval prior to the election of A. G. Bullock in January, 1883. Mr. Bullock is a son of ex-Governor Bullock, a native of Enfield, Conn., born June 2, 1847, a Harvard alumnus, and a member of the Worcester bar. A prominent business man and connected with various social and literary associations, he is widely known and popular. The *Insurance Times* says of him: "He has an enviable record. Under his administration the State Mutual has made definite and steady progress. In eight years he has increased the insurance in force from $14,162,000 to $35,017,951; the assets from $3,000,000 to $6,396,572.16; the annual income from $500,000 to $1,661,163; the annual disbursements to policy-holders from $261,000 to $607,390,69.

Always a strong company, Mr. Bullock brought it up abreast of the times and made it progressive and prosperous.''

The company's home office is a handsome four-story granite front structure, 40x60 feet, at No. 240 Main street, the interior finished in fine woods and plate glass, the arrangements perfect, and the conveniences of all kinds complete. Here may be seen, every working day, twenty busy clerks, and in the private office the president, the secretary, the actuary, the superintendent of the hundreds of agencies, and the medical directors, Drs. Thomas H. Gage and Albert Wood. The board of directors embraces many of the leading citizens and capitalists of Worcester and Worcester county, as follows: A. G. Bullock, P. L. Moen, Thomas H. Gage, E. B. Stoddard, T. W. Hammond, S. Salisbury, Wm. E. Starr, Aug. N. Currier, W. H. Jourdan, Geo. F. Hoar, Albert Wood, Henry M. Witter, Thomas L. Nelson, Josiah H. Clarke and Frank A. Gaskill of Worcester, and Chas. A. Denny of Leicester.

THE STATE SAFE DEPOSIT COMPANY.

A. G. Bullock, President; H. M. Witter, Secretary; Halleck Bartlett, Manager—Insurance Building, No. 240 Main Street—Company Incorporated 1888.

The officers of this company are men of approved character and responsibility, President Bullock and Secretary Witter sustaining respectively the same relations toward the famous old State Mutual Life Assurance Company. The vaults, forming an extension of the last-named company's fine building, No. 240 Main street, are massive and constructed in the most substantial manner from special plans, thoroughly fire and burglar-proof, provided with the latest improvements in safes, doors, locks, etc., built above ground, well-lighted, and constantly under the eye of watchful guardians, night and day. The safes, easily accessible to depositors only—each of whom carries his own key—are of various sizes to suit the requirements of patrons, and are rented at very reasonable rates ranging from $5 upward. Here may be stored, with absolute assurance of safety, every description of valuable papers, securities, jewelry, diamonds, etc., and the same may be reclaimed at any time without the trouble of asking.

A commodious storage vault, fire-proof and otherwise secured, adjoins, where families or individuals may store trunks, boxes, or other packages of valuable clothing, furs, silver and pictures, while absent from the city for the season or for any other reason.

METROPOLITAN STORAGE WAREROOMS.

Household Furniture and Merchandise Storage—Furniture and Other Goods Skillfully Packed for Moving or Shipment—James H. Dickie, No. 6 Barton Place.

Mr. James H. Dickie, an experienced handler of household goods, for twelve years with a leading Worcester furniture house, Christmas, 1889, established a storage warehouse at the corner of Southbridge and Beacon streets, but ere long discovered that he could not find room there for all the goods offered him. In September last he secured the old Worcester Light Artillery armory building, four stories, 50x70 feet, No. 6 Barton place, which he refitted throughout with compartments provided with locks and keys and other improvements for the convenience of patrons and the safety of their goods, each lot being kept separate from all others, and none but the owners having access to them. The entire place is kept neat and clean; no fire is permitted about the premises, and the fire patrol station is next door. Rates are very moderate. Parties who contemplate removal from one portion of the city to another or to distant points will find it profitable to secure Mr. Dickie's services in packing the more fragile and valuable articles of furniture, such as mirrors, pictures, pianos, organs, etc. Barton place runs west from Main street between Pleasant and Chatham.

THE CURTIS MANUFACTURING COMPANY.

Albert Curtis, President and Treasurer; C. G. Stratton, Secretary—Manufacturers of Woolen Goods—Webster Street.

The venerable Albert Curtis, now president and treasurer of the company, founded this noted enterprise in 1835, when, with limited means but boundless energy and sagacity, he began the manufacture of woolens on a small scale as compared to the present output of the mills developed from his early venture. At the age of eighty-four he still participates in the business management, presiding over the destinies of the concern with all of his old-time spirit and looking after the finances in a careful, methodical manner that attests a mind still strong and healthy.

As now constituted the company was incorporated with $100,000 capital in 1880, and is one of the best representatives of that particular industry in this vicinity. The main building is of brick, three stories and basement, 50x100 feet, with which is connected a three-story-and-basement brick structure, 36x70 feet, with an L 25x50 feet, and several smaller brick and wooden buildings at the rear. The mill is what is termed a nine-set plant, completely equipped and provided with both water and steam power, a fine forty-horse engine supplying the latter. From *one hundred and twenty-five to one hundred and fifty* people work in the mill, and the output, quite large and embracing every description of domestic woolen dress goods, is distributed to the trade in all parts of the country through C. G. Ross & Co. of New York, James Talcott of New York, and Wernwheg & Dawson of New York and Philadelphia.

J. J. WARREN COMPANY.

J. J. Warren, President; John M. Warren, Treasurer; Walter F. Davison, Secretary—Manufacturers of Fine Leather and Canvas Goods of Every Description—Warren Building, Washington Square.

The uses to which leather is put are infinite. Aside from harness, saddlery, footwear, belting for machinery, and military equipments, this material is utilized on a grand scale in the manufacture of a great variety of every-day requisites and conveniences for home and travel, such as dressing-cases, collar and cuff boxes, toilet rolls, music rolls, portfolios, straps and belts, cases for manicure sets, fire-arms, medicines, musical instruments,

samples, etc. Canvas is also largely employed for kindred purposes, chiefly in the making of valises, sample cases, extension cases, light trunks, gun cases, shooting jackets aud belts. Among the largest manufacturers of leather and canvas goods in this country is the J. J. Warren Company of this city, incorporated as the Harrall Manufacturing Company in 1883, capital $20,000. For four years the business was prosecuted in Boston, at the expiration of which time the concern was removed to Worcester and reorganized under the present style. The plant is located in the Warren building, at Washington square, opposite the Union passenger station. The three upper stories of the building, affording 18,000 square feet of floorage, are used for the factory, which is fitted up with every appliance that ingenuity can devise to facilitate operations. In all departments —designing, cutting, stitching, finishing and packing —about sixty hands are employed, most of whom are experts, as the producing of the various fine articles furnished by this concern requires much artistic skill and experience. A large proportion of the finest work is necessarily done by hand, but many very ingenious and effective machines are brought into service, with the aid of which large quantities of goods are turned out in a surprisingly short space of time. Five traveling salesmen represent the house in New England, the middle, western and southern States, and transactions embrace the entire country, extending even to principal points in Canada, the company maintaining branch offices at the corner of Washington and Winter streets, Boston; New York, Denver, and San Francisco. Beautifully illustrated catalogues and price-lists are supplied on application. A specialty is made in Sample Cases and work of any description to order at short notice. The Messrs. Warren are residents of Worcester, and Secretary Davison is from Hinsdale, Mass. All are active, earnest business men, and give their undivided personal attention to this enterprise.

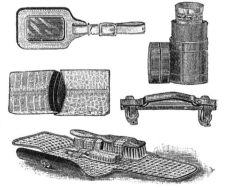

THE WORCESTER MAGAZINE AIR RIFLE.

Manufactured by The Worcester Magazine Air Rifle Co.—J. J. Warren Company, Agents, Warren Building, Washington Square.

The American boy of to-day, whatever his position in life, feels that he has not yet a complete outfit if he does not possess a rifle or a pistol. Unfortunately, such as have been made in the past and called toys have been dangerous to both the owner and his friends or playmates, and too many young men are to be seen who have been injured, more or less seriously, by a shot

from or the bursting of these so-called harmless toys. Within the past few years, however, the air gun has been brought into use, and with these the operator is secured against any explosion of the piece, yet they were all too expensive for any but the wealthy, and were still dangerous to those who might stand in the way of the shot. Now both parents and boys will be glad to know that the Worcester Magazine Air Rifle Company have perfected and are making a new air gun, which competent judges pronounce superior to all others yet produced, and which, because of its excellence and moderate cost, must quickly become popular. This gun, which contains all the best improvements known, is what its name implies — a magazine rifle, but such an one! One hundred charges can be placed in the magazine at one time, and fired off almost as quickly as the marksman chooses. All that is necessary to load the rifle is to lower a lever and return it to its proper position in the stock, which is but the work of a moment. By an ingenious contrivance — something like that of the slot machine — one ball is separated from the rest and put in position during this simple action, the whole being automatic. Then the cost is nominal, for the cost of the whole one hundred rounds of good-sized duck-shot is only *one cent*. But besides this, it has been demonstrated that while the rifle will carry from 200 to 300 yards, and with accuracy for 35 to 40 yards, it is not a death-dealing weapon, for the shot propelled from it will not pass through the skin of a human being. Some excellent practice has been made with this rifle, and a good marksman will be satisfied with it. Indoor amusement at this rate is cheap and attended with but little danger. The rifle is made of steel and iron, and almost the whole of the piece is nickel-plated, making it a very handsome present for Young America. It is gotten up with taste, and is really a thing of beauty, as the cut shows. In length, the rifle is 33 inches, and the unusual length of the barrel gives it precision in shooting. One great item to be taken into consideration is the cost of the rifle, which is not more than half that of the so-called best makes hitherto in existence. Although the "Worcester Magazine Air Rifle" has only just been introduced, the makers have already received orders for several thousand.

C. H. DRAPER,

Livery, Feed and Truck Stable—Furniture and Piano Moving a Specialty—No. 161 Main Street.

Among the best equipped and most accommodating of Worcester's numerous livery stable men is Mr. C. H. Draper, of No. 161 Main street, who has been catering to the wants of the public in the way of horses and wheeled vehicles since 1878, when he started in the business on Lincoln street. He removed in 1885 to his present stand, where, with stables, barns and sheds covering a quarter of an acre adjacent to Lincoln square depot, fitted up with all possible conveniences, including telephone, a great variety of elegant single and double carriages, buggies, etc., and a stud of thirty fine horses, he is better prepared than ever to serve the public. Sixteen attentive and experienced men are connected with the establishment, and careful, polite and well-informed drivers are furnished when desired by strangers and others wishing a pleasant jaunt through the city, the suburbs, or the country in any direction.

In addition to his general livery equipment Mr. Draper is provided with heavy draught horses and trucks, gives personal attention to trucking and freighting, and makes a specialty of furniture and piano-moving. Passengers and baggage are also transferred to and from all trains and all points in the city and environs. Prompt service and reasonable prices is his motto, and patrons may depend upon courtesy and upright dealing.

Mr. Draper, a native of Spencer, is widely known as an honorable business man of large experience in his special line. An Oddfellow, Knight of Pythias and G. A. R. man, he is popular with all classes.

J. S. WHEELER & CO.,

Manufacturers of Iron Planers—No. 23 Hermon Street.

On the opposite page is illustrated the famous Wheeler planer, built in Worcester by the old and reputable house of J. S. Wheeler & Co., and in general use throughout the United States, Canada and Europe. These planers are pronounced, by competent mechanics, unequaled·in point of neatness, economy and effectiveness, convenience, rapid working and durability. This house was established in 1867. About 1878, Mr. Wheeler became sole proprietor, retaining the

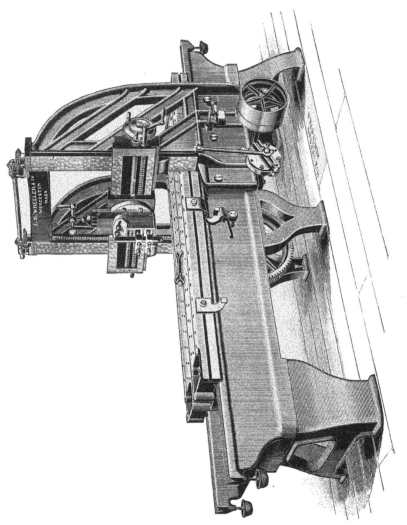

original name and style, and continues to transact a large and prosperous business, occupying one floor, 50 x 120 feet, well fitted up with machinery and steam power, and employing twenty-five skilled mechanics. Formerly a great variety of machinery and special tools were made here, but of late Mr. Wheeler has confined his attention exclusively to the manufacture of the iron planers above referred to, and has recently made many changes in the design of the machine and introduced many improvements, for which there are several applications for patents now pending. He is a practical and experienced machinist, a native of Fitchburg, and has resided in Worcester for the past forty-seven years. An honest man and a good citizen, he enjoys the confidence and regard of all who know him.

BELL CLOTHING COMPANY.

C. F. Pharaoh, Manager—Dealers in Ready-Made and Custom Clothing and Gentlemen's Furnishings—No. 32 Front St.

The art of clothing the multitude well and cheaply has been brought to extraordinary perfection of late years, more especially in New England, where the trade is in the hands of men of taste and experience, and where competition, while honorable for the most part, is yet active and conducted on close margins, much to the advantage of the consumer. The latest addition to the Worcester clothing trade, and one of the most popular and promising, is the Bell Clothing Company, established in the spring of 1890 by Mr. C. F. Pharaoh, formerly of the Star Clothing Company, of which he was one of the founders. Mr. Pharaoh at first occupied a handsome store in the Chase block on Front street, and was already building up a flourishing business when, on the first of May, he formed a copartnership with Mr. J. A. Courtemanche,

likewise an experienced and successful clothing merchant, and the new firm at once secured the great salesroom No. 32 Front street, 25 x 135 feet, which they proceeded to remodel in superb style, putting in an entirely new front, including immense plate glass show-windows and doors, numerous costly counters, shelving, show-cases, cash carriers and all modern improvements. Their stock, vastly reinforced direct from the manufacturers and enlarged by additions in all departments, was gradually removed to the new stand, tastily and conveniently arranged, and, finally, on the evening of June 6, the opening occurred. The *Telegram* of the 5th referred to the event as follows: "The windows were filled with stylish suits and made all the more attractive by a huge bell of vari-colored flowers that hung suspended from the ceiling, the gift conjointly of George H. Grant of J. B. Barnaby & Co., Providence; Joel Feder of Stern, Falk & Co., New York, and W. A. Wetherbee of Schattman Bros., New York, who were present at the opening in company with Seth H. Ingraham of Hawley, Folsom & Romulus, Boston; J. Schattman of Schattman Bros., and Louis Strauss of Leopold, Morse & Co., Boston. Inside, everything usual to well-stocked houses of the kind was found, also a full line of men's furnishings and hats. Potted plants and flowers artistically arranged added to the attractiveness of the scene, which was further enhanced by music by Bemis's orchestra of seven pieces, stationed in one corner of the store. Despite the inclement weather, the house was packed with sightseers, who received as souvenirs of the occasion handsome lithograph cards and natty working caps, distributed by six business-like clerks." The custom department receives special attention, and orders are made up and trimmed at the celebrated Oak Hall tailoring establishment, Boston, and George Snow & Co. of Dover. Stocks are complete, and embrace every article of men's, boys' and children's wear in infinite variety, all novelties in styles and materials being received and put on sale as soon as introduced in the New York market. In every respect this is a model clothing house, and buyers of every nationality will be made at home, there being nine polite salesmen speaking English, French, German, Italian, Scandinavian, Spanish and other tongues. Mr. George Taylor, an accomplished artist, presides over the custom department, and patrons may depend upon good workmanship and perfect style and fit. Messrs. Pharaoh and Courtemanche are courteous gentlemen and thoroughly acquainted with all the details of the trade. Mr. Charles F. Pharaoh, the manager, as before stated, was formerly connected with a leading concern here, and with J. B. Barnaby & Co. of Providence, R. I., the most extensive clothing house in New England— now the J. B. Barnaby Company—maintaining great stores all over the east and west as far as Kansas City. Mr. Courtemanche was long connected with the great Canadian house of Carhalter & Carpenter.

KNOWLES LOOM WORKS.

C. H. Hutchins, President and Treasurer; F. P. Knowles, Vice President; H. H. Merriam, Secretary; Geo. F. Hutchins, General Superintendent—Builders of Open Shed Fancy Looms, Looms for Worsteds, Woolens, Silks, Cottons, Velvets, Carpets, Upholstery, Draperies, Tapes, Ribbons and Suspenders, and every Variety of Weaving Machinery— Cor. Grand and Tainter Sts.

This superb industrial establishment—next to the wire works the most important and influential of those which have made the names of Worcester and Massachusetts famous throughout the civilized world — was founded by two brothers who, bred to diligent labor and denied the early advantages of advanced education, nevertheless achieved, through dint of application and energy, combined with natural inventive talent and business tact, results which, in their effect upon commerce and manufactures of textiles, can be fairly characterized as stupendous. Both were born upon a farm in the town of Hardwick, Worcester county — Lucius J. Knowles, July 2, 1819, Francis B., November 29, 1823. The elder, at the age of fourteen, began an academic course of three years, and, at seventeen, engaged as clerk in a Shrewsbury village store, becoming a partner two years later. Previous to leaving home he had exercised his mechanical genius in the construction of various original machines, and, on engaging in mercantile business, he devoted all of his spare time to the same pursuits, experimenting with reed instruments, steam engines, etc., and, at length, completed a working model of the now famous Knowles safety steam boiler feed regulator. Retiring from mercantile pursuits in 1840, he became interested in and constructed one or more electric motors, and then engaged in the study and development of photography, which art he pursued until 1844, when, having invented a spooling machine, he located at New Worcester as a thread manufacturer. He next, in 1847, removed to and started a cotton warp mill at Spencer, which he abandoned two years later and went to Warren. From 1853 to 1860 he manufactured woolen goods, during that period securing two patents for looms and one for an improved pumping engine valve. In 1862 he started machine shops for the manufacture of his patent feed regulator, and, in 1863, began building his steam pumps. In copartnership with his brother, Francis B., the same year he began the construction of looms at Warren. In 1866 the firm removed to Worcester, where, with a small force of expert workmen, they occupied unpretentious shops in Allen court, whence they removed in 1870 to the (then considered) monster shops at the Junction, about one-third of a mile west of which stands the magnificent plant we illustrate, and which is described further along. Mr. L. J. Knowles, unostentatious and retiring though he was, could not escape his share of public honors and burdens. He received from Williams College the honorary degree of master of arts in 1869, served two terms in the House of Representatives and one in the Senate, and also sat in the Common Council of 1873. He was conspicuous in business circles, and filled many positions of trust in connection with banking, insurance, educational and commercial institutions. Mr. Knowles died suddenly of neuralgia of the heart while on a visit to the National capital, February 25, 1884.

Francis B. Knowles began life for himself at the age of seventeen, with the same equipment— common school and academic training. He taught one term in the Dana public school, and, in 1842, accepted a like position at Gloversville, N. Y., where, for a time, he continued the work of teaching, but subsequently became a traveling salesman in the glove trade, in which he was so successful that April 1, 1845, he engaged in the manufacture of buckskin gloves, and later in the clothing business, which he continued until the formation of the Knowles Brothers copartnership in 1863, after which his business life was identified therewith. He was married twice—in 1845 to Ann Eliza Pool and in 1867 to Hester A. Green, the latter surviving him. After the death of his brother the business was continued under the firm name of L. J. Knowles & Brother until January, 1885, when it was made into a company of which Mr. F. B. Knowles was president until his own death, which also occurred in Washington City, May 15, 1890. He was active and liberal in the cause of religion, and one of the founders of the Plymouth Congregational church. For some years past he made Florida his winter home, owning large bodies of land, orange groves, etc., in that State, and being interested in the Seminole Hotel and Rollins College at Winter Park, and president and principal stockholder of the Winter Park Company. It was during the last year of his life that the new works of the Knowles Loom Company were planned and erected.

THE BUILDINGS.

The buildings, carefully planned by the celebrated Boston mill engineering firm of Lockwood, Greene & Co., are two in number, separated by a 60-foot yard, and extend eastward from Grand street, between Tainter street and the Boston & Albany railroad tracks, a distance of 521 feet. The eastern portion—the machine shops proper—is of four stories, flat roof, fronting 221 feet on Grand and 251 feet on Tainter street, 212 feet on the railroad and 218 feet on the central yard. It is constructed in the form of a hollow square, with court in the center, and each floor affords 40,000 square feet of area. On the Grand and Tainter streets corner of the ground floor is the general office, and, adjoining that, the shipping office. At the corner of Tainter street and the yard is the time-keeper's office, and in the rear of that, fronting the yard, the engine and boiler rooms, chimney, elevator and stair tower. Other stairs are provided at the northeastern and southeastern corners of the central court. The heating and ventilating appliances, of the most approved style, adjoin the boiler and engine rooms, a complete system of pipes and registers extending to all parts of the building, while a fan of immense proportions will supply fresh air in abundance when required. The machine shop is on the second floor, the woodworking shop, draughting and pattern rooms and storage for supplies on the third, and the setting-up and testing rooms on the fourth.

The foundry building, east of the dividing yard, is 180 x 224 feet in area, one story, with monitor roof. Projecting westward, at the north and south sides, are wings, that on the north fitted up with sixteen forges, and that on the south with appliances for cleaning castings, sandpits and annealing apparatus. The forge shop has 3,600 and the cleaning shop 2,000 square feet of floorage. A two-story projection of the foundry, the upper floor of which is used for general storage purposes, connects the forge and cleaning shops with the main foundry, presenting a superficial area of 30,000 square feet. The entire plant is of brick and granite, constructed in the most substantial manner, and on a gigantic scale (already the largest plant for the manufacture of fancy looms in the United States), notwithstanding which large additions are in contemplation.

A description of the working facilities would hardly enlighten the general reader. Suffice it to say that they comprehend everything that can be utilized to advantage, that about 1,000 men are employed, and that from twelve to fifteen looms, complete, are produced daily, embracing every description of weaving machinery. This establishment supplies only the American market,

Hutchinson, Hollingsworth & Co. of Dobcross, England, manufacturing, under the Knowles patents, for foreign trade. The output has doubled during the past five years, and still the demand increases. The Knowles Loom Works is a close corporation, capital $300,000, and most of the stock is held by members of the family and its connections. President C. H. Hutchins is a son-in-law and Vice-President F. P. Knowles a son of the late F. B. Knowles.

JOHN G. JEFFERDS,

Manufacturer of and Dealer in Fertilizers, Tallow, Poultry Feed, Broken and Ground Glues—Works at Quinsigamond.

Mr. Jefferds, a native of the Green Mountain State, who served two years in the war for the Union and retired with the rank of sergeant-major, established himself at Quinsigamond— Worcester's principal southeastern suburb—in 1874, and by the exercise of energy, sagacity and integrity, has built up a flourishing business in the manufacture and sale of fertilizers, tallow,

poultry feed and glues. His premises comprise five substantial two-story frame buildings, respectively 40 x 80, 25 x 40, 30 x 30, 20 x 40 and 30 x 42 feet in superficial area, some of which are fitted up with grinding, mixing and rendering appliances, boiler and engine, and the others utilized for packing and storage purposes. Twenty hands are employed, and the annual product approximates 1,200,000 pounds of tallow, 300 to 400 tons of animal fertilizers, 60,000 to 75,000 pounds of broken and ground glues, and 50 tons of superior poultry food—the latter put up in convenient packages and sold throughout New England. His sales are steadily increasing.

MACULLAR & SON,

Clothiers and Custom Tailors—Nos. 372 and 374 Main Street.

This is a branch of the famous old Boston house of Macullar, Williams & Parker, established many years ago and succeeded by Macullar, Parker & Co.—the latter one of the most reputable business concerns in the modern Athens. Mr. A. Macullar remains at the head of the home establishment, while his son, Mr. F. R. Macullar, has charge here—a position for which he is well fitted by temperament and previous training.

The Worcester store is one of the most attractive in the city, 30x90 feet, richly and tastefully appointed, and superbly stocked with a line of men's, youths' and boys' ready-made fine clothing, such as is carried only by the most exclusive class of clothiers. Commanding the confidence and patronage of the best people of town and country, it is hardly necessary to say that goods are sold entirely upon the irmerits, that no exaggeration or misrepresentation is permitted, and that the one-price system rules—the lowest consistent with good fabrics, stylish cut and first-class workmanship and finish. In connection with the salesroom is an extensive and well-conducted custom-tailoring department, stocked at all seasons with the choicest imported and domestic fabrics, where those who prefer may leave their orders for garments in the full assurance of a perfect fit, the best possible material, trimmings and finish, and style equal to that of any first-class house in Boston or New York, an artist cutter standing ready at all times to serve discriminating patrons. .

WORCESTER CORSET COMPANY.

The Worcester Corset Company--D. H. Fanning, President; F. W. Ruggles, Treasurer — Manufacturers of the Royal Worcester W C C Corsets — Office and Factory, Cor. Hermon and Beacon Sts.; Retail Store, No. 328 Main St.

The Royal Worcester. W C C corsets are universal favorites with American ladies. The Worcester Corset Company, established in 1861, from small and unpretentious beginnings has steadily advanced on the line of improvement and development until it now stands at the head in the production of strictly fine corsets. Experts unhesitatingly pronounce this brand of corsets unsurpassed by any other made on either side of the Atlantic. These corsets combine the very best material and the highest artistic and mechanical skill in their construction,

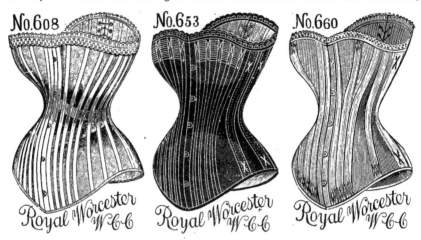

points of superiority which have always in the past, and will ever continue to distinguish this company's goods, which are formed upon the latest and most perfect models, exquisitely finished and fully warranted. They are made of a single thickness of light, strong fabrics, serges, silks, satins and pongees forming the basis of the higher grades; an inside linen band gives ample strength to the waist line; thus the minimum of weight and the maximum of flexibility and strength are secured. In a word, they are a boon to woman; and, being made in more than one hundred styles, each designated by a number, any figure or taste may be readily suited. The trade-marks, together with the style number, are indelibly printed on the inside of all genuine

Royal Worcester W C C Corsets

Medals and diplomas have been awarded the products of this company by juries of expositions wherever exhibited. In the spring of 1888 an act of incorporation was secured; capital, $125,000, which was in May, 1889, increased to $200,000. For many years the works were situated at Nos. 564 and 566 Main street, but the accommodations at last becoming insufficient, they were removed in January, 1890, to the present location, corner Beacon and Hermon streets, and the retail store to No. 328 Main street. Four floors, aggregating over 50,000 square feet, are devoted to the work-rooms and office. A description of the various departments would prove tedious with no resulting advantage to the reader. Suffice it to say that the processes are reduced to an exact system; splendid light and ventilation are provided; the latest and best machinery furnished, and a myriad of bright-eyed, industrious girls is employed, under the direction of experienced and skillful superintendents and forewomen. The Main street store is a favorite shopping place for ladies resident or visiting in Worcester in search of corsets, waists, neckwear, underwear, laces, and notions generally—the most complete store of its kind in New England. The custom department is also here, and many patrons leave their orders for corsets to measure. The company's New York office is at No. 454 Broadway. The Chicago salesroom was recently removed to the fine new building Nos. 260 and 262 Fifth avenue.

DARLING BROTHERS.

Contractors and Builders—Office, Mill and Shops, E. Worcester St.

Perhaps no firm in New England, in any department of industrial enterprise, has made such rapid strides of late years toward celebrity and success on a grand scale as have Darling Brothers, contractors and builders, of this city. Up to the autumn of 1886 they had confined their attention to small local contracts, involving limited capital and the employment of few men, but, having been awarded the contract for building the Norwich & Worcester freight house on Southbridge street, they suddenly shook off their previous apparent indifference and went in to make a reputation, in which effort they succeeded so well that other large contracts soon followed and were executed promptly and satisfactorily, among the most notable being the

Polytechnic Institute instrument house, the monster Knowles loom works, and the elegant new Worcester theater. They have recently completed a beautiful new Baptist church on Pleasant street and a working plant for themselves on East Worcester street, the latter consisting of two two-story frame structures—office, mill and shops, 31 x 113 feet, and engine and dry-house, 28 x 44 feet. The firm erected a number of fine buildings at other points the past year, among them a fire-proof brick and brownstone City hall and memorial building, a granite Union Congregational church (*see engraving*) costing $80,000, and two large granite trimmed brick business blocks at Rockville, Conn. They have now under way a State Normal school building, to cost $102,900, at Bridgewater, and another for the same purpose, to cost $93,529, at Westfield; a $42,775 bank building at Fall River, and another, at Providence, to cost $95,484, in addition to which they are at work upon the new fire-proof Bristol County court-house at Fall River— contract price, $116,000—and upon a $64,435 granite church at Wakefield, Mass. They have recently broken ground for and will push to completion the Grady memorial hospital at Atlanta, Ga., for which they were awarded the contract at $64,012. They recently completed two fire-proof buildings for the Government armory at Springfield, and have secured the contract for a third, to cost $106,950. A $35,000 engine-house at Cottage Farms for the B. & A. railroad company completes the list of Darling Brothers' pending contracts and those completed during last year. Their finished business for 1889 aggregated $500,000; that, for 1890, including contracts made, will not fall short of $750,000. They have employed 726 hands the past year, and have increased the number very considerably with the opening of the present season. A notable feature of Darling Brothers' facilities is the ownership of eighty acres of the celebrated Milford pink granite quarries, whence they are enabled to procure any required quantity of that most beautiful and desirable material, their works at that place being equipped in the best manner and employing seventy-five men in quarrying and cutting. Messrs. Daniel W. and Jasper T. Darling entered the Union army at the ages of sixteen and eighteen respectively. Discharged from the service in 1865, they became apprentices and later journeymen carpenters, subsequently forming a copartnership, which still continues. They owe all of their success to enterprise, industry and the faithful performance of every agreement.

PATSTON & LINCOLN.

J. William Patston and Charles H. Lincoln—Architects—Chase Building, No. 44 Front Street, Room 55.

This business was established in 1885 by Mr. Patston, who came here from Providence, R. I., where he had followed his profession for several years, and earned for himself an excellent reputation as a skilled architect, being engaged on several buildings of merit in that city and neighborhood. Since he has been in Worcester opportunity has frequently offered itself for this gentleman to display his skill, and he has, while building up a good professional reputation, in every instance been able to please his clients. Mr. Lincoln, who is a Worcester man, is so well known for his artistic taste that it were almost superfluous to attempt to introduce him to the people of Worcester. His knowledge of architecture enables him at all times to meet the expressed desire of those who consult him. He became a member of the firm on October 1, 1890, and the two gentlemen, with their practical ability, are competent to carry out any work which may be entrusted to them, while their clients may rely upon receiving prompt attention.

HON. SAMUEL WINSLOW.

Hon. Samuel Winslow was born, the son of Eleazer R. Winslow, in Newton, Mass., February 28, 1827, and is consequently in his sixty-fifth year. He is of Pilgrim stock, descended from Kenelm, a brother of the celebrated Gov. Winslow who came over in the Mayflower in 1620. Receiving a limited education in the Newton common schools, Samuel Winslow set in to learn the machinist's trade, obtaining employment in an establishment making a specialty of cotton manufacturing machinery. Ingenious and industrious, his advancement was rapid, and ere attaining his majority he was foreman over fifty workmen. Coming to Worcester in April, 1855, he and his brother, Seth C., formed a copartnership, established machine-shops, and prospered, adding to their specialties two years later the manufacture of skates, in the form, material and construction of which they made many improvements. The brothers continued in business together until 1871, when, Seth having died, the surviving partner made some changes and additions to the plant and managed it on his individual account for about fifteen years. The Samuel Winslow Skate Manufacturing Company, of which the founder retained control, was organized in May, 1886, and has done and is doing a flourishing business, supplying fine skates for the American, Canadian and European markets. The handsome and perfectly equipped factory on Mulberry street, since greatly enlarged, was erected in 1874.

Mr. Winslow's business sagacity and interest in public affairs have more than once led his fellow-citizens to confer upon him distinguished political honors. He was elected to the Common Council in 1864-65, to the Legislature in 1873-74, to the board of Aldermen in 1885, and to the mayoralty, terms of 1886-87-88 and '89. From 1868 to 1871 he was a trustee, from 1884 to 1886 vice-president, and in 1886 president of the Worcester County Mechanics Association. Married in 1848 to Miss Mary W. Robbins, he has two sons, Frank E. and Samuel E., the latter secretary of the skate company.

THE SAMUEL WINSLOW SKATE M'F'G. COMPANY.

Samuel Winslow, President and Treasurer; Samuel E. Winslow, Secretary—Manufacturers of Ice and Roller Skates—Asylum Street.

Judging from what our reporter has observed, the world is supplied with skates by Massachusetts manufacturers. At any rate it is conceded that the best skates are made in this State, Springfield and Worcester being the principal centers of the industry, while some idea of its ex-

tent may be gathered from the fact that one factory here—that of the Samuel Winslow Skate Manufacturing Company on Asylum street—employs from 50 to 150 skilled workmen. The works were established in 1856. The present company was incorporated in 1886 with $50,000 capital, President Samuel Winslow of the Citizens' National Bank accepting the presidency and his son Samuel E. the secretaryship. Both are Worcester men of prominence in business circles, energetic, enterprising and successful. The skate factory occupies the four-story building adjoining the Winslow & Curtis Machine Screw Company's establishment on Asylum street, 40 feet wide by 307 feet long, another building five stories and 30 feet square, forming an ell 30x50 feet, two stories high, and is thoroughly equipped throughout with appropriate machinery, driven by a 105-horse-power steam engine. Every description of late improved ice and roller skates are made here in immense numbers and are supplied to the trade throughout the world. They are beautiful goods in the most attractive styles, and popular and salable wherever introduced.

Other leading specialties to which particular attention is given embrace fine gear-cutting, high-grade press and punch work, polishing and nickel-plating, the facilities for doing which are unsurpassed.

THE WINSLOW & CURTIS MACHINE SCREW COMPANY.

Manufacturers of Standard Machine Screws and All Kinds of Screw Machine Work —Asylum Street.

Worcester is the principal centre of numerous industries, among which not the least important is the manufacture of the better grades of machine screws, a leading house in this line being the Winslow & Curtis Machine Screw Company, established in 1888 by Messrs. Samuel E. Winslow and A. B. Curtis, the former a native of Worcester and secretary of the Winslow Skate Manufacturing Company, the latter born in Vermont and a skilled practical machinist. The present style was adopted in February, 1890. The works, employing twenty-five hands, are situated on Asylum street, occupy two floors 38x110 feet, and are well equipped with machinery, steam power, and all facilities for turning out large quantities of superior work, including a comprehensive line of standard machine screws in all styles and some other specialties, one of which is the new envelope opener, patented August 21, 1888. It is simply a spring blade of proper length set in a frame so adjusted that when pressed downward it takes off just enough of the envelope at one edge to open it without injury to the contents. This little machine needs only to be seen to be appreciated, and is exported to Germany in large numbers, the methodical people of that country recognizing its convenience and adopting it freely in government and private business offices.

This new company is in a prosperous condition, having a large and growing trade at home and abroad, and will be compelled ere long to increase its facilities, sales already pressing close upon production.

WORCESTER COUNTY INSTITUTION FOR SAVINGS.

Stephen Salisbury, President; Charles A. Chase, Treasurer; Charles F. Aldrich, Clerk of Corporation; Ed. B. Hamilton, General Accountant—No. 13 Foster St.

The Worcester County Institution for Savings was incorporated on the 8th day of February, 1828, and during a continuous existence of more than sixty-three years has ever proved true to the trust reposed in it by its many thousands of depositors, a monument to the upright methods of its administration, and a model of correct financiering. No patron has ever lost a dollar through any fault of the management; interest and dividends have been promptly met on demand, and with the lapse of years the institution has grown in favor, power and influence, until today it ranks with the few ancient fiduciary trusts of this country that have never suffered from serious permanent reverses or failed in the performance of the duties devolving upon them as custodians of the people's savings. How much good this grand old bank has done in the encouragement of thrifty habits among the struggling masses at home and the advancement of public and private improvement and development, by supplying the means necessary therefor, may never be known, but it is certain that successful legitimate enterprise has ample reason to thank the good providence that presides over the vaults of the institution. Deposits are received at any time in sums from $1.00 to $1,000, and draw interest from the first of January, April, July and October. January and July 15 are dividend days. The principal executive officers are named above. Messrs. Henry W. Miller, Albert Tolman and George S. Howe are vice-presidents. Trustees—Joseph Mason, John D. Washburn, Edward L. Davis, Stephen Salisbury, George E. Francis, Wm. H. Jourdan, Thomas H. Gage, Josiah H. Clarke, Charles B. Pratt, A. Geo. Bullock, John W. Wetherell, Waldo Lincoln, George Chandler, Frank P. Goulding, Lincoln N. Kinnicutt, Jonas G. Clark, Charles F. Aldrich, Elisha D. Buffington, Samuel S. Green, Samuel C. Willis, jr., George W. Fisher, Leonard Wheeler, Ed. D. Thayer, jr., George F. Blake, jr. Board of Investment—Stephen Salisbury, Waldo Lincoln, Jonas G. Clark, Albert Tolman, A. Geo. Bullock. Board of Auditors—George E. Francis, George F. Blake, jr., George S. Howe. The bank occupies a portion of the Worcester National Bank building, Nos. 9 to 13 Foster street. Number of depositors, 24,736; total deposits, $11,383,098.80.

WORCESTER CARPET COMPANY.

Wm. Jas. Hogg, Proprietor—Manufacturers of Wilton and Brussels Carpets—Mills and Office, Brussels St.; Salesroom, Cor. Broadway and Worth Sts., New York.

Of all of Worcester's diversified industries none are more worthy of special attention than the

manufacture of carpets as conducted by the Worcester Carpet Company. The enterprise is not, by any means, a new one, having been founded in 1870 by the Crompton Carpet Company, under whose competent management it prospered until 1879, when Mr. Wm. Jas. Hogg, an experienced practical carpet weaver, purchased the plant, and has since successfully directed operations under the name and style of the Worcester Carpet Company. The mills and appurtenances, situated on Brussels street, comprise three three-story brick buildings, two of which are 60 x 120, the other 50 x 100 feet, with which are connected several smaller structures used as dyehouses, store rooms, etc. The office, in front, is entirely separate, commodious and elegantly fitted up. The mills, substantial and handsome, are equipped throughout with the latest improved wool-carding, spinning and weaving machinery, driven partly by water and partly by a splendid 325-horse-power steam engine. The operatives in all departments number 400, and the output, comprising the best grades of Wilton and Brussels carpets, is very large and valuable. The popularity of the goods is shown by the fact that they are handled by the trade and purchased by consumers in every village and town in the United States and the territories. The wools used here are imported expressly for the purpose, and all yarns employed in the manufacture of carpets are made on the premises. The mills are run to their full capacity the year round, and there is no accumulation of stock. The principal office is, as above stated, adjacent to the mills, but the general salesroom, for the convenience of the jobbing trade, is at the corner of Broadway and Worth street, New York city, where all orders should be sent.

CITIZENS NATIONAL BANK OF WORCESTER.

Samuel Winslow, President; Henry S. Pratt, Vice-President; L. W. Hammond, Cashier—Capital Stock, $150,000—No. 425 Main Street.

This ably managed and flourishing institution was organized and chartered as a National bank February 1, 1865, its original incorporation as a State bank having occurred April 9, 1836. The results of the first twenty years under the new auspices were so satisfactory that the charter was extended for a like period, to expire on the first of February, 1905. The board of directors embraces, besides the president and cashier, already named, Messrs. Benj. W. Childs, Hamilton B. Fay, Henry S. Pratt, George B. Buckingham and Fred W. Ward. From first to last the management of this bank has been distinguished for rectitude and conservatism, not unmixed with liberality of the most useful and effective kind, as many a successful business man whom it has assisted when in difficulty can attest. A like spirit has ever been evinced toward public enterprise of a safe and commendable kind, and both city and county are under obligations for timely assistance at various times.

The Citizens National does a general banking business in all that the term implies, and stands equipped and ready to serve the public in the best manner in the matter of deposits, loans, discounts, exchange, collections, etc. Discount day, Mondays. Condition of bank February 26, 1891:

RESOURCES.		LIABILITIES.	
Loans and discounts..................$454,295 37		Capital stock paid in....................$150,000 00	
Overdrafts, secured and unsecured......	54 24	Surplus fund.........................	30,000 00
U. S. Bonds to secure circulation	50,000 00	Undivided profits........................	26,281 47
Stocks, securities, claims, etc..........	30,000 00	National bank notes outstanding..........	45,000 00
Due from approved reserve agents........	54,861 16	Dividends unpaid........................	209 00
Due from other National banks	445 32	Individual deposits subject to check,......	362,958 72
Current expenses and taxes paid........ .	2,751 28	Due to other National banks.............	19,667 86
Premiums on U. S. Bonds..............	3,000 00		
Checks and other cash items.............	6,264 64		
Exchanges for clearing house............	1,565 09		
Bills of other banks......................	2,866 00		
Fractional paper currency, nickels and cents........	126 95		
Specie........	21,572 00		
Legal tender notes......................	3,955 00		
Redemption fund with U. S. treasurer (5 per cent. of circulation)..............	2,250 00		
Total...................$634,117 05		Total.............................$634,117 05	

BOSTON MARBLE AND GRANITE COMPANY.

Monuments and Building Work in Marble, Granite, Brownstone, etc.—No. 53 Central Street—M. A. Murphy, President and Treasurer.

The Boston Marble and Granite Company was established in 1874, but for reasons not necessary to state was not incorporated until 1888, when the cash capital invested was fixed at $25,000 and Mr. M. H. Murphy chosen president, to which have since been added the duties of treasurer. The wisdom of this choice is proven by the prosperity which has marked the company's career under Mr. Murphy's capable administration, much of the finest monumental and architectural stone-work in Worcester and other parts of New England having been designed, contracted for and executed under his supervision and direction. The company's office and salesroom are located at No. 53 Central street, and are handsomely fitted up, exhibiting numerous splendid examples of fine art sculpture, imported and domestic. Adjoining are the shops and yards, covering 12,000 square feet, conveniently and comfortably arranged and fitted up with sawing and polishing machinery driven by a fine fifteen-horse-power steam engine. Twenty-five skilled stonecutters and assistants are regularly employed, and a vast amount of superior work is done in marble, granite, brown, and other varieties of stone, specialties being made of intricate and artistic designs for the construction of monuments and fine buildings. The attention of architects, builders and designers of public and private monuments is invited to this company's excellent facilities. Bids are made and specifications faithfully fulfilled at reasonable prices, with artistic skill and without unnecessary delay.

President Murphy, a native of Boston, is a trained practical sculptor and designer of genius and culture. He has resided in Worcester for some fifteen or sixteen years, and is an energetic, public-spirited citizen, widely known and popular.

STEWART BOILER WORKS,

Manufacturers of Steam Boilers, Penstocks, Tanks, and Plate Iron Work—Works, Albany and Muskeego Sts., on Line of the Boston & Albany and Worcester & Shrewsbury Railroads, One-Half Mile East of the Union Station.

Stewart & Dillon were the founders of this house, starting in 1864 on Manchester street; removing, in 1866, to Cypress street. Mr. Dillon retired in 1869. The business was carried on alone by Charles Stewart till 1872, when Wm. Allen was admitted, and the firm changed to

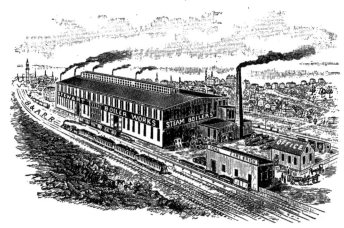

Stewart & Allen, and, in 1878, to C. Stewart & Son—Charles and James C. Stewart. The elder Mr. Stewart withdrew in September, 1888, when the sons, James C., John C. and Charles M., formed the present firm, remaining at the old stand until September, 1889, when they removed to their new shops at Albany and Muskeego streets. The premises are quite commodious, comprising one and one-half acres of land, a one-story wooden structure, 60 x 165 feet, engine and boiler room 30 feet square, and storage sheds. The main shop is completely equipped with the best modern machinery and tools. From thirty to fifty hands are employed, dependent on the season, and a large amount of superior iron and steel plate work is done, the output embracing every description of steam boilers, penstocks, oil, water and dye tanks, and, in short, everything desired in riveted sheet and plate iron and steel. The repairing of steam boilers receives special attention, and parties wanting anything in their line will find everything as represented, and receive courteous treatment. The facilities are first-class and prices fair.

WHITE, PEVEY & DEXTER COMPANY,

Pork Packers—Putnam Lane, near Bloomingdale—Office and Store, No. 13 Bridge St.

Naturally enough, the great export pork-packing centres are situated in the wild and woolly west, where corn is so cheap that it is used for fuel. Some people have a prejudice, however unreasonable it may appear in the eyes of the big monopolists, against meat cured and prepared in a manner at least suspicious. Consequently New England hogs and hog products are steadily recovering their former prestige, and discriminating consumers in this part of the country will buy none other than meats prepared and cured at home. That the demand will continue to grow there can be no doubt, for it is a fact that the finest hogs raised in the United States are bred in Vermont, New Hampshire and Massachusetts, the meat more firm, sweet, juicy and healthy, and the lard clean and sound—such meat and lard as the old-time Yankee farmer knew how to raise, fatten, cure and render.

The pork-packing business, resumed in New England on a small scale more than twenty years ago, has received fresh impetus from the exposures of western methods developed of late, and those reputable houses hereabouts engaged in preparing meats for the home market are more prosperous than ever before. This is especially true of the White, Pevey & Dexter Company of this city, established in 1870, who have hitherto cut and cured a limited supply, but during the past two seasons found it impossible with their restricted facilities to meet the requirements of dealers,'and consumers. They therefore decided to enlarge, and in the spring of 1890 began the erection of new buildings, since occupied, one of which is entirely of brick, four stories in height, 60x130 feet, the other brick and frame, one story, 80x100 feet. A spur track connects the premises with the Boston & Albany railroad, and the carcasses are moved from place to place by means of overhead tracks, wheels and hooks. Improved appliances and conveniences are provided for cutting, curing and smoking meats, manufacturing sausages and rendering pure lard, of which they make a specialty, and, on the whole, this is one of the most complete establishments of the kind in the East, scupulously neat and clean, and all processes conducted by careful skilled workmen (of whom there are one hundred) under the supervision of members of the firm, all of whom are experienced pork-packers. The meats cured here are unsurpassed for sweetness and delicacy of flavor, and special attention is invited to the extra sugar-cured hams and the W., P. & D. brand of lard for which the house is justly famous. Mr. R. G. White is a Vermonter, E. P. Pevey from New Hampshire, and E. C. Dexter a New Yorker. All are enterprising, liberal men, and have succeeded by honest, hard work.

GEORGE BURNHAM & COMPANY.

Frank Reed, Proprietor—Manufacturer of Patent Improved Hand and Power Upright Drills and Clamp Drills—No. 19 Hermon Street.

Of all the appliances of a first-class blacksmith-shop no single one is of greater value than the upright drill, always presuming that that tool is of the best kind. Made in differing styles, the manufacturers claim, each for his own machine, points of superiority over all others, but it is often all a question for each buyer to settle for himself which is really the best. The concensus of opinion, however, seems to be in favor of the

machine that does its work most rapidly, most accurately and at the least expenditure of time, labor and money, and, this view being accepted, there is excellent ground for believing the Burnham patent improved upright drill at least equal to the best and superior to most of its rivals.

Up to November 1, 1889, the above-named drill in several styles was manufactured by George Burnham & Company, established in 1882. On that date Mr. Frank Reed, who for a short time previously had been associated with H. M. Wright, became sole proprietor and gave the concern new blood and a fresh impetus. The shops, situated in the building No. 15 Hermon street, have floor space aggregating 2,100 square feet and are thoroughly equipped with appropriate iron-working machinery driven by steam. Eight men are kept busy in the various departments and an extraordinary amount of excellent work is done, the specialties embracing a full line of Burnham drills in styles varying from No. 0, to No. 8, in weight from 85 to 380 pounds, and in price from $20 to $110. Of the advantages combined in these drills the following are especially worthy of mention, viz: The feed motion is positive and can be adjusted to four rates of speed; the feed levers are made of malleable iron and will not break. The grinding attachment is a solid emery wheel 5 inches diameter, 1-2 inch face, driven by friction from balance wheel; is brought into use by tightening of a thumb screw; it also provides an angular rest for grinding the drill bit correctly. The wheel holder is for drilling tires without resting on the felloe, which is desirable in case of nicely painted work, and all the holes can be drilled without lifting the wheel.

This house also have a stock of twist drills and universal chucks, especially adapted for blacksmiths' drills, threaded to screw on the end of spindles. All parts are made of bar steel and jaws are hardened, not easily broken, or liable to get out of order.

NELSON H. DAVIS,

Wholesale and Retail Jeweler—Burnside Building, No. 351 Main Street.

This is a pioneer jewelry house, founded nearly half a century ago by the noted A. L. Burbank, under whose enterprising management the establishment attained an enviable eminence. On the 14th of August, 1890, Mr. Nelson H. Davis became sole proprietor by purchase, and is

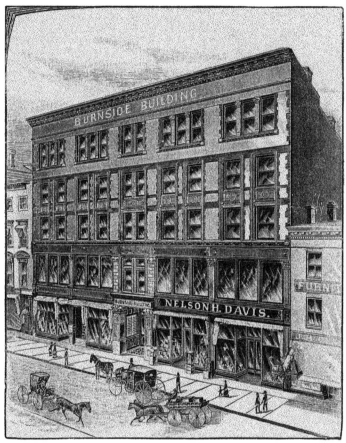

devoting his excellent business talent to the rehabilitation of the old house, the augmentation of its facilities and the extension of its trade, in all of which objects he is accomplishing wonders. The stock, already large and of the most attractive kind, has been greatly reinforced by frequent new invoices of foreign and American goods, and will compare favorably with that of any similar concern in New England. The display is especially rich in set and unset diamonds, solid and stylish gold jewelry, fine domestic and imported gold watches and chains, rare French clocks, sterling silverware, bric-a-brac, bronzes and fancy articles, all of which will be sold at moderate prices and warranted as represented. New accessions to the stock are being continually received, comprising all desirable novelties. Mr. Davis is a young man of spirit and energy, who has made his way to the front by sheer force of character, industry and tact. His clerks and salesmen are selected for their thorough knowledge of the business, combined with that affability and courtesy for which their principal is distinguished. Ladies and gentlemen desirous of inspecting a stock of rare and costly goods such as is seldom shown in the interior should pay a visit to this establishment, where they will receive every attention and be afforded all possible facilities for comparison and selection.

ALBERT H. STEELE.

Successor to Fifield & Steele, Manufacturer of and Dealer in Narrow Fabric Loom Supplies—No. 54 Hermon Street.

Manufacturers of ribbons, tapes and other elastic and non-elastic fabrics will be interested in knowing that they may obtain right here in Worcester whatever they may require in the way of narrow loom supplies and attachments of the best and latest improved styles.   Messrs. Fifield &

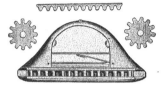

Steele began the. manufacture of this class of devices in 1887, and were quite successful, but Mr. Fifield retired in 1889, leaving Mr. Albert H. Steele in sole control.   The latter has a roomy and well appointed shop, with appropriate machinery—some of which is of his own design for special work—and employs several expert workmen at No. 54 Hermon street, where orders for shuttles, blocks, racks, pinions, lays, etc., are executed at short notice, and careful attention is given to repairs.   Mr. A. H. Steele, who is a native of Vermont, came to Worcester about ten years ago, and since that time has been engaged in the city's mechanical industries of various kinds.   He has also enjoyed and profited by the advantages of the Worcester School for Drawing and other means of acquiuing a practical and technical knowledge of applied mechanics.   He is the inventor of an improved spring spindle fastening, which he uses in his work and for which he has applied for a patent.

NEW WORCESTER THEATER.

Rock & Brooks, Proprietors and Managers—Exchange Street, Near Main.

The New Worcester Theater was completed about the first of May, 1890, and thrown open to the public on the evening of Monday, the fifth of the same month, with "Shenadoah" as the initial attraction.   The crowds who attended on the inaugural night, and the subsequent crowds who have been entertained within its walls, were treated to a sight of what Worcester people never before saw at home, a real theater, perfect in its appointments, beautiful within and without, and complete with conveniences and comforts to which they had theretofore been strangers.   The building itself is a remarkably handsome structure of brick with granite and terra cotta trimmings and ornamentation, elegant in design, lofty and commodious, 65 feet front and of proportionate depth, and cost, with fittings and scenery, about $125,000.   The stage is large—unusually so, the other dimensions considered, and the seating capacity is about 1,400. The pitch of the floors in orchestra, balcony and dress circle is rather steeper than is customary, thus enabling all to obtain a clear view of the stage and the actors, while the galleries are equally desirable coigns of vantage whence "the gods" may see and hurl their thunders with ease and comfort—to themselves at least.   The orchestra circle, raised above the orchestra floor, is especially well arranged, as are the private boxes, and the decorations throughout are quietly sumptuous.   The stage curtain is something of an innovation—velour, embroidered in applique with stained glass jewels and shells interwoven; the box draperies gold tinted silk, arranged in artistic folds, while backs and cushions are of terra cotta plush.   Other draperies and curtains are in keeping.   The box chairs, of shell design, are upholstered with brocade in boquet pattern in cream and rose and cream and electric blue.   Green Wilton is used for the hallway carpets; blue and light Wilton for the main floor; Brussels for the second floor; moquette for the ladies' and Brussels for the gentlemen's waiting-rooms.   Metropolitan opera-house chairs, upholstered in gray-blue plush, are provided for the body of the house.   It is unnecessary to describe the scenery, and it will be passed with the remarks that all desirable modern improvements and many novelties have been introduced, and the same applies to the stage mechanism, which is absolutely faultless.

The approach to this fairy temple is sheltered by an iron awning.   The broad vestibule is separated from the foyer by a stained glass screen, at the centre of which is the ticket office, double doors on either side leading to the foyer, the latter about eighteen feet wide, stairs leading to the gallery from both sides.   On the right and left are the ladies' and gentlemen's dressing rooms, and a cloak-room.   The gallery ticket office is at the end of the foyer, and the gallery entrance and exit fronts the court in the rear.   A partition of stained glass panels separates the foyer from the orchestra.   The theater office is on the second floor, immediately over the vestibule.   Five tiers of large and convenient dressing-rooms are situated at the left of the stage.   All desirable practical safeguards against fire are provided, and the house can be emptied in a very brief time.   Ventilation is also carefully looked after, and the house is lighted throughout by electricity, while electric bells and speaking tubes connect the main office, the ticket office, the orchestra and the stage.

The firm of Harris & Rock secured the first five years lease of the new dramatic temple, dating from August 1, 1890. Mr. Harris is junior member of Rich & Harris, well-known theatrical managers, and the demands upon his time and labor at other points during the season are so exacting that it was found impracticable for him to devote much attention to his Worcester interests; Mr. Rock bore all the burden at this point without reaping any corresponding advantage; so it was decided to make a .change, and Mr. W. F. Brooks, previously identified with the Security Associates, joined Mr. Rock in purchasing Mr. Harris' interest, the transfer to date from June 1, 1891, when the names of Messrs. Rich & Harris will be superseded by those of Rock & Brooks, whose object it will be to sustain and improve the high reputation already won by the New Worcester Theater.

LINCOLN HOUSE.

George Tower, Proprietor—Corner Main and Elm Streets.

Of hotels Worcester boasts several that compare favorably with those of any New England city of equal population. Among these is the well-known and popular old Lincoln House, centrally located at the corner of Main and Elm streets, that for fifty-six years has catered to the comfort of transient and permanent guests under the management of various proprietors, it having been first opened by the late D. F. Brigham as long ago as 1834. The building has been remodeled, enlarged and vastly improved since then, and as it now stands is a handsome and substantial three-story brick structure, with mansard roof, fronting 127 feet on Maple and 124 feet on Elm street. It contains, besides office, reading and sample rooms, public and private parlors, spacious dining-room, etc., eighty-four elegantly appointed sleeping apartments, beautifully furnished, clean, cosy and well lighted, with connecting bath-rooms, toilet rooms with running water, gas, electric call bells, and all modern conveniences. One hundred and fifty guests can

be comfortably accommodated, and on occasion two hundred may be fed and sheltered without too much crowding. It is hardly necessary to speak of the *cuisine*, the tables and the attendance further than to state that they are unexcelled. The house is largely patronized by transient boarders at all seasons. Rates are moderate—$2.50 per diem, with special terms to commercial travelers who make the Lincoln headquarters.

Besides conducting the Lincoln acceptably and successfully for the past twenty years, Mr. Tower is proprietor of and in the season personally manages Tower's Hotel, at Falmouth Heights on Vineyard Sound—a most desirable summer resort, where the thermometer seldom rises above 78 degrees, or falls below 62 degrees; average, 70 degrees. The house will accommodate one hundred and fifty guests. It is reached via the Old Colony railroad, opens June 15, and is patronized exclusively by unpretentious, ease-loving, wealthy people, who find here every desirable luxury and convenience, including sea air, warm baths, boating, fishing, steamboat excursions, skating, bowling, billiards, delightful drives with fine horses and carriages, a sumptuous table, attentive servants, etc., at reasonable rates.

CROMPTON LOOM WORKS, WORCESTER, MASS.

M. C. Crompton, President; Horace Wyman, Vice President and Manager; Justin A. Ware, Secretary and Treasurer—Manufacturers of Looms for Fancy Woolen, Cotton, Silk and Carpets—Office, No. 110 Green St.

The Crompton loom is in general use, and, with recent improvements, ranks with the most ingenious and perfect machinery employed in the manufacture of textile fabrics. William Cromp-

ton, the inventor of this loom in its original form, was a native of Lancashire, England. He immigrated to this country in 1836, and the ensuing year was granted a patent upon his device. He continued to experiment with, improve and construct his loom until 1849, when he was succeeded in business by his son George and Merrill A. Furbush, under the style of Furbush & Crompton, which firm continued and prospered till 1859, when Mr. Furbush retired and

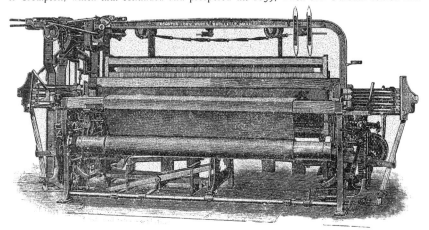

located in Philadelphia. Mr. George Crompton then continued as sole proprietor of the Crompton Loom Works until his death in December, 1886. The present corporation was formed in January, 1888, with capital stock to the amount of $550,000. Only the best obtainable inventive and mechanical talent is employed, and the one object of the corporation is to render the Crompton loom as near perfect as human ingenuity can make it, and keep in the lead of all competition. Our first loom engraving shows the high speed "1889" horizontal 25-harness Crompton loom, the latest novelty, and an improvement over everything that preceded it in that style of loom. Our second cut illustrates the Crompton "1889" double-beam 36-harness fancy loom. Both of these looms are of the "close-shed" type, a specialty of these works, guaranteeing smoothness of fabric and ability to weave any and all difficult patterns. A technical description of these machines would not interest the general reader, and would be of little or no value to those familiar with weaving devices, so we omit it with the single remark that in design, material, workmanship, finish, durability and adaptability to the service for which they are intended, and for rapidity of operation, they are unexcelled. Built expressly for weaving fancy worsteds and woolens, together with other styles adapted for cotton and silk goods and carpets, they perform all that is expected of them and give unvarying satisfaction.

The Crompton looms are in use in the mills of this country, Europe and South America, and the increasing demand is the best testimony to their value. The Crompton Loom Works are situated on Green street, the office being No. 110, itself a beautiful structure, commodious, con-veniently arranged and finished in art wood-work, with appropriate decorations. The main factory buildings are of brick, which, together with the many wings and additions, cover three acres of land, and form a hive of industry such as is seldom seen, fitted up with all requisite machinery, much of which is of special design and construction, and giving employment to a regiment of well-paid, contented and expert mechanics. One building is devoted entirely to experimenting with and perfecting new ideas and improvements in looms and their attachments, and it is largely to this plan that is due the extraordinary degree of excellence attained. The productions of these works cover the entire range of textile weaving.

WILLIAM J. ESTEY,

Restaurant and Caterer—No. 411 Main Street.

Mr. William J. Estey is one of Worcester's best-known and most-popular citizens, formerly a member of the City Council for two years. A native of Greenwich, he left the farm at nineteen, and has since engaged in a variety of occupations, among them the shoe business, traveling and selling over the counter for several years. He is now forty years of age, hale and hearty, a Freemason and Oddfellow, genial and companionable. On the 25th of April, 1890, Mr. Estey opened a spacious and elegantly appointed first-class restaurant on the second floor of No. 411 Main street, where all the substantials and luxuries obtainable in this market are served at any hour of day or night to regular or transient customers, at moderate prices. The cookery is equal to that of any hotel in New England and the service especially good. In connection with this establishment Mr. Estey makes a specialty of catering for balls, parties, public and private dinners, banquets, luncheons, and similar occasions. No pains or expense are spared to render satisfaction, and, provided with every possible facility, ample means, a superb *chef*, and an army of attentive waiters, failure is impossible.

WALDO HOUSE.

Lorenzo B. Start, Proprietor—Waldo Street.

The Waldo ranks with the noted hotels of interior New England, having been opened about forty years ago by a Mr. Russell Lamb, who subsequently retired and was succeeded by Messrs.

R. N. Start & Co. For more than thirty years that firm conducted the house successfully, and it was under their capable management that the hostelry became famous, and was gradually enlarged by additions from the little twenty-room tavern of the forties to the handsome and commodious hotel of the present day, containing 140 rooms and ample accommodations for 200 guests. A Mr. Brooks was temporary host from April, 1889, to August, 1890, when Mr. Lorenzo B. Start returned and resumed charge — an event which augurs well for the house and its numberless occasional guests' comfort and pleasure. Situated near the new Worcester theater and always a favorite resort of the profession, the traveling actor and actress will be especially pleased to again meet and be cared for by Mr. Start. The structure, substantial and attractive, is practically fire-proof. It is lighted throughout by gas, provided with hot and cold water and baths, electric call bells, billiard-room, barber-shop, and every desirable modern convenience. The elegantly appointed dining-room will seat one hundred guests, and the tables are abundantly supplied with the best of everything edible, prepared by an experienced staff of cooks and served by polite and attentive waiters. The sleeping apartments are sweet and clean, the beds inviting and restful, and the furniture and appointments all that could be desired. The house was but recently refurnished and refitted throughout, rendering the spacious office, reading and sample rooms and parlors more than ever attractive. Mr. Len. B. Start has passed the greater part of his life in the Waldo, is widely known and popular, and hopes to receive a share of the patronage of the traveling public.

WORCESTER PANTS MANUFACTURING COMPANY,

Manufacturers of Men's, Boys' and Children's Pants—Nos. 7 and 9 Washington Sq.

Specialism is no longer confined to the professions. Manufacturers have learned that by giving exclusive attention to certain articles they arrive at a degree of perfection as regards quality of workmanship and economy of time and labor that is unattainable by those who distribute their energies over a broader field and attempt too much. In no department of industry is this more apparent than in the making of clothing for the multitude, hence we find some establishments devoted to the making of certain kinds and grades of underwear, others to shirts, others to collars and cuffs; another class makes only coats and vests; still another produces overcoats, and finally the construction of bifurcated nether garments, otherwise called pantaloons — "pants" for short — is rapidly becoming concentrated in the hands of a few enterprising individuals and firms, who, provided with improved machinery and other facilities and adhering to popular styles, are enabled to supply the market on better terms and with a greater variety of goods in better fabrics and better workmanship than were ever before offered. A leading representative of this important industry is the Worcester Pants Company, established in 1888 by Messrs. E. Epstein and A. I. Asherowsky, and occupying one floor, 50 x 117 feet, of the large brick building Nos. 7 and 9 Washington square. A complete equipment of sewing machines and other requisite appliances are run by steam, and about fifty hands are steadily employed in filling orders for medium grade pants for men's, boys' and children's wear, the output going to jobbers and wholesale dealers in the New England States and New York. Messrs. Epstein and Asherowsky are wide-awake business men, enterprising and progressive, and are fast making for their house a first-class reputation while steadily extending their trade. This firm recently added another floor to their premises. All goods are bought direct from the mill, and all work is made inside the factory, as they have all necessary facilities for the purpose.

CITY NATIONAL BANK.

Calvin Foster, President; Nathaniel Paine, Cashier—Cor. Main and Pearl Streets.

The City Bank dates from 1854, when it was chartered under the State banking law of Massachusetts. For a period of ten years the institution continued to prosper as a fiduciary agent under the original auspices, and was then reorganized and reincorporated as a National bank in 1864. How successful it has been during the past twenty-seven years may be inferred from the official statement, which shows capital, $400,000; surplus and undivided profits, $217,313; loans and discounts, $1,634,020.75. The City National does a strictly legitimate business in deposits, loans, discounts, mercantile paper, drafts, collections, etc., allowing interest on special deposits, and has been one of the most powerful factors in Worcester's industrial, commercial and civic growth. The officers are named above and are noted as capable financiers. The board of directors embraces some of the city's most progressive, enterprising and substantial business men and capitalists, as follows: Calvin Foster, president, Lewis Barnard, Loring Coes, Wm. W. Rice, Wm. E. Rice, Arthur M. Stone, Thomas Gage, Henry M. Witter, and Edward D. Thayer, jr. Herewith is submitted the report to the Comptroller of the Currency of date February 26, 1891: ·

RESOURCES.

Loans and discounts....................$1,634,020	75
Overdrafts, secured and unsecured.....	688 74
U. S. bonds to secure circulation········	50,000 00
Stocks, securities, judgments, claims, etc.....	1.150 00
Due from approved reserve agents......	44 225 84
Due from other National banks ·········	23,252 14
Current expenses and taxes paid.......	5,004 49
Checks and other cash items............	5.194 00
Bills of other banks......	6,805 00
Fractional paper currency, nickels and cents.......................................	440 69
Specie.....................................	55,503 85
Legal tender notes.........................	23,761 00
U. S. certificates of deposit for legal tenders...................................	50,000 00
Redemption fund with U. S. Treasurer (5 per cent. of circulation)...............	2 250 00
Total................$1,902,386	50

LIABILITIES.

Capital stock paid in.....................$400,000	00
Surplus fund.....	100,000 00
Undivided profits.........	117,313 35
National bank notes outstanding.........	45,000 00
Dividends unpaid.........................	60 00
Individual deposits subject to check......1,180,935	88
Due to other National banks ·······	59,077 27
Total.... ....$1,902,386	50

J. J. SAWIN,

Naphtha Oil Extractor, Manufacturer of Chip and Naphtha Grease—Rear of No. 220 Shrewsbury Street.

Mr. Sawin, formerly a resident of Natick, Mass., was the pioneer extractor of oil from upper leather used in the manufacture of boots and shoes, and more particularly from scraps, the latter being especially adapted, after treatment, to the making of ladies' shoe heels. Though his process was patented in 1875, he has never as yet enforced the law against infringers. He began his experiments in 1867, and in 1869 regularly established himself in business at Natick, Eben E. Phillips, the well-known Boston manufacturer, being the first to recognize the value of Mr. Sawin's discovery and purchased his product.

Mr. Sawin completed his preparations and apparatus and engaged in the extraction of grease by the use of naphtha at Natick in 1874, remaining there until 1882, when he removed to Worcester because of its more central location and greater accessibility. In the rear of 220 Shrewsbury street, he has erected extensive works, comprising several frame buildings, one for the extraction of naphtha grease and the preparation of upper leather, heel and lining stock, another utilized as a chip grease factory, and a third for boiler and engine, the latter of seventy horse-power. Employing six men, he produces annually 1,100 barrels of naphtha grease and 2,000 barrels of chip grease, which is disposed of to manufacturers of curriers' hard grease and soap boilers, considerable quantities being exported. Fully one-third of the Massachusetts output of naphtha and chip grease comes from this factory, the largest and most complete in the State.

HOLLAND & HAVENER,

Dealers in Bicyles, Tricycles, Athletic and Sporting Goods—Gymnasium Apparatus—
Instruction in Fencing, Boxing, etc.—No. 507 Main St.

This, the only exclusively sporting goods house in Worcester county, was founded in 1877 by
Hill & Tolman, who succeeded in making it famous and profitable. Those gentlemen, however,
 retired on the formation of the present firm,
Messrs. Lincoln Holland and Lud C. Havener, in
1889. Both are experienced in the sporting goods
trade and widely and favorably known to the
general public, Mr. Holland, a native of Worcester, twenty-nine years of age, having been at one
time with Hill & Tolman and subsequently in the
same business on his own account, while Mr.
Havener is a professor of gymnastics and was
formerly an instructor of the Boston Athletic Club
and in several of the largest Y. M. C. A. gymna-
siums of the country. In rear of the salesroom is
a private gymnasium presided over by Mr.
Havener, who gives regular lessons to a large and
growing class. The firm carry a general and
varied stock of bicycles, tricycles, athletic, gym-
nastic and sporting supplies and apparatus, etc.,
and have a liberal patronage from clubs and
individuals. The store, handsomely arranged, is
quite large, 35 feet front and 100 feet deep,
including the gymnasium, boxing and fencing school in rear. Broad and lofty plate glass windows admit ample light, showing the whole attractive interior. They also conduct a well-
appointed riding-school at No. 215 Front street, and a branch store at
Cottage City. The goods sold here are of standard excellence, selected
by the firm especially for this market, and include as leading specialties
a line of safety cycles for both sexes, made by the most reputable manufacturers and warranted. They have a completely equipped shop at
No. 19 Allen street, where every description of cycle repairs are made
in the best and neatest manner. Wheels are also rented by the hour,
day, week, or month, so that strangers visiting the city need not forego
exercise and practice. Among the machines in stock the buyer or
renter has choice of the following list, the places of manufacture being
appended: Columbias, Hartford, Conn.; Victors, Chicopee Falls,
Mass.; Broncho (Chainless), Westboro, Mass.; Hartford, Hartford,
Conn.; Hickory (Ladies or Gents), Newton, Mass.; Diamond, Worcester, Mass.; Giant (Ladies or Gents), Toledo, Ohio; Premium
(Ladies), Washington, D. C.; Nonpareil (Boys), Chicopee, Mass.;
Lovell (Girls), Washington, D. C.; Little Beauty (Boys), Washington, D. C.; H. & H.
Safety (Boys), New York. Any other style furnished to order.

Fac-simile, John Clark-
son's arm. Pitcher Bos-
ton League team.

E. J. SOMERS,

Manufacturer of Tacks—Fine Shoe Tacks a Specialty—No. 17 Water Street.

One of the curiosities of manufacturing history is the development of the tack industry. In
some form or other the tack has become indispensable to many trades, and the demand is constantly increasing. Hence the growth of an interest that in its beginnings seemed almost
puerile. Like pins, everybody uses them, and like pins, it would be difficult to say what becomes of tacks all, though it is evident that, unlike pins, they are not finally lost and never
found, for every tack has its mission and usually sticks strictly to business.

Somers Bros. began the manufacture of tacks at No. 68 School street, Worcester, in 1885,
and soon controlled a flourishing trade. In September, 1889, the firm dissolved, Mr. J. S.
Somers assuming sole ownership. He occupies a part of three floors, fitted up with tack machines of the latest improved design, driven by steam. These machines are automatic in action,
simple and perfect, and one man can easily attend eight of them. They turn out every description of tacks in great quantities, and Hungarian and hob nails as required, but a specialty is
made of fine shoe tacks, for which there is an extraordinary demand in this market. Orders to
any extent are promptly filled at lowest figures, and the trade throughout New England, New
Jersey and Pennsylvania is largely supplied from this source.

Mr. Somers was born and reared in Worcester, is an experienced practical workman, and a
young man of rare energy and business capacity.

FREELAND J. ELLIS,

Golden Rule Dining and Ice Cream Rooms—No. 476 Main Street.

The Golden Rule is a popular and well patronized institution of Worcester, established in 1882 by Mr. Thomas.Gray, to whom Mr. Freeland J. Ellis succeeded in July, 1890, subsequently removing from 500 Main street to the second floor of the elegant Taylor block, entrance at 467 Main street, one flight of broad and easy stairs leading to the rooms, which are lofty, perfectly lighted, cheerful and attractive, and cover floorage 50x80 feet, with ample seating capacity for 150 guests at once. The appointments are not gaudy but quietly elegant, suggesting plenty and substantial comfort rather than empty display, and the effect is seen in the character of the customers, solid, unpretentious business and professional men and women from all parts of the city, with a sprinkling of transient visitors from the country and adjacent villages. The tables are abundantly provided with the best and most wholesome meats, poultry, fish, game, vegetables, fruits, pastry and dainties, all in their season, skillfully and appetizingly prepared by experienced and careful cooks, and promptly served by a corps of tidy and attentive waiters. Breakfast, dinner and supper are served *a la carte*, and moderate charges prevail.

Mr. Ellis is personally a genial, accommodating and hospitable gentleman, who supervises his establishment with a watchful eye, and is never so happy as when his rooms are crowded with well-pleased patrons. He was formerly associated with Mr. Henry E. Capen in the management of the Silver Lake Hotel, Katahdin Iron Works, Me., one of the most fashionable pleasure resorts. Subsequently he was for three years one of the foremen of the Union Water Meter Company of this city, resigning to start his present enterprise. He is a Freemason, past junior warden of Mt. Kineo lodge No. 109, Maine, and past recording and financial secretary of Good Cheer lodge No. 37, I. O. O. F., of the same place. He is also a member of the Worcester Continentals, and visited Philadelphia with that corps last summer.

Mr. Charles T. Locke, the accomplished *chef* of the Golden Rule, is an affable and obliging gentleman, who has since 1875 presided with skill and success over the *cuisine* of leading hotels and restaurants in Philadelphia, Boston, Bar Harbor, Hampton Beach, Jacksonville, Fla., and elsewhere.

F. A. ATHERTON.

Manufacturer of Refrigerators of All Kinds—The Boulevard, Near Elm Park.

A good, reliable refrigerator is a necessity in every well-regulated household, while the butcher, the grocer, the dealer in dairy products, fish, game, fruits and other perishable commodities, could hardly do business without its aid. This is one of the modern inventions in which everybody is directly or indirectly interested, because by enabling the housekeeper or the merchant to preserve fresh edibles indefinitely, it makes them much cheaper than they would otherwise be, thus assuring sound, sweet food and consequently good health. In a word, the cheapest article in the market is a first-class refrigerator, which study and experience, combined with mechanical skill, have brought to a degree of perfection that leaves nothing to be desired. One of the most noted New England nmanufacturers of refrigerators is Mr. F. A. Atherton, who, having learned the trade with his father, engaged in business for himself in 1875 on Grove street, where he built commodious shops, and remained until the summer of 1889, when, having bought the paternal plant on the boulevard, he

erected an addition thereto and now occupies two two-and-one-half story frame buildings each 45x85 feet in dimensions, with brick engine-house attached. Here equipped with a complete outfit of wood-working machinery and a twenty-five horse-power steam engine, and employing a competent force of skilled workmen, he is prepared to fill promptly and in the best manner all orders for his celebrated refrigerators, which are unsurpassed for all good qualities. These are built in any style or size desired, from the smallest domestic refrigerator to the largest and most elaborate for the use of hotels, meat dealers, milk and butter dealers, grocers and others. Intending buyers are invited to inspect his work and prices, at No. 117 Park avenue. Old refrigerators bought, sold or repaired.

THE WARE, PRATT COMPANY.

Custom and Manufacturing Clothiers and Dealers in Men's Furnishing Goods—Nos.
408 and 412 Main St.—W. W. Johnson, President; H. S. Pratt, Treasurer;
Charles E. Black, Secretary.

This great leading clothing house — the most extensive in Worcester or in the State west of
Boston—had its origin in a small tailoring and ready-made clothing store established by Mr. A.
P. Ware in 1847. Eleven years later a new firm was organized under the name and style of A. P. Ware & Co., to whom Ware, Pratt & Co. succeeded in 1869, and enjoyed uninterrupted prosperity until its dissolution and the incorporation of the existing company January 1, 1888, capital stock $100,000. The officers, named above, rank with Worcester's best and most popular business men. President Johnson, who entered the service of A. P. Ware & Co. as a clerk many years ago and advanced step by step to a copartnership, was selected for his present responsible position in recognition of his great executive ability on the organization of the company. Treasurer Pratt was Mr. Ware's first partner in the firm of Ware & Pratt, has been connected with the house for thirty-five years, is noted for energy, tact and enterprise, is reputed the most astute and far-sighted clothing man in New England, is a director of the Citizens' National Bank, a member of the Worcester Club, and a liberal, progressive and respected citizen. Secretary Black, experienced, alert, accurate and efficient, has the unbounded confidence of his associates in business and of the community at large. One hundred people are employed in all capacities, and that they are kept busy is attested by the volume of transactions, averaging $236,000 per annum, about
$65,000 of which is credited to the custom tailoring department, the largest, best managed and
most comprehensive in New England, employing several expert cutters and numerous skillful
tailors, carrying an immense and varied stock of fine and medium foreign and domestic woolens,
and favored with the patronage of legions of well-dressed men in all walks of life. The
beautiful and commodious five-story brick structure illustrated herewith is situated at Nos. 408
and 412 Main street. It is 49 feet front by 137 feet deep, and was originally erected for the
accommodation of the concern when Ware & Pratt and A. P. Ware & Co. consolidated,
occupying it for the first time March 10, 1869. Three immense floors are now devoted to the
business, and every department—custom tailoring, wholesale, manufacturing and sales—is complete in itself. It would be difficult to describe each in detail. Suffice it to say that the house
buys heavily for cash directly from mills and importers, is at all times supplied with the latest
styles of fabrics in abundance, closely follows the fashions from season to season, and is prepared
to meet promptly all fair competition in the essentials of quality, cut, fit and workmanship,
whether the garment be selected from the ready-made stock or ordered direct from the tailoring
department. And operations are not confined to gentlemen's attire alone, the company showing

the finest, largest and most varied assortment of youths', boys' and children's suits and single garments, and goods from which to make others to measure, ever exhibited in this market. We designed speaking at length of the furnishing goods department, but have already extended this notice to unusual length, and in this connection will simply say that no labor or pains are spared to provide for rich and poor alike in the matter of shirts, collars, cuffs, neckwear, underwear, and all of the requisites of a neat appearance and personal comfort. The stock embraces all grades and styles, and prices are always as low as any reasonable being could expect.

R. E. KIDDER,

Manufacturer of Kidder's Patent Universal Sawing Machine, the Lightning Copying Press, Patterns, Models, etc.—No. 35 Hermon St.

The engraving represents Kidder's new patent "Universal" sawing machine, with latest improvements, the design in the construction of which is to make a saw bench that will cover a

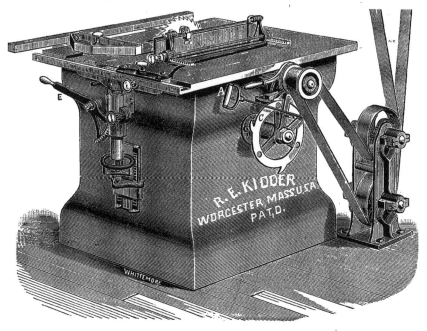

large variety of work, and, at the same time, make all of the changes quickly and still maintain sufficient driving power for any work that may be required. The workmanship in this machine is first-class in every respect. Some of the advantages claimed for this machine are thus summarized: First—It has three arbors, any one of which can be brought into axial line instantly and ready to run, the other two remaining at rest. No time lost in changing from splitting to cutting off, and *vice versa*. In fact, all three of the saws can be changed in less time than it takes to change one on any other saw made. This makes it adapted to a greater variety of work without any loss of driving power. The time saved in manipulating this machine will soon pay for it. No pattern, cabinet, or job shop can afford to be without it. Second—The great difficulty that is found in all other double saws that change by rotating—namely, the lack of driving power—is entirely overcome in this machine. The driving belt is a long one, and always of the same length. This machine will, with a four-inch belt, saw four-inch hard-wood stock. This has been fully demonstrated. Third—The gauges are light, accurate and strong; more easily, quickly and accurately adjusted. The cutting off has always a square and mitre without any change; also any angle between 0 and 45°. The splitting gauge can be more quickly and accurately set on any angle from 0 to 45° than any other. Fourth—The table is instantly and easily raised and lowered for rabbeting, grooving, etc., by means of a balance weight, not shown in cut, in connection with lever *E*. This machine is fully indorsed by many competent judges, some of whom have sent Mr. Kidder valuable testimonials, among them the Pond Machine Tool Company, Chas. P. Johnson, the well-known stair builder, Geo. L. Brownell and Prentice Bros., of Worcester: the G. H. Bushnell Company, founders and machinists, of Thompsonville, Conn.; Chas. A. Bennett, principal of the St. Paul (Minn.) Manual Training School, and many others. These machines are shipped to all parts of the States, and are taking

the lead wherever introduced. Mr. Kidder is also manufacturing the "Lightning" copying press in three styles (A, B and C), and in great numbers to meet a demand which sprung up as soon as the press was placed on the market. Style C is shown herewith. This press is neat, light, convenient, and in all respects much superior to the letter presses hitherto in vogue, besides being cheaper. He is moreover the manufacturer of the Kidder patent library, academy, artist's and "Artist's Friend" drawing tables and easels, combining many and valuable improvements upon anything of the kind ever heretofore made. In addition to these leading specialties, he gives careful and skillful attention to the construction of working models for inventors, and patterns of all kinds for machinery, architectural iron work and all purposes for which castings are used. Mr. Kidder has been established here since 1870. His office and manufactory are located at No. 35 Hermon street; he is well provided with all of the latest improved machinery and skilled workmen, and does a flourishing business, principally with New England parties. He was born at Wardsboro, Vt.

W. E. W. FELT,

Succeeding Felt & Prescott — Plain and Fancy Mercantile Job Printer — No. 392 Main Street.

One of the neatest and most perfectly equipped job printing establishments of inland Massachusetts is situated at No. 392 Main street. It was started at Nos. 37 and 39 Pearl street in 1886 by Mr. W. E. W. Felt. On the first of November, 1888, Mr. W. W. Prescott an accomplished workman, was taken in as a partner, and the firm soon attracted an excellent patronage from that portion of the business community who recognize and appreciate skillful combinations and artistic effects as expressed in the tasty arrangement of types, rules, borders and colors. For reasons not necessary to state Mr. Prescott retired on the 22nd of May last, when Mr. Felt resumed sole management of the business. The plant, occupying one floor 20x45 feet, comprising a subeth line of plain and fancy job, card and body type suited to the class of work to which he confines his attention, four improved new job presses, and a fine electric engine that supplies all the power required. Additions are constantly being made to the outfit, particularly in the matter of type, the founders bringing out new styles every week or two and the enterprising printer being compelled to keep up with the procession,—which by the way, was the origin of the old composing-room gag involving the impossibility of keeping a wife or a printing office in running order without plenty of new dresses. It is a fact that the type used in a modern job printing office is seldom worn out; it is discarded often when scarcely injured by actual service, to make room for fresh novelties. Mr. Felt is a native of New Hampshire, is not only a very superior printer, but a progressive business man and good citizen, and we unhesitatingly commend him to the favor of the public at large who require nice printing of any kind, from a newspaper or full-sheet poster to the daintiest wedding, invitation or address card.

C. B. COOK LAUNDRY COMPANY.

R. H. Kenyon, President; C. B. Cook, Treasurer and Manager—Steam Laundry, Barton Place.

A visit to and inspection of the various departments of the above-named company's great laundry is full of interest and instruction. The building itself, fronting on Barton place, convenient to Main street and other principal thoroughfares, is a substantial four-story brick structure, erected in 1889 by Mr. C. B. Cook, who established here the famous Worcester Collar Laundry and built up an immense patronage.

July 1, 1890, the present company was organized, Mr. R. H. Kenyon assuming the presidency, while Mr. Cook acts in the dual capacity of treasurer and manager. The capital invested is nominally $20,000, though doubtless the building, machinery, appurtenances and good-will represent a much larger sum. The equipment is complete, embracing all the latest and most approved new devices for cleansing and ironing garments with the least possible injury to the fabric, a fine steam boiler and engine furnishing hot water and power, which are distributed to all parts of the laundry where required by means of pipes, shafting and belts. About forty skillful and well paid operatives are employed, and the 8000 square feet of floorage devoted to the laundry is a continuous scene of bustle and cheerful toil from morning to night every day in the week. It is hardly necessary to state that the work done here is of the very best, unexcelled anywhere, specialties being made of gentlemen's shirts, collars and cuffs and ladies' fine white goods. A very extensive trade is the reward of care and skill, the best and most fastidious people of the city and of the adjacent towns and villages sending their work here regularly through branch offices and agencies, several of which have been established over the border in New Hampshire and Connecticut and add materially to the volume of business.

President Kenyon, who has had considerable experience in this branch of industry, was for several years connected with the Fall River Laundry. Mr. Cook made his first bow here as proprietor of the Worcester Collar Laundry in 1880, and by the exercise of tact, energy and integrity has made the establishment one of the largest and finest in New England. He continues to personally supervise the laundry.

PORTER & GARDINER,

Last Manufacturers—No. 25 Union St.; Boston Office, No. 115 Summer St.

Mr. Samuel Porter, the present senior partner, was the founder of this house, which he established in 1866. Later he sold out to Colby, Swan & Co., and subsequently purchased Mr. Swan's interest, when the style became Colby & Porter, and so continued until November, 1887,

when Mr. Colby retired and Mr. Thos. W. Gardiner, who had for some years performed the duties of superintendent, joined Mr. Porter and the present style was adopted. Mr. Porter, a native of Brockton, devotes his attention to the office work, sales and outdoor affairs of the house, while Mr. Gardiner, a practical model-maker, looks after the mechanical department. They have recently completed the fitting up of a new brick factory at No. 25 Union street, the dimensions of which are 40 x 127 feet, five stories high, with dry-houses capable of kiln-drying 80,000 blocks at one time, so there need be no lack of dry lumber from this house, which is certainly a model establishment, equipped with the requisite and peculiar machinery, special tools, etc., appropriate to last-making, steam power and all conveniences. The working force of expert mechanics numbers thirty, and the output averages fully 15,000 pairs per month of boot and shoe lasts in all grades, especial attention being given to orders for fine work in new styles. These lasts are disposed of to manufacturers of boots and shoes and dealers in shoe factory supplies all over the United States, and the concern is kept busy supplying the demand. The Boston office, where Mr. Porter may be found on Wednesdays and Saturdays, is at No. 115 Summer street.

HOTEL PARKER.

A. H. Kendrick, Proprietor—Nos. 1, 3 and 5 Walnut Street.

Few cities of equal or approximate population are so abundantly provided with hotels of all classes as is Worcester, where vast numbers of residents habitually board in preference to keep-

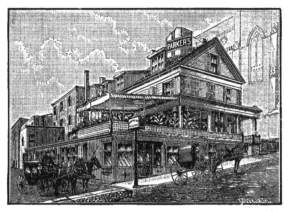

ing house. Among the most popular and home-like of the minor hotels the Hotel Parker deserves especial mention. The building, a view of which we print herewith, is of wood, irregular but attractive architecturally, and covers ground 80 x 170 feet. It is of three stories, conveniently situated, opposite Mechanics Hall and near Main street, lighted by gas, heated by steam, and contains a neat office, reading-room, pool-room, barber-shop, public and private parlors, and forty sleeping apartments for guests, all of which are comfortably furnished, clean and spacious. The table is first-class, abundantly supplied with the best meats, poultry, fish, vegetables, fruits, etc., in the market, skillfully prepared and served by attentive waiters. The Parker was opened by J. B. Parker, in 1885. Two years and a half later Mr. A. H. Kendrick, a native of North Brookfield, became proprietor. Solicitous to please, he devotes his entire time and energies to securing for his house a liberal support from the traveling and boarding public, and has been quite successful. No labor or pains are spared to make guests comfortable and at home. Rates are quite reasonable.

IVER JOHNSON & CO.,

Manufacturers of Fire Arms, Bicycles and Police Goods—Nickel Plating—No 44 Central Street.

No city of equal or approximate population in the world can boast such a diversity of manufactures as are clustered together within the corporate limits of Worcester, producing vast quantities of textile fabrics, machinery, hardware specialties, wooden, leather, steel, iron and brass goods, fire arms, cutlery, clothing, sporting goods, etc. One of Worcester's most notable industrial establishments is that of Iver Johnson & Co., founded by Johnson, Bye & Co. in 1871. Mr. Bye retired in 1882, since which time Mr. Johnson has been sole proprietor under the present style. The plant is a large one, consisting of a quadrangle of three and four-story brick buildings, 100 feet square, each side 30 feet wide, with a

40-foot court in the center. The equipment of machinery is comprehensive and valuable, including lathes, planers, drills, trip-hammers, etc., and a complete outfit of special tools and appliances, not the least important of which is a costly set of modern improved nickel-plating apparatus—the whole driven by a 160-horse-power steam engine. The works are arranged with an eye to thoroughness and convenience, and give employment to from 250 to 300 hands. A great variety of goods are made here, embracing several styles of shot guns and revolvers, (among the latter the "Swift," "Defender," "American Bull Dog," and "Boston," all superior weapons); bicycles in several patterns, police goods, etc., which are supplied to the trade everywhere through the famous house of John P. Lovell & Co., No. 147 Washington street, Boston. Mr. Johnson, a Norwegian by birth, has lived in this country since boyhood. He is a much respected citizen and president of the Worcester Loan Association.

BLAKE, BOUTWELL & CO.,

Wholesale Iron and Steel, Heavy Hardware, Sheet Iron, Roofing Tin, Copper and Zinc, Carriage and Wagon Woodwork, Carriage Makers' and Blacksmiths' Supplies—Bridge, Mechanic and Foster Streets.

If the business men of any section of this broad land are laying the flattering unction to their souls that New England is losing her grip, a journey from Boston to the New York State line, with stops of a day or two at the principal points on the route, will surely dissipate that impression. It is questionable if any city in the United States, of equal population, can make such an exhibit of industries and commerce as can Worcester, and among the most conspicuous and creditable of her mercantile houses is the one named above — Blake, Boutwell & Co., who occupy the notable triangular structure fronting on Bridge, Mechanic and Foster streets, 65 feet long on each face, four stories in height, built of brick with rough-cut brownstone trimmings — an architectural feature of the city, erected in 1886 and owned by Mr. G. F. Blake, jr., head of the firm. This house dates from 1876, when Mason & Lincoln established themselves in Worcester as general wholesale hardware merchants—a pursuit which they successfully prosecuted until 1884, when Blake, Boutwell & Co. (G. F. Blake, jr., and G. S. Boutwell) purchased the stock in trade and good will and supplanted the old firm. Vast changes and improvements in methods have been made since then, and the present firm has multiplied resources, facilities and transactions until their field of operations embraces the most desirable portions of Massachusetts and adjoining States. Ten men are employed, including book-keeper, clerks, salesmen, porters and teamsters, and three teams are kept constantly busy handling consignments and shipments and in city deliveries. Blake, Boutwell & Co.'s leading specialties come under the heads of iron and steel and heavy hardware, of which they carry comprehensive lines. They also keep in stock and furnish to order a choice assortment of galvanized, Harvey's cleaned, common and Russia sheet iron, sheet copper and zinc, carriage-makers', wagon-makers' and blacksmiths' supplies of all kinds, and a complete line of vehicle woodwork — shafts, spokes, rims, wheels, etc.—all of which are furnished to the trade on favorable terms. The house has the Worcester agency for and carries large stocks of William Jessop & Sons' cast steel, LaBelle cast steel, and James Royston's Son & Co.'s hardened and tempered steel wire of all gauges. Here is also shown a superior line of improved portable forges. Mr. Blake is a native of Boston and Mr. Boutwell of Lyndeboro, N. H. They are representative business men and leading citizens.

MASON & RISCH,

Manufacturers of Vocalions—Office and Factory, Nos. 5 to 15 Summer St.; New York Office, No. 18 E. Seventeenth Street.

The Vocalion is an organ constructed on the principles of the pipe-organ. In each of these instruments the tone is produced by the stationary vibrations of columns of air. They differ, however, in two very important particulars, *i. e.*, in the method adopted for producing the stationary vibrations, and in the size of the chambers to which the stationary vibrations are confined. In the vocalion metallic reeds are employed to produce the vibrations; in the pipe-organ air reeds perform this function. The former require chambers of small capacity, the latter chambers (pipes) of large capacity. By this ingenious device of substituting the metallic reed for the air reed, tones are obtained which have all the purity and power of those obtained from pipes, entirely free from the snarl and twang which renders so disagreeable the tones of a common reed-organ. The small size of the chambers required for the vocalion enables the manufacturers to compress the space necessary for a many-voiced organ into dimensions suitable for the parlor and moderate-sized churches. From this description of the method employed, of producing pure pipe-tones from reeds, the importance of the vocalion as a musical instrument, capable in every respect of replacing the more costly and bulky pipe-organ, will be at once apprehended. *The Vocalion*, in its method of producing tone, as well as in its construction, is a patented invention, and is the outcome of many years of labor and experiment involving large expenditure. The idea is copied from nature's method of producing tone — the method that is undeniably the best—and which, as far as is practicable, is embodied in the vocalion. This will be clear by instancing the tone-making apparatus of the human throat. The lungs are the bellows; the muscles which inflate the lungs are represented by the foot treadles or the bellows-lever of the organ; the vocal chord or the larynx of the throat is a reed; the tube or throat which contains the vocal chord develops the tone and delivers it to the mouth; there it is reinforced and further qualified before its final emission. Tones produced on this plan have purity, beauty, variety, intrinsic music value, power, and (highly important) carrying property. These qualities are peculiarly the property of the Vocalion Organ, hence its name " *Vocalion*,"

6

a named coined and given the instrument to emphasize the manner in which its tones are produced.   *The Vocalion* is a rival, in the variety and excellence of its registration and tonal qualities, of a richly voiced pipe-organ costing more than double its price, and, for the reasons already given, is in many respects superior to the pipe-organ of equal capacity.   The points of resemblance between the vocalion and the pipe-organ are: The tone is undistinguishable one

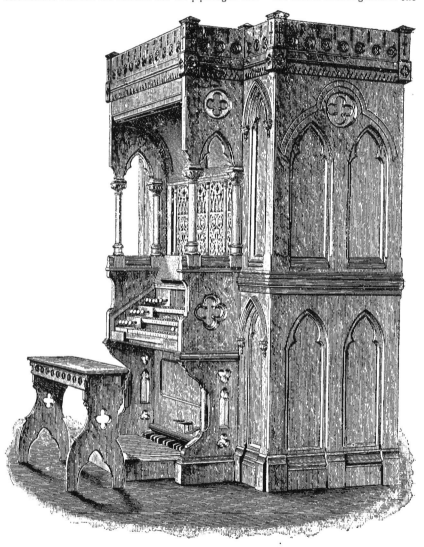

from the other; the vocalion is played like a pipe-organ.   The vocalion and the pipe-organ are both large wind instruments, the wind being supplied from the bellows by pressure and not by suction, as in the cabinet organ.   The vocalion and pipe-organ bellows, wind-chest and feeders are the same in principle and construction, as well as in operation.   The vocalion and pipe-organ key-boards, registration, stop-action, as well as the mechanical registers, are similar in both instruments.   The vocalion resembles the pipe-organ in the beauty and variety of its tones, and in its purity, power, dignity and pervading quality.   The vocalion resembles the pipe-organ.

in its capability for beautiful and varied registration. The vocalion resembles the pipe-organ in its adaptability for the interpretation of music, drama, and all devotional and liturgical music. The advantages of the vocalion over the pipe-organ are thus summed up: It costs one-half the price of a good pipe-organ of equal capacity. It costs little or nothing to keep in order—requiring little tuning. It occupies one-quarter the space of a pipe-organ of similar capacity. It is movable without being entirely taken to pieces. It is constructed so that each reed, having its own separate tone-chamber, can be removed with ease, and without disturbing the action. It has 58 notes to each tone in the manuals, and no tone borrows from another for the lower 14 tones, as is frequent in pipe-organs. It is ready for use on being unpacked. The two-manual vocalion requires no special mechanical skill to remove from the case and set up in position. The vocalion in its original form was the invention of James Baillie Hamilton of London, Eng., and the name was coined and conferred by Rt. Hon. Wm. E. Gladstone. Mr. M. S. Wright of Worcester subsequently devised and added important improvements, and later the interests of both inventors were purchased by the New York Church Organ Company, who fitted up the factory in this city, but before the vocalion was placed on the market Messrs. Mason & Risch, residents of Toronto, Canada, bought the plant, patents and rights, made additions and improvements, and secured the services of Mr. Wright as superintendent. Mr. Wright is an experienced and skillful builder of this class of instruments. Mr. A. J. Mason, a nephew of the senior partner, is general business manager. Both members of the firm are shrewd men who invested their capital here in the confident anticipation of profitable results—an anticipation which it is safe to say they will realize, as the vocalion needs only to be seen and heard to be appreciated, and sales already approach the present limit of productive capacity.

The factory building, entered by an imposing Norman arch, is of brick, five stories, 50x115 feet, and is perfectly equipped in all departments, the usual output being supplemented by an entirely new plant of special reed-making machinery of the latest style. A fine boiler and engine supply ample heat and power, and fifty skilled artisans are employed. The output goes to all parts of the United States, to England, Australia, Japan and other countries, and no word of complaint has ever reached the manufacturers.

C. H. HILDRETH, 2d,

Livery, Hacking, Board and Feed Stables—No. 10 Sever Street.

Of all the advantages of city life none are more attractive than the ease with which one may be transported by public or private conveyance from point to point. The hackney coach is a peculiar institution of the city, as is the livery stable. Worcester's most prominent livery and hack man is Mr. C. H. Hildreth, 2d, (junior), formerly of No. 20 Market street. On the first of March, 1890, Mr. Hildreth purchased the well-known stables of Mr. Charles F. Henry, No. 10

Sever street, and having made some necessary additions and improvements, removed his own stock of horses, carriages, etc., thereto, consolidating both under one management. The premises are the largest and the plant the most complete of the kind in Worcester, the former covering ground 150 x 250 feet with palatial stables, carriage-houses, store-house and capacious yard, while the latter comprises thirty or more fine horses and about fifty stylish vehicles of various kinds, including a number of handsome hacks, several elegant landaus and coupés, and many tempting double and single pleasure carriages, buggies, etc. Nine men are employed, including hostlers, drivers and other assistants. A specialty is made of furnishing hacks and carriages for pleasure parties, weddings and funerals, and for shopping and visiting. A coupé stand is maintained at No. 369 Main street and a hack stand at the Bay State House. Calls by telephone receive prompt attention. Experienced, liberal and obliging, Mr. Hildreth is popular and does a flourishing business. His efforts to please are ably seconded by Mr. Z. H. Dean, long in the employ of Mr. Henry and a favorite with all former patrons of that gentleman. Rates are reasonable and service first-class.

C. W. HUMPHREY,

Manufacturer of Paper Boxes of All Kinds—No. 42 Southbridge Street.

The manufacture of paper boxes is an industry of large proportions in which Worcester excels, there being several large factories here. One of the most prominent and best patronized

is that of Mr. C. W. Humphrey, situated at No. 42 Southbridge street. It was established about 1880 by a Mr. Marcy, who sold out subsequently to a Mr. Cook, to whom Mr. Humphrey succeeded in 1882. One floor of 800 square feet is occupied by the machinery —shears, dies, cutters, etc.; steam power is rented—and from fifty to sixty operatives are employed, and the output is very large, comprising every description of paper boxes for the use of manufacturers of shoes, slippers, confectionery and other goods susceptible of being so packed. While the local demand is liberal, orders are constantly being filled for shipment to New England points, and to New York and other States, and Mr. Humphrey is kept busy at all seasons. His facilities for manufacturing enable him to supply the above and other trades with every description of first-class boxes at most moderate prices, and also to undertake orders for any desired quantities, which are always promptly executed. Mr. Humphrey was born at Brockton, and has been a resident of Worcester for the past twenty-five years, where he is highly respected by all who know him.

SUMNER PRATT & CO.,

Cotton and Woolen Manufacturers' Agency—Dealers in Machinery, Wool Stock and Mill Supplies —No. 22 Front Street.

This is a pioneer house—one of the oldest in continuous existence in this vicinity. It was founded as long ago as 1847, by the late Sumner Pratt, and after an honorable and active career of forty-four years is as strong and enterprising as ever—more so if possible—maintaining its representative position in the front rank of the trade and transacting an annually expanding business with mill-owners throughout the United States. The present firm, composed of Messrs. W. H. Crawford and Frederick S. Pratt, dates from 1870. The first-named is a native of Oxford, while Mr. Pratt, a son of the original senior member, was born, reared and received his preparatory training in this city, having been connected with the famous old house almost from boyhood in the various capacities of salesman, clerk, bookkeeper and partner. Both are energetic business men and public-spirited citizens of high personal and commercial standing.

The building occupied by Sumner Pratt & Co., at No. 22 Front street, is worthy of the house. It was built by the elder Mr. Pratt and is an ornate four-story brick structure with brownstone trimmings, 38 feet front by 125 feet deep. Three floors are utilized for storage, salesrooms and office, and an immense stock is carried, comprising every description of woolen and cotton mill machinery and appliances, wool stock and mill supplies. The house has the sole agency here for many leading manufacturers of mill machinery, and is prepared to execute all orders at short notice, in the best manner, and at factory prices. Buyers and consumers of wool stock and mill supplies are also offered the most liberal terms and inducements.

JOHNSON & BASSETT,

Manufacturers of Self-Operating Wool-Spinning Machinery, Heavy Pattern Mules adapted for 300 to 500 Spindles, Medium Weight Mules adapted for 240 to 360 Spindles, Self-Operating Jacks adapted for 200 to 288 Spindles, Automatic Bobbin Winders and Spindle Band Tension Regulators—Corner of Foster and Bridge Streets (near Union Depot).

The firm of Johnson & Bassett was organized and the manufacture of automatic spinning machinery begun in 1870, the house being then established at No. 186 Union street, where the business was continued until 1886. Through the death of Mr. Johnson in 1880 the undivided ownership and management devolved upon the surviving partner, Mr. Joseph M. Bassett, a skilled and experienced mechanic and business man who has proved himself equal to the demand upon his physical and mental powers and continues the business as before, retaining the original style in honor of his deceased friend and partner and extending his trade to every State and hamlet in the Union that contains a woolen mill. Owing to the increase of business, and the consequent necessity for more extended facilities, it was essential that more commodious quarters be secured, and the requirements were fully met by the erection by Mr. Bassett, in 1886,

of the very handsome and substantial factory building, illustrated by the above engraving, solidly constructed of brick, four stories and basement, 62x125 feet, most advantageously situated at the corner of Foster and Bridge streets, near the Union depot.

The self-operating woolen mules, jacks and jack-heads made here are so universally known and approved as to require no technical description, nor, in fact, have we space at command therefor. Full particulars, illustrations and descriptions are furnished on application. The works are perfectly equipped in every department with ingenious special machinery and a 60-horse-power steam engine, and from eighty to one hundred skilled hands are employed. The present outlook of the business gives indications of largely increased demands upon the factory for its goods in the near future, which can be readily met, its capacity being fully equal to all probable requirements.

Mr. Bassett is a native of Vermont, who has resided and been actively engaged in business in Worcester during most of his life.

CENTRAL NATIONAL BANK OF WORCESTER.

Joseph Mason, President and Solicitor; Henry A. Marsh, Cashier—No. 452 Main Street.

This bank was chartered and organized as a State bank in 1829, under the name of the Central Bank of Worcester. May 18, 1864, it was reorganized under the National banking act, and took its present name. During the period of its existence as a State bank, and since, it has sustained a deserved reputation for prudence, sagacity and fidelity in its business transactions. Its banking rooms are large and convenient, and its customers always receive prompt and courteous attention. Its board of directors meets every Monday, and consists of the following named gentlemen: Joseph Mason, Philip L. Moen, Thomas L. Nelson, Samuel R. Heywood, Augustus N. Currier, Waldo Lincoln, George W. Knowlton, Henry A. Marsh and C. Henry Hutchins. The subjoined report of the bank shows its condition February 26, 1891:

Resources — Loans and discounts, $1,274,844.19; overdrafts, secured and unsecured, $341.41; U. S. bonds to secure circulation, $50,000; stocks, securities, claims, etc., $11,400; due from approved reserve agents, $72,723.58; current expenses and taxes paid, $5,233,63; premiums on U. S. bonds, $5,000; checks and other cash items, $11,266.57; bills of other banks, $6,836; fractional paper currency, nickels and cents, $451.24; specie, $39,177.21; legal tender notes, $12,500; U. S. certificates of deposit for legal tenders, $20,000; redemption fund with U. S. treasurer (5 per cent. of circulation), $2,250; total, $1,516,993.83. Liabilities—Capital stock paid in, $300,000; surplus fund, $100,000; undivided profits, $42,057.10; National bank notes outstanding, $45,000; individual deposits subject to check, $981,145.22; demand certificates of deposit, $33,642.06; due to other National banks, $15,149.45; total, $1,516,993.83.

WM. H. BROWN,

Machinist—Manufacturer of Carders' Tools—Lewis' Patent Card Clamps, Ratchets, Hammers, Gauges, Tubes, Scrapers, etc.—No. 81 Mechanic Street.

If skill, ingenuity and long experience count for anything, Mr. Wm. H. Brown has a just claim to pre-eminence in his particular field of industry. A native of New York and a practical tool-maker, he established himself in this city in 1855—thirty-six years ago—and has steadily

pursued the even tenor of his way, devising and adopting improvements from time to time until he now turns out a line of specialties that for simplicity, effectiveness, excellence of material and workmanship is unsurpassed. He occupies one floor, 20x38 feet, at No. 81 Mechanic street, where he has a complete outfit of appropriate steam-driven machinery, employs several workmen, and is prepared to fill promptly all orders for carders' tools, ratchets, hammers, gauges, tubes, scrapers, etc. He is sole manufacturer of Lewis' patent card clamps, and gives attention to machine jobbing and repairs of every description.

HENRY E. DEAN & CO.,

Manufacturers of Standard Wire Goods, Special Hardware and Housekeeping Goods, Spring Steel Wire Wagon-Seat Cushions, Steel Wire Brushes, Wire Window and Elevator Guards, Office and Desk Railings, Screens, etc.—No. 180 Austin Street.

Mr. Lewis Dean began the manufacture of wire goods in Oakham, Mass., in the year 1857. Being an ingenious and capable man, he gradually built up a large and prosperous business, to which his son Henry E. succeeded some years ago, subsequently erecting and removing to his present place, No. 180 Austin street—a substantial three-story frame factory, 40x75 feet, with commodious salesroom and office adjoining. The establishment is equipped in the most effective manner throughout, most of the improved appli- 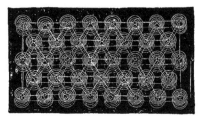auces being of Mr. Dean's own invention, among them a machine specially designed for making the "Dean" spring steel wire wagon-seat cushion that attracts immediate and wondering attention. One hundred and fifty hands are employed, and Mr. Dean's market may be called world-wide, his goods being sold in all parts of the United States, Canada, Great Britain, Belgium, Australia and other countries. He manufactures almost everything coming under the head of standard wire goods, including office and desk railings and screens, window and elevator guards, steel wire brushes, sieves, lime and sand screens, coal screens, special hardware and housekeeping con- veniences of every description, such as broilers, toasters, glove pot-cleaners, portable plate- racks, doughnut lifters and skimmers, potato-mashers, spiral egg-beaters, culinary rollers, rat and mouse traps, etc., together with dish-covers, vegetable boilers, dish-drainers, potato-fryers, egg-whips, corn-poppers, conductor strainers, horse and ox muzzles, sponge baskets, "Perfec- tion" pillow-sham holders, and countless other devices for use and ornament. Special atten- tion is invited to the steel wire cushion illustrated herewith, which is positively unrivaled as a seat for wagons, carriages, sleighs, railroad cabs, fire engines, etc. It is made to order of any desired size, may be used either with or without a cushion or blanket, and is practically indestruc- tible. Among the facilities of the establishment should be mentioned two looms for the making of coarse wire cloth, while twenty-four others for the weaving of finer grades are kept busy else- where. Mr. Dean keeps several energetic salesmen in New England and the middle States.

WORCESTER STORAGE COMPANY.

Horace Wyman, President; George A. Stearns, Jr., Treasurer—Fire-Proof Ware- house, No. 29 Gold Street Court.

The public fire-proof storage warehouse idea, though not a new one, seems never to have been put into actual operation at this point until 1889, when the Worcester Storage Company, capital $13,000, was incorporated and the commo- 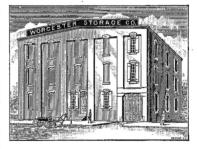dious three-story brick structure 60x60 feet, No. 29 Gold street, erected. Our cut gives a general view of the building, which, constructed upon approved principles, provided with iron-faced shutters, and isolated from others, offers the maximum of protec- tion from conflagration—a condition still further en- hanced by precautionary regulations against the making of fires for any purpose or smoking on the premises. As a consequence, low rates of insurance upon merchandise stored here are freely offered by responsible underwriters. The internal arrange- ments are as nearly perfect as is attainable, a power- ful hydraulic elevator being provided for the raising of goods by the wagon-load to the upper floors, where are found a number of rooms of various sizes for rent to parties desirous of keeping their property separate from that of others. The convenience and security of a warehouse of this kind can hardly be overestimated. Residents who intend a prolonged absence from the city find here perfect safety for their furniture, trunks, packages and other valuables of a bulky nature, while merchants, manufacturers and others may store with the company every description of merchan- dise, machinery, vehicles, etc., with the assurance that they will be well cared for and restored in first-class condition.

COES WRENCH COMPANY.

Loring Coes, President; John H. Coes, Treasurer; F. L. Coes, Secretary—Manufacturers of the Original L. Coes' Genuine Patent Knife-Handle and Mechanics' Screw Wrenches—Mill Street, Coes Square.

The Coes wrenches have been before the public and in daily use by mechanics and others for more than fifty years, and are to-day more popular and salable than ever before. The latest

and best improvement in wrenches, known as L. Coes' "Genuine " patent knife-handle wrench, is thus described: 1. The ferrule frame and tip of handle are cast in one piece, with shank of bar solidly keyed into same, thereby preventing the possible displacement of either ferrule or tip.

The iron frame is covered on either side by blocks of southern dogwood or persimmon, solidly riveted to the sides. The utility of this invention is apparent and a decided improvement over all other wrench handles. 2.— The bar of wrench is made straight the whole length, full size of the larger part of the wrench, and will stand nearly one-third more strain, when the jaw is used opened half the length of the screw, than the so-called "reinforced " or "jog bar." 3.—The jaw is made with ribs on the inside: these run the length of the jaw, with a full bearing on the front of the bar, and in connection with the projecting sides of the jaw (secured by patent) make the jaw fully equal to any strain the bar may be subject to. The barrel of jaw has also been enlarged, to take a larger and longer screw, which enables the wrench to take a larger nut than any now in the market.

For the improved "Mechanics' " wrench it is claimed that it is equally strong and serviceable with the "Genuine," the bar and jaws are of the same size, the quality of stock identical, and each wrench thoroughly case-hardened. The majority of wrench users care nothing for fine finish, requiring a strong tool for actual work, and this is just suited to their wants. A recent improvement consists of a cup tip firmly riveted to end of shank, which prevents splitting and loosening of the handle.

L. and A. G. Coes founded this industry in 1841. In 1888 the present company was incorporated, capital $100,000. The Coes Wrench Company operate two factories, one located at Coes square and the other at Webster square. Both factories are fully equipped with special machinery which is adapted to the rapid and accurate production of the class of goods manufactured. The machinery is driven partly by water and partly by steam power. One hundred and thirty workmen, comprising many skilled mechanics, are employed. The selling agents are: J. C. McCarty & Co., No. 97 Chambers street, and John H. Graham & Co., No. 113 Chambers street, New York.

H. E. SMITH & CO.,

Manufacturers of and Dealers in Boots, Shoes and Rubbers—Proprietors of the Unequaled "Nox 'Em All" Shoe—Nos. 15 and 17 Mechanic Street.

The man who can and does say the right thing at the right time in the right way—who gives a catchy and appropriate name off-hand to a catchy and useful idea or thing—is a born genius and capable of great things. No better exemplification of this occurs to us than is afforded by the renowned "Nox 'Em All" shoe, originated—goods and name—by the firm of Childs, Smith & Co., now H. E. Smith & Co., Nos. 15 and 17 Mechanic street, Worcester. This shoe—empathically the poor man's friend—is especially designed for the use of those with whom durability is a prime object, and in that respect has no rival, being made of the best selected waterproof grain, the soles standard fastened, the most careful workmanship displayed throughout, and no pains or expense spared in perfecting this particular brand of shoe and bringing it to the notice of dealers and consumers. The result is that the "Nox 'Em All" is received with general and rapidly increasing favor east, west, south, wherever introduced, and that department of the factory is driven to its utmost capacity to meet the demand.

The old firm of Childs, Smith & Co. was established in 1875, soon winning and always maintaining a prominent position among the more reputable representatives of the boot and shoe industry and conducting in conjunction with their manufacturing business the handling of boots, shoes, and rubbers at wholesale. Success was assured from the start, and ere long they moved to and occupied the imposing five-story brick building Nos. 15 and 17 Mechanic street, affording 16,000 square feet of floorage. Eighteen clerks and assistants are employed here; seven travelers represent the house in all parts of the country, and transactions exceed $600,000 annually, the territory covered embracing nearly all of New England and the middle States, a portion of the central west, and some parts of Canada. The leading specialty is the "Nox 'Em All" shoe, though every description of footwear is sold.

On the first of last July Mr. H. E. Smith succeeded to the sole proprietorship and management, under the style of H. E. Smith & Co. He was born at North Brookfield, the son of a shoe manufacturer, is nearly fifty years of age, and has been familiar with every phase of the trade "since infancy" as he himself expresses it. He entered upon his business career in 1866, after four years and ten months' service in the Fifteenth Massachusetts volunteer infantry (in which he rose to a lieutenancy). Since his return from the big war Col. Smith has rendered excellent service as an officer of Battery B, Worcester Light Artillery. He was a charter member of and has since commanded the Worcester Continentals. At the 250th anniversary of the Ancient and Honorable Artillery Company of Boston he was elected commander of that distinguished organization.

Mr. Smith may be fairly characterized as the architect of his own fortunes, which have steadily "waxed" more and more easy and give evidence of "lasting". In his case, at least, there "seams" to have been "nothing like leather," which has lifted him from "peg to peg" to the "upper" walks of commercial life by the "sole" force of industry and integrity. A pleasant, genial gentleman, always ready with a jest and a smile, his worst enemy (if he has one) could not harbor a wish to see him "strapped," "out at toes" or "run down at heel."

MRS. MARION B. WARE,

Manufacturer of Mattresses and Fillings—Dealer in Feathers, Pillows, etc.—Tatnuck, Near Corner of Pleasant and Chandler Streets.

This enterprise was started by Mr. J. E. Ware at Ashland in 1875. He subsequently removed to Worcester, where for some years he prospered, but was at last overtaken, a year or two ago, by business difficulties and forced to suspend. An arrangement having been effected with creditors, his wife assumed the direction of affairs and the concern is continued in her name. The premises comprise twenty acres of land, with dwelling, barn and appurtenances, and a two-story mill equipped with shoddy-picking and other machinery and a sixty-horse-power steam engine. From twelve to fifteen operatives are employed, and the output embraces all grades of mattresses, white and gray wool, cotton, excelsior, husk, fiber and hair fillings, feathers, pillows, cushions, cotton and wool flocks, seagrass and other materials. Trade extends throughout New England, New York State, south to Richmond, Va., west to Omaha, and east to Halifax and Frederickton, N. B.

AMERICAN AWL COMPANY.

H. A. Southwick, Superintendent; C. A. Hardy,. Traveling Salesman—Manufacturers of and Dealers in Shoe Manufacturers' Tools, etc.—No. 195 Front Street.

It is a question if the American Awl Company could have selected a better field of business operations than Worcester, which is the centre and to a great extent the base of supplies of the great shoe manufacturing section of the United States. The house was founded in 1876 by Mr. H. A. Southwick, Mr. C. A. Hardy acquiring an interest and becoming associated as a copartner in 1880. Occupying one entire floor, 60x120 feet, at No. 195 Front street, fitted up with

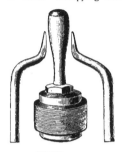

improved metal-working machinery and provided with steam power, the company employs eight skilled hands and produces great quantities of superior tools especially designed for the shoe industry, besides handling as agents and jobbers a variety of specialties made elsewhere. Of their own manufacture, the attention of the trade is invited to a choice line of raw-hide mallets, wax thread needles and awls; "New Era," "Varney," and "Champion" pegging awls, etc., lasting machine awls and drivers; "Bigelow," "McKay" and "National" heeling awls and drivers; awls and drivers for heel-slugging machines, etc., while they carry large stocks of McKay needles, shoe knives, extension blades and handles, etc., of others' make, and are agents for the sale of the celebrated "Excelsior" needles. The house also has the special agency and will fill orders from farmers and others for Whitley's solid steel mower, manufac-

tured by the William N. Whitley Company (formerly the Champion Mower and Reaper Company) of Springfield, Ohio. This concern ranks with the most reputable in the country, and has established flourishing connections in almost every State in the Union. The senior member, Mr. Southwick, is a native of Mendon, Mass., and a machinist by trade. He has personal supervision of the manufacturing department. Mr. Hardy, a practical machine paper-knife maker, represents the house on the road.

BAY STATE HOUSE.

Douglass & Brown, Proprietors—Corner of Main and Exchange Streets.

The Bay State ranks with the most famous of New England hotels, and, being first-class in all respects, easily distances all local competitors. It is the regular stopping-place of wealthy and distinguished visitors to Worcester, headquarters for the more exclusive class of commercial travelers, and the home of many retired business men and their families, who find here all the comforts and conveniences, privacy and luxury of domestic life, with none of the cares and an-

noyances that mar the pleasure of a private establishment. The Bay State was erected about twenty-five years ago, but has undergone many changes of management. The building, belonging to a stock company, has been several times enlarged and remodeled, and, as our engraving shows, presents an imposing appearance. It is of brick, four stories and basement, 80 feet front by 100 feet deep, substantially constructed, practically fire-proof, and fitted up with every provision for the safety of its inmates. The principal entrance from Main street leads to the spacious rotunda and elegant office, paved with tessellated marble, lofty and richly frescoed. On this floor are the main hall, public parlors, reading and sample rooms, etc. In the basement are the splendidly fitted billiard-room, the kitchen, pantries, store-rooms, and other appointments pertaining to the service. On the second floor are the great dining-hall, 40x80 feet, capable of seating three hundred persons, private parlors, reception room, etc. On the upper floors are the sleeping apartments and private sitting-rooms, one hundred and thirty-two in number, arranged singly and *en suite*, commodious, handsomely furnished, richly carpeted and upholstered, clean, sweet, airy, with large windows, lighted by gas and fitted up with electric bells, hot and cold water and all conveniences, including bath and toilet-rooms. A fine passenger elevator connects all the upper floors with the rotunda, and makes access to the top of the house as convenient as the second story.

It is hardly necessary to say more of the table and the *cuisine* than that they are perfect, the latter presided over by a noted *chef* and a lieutenant scarcely less accomplished than his principal. The service is first-class in every departmennt, and the guest of the Bay State who does not enjoy life will have only himself to blame, as all the facilities of luxurious living are supplied in superabundance. Rates, graduated from $2.50 to $3.00 and $3.50 per day, are exceedingly moderate, accommodations considered. A fine laundry and livery stable are connected with the house, and hacks run to and from the house, connecting with out going and incoming trains at all hours of day and night.

Messrs. Frank P. Douglass and Charles Brown assumed the proprietorship and direction of the Bay State in 1888, both having been long identified with hotel-keeping. They have made many important improvements in the internal arrangements, refurnished the house throughout, and, giving their undivided attention to their business, have largely increased their personal pop-ularity and the patronage of the hotel. They are ably seconded by Messrs. E. S. Douglass and E. L. Church, clerks.

WRIGHT & COLTON WIRE CLOTH COMPANY.

George F. Wright, President; S. H. Colton, Treasurer; George M. Wright, Manager — Manufacturers of Power Loom Wire Cloths, Galvanized Poultry Netting and Fencing.

The manufacture of wire cloth is one of those industries which, of comparatively recent origin, quickly demonstrated its usefulness and has already taken a prominent place among the

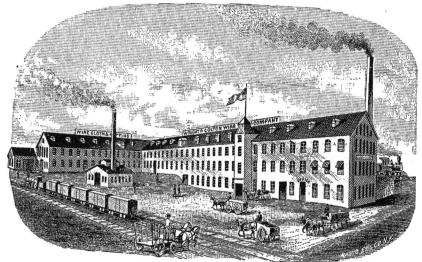

established standard interests of the country, and of which the Wright & Colton Wire Cloth Company is one of the conspicuous representatives. President Wright was the founder of the Wright Wire Cloth Company, formerly of Palmer, established in 1885, reorganized in 1889 as the Wright & Colton Wire Cloth Company, capital $50,000, and removed to Worcester on the first of January, 1890. The premises now occupied are convenient and well suited to the purpose, comprising a commodious two-story brick building 60 x 420 feet on Hammond street near the Boston & Albany and New York & New England railroad tracks. The machinery equipment is first-class and includes a great number of power looms and special appliances designed for the making of every description of steel, iron, brass and copper wire cloth and twisted nettings, all driven by a ninety-horse-power steam engine. Seventy-five hands find employment in the mill, and the output is large and rapidly increasing. Specialties are made of high grade locomotive steel spark netting, fanning mill, hardware, and fruit-drying wire cloths, twisted nettings and improved twist warp wire lathing. The goods made here are in all respects of the best quality; orders are being booked from all parts of the country, and the outlook for a prosperous career is most flattering.

FOWLER & COMPANY,

Manufacturers of the "Perfection" Sash Curtain Rod Fixtures — No. 65 Beacon St.

The device herewith illustrated so nearly explains itself that but a few words of description are necessary. The rod used is the ordinary curtain rod, to which at each end the fixtures are

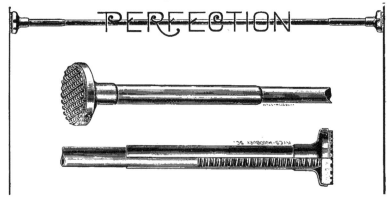

applied, the corrugated rubber button attachment preventing the fixture from marring the casings. The directions for putting up are appended: Cut the rod three inches shorter than the space to be filled. File burr from ends. Apply the fixtures to the rod, and the spiral springs inside of the fixtures, yielding to pressure applied at the ends, will allow the rod and fixtures to be adjusted into the space they are to occupy, where they will be held by the force of the springs and the friction of the rubber. No screws or nails being used, no holes are left in the window casing, if it is desired on account of the shrinking of the curtain to drop the rod a little, or, for any reason, to remove it altogether. A slight mistake in cutting off the rod does not spoil it, the springs in the fixtures adjusting themselves to the change. Messrs. H. A. Fowler and J. H. Lingley, the inventors, commenced the manufacture of this superior curtain fixture on Pearl street in July, 1889, and soon built up a good trade, the article selling on sight. On the first of January, 1890, having organized the present firm of Fowler & Company, the works were removed to No. 65 Beacon street, where, with a complete outfit of special machinery and tools and a sufficient force of capable workmen, they expect to fill all orders without delay.

JOHN J. ADAMS,

Manufacturer of Boot and Shoe Machinery—Patent Improved Sole Cutters a Specialty— No. 85 Mechanic Street.

Situated geographically in the very heart of the greatest shoe manufacturing region on the globe and possessed of all of the commercial and industrial advantages necessary to maintain her supremacy in this respect, Worcester is naturally the principal center where are constructed the various forms of improved machinery and special tools required by the trade. Prominent among those who have contributed to the city's fame in this respect is Mr. John J. Adams, or, more accurately, the establishment of which he is now the head, founded in 1878 by Edwin Fisher, to whom Mr. Adams succeeded in 1880. The works occupy one floor, 20 x 80 feet, of the large brick building No. 85 Mechanic street, and contain a complete outfit of iron-working machinery and appliances, steam power, etc., giving employment to six trained mechanics and turning out a considerable volume and great variety of superior work, the specialties embracing a general line of high-grade shoe machinery and patent improved sole cutters of the best class. In addition, Mr. Adams gives prompt and skillful attention to all orders for repairs of the machinery named, steam engines, etc., and to machine jobbing generally. He was born, reared and learned his trade in Worcester, is an expert machinist, an enterprising business man, and popular with all who know him.

EVANS & CO.,

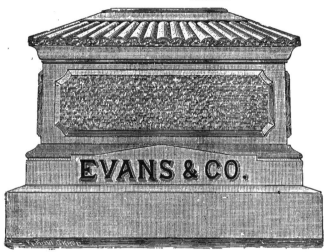

Manufacturers of and Dealers in Foreign and American Marble and Granite Monumental Work — Fine Polished Granite Work a Specialty — Salesroom and Steam Mill, No. 131 Central St., Near Summer. From time immemorial it has been the custom of all civilized peoples to erect memorials to their loved and honored dead, and in no age has this beautiful and appropriate custom been so general as in our own — the era of the world's greatest enlightenment and best development, moral, mental and physical. That stone should have been originally chosen as the material for the construction of monumental piles is not surprising, inasmuch as, in the then undeveloped state of sciences and mechanics, it was at once the most beautiful and the most enduring substance obtainable. That the ancients attained to great skill in the art of preparing stone for the purpose and achieved wonders in the uprearing of such structures is attested by the pyramids, and other old world remains that, antedating history, still challenge the admiration and curiosity of mankind. Worcester is particularly well situated with reference to supplies of superior marble and granite, the choicest quarries on this continent being within convenient reach, and consequently the monument industry flourishes here, a leading representative thereof being the house of Evans & Co., founded many years ago by Mr. A. M. Evans, who is still at its head with Messrs. H. F. Stedman and H. E. Chandler as his associates — one of the busiest and most liberal establishments in New England, the proprietors at the time of the late labor troubles having promptly increased wages beyond the demands of their employé. The office, salesroom, steam mill and worksheds at No. 131 Central street are commodious, completely equipped, and cover ground 60x175 feet (2,000 square feet), running the machinery, derricks, etc., by means of a sixty-horse-power steam engine. Granite and marble-cutters, sawyers, polishers and assistants to the number of twenty-five or more find steady work here, and the business of the house is very large and constantly increasing, the demands upon its resources coming principally from the New

England States, though frequent orders are executed for shipment to all parts of the country. The facilities are ample, and parties in want of anything in Evans & Co.'s line, from a simple marble slab to an imposing American, Swedish or Scotch granite monument, from a headstone to a group of artistic statuary, are invited to call upon or communicate with the firm in the full assurance of superior work and upright dealing.

WM. H. BURNS & CO.,

Manufacturers of Ladies' Muslin and Cotton Underwear—No. 69 Park St.—Branch
Warehouses: No. 402 Broadway, New York; No. 15 Avon St., Boston; No. 138
State St., Chicago.

The handsome and commodious brick block shown in the accompanying cut is the second
erected by this firm since its establishment in 1883, the first soon proving inadequate to the
requirements of the business. As at
first constituted the house was
styled Baker & Burns—John S.
Baker and W. H. Burns—but, the
senior member retiring, Mr. Harry
S. Green became Mr. Burns' associate and the style was changed to
W. H. Burns & Co. The factory is
of five stories, covers 50,000 square
feet of ground, and the four upper
floors are used by the firm for
manufacturing purposes, the lower
story being rented to several retail
merchants, Burns & Co. reserving
52,000 square feet of floorage for
their own use — none too much, as
their transactions are expanding
with unprecedented rapidity and
the pressure upon their productive
capacity increases in like ratio. At
present they employ 450 people, females for the most part, and have in all 650 sewing machines
specially designed for this particular class of work, constructed to order by the leading
manufacturers of the country. The production averages 550 dozen garments, worth at first
hands from $2,500 to $3,000, daily. These garments, which comprise every form of muslin and
cotton underwear for ladies and misses, in all styles and grades from the finest to the most
ordinary, are noted for accuracy of fit, excellence of material, workmanship and finish,
durability and attractiveness, and are handled by the trade all over the United States. During
the year 1889 Burns & Co. cut and made up two and a half million yards of cotton cloth from
the Lawrence, Lewiston and Providence mills. They also imported, and continue to import for
their own consumption, vast quantities of Hamburg embroidery from Switzerland, laces from
France, Spain and Austria, so-called Irish lace from Nottingham, England, and pearl buttons
from Vienna—the price of which latter commodity, by the way, will be nearly or quite doubled
by the new tariff. It is unnecessary to dilate upon the personality of Messrs. Burns and Green;
their industrial and commercial enterprise and the results achieved is the best possible comment
upon their capacity and extraordinary energy. Branch offices have been established for the
convenience of buyers in Boston, New York and Chicago.

J. C. SPEIRS & CO.,

Manufacturers of Drop Forgings of All Kinds—Cor. Nebraska and Winona Streets.

Drop forgings are in constantly increasing request among manufacturers of hand and machine
tools, light and heavy machinery, vehicles, etc., and the supply is never greater than the demand
in the better grades. Of those who have recently engaged in this industry we know of none
who have better prospects or are more worthy of notice than the new firm named above, who,
as Speirs & Moore, established themselves at the corner of Nebraska and Winona streets and
started their works in April, 1890. Messrs. J. C. Speirs and A. L. Moore, both young and
enterprising business men, expert mechanics, industrious and capable, succeeded well, but on the
30th of October Mr. Speirs purchased Mr. Moore's interest and changed the style to J. C.
Speirs & Co. Their factory is a one-story frame building 40 x 110 feet, with 25 x 25-foot L for
boiler and engine, built especially for them and thoroughly equipped with newly improved
machinery of the best class. They commenced with eight skilled employes, but confidently
expect to enlarge their facilities and extend their trade to all parts of the country, making
specialties of high grade drop forgings, such as bicycle, tricycle, fire-arm, sewing machine and
machine tool parts, wrenches, etc. Estimates are cheerfully furnished and prompt attention is
given to orders large or small.

NORCROSS BROTHERS,

Contractors and Builders—Office, No. 10 East Worcester St., Near Union Passenger Station.

This great leading firm of contractors, which in acquiring for itself a national reputation has at the same time reflected credit upon and aided in extending the fame of Worcester to every section of the land, is composed of Messrs. James A. and Orlando W. Norcross, natives of Maine.

ALLEGHENY COUNTY BUILDINGS,
Pittsburg, Pa.

They were first established at Swampscott, Essex county, as carpenters and builders on a modest scale in 1864. Four years later they removed to this city and began laying the foundations of the vast business enterprise of which they are now the proprietors and managers. Their office is situated in the large four-story brick building No. 10 East Worcester street, containing also their extensive planing mill and woodworking shops, equipped to perfection. Connected therewith, and lying alongside the Boston & Albany tracks, are commodious lumber and stone yards. A great many men are employed here, but their number is insignificant compared with the total working force of the firm, quarrymen, granite and freestone cutters, mill hands, masons, bricklayers, etc., scattered all over the country, the house owning valuable granite quarries at Milford, Mass., and Stony Creek, Conn., and freestone quarries at East Longmeadow, Mass., near Springfield. A fortune is invested in machinery alone for the manipulation of stone. Branch offices are maintained at Huntington avenue, Boston, and No. 48 West 125th street, New York city, where parties contemplating the erection of buildings of any kind will be made welcome and afforded every facility and convenience in the way of practical suggestions, estimates, etc. The real career of this truly representative firm began subsequent to its location in Worcester, with their first important contract, the construction of the Congregational church at Leicester, in which was displayed such good taste, mechanical excellence and prompti-tude that the standing of the brothers was at once established. Contracts thereafter rapidly succeeded each other, and by the close of 1870 they had completed the Crompton block on Mechanic street, the First Universalist church and the Wor-cester High School building. Since then they have undertaken and carried out many important building contracts in this and other cities — among them the Allegheny county court-house and jail at Pittsburg, Pa., the largest and finest structure of the kind in America, designed by that prince of architects the late

CHAMBER OF COMMERCE,
Cincinnati, Ohio.

H. H. Richardson; the Cincinnati Chamber of Commerce building; the Howard Memorial Library at New Orleans; the Union League club-house, New York; the Algonquin club-house, Boston; the Vermont University, Burlington; the Union Theological Seminary, New York; the vast Marshall Field (wholesale department) building, Chicago; the Lionberger building, St. Louis; the Trinity church, Boston; the St. James church, New York; the South Congregational Church, Spring-field, Mass.; the Union depot and massive railroad arch over Main street, Springfield, and many other notable examples of modern architecture and engineering. They are now engaged upon a number of important contracts, of which we may name the State street Exchange, the new Ames building, and the State House extension, all in Boston, and several churches in New York. Both members of the firm are leading and public-spirited citizens, but too much immersed in their business to mingle much in public affairs, though Mr. James A. Norcross was a member of the City Council in 1877. The junior partner, Mr. Orlando W. Norcross, served one term of enlistment in the Fourteenth Massachusetts heavy artillery during the late civil war. Below are named some of the buildings erected by Norcross Brothers, with date and cost of each: Public Buildings—Hampden County court-house, Springfield, Mass., contract, 1872; cost, $175,000; Woburn library, 1877, $80,000; Ames library, North Easton, Mass., 1877, $36,000; North Easton town hall, 1879, $50,000; Crane memorial library, Quincy, 1880, $44,000; Albany city hall, 1881, $295,000; Allegheny County court-house and jail, Pittsburg, Pa., 1885,

$2,500,000; Cincinnati chamber of commerce, 1887, $530,000; Howard memorial library, New Orleans, La., 1887, $98,000; Malden library, 1885, $90,000; New London library, 1889, $39,000; Warder library, Springfield, Ohio, 1889, $63,800; Boston chamber of commerce, 1890, $373,800; State house extension, Boston, 1889, $627,300. Club Houses—Union League club house, New York, 1879, $255,000; Boston Art club house, 1881, $54,000;. Algonquin club house, Boston, 1886, $177,000. Private Residences—Newport, Annie W. Sherman, 1875, $40,000; Boston, Oliver Ames, 1882, $68,000; Boston, C. A. Whittier, 1881, $107,000; Albany, Grange Sard, jr., 1882, $32,000; New York, block for Union Theo. Seminary, 1883, $60,000; Wellesley, Brownlow Hall, 1883, $60,000; Cambridge, A. Aggassiz, 1883, $95,000; Washington, D. C., B. H. Warder, 1886, $112,000; Great Barrington, "Kellogg Terrace," 1885, $600,000; Boston, John F. Andrews, 1885, $140,000; Boston, C. C. Converse, 1886, $55,000; South Lancaster, John E. Thayer, 1886, $85,000; Chicago, Ill., J. J. Glessner, 1886, $85,000; Dedham, Mass., A. W. Nickerson, 1887, $175,000; Springfield, Ohio, A. S. Bushnell, 1887, $90,000; Cambridge, Mass., E. H. Abbot, 1889, $116,400. Educational Structures —Worcester High School, 1870, $120,000; Latin High School, Boston, 1878, $170,000; Harvard College gymnasium, Cambridge, 1878, $91,000; Harvard College, Sever hall, 1878, $104,000; Harvard College law school, 1882, $136,000; Union Theological Seminary, New York, 1882, $286,000; Vermont University, Burlington, 1883, $92,000; Lawrenceville school buildings, New Jersey, 1883, $320,000; Durfee high school, Fall River, Mass., 1886-7, $200,000; Crouse Memorial College, Syracuse, N. Y., 1888, $220,000; Osborne Hall, New Haven, Conn., 1888, $140,000; Mission school, New York, N. Y., 1889, $30,000; Williams Memorial Institute, New London, Conn., 1889, $70,000. Business Blocks—Crompton's block, Worcester, 1868, $75,000; Cheney block, Hartford, Conn., 1875, $337,000; Ames warehouse, Boston, 1882, $133,000; Turner building, St. Louis, Mo., 1883, $208,000; Marshall Field building, Chicago, Ill., 1885, $900,000; N. Y. Life Insurance building, Omaha, Neb., 1887, $525,000;. N. Y. Life Insurance building, Kansas City, Mo., 1887, $520,000; Burnside building, Worcester, 1886, $92,000; Lionberger building, St. Louis, Mo., 1888, $275,000; F. L. Ames building, Boston, 1889, $650,000; F. L. Ames building, Boston, 1890, $350,000; Boston Stock Exchange, 1889, $1,500,000; Bradley building, Boston, 1890, $70,000; Weeks building, Boston, 1889, $44,000; F. L. Ames building, Boston, 1889, $280,000. Churches— Congregational church, Leicester, 1866, $30,000; Congregational church, South Adams, 1867, $20,000; First Universalist church, Worcester, 1870, $30,000; South Congregational church, Springfield, Mass., 1870, $150,000; Trinity church, Boston, 1873, $390,000; Norwich Congregational church, 1873, $90,000; All Saints' church, Worcester, 1875, $95,000; Trinity church parsonage, Boston, 1879, $28,000; Winthrop Congregational church, Holbrook, 1879, $22,000; Grace church, New Bedford, 1880, $40,000; Presbyterian church, Albany, N. Y., 1882, $80,000; First Spiritual temple, Boston, 1883, $120,000; St. James' Episcopal church, New York, 1883, $130,000; Newton Baptist church, Newton, 1885, $43,000; St. John's church, New York, N. Y., 1889, $390,000; St. John's church, Stamford, Conn., 1890, $128,000; Holy Trinity church, New York, N. Y., 1888, $180,000. Norcross Brothers also built the Ames Memorial monument at Sherman, Wyoming Ter., at a cost of $62,000. It has medallions of Oakes A. and Oliver Ames on either side, cut on the solid stone, sixteen times life size. This monument is situated on the highest elevation of the Rocky Mountains that is crossed by the Union Pacific railroad, and commands an extensive view from this road.

LUTHER SHAW & SON,

Brass Founders and Manufacturers of Babbitt Metal and Solder—Works, No. 29 Jackson Street.

A great engine and machine building center, Worcester offers many advantages to the skillful brass founder—inducements that have brought hither several noted masters of that art, among them the firm of Luther Shaw & Son, who established themselves here in 1880. The success of the concern was immediate, and a fine business was being built up when, four years later, the senior member, Mr. Luther Shaw, died, leaving all of his interests in the hands of his son, who entered business with him in 1880. The surviving partner is a thorough practical brass-worker and an enterprising young business man, and as sole proprietor is making for his house a high and deserved reputation for fine workmanship and promptitude in the execution of orders. The foundry and shops at No. 29 Jackson street, occupy the entire brick building, two stories and basement, 40 x 40 feet, the basement being used for storage, with foundry on the first and pattern shop on the second floor. Five expert workmen are employed, and every convenience provided. The specialties comprise brass castings of every description, together with composition, zinc, lead and white metal castings for all conceivable purposes, and the manufacture of Babbitt metal and solder for the trade.

UNION RAILROAD STATION, SPRINGFIELD, MASS.—BUILT BY NORCROSS BROTHERS.

7

E. O. KNIGHT,

Manufacturer of and Dealer in Engines and Boilers, Appliances and Engineers' Supplies—No. 142 Union Street.

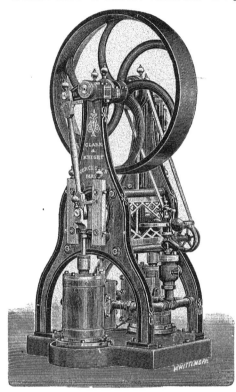

Worcester mechanics excel in the construction of engines, boilers and kindred devices, not a few of the most valuable improvements in this line having originated here. A prominent representative of this industry is Mr. E. O. Knight of No. 142 Union street. Mr. Knight is a native of Lincolnville, Me., a practical engine-builder of large experience, and was the junior member of Clark & Knight, established in 1878. Mr. Knight succeeded to the sole proprietorship in 1884. His equipment of special tools and machinery embraces all that is requisite, and he transacts a large business in manufacturing new and repairing old engines and boilers, besides buying, selling and exchanging second-hand engines on liberal terms. He is also agent for and carries a large stock of Waters' governors, automatic injectors, lubricators, heaters and engineers' supplies of all kinds. Orders for new work or jobbing of any kind are given immediate and skillful attention.

The Clark & Knight vertical engine illustrated herewith is so simple as to be readily understood by even a novice, while it is at the same time a most perfect and effective machine, capable of developing great power without undue strain or danger of "running through itself," as it is technically called. The material, workmanship and finish are of the highest order, and, in a word, nothing has been left undone to place and keep this engine in the front rank of those employed for light manufacturing and kindred purposes.

PRATT & INMAN,

Importers, Wholesale and Retail Dealers in Iron and Steel.—Nos. 15 and 17 Washington Square.

The oldest and one of the most extensive houses engaged in supplying Central Massachusetts manufacturers and mechanics with iron and steel in all grades is named above. Founded in 1829 by Joseph Pratt & Co., for forty years the concern had no local rival and controlled the market throughout this region. When it is remembered that Worcester has been an important manufacturing centre almost from the beginning of this century, it will not be difficult to comprehend that the transactions of this house must during its long career have aggregated an immense total and that it must have wielded vast influence in the industrial development of the city and county. It is unnecessary to follow the various changes that have taken place in its *personnel*. Suffice it to say that in 1853 the present style was substituted for that of J. H. Pratt & Co. The firm now consists of Messrs. F. H. and W. H. Inman, though the title Pratt & Inman is retained. The premises embrace two floors 40 x 120 feet each at Nos. 15 and 17 Washington square, and are constantly stocked with full lines of choice merchant bar, rods and other forms of choice iron and steel, such as are required in this market, and which are supplied in quantities to suit at lowest quotations and on favorable terms. Buyers and consumers of this class of materials are invited to call and inspect stock and facilities in the full assurance of honorable and liberal dealing.

GEORGE E. WEBB,

Builder of Row Boats, Sail Boats and Steam Launches—Pleasure Boats for Hire— Lake Quinsigamond.

·Probably no sheet of water of the same extent in the world is so crowded with pleasure craft in the season as Lake Quinsigamond, nor can any similar lake boast the same facilities tor boat-building. Of yards devoted to this industry there are two—one (which is the oldest) at the upper end of Lincoln park, conducted by Mr. George E. Webb and completely equipped for the construction of any style of craft. This enterprise was established in 1872 by a Mr. O'Leary, who sold out to Mr. Webb in 1887. Provided with ample water front, boat-house; floats and shops, Mr. Webb employs several skilled workmen and is prepared to contract for building any kind of boat from a steam launch to a twelve-pound canoe or racing shell. Of the latter class he makes a specialty, and has built many of the fastest ever put in the water. Of launches

he has designed many, some of which are kept here and others have been sent to other points. The two neatest and swiftest steam launches on the lake are from his shop, one 25 feet long to carry eighteen passengers, James A. Norcross owner; the other 18 feet long, O. A. Jefts owner. He has also built many boats of all styles for the local boat clubs. Besides building boats for sale and to order, Mr. Webb owns sixty-five small craft (including skiffs, canoes and shells) and three sailing craft which are kept for hire, and those desiring a pleasure sail on the lake will be accommodated at moderate prices. His craft are all kept tight, dry and clean, provided with cushions, and all conveniences.

Mr. Webb is a native of Lowell, a polite and obliging man, and an amateur oarsman with a record. He is also a practical boat-builder, for several years was the only one on the lake, and has made a first-class reputation as a practical designer and builder of all kinds of boats.

LAKE VIEW HOUSE,

H. W. Goodnow, Proprietor — West Shore, Lake Quinsigamond.

Lake Quinsigamond is the great summer attraction of this vicinity, and much has been done to render it a pleasure resort worthy of the city and of the State. One of the latest important permanent improvements was the erection of the Lake View House, opened to public patronage by the enterprising proprietor June 17, 1889. The building, occupying a beautiful elevation above the lake shore and convenient to the water side, is an architectural ornament, 44 feet square, four stories in height, with broad verandas on two sides facing the lake on a level with the lower floor and extending all around the house at each upper story. At the summit is a lookout that commands a view of the lake and surroundings in every direction for many miles. Within the arrangements are in keeping with the exterior. The bijou of an office is fitted up in beautiful style, as is also the commodious dining hall and refectory. There are twenty-two private rooms for guests, each communicating with the office by means of electric bells, and all elegantly furnished, as are the parlors. Lighted throughout by gas and electricity, with hot and cold water, baths, telephone connection, a luxurious table and attentive service, with all modern comforts and conveniences, it is difficult to realize that one is not in the heart of the city. Mr. Goodnow, the proprietor, owns two elegant miniature steamers—the *Media* and the *Marion*—that ply regularly on the lake during the season, carrying pleasure-seekers to all points of interest at nominal fares. The landing is but a few steps from the house, and multitudes avail themselves of the facilities thus afforded for a sail upon the placid waters. Tourists, pleasure and wedding parties can find no more enjoyable spot or better accommodations than are afforded by the Lake View with its shady surroundings, airy parlors, elegant refreshment rooms and numberless other attractions. Mine Host Goodnow is a well-known feature of the lake, where for several years he presided over the clambakes for which the shore is famous, his popular *habitat* being Goodnow Landing. He hails from Clinton, is a genial boniface and a liberal, enterprising, popular man. The season opens May 1 and continues until closed by approaching winter.

W. C. YOUNG & CO.,

Manufacturers of Machinists' Tools—No. 17 Hermon Street.

When one reflects upon the vast amount of machinery in use and constantly in course of construction and repair, it is not difficult to understand that the industry of making tools for the use of machinists must be an important one. New England is the very home of this industry, and Worcester the progressive is one of its principal centers. A leading house in this line is the one named above, established in 1879 and occupying the building No. 17 Hermon street. Mr. W. C. Young, sole proprietor and a native of Leominster, this county, is a practical and thorough machinist, who in a career of many years has made numerous valuable improvements

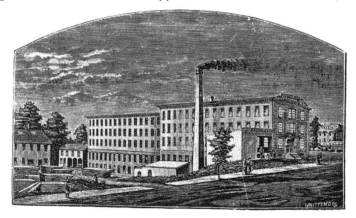

in the appliances to which he devotes his attention. His equipment of iron and steel-working machinery is complete, and includes two 80-horse-power boilers and a 100-horse-power engine. A working force of thirty skilled mechanics is employed, and the output, unexcelled for neatness and effectiveness, is sold all over the United States, in addition to which there is a large and growing foreign demand. The machinery and tools made here comprise a superb line of devices for the use of iron and woodworkers, among the more noticeable of which may be mentioned screw-cutting engine lathes, screw-cutting foot-power lathes, screw-cutting bench lathes, hand lathes, back-geared hand lathes, plain bench lathes, wood turners' lathes, pattern-makers' lathes, amateur foot lathes, chuck lathes, slide rests, "Standard" lathe tools, etc., and the celebrated Taft's punches and shears for working iron, steel and brass up to five-eighths of an inch in thickness.

LORING COES & CO.,

Manufacturers of Machine Knives, Cutters, Plates for Dies, etc.—Corner Coes and Mill Streets.

It is now just sixty years since ·Moses Clement, an ingenious mechanic of the highest class, began the manufacture. in this city of machine knives and similar appliances which he continued for many years, being succeeded by L. Hardy & Co., and they by L. & A. G. Coes. This firm continued in business, extending their facilities from time to time and making a national reputation for superiortiy of product until 1869, when Mr. Loring Coes became sole proprietor, and, under the style of Loring Coes & Co., still conducts the industry on a growing scale at the old stand on Coes street, corner of Mill. The plant is an extensive and valuable one, comprising one main building of two and a-half stories, 40x100 feet, engine-house and storage

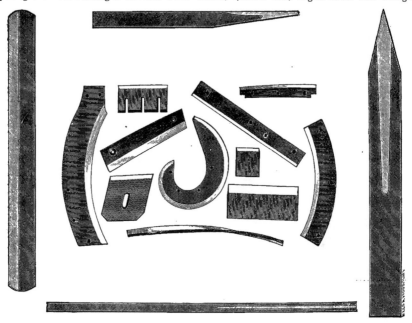

building. The machinery outfit, embracing all requisite special tools and appliances, is first-class and driven partly by water and partly by steam power. A sufficient force of skilled workmen is employed, and the output very heavy and valuable, comprising every description of machine knives, shear blades and strips, plated stock, moulding cutter plate, die stock for leather, cloth and paper-cutting dies, lawn mower and hay-cutting knives and paper blades.

Mr. Coes was born and has passed a long and useful·life in Worcester, where he is universally respected as an upright and public-spirited citizen.

BOSTON CLOTHING COMPANY,

Dealers in Men's, Youths' and Boys' Clothing—Nos. 196 and 198 Front Street.

More than fourteen years ago—in 1876—Mr. Jacob Godinski established the Boston Clothing Company at No. 192 Front street, where he remained until October last, when, his growing business demanding greater space and better facilities, he removed to Nos. 196 and 198 on the same street, where, occupying a splendid 44 x 125-foot salesroom fitted up with plate glass front and other modern equipments and appointments that cost $3,500, he is prepared to show his customers a magnificent stock of goods, comprising every grade of ready-made clothing for men, youths and boys, underwear, furnishings, hats, umbrellas, canes, fancy articles, etc. He also carries a choice line of ladies' garments in popular fabrics, which, like those for the males, are sold at lowest cash figures. Mr. Godinski employs nine assistants, and his transactions for 1889 aggregated over $200,000.

M. E. HALL,

Merchant Tailor, Ladies' Dress and Cloak Maker, Dealer in Cloths and Tailors' Trimmings—Garments Neatly Cleaned and Repaired — No. 203 Main Street.

No excuse short of abject poverty will serve the ill-dressed resident of Worcester, facilities for obtaining good clothing are so abundant. Among the oldest and most reputable tailoring houses

is that of Mr. M. E. Hall, No. 203 Main street, established fifty-five years ago by L. W. Sturtevant, to whom Mr. Hall succeeded September 1, 1880. The premises consist of six rooms, two of which are devoted to the sales department, one to the use of the cutters, one to the tailors, and the remainder to the dress and cloak department — the latter started in the beginning of May, 1890, and presided over by an experienced and competent lady modiste. Eight first-class hands are employed, and the house is kept busy on custom work for city patrons, both ladies and gentlemen, special attention being given to orders for fine tailor-made garments for the former and fashionable clothing for the latter. Mr. Hall has also superior facilities for designing and making coachmen's and footmen's liveries, riding and hunting suits, and invites attention to his large and varied stock of fabrics suitable for those classes of garments. A cleaning and repairing department is also conducted in connection with the shop, and great care is taken with all work of that kind. In the department of ladies' tailoring special facilities are provided, and orders are executed in a style equal to that of the most celebrated metropolitan ladies' tailors, while prices are much lower. Mr. Hall, who is a trained practical cutter, is a native of Worcester, learned his trade in Boston, and is master of all its details. Young, energetic, industrious and ambitious, he has before him the prospect of a useful and successful career.

L. W. PENNINGTON,

Designer, Manufacturing Jeweler and Diamond Setter—No. 81 Mechanic Street.

The manufacture of jewelry and society emblems from original designs is an industry in which art culture and inventive genius combine with a high order of trained manual skill to produce articles in the precious metals that shall at once please the eye and serve some purpose of utility or adornment. Thorough masters of this art in all its branches are comparatively few in number, and when found are usually kept busy as bees on orders from all classes of customers. One of the most accomplished and successful designing and manufacturing jewelers of whom we have any knowledge is Mr. L. W. Pennington, who occupies the second floor, 15 x 38 feet, No. 81 Mechanic street, where he has a superb equipment of late improved machinery and appliances, steam power, all requisite conveniences, and employs five or six experts. As before intimated, Mr. Pennington's specialty is the designing and execution of fine work in the precious metals and the making of novelties in jewelry, military, civic and society badges and emblems and similar work of the best grade. He is also a diamond-setter of rare skill and judgment, and gives careful attention to orders for electro-plating, gilding, acid coloring, oxidizing, and repairing and lapping of every description. Parties having in their possession broken or worn-out plate, jewelry or other articles of gold or silver will find here a ready sale at full prices. Mr. Pennington is of English birth, came to America sixteen years ago, and was engaged in business at Providence for several years previous to coming here in 1887.

CLARK MOULDING WORKS.

M. E. Clark, Treasurer and Manager — Factory and Salesroom, No. 7 Harris Court; Entrance from No. 15 Jackson Street.

This flourishing enterprise originated in a small curtain pole ring business established some years ago by Mr. M. E. Clark. His success was so pronounced that in 1888 it was deemed advisable to increase facilities and output by investing larger capital, whereupon the present concern was incorporated with $7,000 stock, Mr. Clark assuming the general management and later the treasurership. The plant comprises a large four-story frame factory building, the salesroom being situated on the ground floor facing Harris court, reached by way of Jackson

street from Main. Upstairs are the shops, fitted up with appropriate woodworking machinery, particularly noticeable features of which are several special machines for turning wood rings and curtain and portiere poles, the invention of Mr. Clark himself. The force of skilled workmen in the factory varies from twelve to twenty, as may be required, and the output, embracing the latest styles in fine cornice poles and trimmings, picture frame mouldings, room mouldings, etc., is very large and valuable. A complete assortment of these devices, together with samples of sweep poles, angle joints and brass trimmings, is exhibited in the salesroom, where orders are received for large or small lots. The goods are also being introduced elsewhere, and already a liberal demand exists for them as far east as Bangor, Me., south to Washington, in Pittsburg, throughout Ohio, as far west as Minneapolis, and even in the Canadian cities. Mr. Clark is a practical mechanic of sixteen years' experience in this and kindred industries. He began by serving a regular apprenticeship to picture-frame working, and was subsequently for five years foreman and salesman for the Worcester Moulding Company — a position which he resigned in 1887 to put in operation his machine for turning curtain-pole rings, now a prominent feature of his extensive business. This wonderful device, after many failures by others, he finally perfected and patented in 1888 — a machine that at once multiplies production and cheapens cost. The old method was to make each ring from a separate block; by the new a stick of proper dimensions six or eight feet long is introduced, the machine started, the knives revolve both right and left, and the rings are thrown off faster than several men could make them on the old-style lathe.

H. H. MASON,

Manufacturer of Cutlery—Grinding, Polishing and Repairing—No. 195 Front Street.

It is not an unusual thing to hear it asserted that for some reason American cutlers cannot produce fine goods that will equal the same grades and styles made in England, and that the workmen of no other nation can successfully compete with our peculiarly skillful British cousins.

There is unquestionably some ground for distrusting the ordinary run of German and American pocket cutlery, razors, surgical instruments, etc., but it is unadulterated nonsense to say that the American mechanic, who excels in all other avenues of industry, must of necessity fail when a reliable blade is required of him. The simple fact is that we have become accustomed to dependence upon England for this class of goods, which for many and sufficient reasons are made in the mother country more cheaply than here, and when offered our choice between an English and an American pocket-knife or kindred article, the price being the same, nine buyers out of ten will choose the former; consequently it does not pay to manufacture the more costly grades here on a large scale, and it is only once in a great while that we find a home cutler who devotes his attention to producing the very best. Such a one is H. H. Mason, who opened a shop at 195 Front street, Worcester, September 1, 1889. Here, occupying one floor 28x35 feet, and provided with special machinery and appliances driven by steam, he is prepared to respond to all demands upon his skill in a manner calculated to reflect credit upon his country and himself. Pocket-knives in any style are made to order or rebladed from choice English steel and warranted; razors are concaved, honed and re-handled equal to new; table cutlery, carving and butcher-knives, pocket-knives, shears and scissors ground, sharpened, repaired and polished in the best manner, and special attention given to putting in perfect order and making surgical instruments. Satisfaction is guaranteed to all customers. Mr. Mason has a fast-growing trade at home and throughout New England, and does considerable work to order for New York dealers. He has a secret process for engraving on steel blades which does the work quickly, cheaply and beautifully.

Mr. Mason is a native of Waterbury, Conn., and during the civil war was a sergeant of the Second Connecticut volunteer heavy artillery. He is also an active member of the G. A. R.

SHEDD & SARLE,

Civil Engineers and Surveyors—Room 36, Knowles Building, Worcester; Room 15, Masonic Temple, Nashua, N. H.; No. 74 Westminster Street, Providence, R. I.

The profession of civil engineer is one that requires for its successful prosecution severe and unremitting application, energy, patience, mathematical accuracy and a high order of intelligence, together with careful training of the p 'ceptive and descriptive faculties and a never-failing fund of general information concerning topography, land and building laws and kindred matters that may be drawn upon at will. It is not surprising, then, that so many fail to achieve either fame or fortune in its uninviting paths, or that so few, comparatively, of those who seek favor and distinction by means of the theodolite, the level and the drawing table succeed in rising above mediocrity. Among the most successful young civil engineers in New England may be named the firm of Shedd & Sarle, established in 1888 and composed of Messrs. Edward W. Shedd, a native of Brookline, Mass., and O. Perry Sarle, jr., born at Warwick, R. I. These gentlemen are worthy and well-equipped representatives of a difficult calling, and are making for themselves an excellent reputation besides securing a patronage that keeps them and their six competent assistants very busy, at home and in adjoining States. They give especial attention to surveying in all its branches, to the planning and supervison of drainage, and to the preparation of maps, in which they excel, as is shown by a recent series made for the city of Woonsocket that display extraordinary cleverness and attention to details. The writer of this has had frequent occasion to visit Shedd & Sarle's Worcester office, and has seen and admired much of their work, among the most notable examples of which may be mentioned an intricate map of the city in sections for the use of the Gas Company, showing the mains; a large map for the Electric Company, indicating location of poles and lights; a large map for the Street Railway Company, showing the course of the various lines; preliminary surveys, plans and estimates for four electric and two steam railways. They are also doing the engineering for the Worcester and Nashua street railway companies, and are kept pretty busy at all seasons, their duties taking both of the firm and their entire force of assistants into the field during the worst weather of the past winter. Shedd & Sarle's Worcester office, one of the most desirable in the city, is room

36 on the fifth floor of the Knowles building, reached by elevator, and commands a very fine view of the eastern half of the city and the hills beyond. A call will convince any one that their facilities and resources are equal to all reasonable demands. They have another office at Nashua, N. H. (room 15, Masonic building), where two competent assistants are employed, and are also associated with the firm of Shedd, Sarle & Shedd, No. 74 Westminster street, Providence, R. I. Worcester telephone connections—Office, 411-4; E. W. Shedd's residence, 5-5; Providence telephone call, 1066-2.

G. W. INGALLS & CO.,

Manufacturers of Organ Reed Boards, Vox Humanas, Octave Couplers, and Tremolos—No. 25 Hermon Street.

Manufacturers and lovers of the church and parlor organ will be interested in a brief sketch of this concern, one of the most famous of the kind on the globe. Mr. G. W. Ingalls, the veteran

improver and maker of organ attachments, is a native of New Hampshire, and early manifested genius for the kind of mechanical work to which his life has been devoted, entering a factory in 1842. He subsequently established himself in business at Concord, N. H., where he remained, devising and perfecting improvements, until 1866, when he removed to Worcester and began manufacturing upon a more extended scale. Successful from the first, the demand for his products steadily increased and his facilities and transactions expanded until at this time his factory, situated at No. 25 Hermon street, requires for its accommodation two floors each 50 x 100 feet, equipped with the most approved special machinery, the plant representing an investment of a considerable amount of money. About fifty specially trained artisans are employed, and the output, mostly order work for American and foreign organ builders, is very large and valued at many thousand dollars annually, consisting of the latest improved organ reed boards, vox humanas, octave couplers, tremolos, etc., unsurpassed if equaled by the work of any other maker. Among the other distinctions conferred upon Mr. Ingalls for his achievements in this field of effort was the grand diploma conferred at the Centennial Exhibition, Philadelphia, 1876. Mr. Ingalls is an elderly gentleman of culture and courteous manners, entirely devoted to his art. He is a good citizen and universally respected.

COATES CLIPPER MANUFACTURING COMPANY,

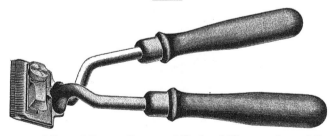

Manufacturers of Coates' Patent Horse and Barbers' Clippers, Coates' Patent Nail Cutter, and Kidder's Patent Improved Awl and Tool-Holder and Plumb-Bob Combined—Nickel Platers—No. 237 Chandler St., Worcester, Mass.

A. A. COBURN,

Boat Builder—Lincoln Park, Lake Quinsigamond.

Mr. Coburn is one of the best-known figures connected with Worcester's great pleasure resort, with which he has been identified during the past fifteen years or more.   At first, and up to 1881, he confined his attention to providing boats of all kinds—a venture that proved popular

and·profitable and in the·prosecution of which he accumulated a large fleet of small craft, mostly built by and for himself.   Ten years ago he began the business of building boats for others, and has made for himself an enviable reputation for taste, skill and ingenuity, having perfected many improvements and evolved new styles of water craft that capture the fancy of lovers of aquatic sports. One of his greatest successes was the noted "Adirondack," unequaled in point of elegance of design, combined with strength, speed and steady sailing qualities. This style of boat is in general use for pleasuring all over New England, and gives unvarying satisfaction. Mr. Coburn has a spacious boat-yard and landing on the lake front, and near by are his shops, where four skilled workmen are employed the year round; at times even more help is required. Local oarsmen and amateurs are his regular customers, and he does a thriving and steadily increasing business year by year as this most healthful muscle and lung-developing exercise grows in public favor. The factory is 30x50 feet in dimensions, two stories in height and completely equipped for the purpose of modern boat-building. Mr. Coburn introduced in the fall of 1889 new machinery propelled by steam so as to expedite his work of boat-building, in order to meet the rapidly increasing demands made upon him for his product in water craft. His success is due to consummate skill and care in the conduct of his business, coupled with the exercise of honorable methods in all his transactions with customers. A cut of the boat-house and factory is presented herewith.

PELLETT BROTHERS,

Contractors, Masons and Builders—No. 47 Wellington Street.

Messrs. T. A. and John C. Pellett are natives of Brattleboro, Vt., where the senior brother was in business prior to his removal to Worcester, and where he left many memorials of his

skill in building. He has had many years' experience in his calling and is a thoroughly competent builder. The copartnership of the brothers was formed in 1888, and has proved advantageous to themselves and to their patrons, as is shown by the largely increased business they transact, their disbursements for wages alone the past year aggregating $20,000 or more Their stone and storage yards are in the rear of 47 Wellington street, and are about 100 feet square. Here is kept on hand a large stock of pink and gray granite, Longmeadow sandstone and other materials, and a number of men are steadily employed getting them into shape for use. The private hotel in front was erected by and belongs to the firm, and is an ornament to that part of the city, four stories in height, 50x60 feet, constructed in the most durable and tasty manner of brick with stone trimmings and marble pillars along the facade. They were also the builders of the magnificient new St. Paul's church on Chatham street, near Main, one of the finest ecclesiastical structures in the State. Contracts are made and buildings erected in any part of New England. Estimates submitted at short notice.

PRESPEY PERO.

Hermon Street Foundry—Manufacturer of Tool, Machinery and Ornamental Castings—Office, No. 35 Hermon Street.

The foundryman fills an important place in industrial economy—it would hardly be an exaggeration to say the first place, since without his aid it would be impossible to construct most of the machinery by means of which other productive industries are prosecuted. Of the many representatives in this city of this leading interest few have achieved a more enviable reputation than Mr. Prespey Pero, whose specialties embrace every description of tool, machinery and ornamental iron castings, the local demand for his superior work keeping him busy at all seasons. Mr. Pero's office is at No. 35 Hermon street, where he will be found ready to receive orders during business hours. His foundry, equipped with every requisite appliance, 50x120 feet in area, is at the rear, where forty expert moulders and assistants are employed.

Mr. Pero was born in Canada, but came with his parents to Worcester during infancy, and is to all intents and purposes a thorough American. About eighteen years ago, being an accomplished and experienced practical foundryman, he built and started his present foundry for a Mr. W. E. Phelps, who retired from the business in 1877, Mr. Pero becoming the purchaser and proprietor.

NON-SECRET ENDOWMENT ORDER.

Herbert McIntosh, A. M., Supreme President and Counsellor; ʇ. O. H. Woodman,
Supreme Secretary ; Wm. F. Ewell, Supreme Treasurer—Office of Supreme Secretary, Burnside Building, No. 339 Main Street, Worcester.

ʻ ʃ ͞ The Non-Secret Endowment Order presents a most attractive plan of investment that cannot fail ʻof ͵commending itself to the thrifty mechanic, clerk, professional man,ʻ small tradesman
and others whose independence is sufficiently precarious to render the certainty of a fixed income when ill, a few hundred dollars at a specified time as theʻ fruit of an investment, or a moderate sum for the immediate use of the survivors in case of death, an object worth providing for

at small expense.
The Order was in-
corporated u n d e r
the general laws of
Massachusetts, Sep-
tember 17, 1889,
and though but a
year and a half old,
a l r e a d y boasts a
m e m b e r s h i p of
more than 5000
and steady and rap-
id gains wherever
introduced. T h e
Supreme Secretary's
office is in this city,
in the B u r n s i d e
building, No. 339
Main street, which
is also general head-
q u a r t e r s of the
Order. There are
four local assemblies
in Worcester, and
we are assured by
intelligent members
that the workings of
the institution are in
all respects perfect
and without friction.
Absolutely non-
secret, the objects
of the order are to
furnish some protec-
tion to its members
at a c t u a l c o s t.
There is nothing
speculative about it,
no life insurance
feature as such, and,
though inculcating
fraternal sentiments,
its members are not oath-bound or otherwise hampered morally. The cost of admission, including entrance and charter fees, registration and certificate, is six dollars; women as well as men
are eligible to membership and official position, and assessments and benefits are graduated
thus :

Amount Paid on each Assessment.	Weekly Benefit when Sick or Disabled.	Amount paid at end of five years, less Benefits received.
$1 50	$20 00	$500 00
1 20	15 00	400 00
90	10 00	300 00
60	5 00	200 00

Sick benefits are charged with interest at six per cent., and what remains to the credit of the
certificate, less payments made on account of such illness, is paid in full to the holder at the expiration of the five-year period. Should a member die within two years his accrued assess-

ments, less sick benefits and interest; will be paid to his representatives; if after two years, such proportion of the full benefit will be paid as represents the time during which he was a member. The feasibility and practical common-sense of the plan is entirely demonstrable in theory, and in practice is proved every day.

Any one of good character and in good health may become a member—by charter in the formation of assemblies; afterward by petition and ballot. Dues cannot exceed four dollars per annum, but assessments are made every month if the funds are needed to meet obligations. There are no grand or State bodies, and therefore no expense on that account, all the business of the order being managed direct from this city. We append a list of the supreme officers, trustees, etc.: Herbert McIntosh, A. M., Supreme Pres. and Counsellor, Worcester, Mass.; J. O. H. Woodman, Supreme Secretary, Worcester, Mass,; William F. Ewell, Supreme Treasurer, Worcester, Mass.; Edgar R. Howe, Supreme Organizer, Worcester, Mass.; Samuel F. Myrick, Supreme Vice-President, Worcester, Mass.; E. H. Trowbridge, M. D., Supreme Medical Examiner, Worcester, Mass.; C. C. Fuller, Supreme Instructor, Worcester, Mass.; Wm. L. Robinson, Supreme Conductor, Worcester, Mass.; Charles G. Hastings, Supreme Guardian, Manchester, N. H.; B. F. Robinson, A. M., Past Supreme Pres., Worcester, Mass. Trustees of the Corporation: Hiram H. Ames, Chairman, Worcester, Mass.; Ray W. Greene, M. D., Clerk, Worcester, Mass.; James Pursey, Worcester, Mass., J. R. Fitzpatrick, D. D. S., Worcester, Mass., Henry W. Holland, Worcester, Mass. Supreme Advisers: Gilbert G. Davis, Worcester, Mass., Henry R. Wheeler, Worcester, Mass., D. L. Merrick, Brattleboro, Vt. Supreme Financiers: Herbert M. Wilson, E. H. Franklin, George S. Coleman, Worcester, Mass.

JOS. A. SAWYER & SON,

Machine Jobbers and Manufacturers of Special Machinery — No. 47 Hermon Street.

The cut herewith presented shows the arrangement of friction pulleys, shafting and hangers as made by Jos. A. Sawyer & Son for running sewing machines by power. Thousands of these are in use in corset factories, shoe factories and other establishments. By virtue of their simplicity and durability they give unvarying satisfaction. Mr. Joseph A. Sawyer established himself in Worcester as a builder of special machinery in 1865, and gradually made for his enterprise a high reputation. About eighteen years ago he took into partnership his son Thomas J., who is now sole proprietor under the former  style of Jos. A. Sawyer & Son, the father dying in the spring of 1888. The shops, fitted up with improved machinery and a fifteen-horse-power steam engine, and giving employment to several expert workmen, is situated in the building No. 47 Hermon street, taking up one entire floor, 38 x 75 feet. Here, besides the device illustrated above, is made a great variety of machinery for special purposes, including a combined hand and power planer for iron work, of excellent design and workmanship, weighing about 1,100 pounds and planing over a surface three feet long, fifteen inches wide and thirteen inches high; scouring and stoning machines for finishing the edges of boot and shoe heels, imitation stitch-marking machines, steam-heating wax cups, double-crank foot-powers, superior exhaust fans for drawing dust from machinery, etc. The house also deals in wax thread sewing machines and duplicates of every description. Mr. Thomas J. Sawyer was born in New Jersey, and since 1865 has lived in Worcester. He is an energetic, thorough-going and successful practical mechanic and business man.

WORCESTER STEAM BOILER WORKS,

William Allen & Sons, Proprietors—Office, No. 57 Green Street.

These works were succeeded to by the present proprietors about fifteen years ago, and are constantly busy in the manufacture of first-class steam boilers of the various types and all kinds

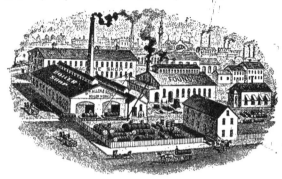

of steam machinery and bolt iron work. Among the specialties manufactured by this concern are dye-wood extractors, bleaching kiers, steam boxes and the Allen improved steam heating boiler for low-pressure heaters for dwellings and business blocks. The plant covers about one and a half acres, near the centre of the city, and consists of commodious boiler shop, machine and woodwork shops, foundry and building room, all of brick, with spur tracks from the various railroads centering in the city, making the delivery and shipment of goods easy and convenient. About 150 hands are constantly employed in the various departments. The house aims to make nothing but the best of work, and their reputation

is such that their goods are sent to all parts of the country, boilers of their manufacture being found in every State of the Union from Maine to California. The patented improvements of their boiler front are such as to cause an ever-increasing demand for their work. Among the recent batteries put in by this firm are twelve 100-horse-power boilers at the Melville Rubber Company's Works, Melville, Mass., and ten, each of 125-horse-power, at the works of the

Woonsocket Rubber Company, Woonsocket, R. I. Many plants are being put up for electric light companies, and among these are eight boilers of 150-horse-power each for the Worcester Electric Light Company, and three of 100-horse-power each for the Nashua (N. H.) Electric Light Company. The boilers and dyewood extractors of this company are to be found also in Mexico, Central America and South America, and their dyewood extractors are sent into Canada as well.

J. E. SNYDER,

Manufacturer of Upright Drills—No. 17 Hermon Street.

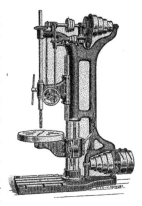

The manufacture of upright drills for the use of machinists, blacksmiths and ironworkers generally is a much more important industry than is imagined by those not interested in the handling of machinery. Several large Worcester concerns are devoted exclusively to the construction of this class of devices, none of whom are more widely and deservedly popular than the house of J. E. Snyder, whose drills are in use all over the United States and exported to foreign countries. The firm when established in 1883 was Currier & Snyder, but dissolved in 1888, when Mr. Currier retired and Mr. Snyder took sole charge. The plant is a complete and valuable one, including all necessary machinery, tools and appliances, driven by steam, and occupies one floor, 40 x 100 feet, of the building No. 17 Hermon street. From fifteen to twenty expert mechanics are employed, and a very large amount of first-class work is turned out, Mr. Snyder confining his attention to upright drills exclusively, which he makes in several styles. Our cut represents the new 28-inch drill, greatly improved and perfected and unexcelled for effectiveness and all good qualities. Mr. Snyder, a native of this State and a thorough practical machinist, personally superintends his works and critically inspects every job turned out of his shop.

JOHN KIRSCHNER & SONS,

Plain and Fancy Job Printers—No. 406 Main Street.

Printing establishments are of all classes, big, little, good, bad and indifferent, and the trade is no exception to the rule that fine workmanship is just as likely to be obtained from a small concern as from a large one, while it is a maxim of the craft that a medium-sized office, carefully managed and employing skilful and accurate workmen, is much more profitable, in proportion to capital invested, than a large one. This holds good in the case of John Kirschner & Sons, who own and operate one of the neatest and most profitable little printing houses in the country, employ no journeymen, do all the work themselves, and earn a comfortable living, while it is more than suspected that their bank account is out of all proportion to their pretensions. At any rate their expenses are comparatively light; they turn out tasty and fetching cards, note, letter and bill-heads and a general line of small mercantile printing, charge reasonable prices, and have little to worry them. Messrs. Kirschner & Sons' office is at No. 406 Main street, third floor. They have a comprehensive assortment of appropriate new type and material and two modern improved job presses, and, being all practical and skillful printers, they fill orders promptly for plain and fancy work. Mr. John Kirschner is of German birth; his sons, Richard H. and George F., are Americans.

NEWTON DARLING.

Manufacturer of Satinets—Chapel Street, Cherry Valley.

This mill, situated upon the site of a former one, burned in 1887, is an important addition to the industries of the vicinity, and cannot well fail to score marked success. It was completed in October, 1888, and is consequently new in all its appointments and of capacity entirely disproportioned to outward appearance, the machinery equipment embracing the latest and most valuable improvements. Mr. Darling had the advantage of several years' previous experience in the same branch of business in connection with his brother, and brought to his present enterprise great skill, energy and capacity. Exclusive attention is given to the manufacture of high-grade satinets, for which there is increasing demand (the output of this mill ranking with the best and in great favor with clothing manufacturers). Bacon, Baldwin & Co. are selling agents' Franklin street, New York.

EZRA SAWYER,

Manufacturer of the Patent Magnetic Separator—No 33 Hermon St.

As is well-known, there is in all machine shops and metal-working establishments a vast deal of waste occasioned by the loss of materials that in the processes of turning, filing and polishing have become so inextricably intermingled that hitherto little or no effort has been made to separate them. Our cut represents a remarkably ingenious and effective magnetic metal separator, devised and patented by Messrs. Ezra Sawyer and B. Fitts, and now manufactured by the former at No. 33 Hermon street, Worcester. It is a simple machine, has been found exceedingly useful for separating particles of iron and steel from brass, copper, composition, etc., and is employed for that purpose in many leading shops throughout the country. The wheel shown in the cut contains three hundred and sixty magnets, to which the iron adheres, and is carried to a brush cylinder in the rear of the machine and there removed, while the brass and other foreign substances fall into the box in front. Its utility and capacity for this kind of work are wonderful, the separation being thoroughly made with the least possible labor and trouble. The machine pays for itself in a short time in the saving of time and labor, to say nothing of the improved quality of stock thus treated. Brass stock, cleansed with the machine, can be used for the best kinds of work. A No. 1 machine is large enough for an ordinary shop, while the No. 2 machine has a little more than twice the capacity. No. 3 is twice the capacity of No. 2. The machine may also be used for separating iron from emery, granular rubber, ores, etc., and is doubtless capable of various other applications. Mr. Sawyer's shop is well-equipped to fill orders promptly, a notable feature being a special magnetizer for charging the magnets used in the separator. He devotes his entire time and attention to this business, and orders are promptly executed. Prices of the newly improved separator: No. 1, $135; No. 2, $225; No. 3, $350.

P. E. SOMERS,

Manufacturer of Tacks and Hungarian Nails—Fine Shoe Tacks a Specialty—No. 17 Hermon Street.

Mr. Somers was formerly a member of the firm of Somers Bros., tack manufacturers, established 1884, and which dissolved September 13, 1889, Mr. P. E. Somers continuing on his individual account at the old stand, No. 17 Hermon street. One floor, 35x95 feet, of the building has so far sufficed for his requirements, but his trade is steadily growing, and the indications are that he will need more room ere long. At present thirty tack machines are run up to their capacity and employment is furnished to twelve hands, the output of tacks, hungarian nails, etc., large in quantity and value, being disposed of to the trade east, west and south. Fine shoe tacks is the leading specialty, and for these the demand is fully equal to the facilities of manufacture. Only the best material is used, and the goods made here are unsurpassed in point of excellence, while prices are as low as can be made anywhere. Twelve of the tack machines now running were built from patterns made by himself, and are superior to any others in use.

Mr. Somers is of Irish birth, coming to this country in childhood. He is a practical and experienced tack-maker, and a liberal, courteous business man.

G. S. & A. J. HOWE,

Wholesale Dealers in Oils, Dyestuffs and Chemicals—Sole Agents for Harkness' Saponified Red Oil—No. 20 Foster Street.

The commercial center of a great manufacturing district, and herself the seat of magnificent industries that consume vast quantities of those commodities, Worcester is necessarily an important market for oils, dyestuffs and chemicals used in the arts. A leading representative of this interest is the famous old house of G. S. & A. J. Howe, established in 1851. The members of the firm were brothers. Mr. A. J. Howe died thirty-five years ago, but the surviving partner has continued the business under the original style for nearly forty years — how successfully is attested by the immense and constantly growing trade throughout central Massachusetts and portions of Rhode Island and Connecticut. The house also has the sole agency for the celebrated Harkness' saponified red oil, prepared at Cincinnati and extensively used by manufacturers of woolen goods.

THE WORCESTER FIRE APPLIANCE COMPANY.

W. H. Raymenton, M. D., President; Henry S. Pratt, Vice-President; John C. Dewey, Treasurer— Manufacturers of the Worcester Chemical Fire Pail and Dealers in Fire Appliances of Every Description —No. 38 Front Street.

An entirely new claimant for public confidence—one whose pretensions are based upon actual trial—is the Worcester Chemical Fire Pail, non-evaporating, non-freezing, thoroughly reliable, and recommended by the highest authority, among its indorsers being the New England Insurance Exchange, the Factory mutual insurance companies, Edward Everett, special agent of the Fire Insurance Association of England (United States branch); the Washburn & Moen Manufacturing Company; President Charles Coburn of the Lowell Underwriters' Association; Chief Hosmer of the Lowell Fire Department; the Worcester *Spy*, Boston *Herald* and *Post;* the Providence *Journal*, and many other competent parties who have seen the device tested under trying circumstances.

The Worcester Chemical Fire Pail is made of glass, and incased in a corrugated tin jacket, open at the top. The pail is filled with eight quarts of a chemical liquid, hermetically sealed by means of a soft tin foil cover, the latter protected by a loose-fitting tin cover which is automatically removed when the pail is taken from the hook for use. The chemical used contains no acid and will not injure the hands or clothing; nor will it freeze, evaporate, or lose its strength with age. Coming in contact with a flame, the fluid generates a gas that kills the fire instantly. The Worcester Fire Appliance Company was incorporated with $50,000 capital in 1888, and has offices and shops at 38 Front street. The company has also recently added a general stock of fire extinguishing apparatus from other makers.

Dr. W. H. Raymenton, the president, is a director of the Historical Society, Vice-President Henry S. Pratt is a prominent manufacturing clothier; and Treasurer John C. Dewey is a son of Judge Dewey and a successful patent attorney.

McCLOUD, CRANE & MINTER,

Manufacturers of Nuts and Screws—No. 57 Union Street.

Vast quantities of bolts, screws and nuts are required by machinists and woodworkers, and

the manufacture of these requisites is an industry that grows with the population and development of the country. Among the most extensive and most noted producers is the firm of McCloud, Crane & Minter of this city, organized in 1884 by the consolidation of Henry Minter, established 1868, with McCloud & Crane, who embarked in the same business in 1872. All of these gentlemen are capable and competent managers, and all are practical mechanics who began their several careers at the bench, working upward through the grades of apprentice and journeyman to that of master. Their premises, No. 57 Union street, comprise a commodious three-story brick building.45x90

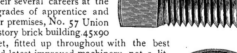

feet, fitted up throughout with the best and latest improved machinery, not a little of which is of special design and construction, all driven by a fine thirty-five-horse-power steam engine. They employ steadily forty-five hands, and their output, comprising every description of iron and woodworkers' nuts and screws of superior quality, is in general use by builders of light and heavy machinery, carriages, etc., east and west.

8

BOSTON STORE.

Denholm & McKay Company—A. Swan Brown, President; James J. Hughes, Vice President; R. John McKay, Secretary; Thomas Hamilton, Treasurer—Retail Dealers in Dry Goods, Carpets, Notions, etc.—Jonas G. Clark Block, Nos. 484, 486, 488 and 490 Main Street.

This house was founded twenty years ago by W. A. Denholm and Wm. C. McKay. The latter died in 1884, and Mr. Denholm continued under. the style of Denholm & McKay until

March last, when he too went the way of all flesh, but prior to that event Messrs. J. J. Hughes and R. John McKay (the latter a younger brother of W. C. McKay) had been admitted to the firm as junior partners. A clearing sale, the largest known in the history of Worcester, enabled the surviving members to settle with the Denholm estate, and soon afterward the Denholm & McKay Company was incorporated under the laws of New Jersey; authorized capital, $250,000; paid up capital, $200,000. In addition to the officers named in our caption, the directory includes the names of Walter Callendar and John McAuslan of Providence, R. I., James Thompson of Hartford, Conn., and A. B. Wallace of Forbes & Wallace, Springfield, Mass., and all are prominently identified with the celebrated Syndicate Trading Company, which controls a vast and growing trade all over New England as well as the west, the transactions of Denholm & McKay alone averaging nearly a million dollars annually for several years past. The new company confidently anticipates, under a more liberal policy, a very material increase of sales, and will employ 200 to 300 people in all departments. The Denholm & McKay Company will continue to occupy four floors and the basement of the great five-story Jonas G. Clark block; principal entrance, Nos. 484 to 490 Main street; dimensions: basement, 84 x 132 feet; first or ground floor, 84 x 132 feet; second floor, 84 x 132 feet; third floor, 84 x 120 feet; fourth floor, 84 x 120 feet; total, 53,424 square feet of floorage. Important alterations and improvements of the interior have recently been made, the stairways enlarged, the old basement doors bricked up and new ones made, and a portion of the space hitherto set aside for the wholesale department remodeled and turned over to retail purposes. The basement is devoted exclusively to the display of household and kitchen utensils and appliances, silver-plated ware, pictures, Japanese goods and kindred commodities. The first floor— the grand bazar — appropriately and conveniently arranged in departments, is set apart for the exhibition and sale of staple dry goods at retail—dress, fabrics, silks, velvets, white, black and colored goods and prints, linens and cottons, domestic and imported, boots and shoes, hosiery, gloves, gentlemen's and ladies' furnishing goods, ribbons, laces, notions, books, stationery, etc. On the second floor are the offices of the company and the private offices of the individual members; the millinery, cloak, suit, shawl, ulster and ladies' underwear departments. On the third floor are shown immense and comprehensive lines of carpets, rugs, mattings, upholstery goods, window curtains of every description, draperies, shades and fixtures. The fourth floor is devoted to stock room, and part of this floor is also fitted up for the use of the carpet-fitters, several of whom are kept busy at all seasons. Upon the whole, this may safely be pronounced the most extensive, as it is the most enterprising and successful dry goods house in the State, outside of Boston. President A. Swan Brown is likewise president of the Syndicate Trading Company, already referred to. Vice President J. J. Hughes, a member of the old firm, has had many years' experience in the dry goods trade of Worcester. Secretary R. J. McKay is of Canadian birth and Scotch descent. Both have been in the employ of or partners of the old firm for nineteen and twenty years respectively. Treasurer Thomas Hamilton, during a period of fifteen years, under power of attorney from the deceased partner, acted in the capacity of chief book-keeper for the late firm of Denholm & McKay, giving daily evidence of rare business ability and probity.

PEOPLE'S SAVINGS BANK.

Samuel R. Heywood, President; Calvin Foster, A. N. Currier, Thomas M. Rogers, W. W. Rice, Philip L. Moen, Warren Williams, Vice-Presidents; Charles M. Bent, Treasurer—No. 452 Main Street.

The thrifty habits of New England people, and more especially of Massachusetts people, have long been proverbial. It is not wonderful, therefore, that the savings bank system has been here brought it to its greatest perfection, reckless speculation prohibited and the strongest possible safeguards thrown around these institutions for the protection of depositors, the statutes of Massachusetts for the regulation of savings banks, embracing in their provisions all that can be desired and providing a model upon which those of many other States are framed. The industrious mechanic, the widow and orphan place their surplus funds here for investment, without hesitation or anticipation of subsequent loss, and it is a reassuring fact that of late years no serious disaster has occurred to lessen public confidence.

Among the many prominent savings institutions that find employment for and pay liberally for the use of money, none enjoy a better reputation or higher standing than the People's of Worcester, incorporated May 13, 1864. The officers, named in our caption, are among the city's most public-spirited and responsible citizens. The board of managers is composed of the same stamp of men, and embraces Messrs. Henry A. Marsh, Harlan P. Duncan, James P. Hamilton, John S. Baldwin, Horace Wyman, Samuel D. Nye, Francis A. Gaskill, Theodore C. Bates, Edwin T. Marble, Edward F. Bisco and Samuel Winslow. October 31st last the books showed deposits aggregating $5,562,664.06. Deposits in any amount from one to one thousand dollars are received at any time and credited with interest from the succeeding quarter day—February, May, August and November 1—and all taxes are paid by the corporation. Semi-annual dividends due February and August. The banking house is conveniently situated at No. 452 Main street, a handsome marble front structure of four stories and basement, the offices being located on the ground floor.

ELIZABETH A. BUTLER.

L. B. Butler, Agent—Manufacturer of Extra Oxford Satinets—Valley Falls.

The late John A. Hunt built a woolen mill upon this site about thirty years ago, which was subsequently burned to the ground, erected the present building of brick, 32x90 feet and four stories in height, at a later period, Mrs. Elizabeth A. Butler becoming the purchaser in 1886 and placing Mr. L. B. Butler in charge as agent. It is a two-set mill, equipped for the production of extra Oxford satinets, and of these large quantities are made, Messrs. Brigham, Mann & Co., of New York, acting as selling agents.

AMES PLOW COMPANY.

President, Geo. Von L. Myers; Treasurer, C. J. Whittemore—Manufacturers of and Dealers in Farming Implements and Machines — No. 84 Prescott Street; Boston Office, Quincy Hall.

The works of the Ames Plow Company were founded by Joel Nourse in the early thirties. Oliver Ames & Sons became owners in 1861, and they were succeeded at a later date by the Ames Plow Company. The works, which extend from No. 84 to No. 100 Prescott street, inclusive, cover a considerable body of land, the buildings comprising the woodworking and finishing shop, L-shaped, 80 x 400 feet, four stories in height; the forge, one story, 80 x 100 feet; the foundry, one story, 80 x 200 feet; cutting, grinding, tumbling and fan rooms; engine and boiler-house containing a 250-horse-power steam engine; pattern-shop of four stories, 20 x 100 feet, containing patterns of everything made on the premises since Joel Nourse first engaged in business; sand and coal-houses, furnaces and cupolas of six or seven tons average daily capacity—all brick and of the most substantial character; a spur track connecting the packing department with the various rail-roads, by which several car-loads are shipped daily. The equipment is complete, the export trade is large, great quantities of plows and agricultural implements and machinery being shipped to English agents for transfer to Australia and South Africa, besides heavy shipments to those countries, to Mexico, the West Indies, Central and South America. One hundred and eighty mechanics and helpers are employed here, and about 8,000 plows are made annually. The Ames family are large stockholders in this establishment. Mr. P. S. Rich has been superintendent of the factory for fifteen years. The company's Boston office, to which all communications should be addressed, is at Quincy Hall.

C. L. BLAIR,

Portrait and Landscape Photographer—Artist in Crayon and India Ink—Chase Building, No. 44 Front Street.

It is now about fifteen years since Mr. Blair established himself as a photographer in this city, locating at first on Main street, whence he removed in 1887 to his present commodious quarters on the seventh floor of Chase building, No. 44 Front street. Here, domiciled in elegantly appointed rooms, fitted up with every desirable convenience, including the latest improved photographic apparatus, faultless light, and every conceivable requisite for taking, developing and finishing the highest grade of pictures, he enjoys a generous and increasing patronage at the hands of the very best class of people, city and country, many coming from all parts of the county in order to avail themselves of his recognized skill. Besides making photographic portraits in the highest style of the art, Mr. Blair devotes special attention to orders for art pictures in crayon, pastel and India ink, and gives uniform satisfaction in each and all branches.

Parties desiring outdoor work—landscapes, photographs of public and private buildings, churches, machinery, merchandise, etc., will find Mr. Blair thoroughly prepared to serve them in the best possible manner, promptly and at reasonable rates. Himself a skilled and experienced practical photographic artist, he employs only the most capable and competent help, and turns out only the best possible work.

L. HARDY & CO.,

H. A. Hoyt, Proprietor — Manufacturers of Woodworking Machine Knives, Paper Cutter, Leather Splitting, Stripping and other Knives — Shear Blades and Strips for Cotton and Woolen Goods, Die Cutter Stock, etc.—No. 9 Mill Street.

The celebrated house of L. Hardy & Co. was founded many years ago, and its products are familiar to planing-mill men, leather, textile fabric and agricultural machinery manufacturers all over this continent. Mr. H. A. Hoyt, a practical and experienced mechanic, succeeded to the proprietorship of the works in 1873, and under his capable management they have maintained and increased their former well-earned prestige. The shops at No. 9 Mill street comprise a one-story frame building 40 x 90 feet, fitted up with steam power, punch cutter, trip hammer and a complete miniature rolling mill. Six competent workmen are employed, and the output is quite large and of the best quality, embracing every description of woodworking machine knives, planers, moulding knives, blanks, finished or in stock; paper-cutter, leather-splitting and stripping knives; straw-cutter, ensilage, lawn-mower, meat-cutter, cork-cutter, rag-cutter and bone knives; shear blades and strips for cotton and woolen goods, and die-cutter stock for boots and shoes, together with welded stock of all kinds, rolled to any desired thickness. Orders are filled with dispatch on reasonable terms and at rock bottom figures.

HARWOOD & QUINCY MACHINE COMPANY.

George S. Harwood, President; Sidney S. Harwood, Treasurer; George Hill, Clerk; E. H. Wood, Managing Director—Manufacturers of Woolen Machinery—No. 50 Lagrange Street, Worcester; Office, No. 220 Devonshire Street, Boston.

For more than half a century Worcester has been famous for the extent and variety of her machinery manufactures, covering almost every description of time and labor-saving devices.

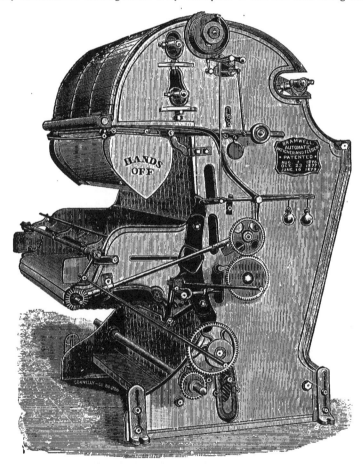

Producers of woolen goods all over this continent are familiar with her fame and claims to superiority in the construction of appliances for simplifying and perfecting their work, and the palm of excellence so fairly won seems likely to remain in the hands of her mechanics for a long period to come. Of those who during the past dozen years have contributed to this result none deserve greater credit than the Howard & Quincy Machine Company, established in 1860 and incorporated in April, 1881, with $20,000 capital. The officers, named above, are all residents of Boston, with the exception of Managing Director E. H. Wood, who makes his home in Worcester and has immediate charge of the works. The latter, situated on Lagrange street, occupy the first and second floors, each 40 x 110 feet, of a plain, substantial three-story brick building, with commodious blacksmith shop adjacent. The machinery equipment, driven by a twenty-five-horse power engine, is first-class, and embraces many special features peculiar to this plant and not necessary to describe, but adequate to any demand upon the company's resources. The specialties comprise a complete line of the latest improved woolen machinery, including everything required in the manufacture from the raw wool of fabrics in all grades. Especial attention is invited, among other valuable novelties, to the Bramwell wool card feeder, unrivaled for uniformity and general excellence of its work. More than 8,000 of these are in use, and they are unanimously declared the only complete machine of the kind ever offered to manufacturers. The general offices of the company are at No. 220 Devonshire street, Boston, where those interested will be afforded an opportunity of inspecting the various machines and appliances made in these shops.

NEW ENGLAND SHEAR MANUFACTORY.

John Jacques & Son—Manufacturers of Shears for Cutting Tin, Paper and Cloth—No. 45 Webster Street, Webster Square.

The manufacture of shears and kindred devices is one of those industries in which New England excels, goods of this kind from her factories competing successfully with those of the

 British and Germans in their own markets, while in this country a foreign-made implement for the same purposes is regarded as a curiosity. Among the successful representatives of this interest must be classed the firm of John Jacques & Son, No. 45 Webster street. The concern was founded in 1855 by William Kean, who was succeeded by John Toulmin, and he by George Rowe, from whom Messrs. Jacques purchased the plant, which, under their management, has been entirely

remodeled and much enlarged, the premises now comprising a handsome frame machine shop 31 x 48 feet, with 20 x 22-foot annex, the whole equipped with appropriate machinery and appliances and giving employment to a competent force of skilled workmen. The firm manufacture a very superior line of shears, but make leading specialties of a new and superior style of improved cutters and shears of all sizes and styles for cutting paper, tin, sheet-iron, and thin material generally. These devices give the best satisfaction wherever tested, and the demand is rapidly increasing. Orders are promptly filled, and those interested are advised to inspect goods and prices before purchasing.

WM. S. HAGAR,

Manufacturer of and Wholesale Dealer in Worcester Ginger Ale, Soda Water, Tonic, Temperance Beers, Fruit Syrups, Dr. Horton's Indian Blood Purifier and Cough Mixture, Standard Neura-Cura, etc.—Nos. 39 and 41 Exchange Street.

Mr. Wm. F. Brooks started this establishment in 1875, and conducted it quite successfully until its transfer to Mr. Wm. S. Hagar in October, 1886. The present owner put into it money, skill, industry and enterprise, and has consequently prospered in an extraordinary degree. The plant is an extensive one, conveniently situated, with factory and bottling department in the 30 x 60-foot basement of No. 39 Exchange street and salesroom and office on the ground floor of No. 41. His manufacturing outfit is first-class, and the charging of fountains and bottling is done by means of Tufts' improved apparatus, from five to eight men being employed. Mr. Hagar manufactures and deals at wholesale in pure and delicious summer beverages, including Worcester ginger ale, soda water and syrups, tonics, and a list of temperance beers that includes strawberry, pine-apple, birch, root, white, pear, etc., bottling and selling from 400 to 500 dozen daily during the season, besides filling syphons and charging fountains. He also bottles the celebrated genuine Standard Neura-Cura (nerve restorative), and is proprietor and manufacturer of the wonderful Indian Blood Purifier and Indian Vegetable Cough Mixture, prepared from the original formulas of the late Dr. Wm. Horton, who practiced medicine in Worcester for forty years. Mr. Hagar has controlled these remedies for the past three years, and the sale has steadily increased throughout New England, the demand exceeding the supply hitherto, though he has recently increased manufacturing facilities and is establishing new agencies all over the country. The purifier is a combination of pure roots and herbs, unequaled as a blood purifier and system regulator—a radical cure for rheumatism, neuralgia, scrofula, liver, stomach and kidney troubles, eczema, salt rheum, itching and burning diseases of the skin, and diseases arising from an impure state of the blood. The cough mixture is likewise a most efficacious and valuable medicine.

W. F. BURGESS & CO.,

Builders of Engines, Pumps, Band Saw Machines, etc., and General Jobbers — Nos. 140, 142 and 144 Union Street.

Burgess & Wade founded this house, when, in 1885, they established an unpretentious machine shop at No. 66 School street, but Mr. Wade retired in 1888, and Mr. Walter F. Burgess continued alone until the 15th of December last, when Mr. Henry A. Mower became associated with him. January 1 they removed to No. 6 Manchester street, but the demands upon their skill and resources increased so rapidly that more space and greater facilities were found imperatively necessary, and they secured a lease for eleven years of the three-story 60 x 60 foot brick building Nos. 140, 142 and 144 Union street, which, remodeled, refitted with a new and augmented machinery plant and appliances, including a forty-horse-power engine, they occupied May 1. Here they employ from ten to twelve expert machinists, and are prepared to execute at short notice orders for the construction of anything in their line, making leading specialties of steam engines, pumps, band saw machines and woodworking machinery generally, and the repair of machinery of all kinds. They are also the inventors of a new and greatly improved wood pulley (patent pending), to which they invite the attention of those interested in this class of devices. Mr. Burgess, a thorough practical machinist and a recognized authority on the subject of machinery, is a native of Connecticut, has resided here for seventeen or eighteen years, and is a well-known citizen. Mr. Mower was born at West Brookfield, and is an experienced and ingenious practical mechanic — in fact, an inventor of note — formerly for four and a-half years in the employ of the Thomson-Houston Company, tool department. He is also a prominent Freemason. These gentlemen are frequently consulted in reference to the construction of new machinery, and their services are in constant demand both in and out of the city—in fact, all over New England.

THE BRUNSWICK.

Haradon & Robinson, Proprietors—Nos. 159 and 161 Front Street.

On Monday, April 20, 1891, the New Brunswick was opened for the accommodation of the hotel-supporting public, and on the evening of that day the house was brilliantly illuminated and a reception held, many hundreds of residents and strangers in Worcester availing themselves of the invitation extended through the daily press to inspect the interior arrangements; and the verdict was one of unvarying approval. The building, of brick, five stories in height, 40 feet front and about 100 feet deep, presents a rather plain exterior above the first story, but in re-modeling and refitting the interior for the present purpose the owner—Mr. R. C. Taylor—has indulged a refined taste without much apparent regard for expense. The entrance is at No. 159 Front street, corner of Eaton place. To the left—No. 161—is a tastily fitted bar and billiard room, and to the right are two spacious stores. A broad and easy stairway leads up one flight to the office, which is in fact a miniature rotunda with stairs and elevator at the east side, reading-room in front, dining-room and parlor, connected by folding doors, on the west side, and cloak and baggage-rooms, lavatory and toilet room in rear. At the south end of the dining-room, and communicating with the kitchen on the fifth floor by means of speaking tubes and dumb waiters, is the carving and serving-room. A capacious refrigerator and bath-room take up the remainder of this floor, which is artistically finished in black birch, with maple flooring. The fittings and furnishings are of a character to correspond with the apartments themselves, the office desk, reading and dining-room furniture being of quartered oak, neat, strong and handsome, though not gaudy, and electric bells connect with the thirty-four sleeping and sitting-rooms, arranged singly and *en-suite*, on the three upper floors. Each of these rooms and suites is fitted up in the most unpretentious yet comfortable manner, furnished in art oak and ash, with spring and hair mattresses and dainty bedding, body Brussels carpets in a variety of tasteful patterns, marble set-bowls, hot and cold water, radiators for distributing heat, lace curtains, and all desirable conveniences, an air of quiet elegance prevading each. Of the decorations throughout in wainscots, paint, paper and overhead frescoes, it is enough to say that they are in keeping with the spirit that designed and the art that executed the entire work. The whole house is perfectly lighted by gas; a fire escape communicates with every room, and a fine new fast passenger elevator carries guests to and from each floor.

Messrs. Melvin E. Haradon and Levi W. Robinson, lessees of the Brunswick, are widely and favorably known to the traveling public. The former, born at Sturbridge, Worcester county, was long connected with the Nassawanno at Palmer and the Cooley at Waterbury, Conn., while Mr. Robinson, a native of Hampshire county, became popular as proprietor of the Waverly in this city. Mr. William C. Hitchcock, who so acceptably fills the position of chief clerk, was literally born in and has pursued the hotel business for nearly thirty years.

HOPEVILLE MANUFACTURING COMPANY.

George A. Bigelow and Newton Darling, Lessees—Manufacturers of Satinets—Sutton Lane, South Worcester.

This very complete mill plant was established in 1870 by the Hopeville Manufacturing Company. The Hopeville Manufacturing Company, E. D. Thayer, President and Agent, and Alex Bigelow, treasurer, was organized in 1870, and still owns the property. During the past fall and early winter the mill was thoroughly overhauled, new machinery added, embracing the latest improvements, and recently started up with greatly increased facilities. The plant—what is technically known as a three-set mill, although only two sets of cards are run regularly at the present time—occupies a three-story brick and frame building 38x72 feet, with which is connected a three-story picker-house 20x30 feet. About forty hands are employed, and the thirty-two looms and other machinery are driven by two turbine wheels and an 85-horse-power steam engine. The present capacity is about 500,000 yards per annum, which it is intended to greatly increase. The product, satinets exclusively, is of fair quality, and is sold through Bacon, Baldwin & Co., Franklin street, New York.

WORCESTER OIL WORKS.

Clarkson A. Spencer, Agent—Manufacturers of Cylinder, Engine, Machine, Signal, Elaine, Wool, Neatsfoot and All Kinds of Lubricating Oils—Mill Soap a Specialty—No. 464 Park Avenue.

This concern, originally established at Binghamton, N. Y., removed to Worcester and started works at No. 84 Southbridge street in 1879, subsequently erecting and occupying the present plant—a two-story-and-basement frame, 20x75 feet—at No. 464 Park avenue. A part of the first floor is utilized for office purposes, the remainder for storage, while manufacturing operations are carried on in the basement and in the second story. Several men are employed, and the house, managed by Agent C. A. Spencer, transacts a large and growing business with the mill owners and machinists of Worcester, central Massachusetts and New England generally, supplying them with superior lubricants, including high-grade cylinder, engine, machine, dynamo, signal, bolt, neatsfoot, lard, whale, sperm, and the celebrated " Elaine "—the latter an unequaled wool oil, of which a leading specialty is made, prompt and careful attention being given also to orders for the best grades of mill soap for the use of fullers.

M. E. SHATTUCK & CO.,

Manufacturers of Fine Cigars—Wholesale and Retail Dealers in Cigars, Tobacco and Smokers' Articles—No. 417 Main St.

By reason of her geographical position and accessibility by rail, Worcester possesses many advantages of which her enterprising merchants are quick to avail themselves, thus making her a leading inland market for certain classes of commodities, not the least important of which come under the general head of cigars, tobacco and smokers' goods. A leading representative of this trade — probably the most extensive in the city — is the house of M. E. Shattuck & Co., who occupy the first and second floors and basement, each 25 x 90 feet, at No. 417 Main street. Mr. Shattuck may fairly claim to have founded the concern, as, when he took it off the hands of Essman & Haas in 1858, it was only a small cigar store, doing a limited retail business. Capable and enterprising, Mr. Shattuck increased facilities and extended operations from time to time until he found himself after awhile at the head of a flourishing establishment, with a successful cigar factory attached. Four years ago, in order to still further augment and extend the business, he admitted to partnership Messrs. James A. Clemence and J. H. Dally, the first-named having been in his employ since 1860 and the second since 1870. At present the house commands a trade that embraces all of New England and enjoys the confidence of dealers to an unusual degree. From thirty to forty men, including clerks, local and traveling salesmen and cigarmakers, are employed, and transactions for 1889 footed up $100,000. Besides handling great quantities of imported and domestic cigars of others' make, the firm produces its own specialty in the popular " 444 " cigar, a favorite with smokers wherever introduced. All leading brands of plug and fine-cut chewing and smoking tobaccos, cigarettes and snuffs are carried in stock, together with a large and varied assortment of smokers' articles, and favorable figures and terms are quoted to the trade. From 30,000 to 40,000 cigars are made on the premises weekly. Mr. Shattuck, born in Vermont, has resided here since 1853. He is a Free Mason, an Odd Fellow, and a public-spirited citizen. Both of his partners are Odd Fellows, Mr. Clemence a veteran of the war, and all are highly esteemed in this community.

D. H. EAMES & CO.,

Clothiers—Cor. Main and Front Sts.

It is now forty years since the firm of D. H. Eames & Co. was founded and established the mercantile house which· has ever since been one of Worcester's most noted business features. Its influence upon the clothing trade of this city has been especially salutary, one of the reforms being the establishment of the strictly one-price system upon a cash basis, doing away entirely with the dickering, haggling and "jewing" that had previously attached to and degraded this branch of commerce, more, perhaps, than any other. This step, with the resolute determination to sell their goods exclusively upon their merits, without misrepresentation or exaggeration, soon fixed the status and reputation of D. H. Eames & Co., giving them a standing which has been maintained through every vicissitude and enabling them to build up an immense and profitable trade without the adventitious aid of sensational advertising — a trade based upon personal and commercial rectitude and reliability, and which embraces all classes of the community, from the learned professions to the day laborer. D. H. Eames & Co. not only have one price (and this is marked in plain figures on everything they sell), but they guarantee their prices to be the lowest obtainable for goods of equal value, and refund the money cheerfully if anything purchased of them is not satisfactory in every particular. D. H. Eames & Co.'s salesrooms occupy the most.conspicuous retail corner in the city, fronting 100 feet on Main and Front streets, handsomely fitted up with all modern conveniences, including spacious show windows on both fronts; the basement, 35 x 100 feet in area, is well lighted, and is one of the best salesrooms in the city. A competent staff of polite, attentive and well-informed salesmen is employed, and the customer, whether rich or poor, is made welcome and no pains spared to show him the goods he wants, while styles, make, fit and price are sure to please. Every description of clothing in all desirable grades for all ranks and conditions of buyers are carried in great variety, and patrons may depend upon every representation made by the salesmen.

F. H. KENDRICK, D. D. S.,

Suite 3, Knowles Building, Cor. Main and Chatham Streets.

Some alleged scientist, basing his calculations upon what he is pleased to call natural laws, the past experience of the race and physical degeneration consequent upon contact with a gradually developing civilization, has declared that the time is not far distant—say two or three centuries—when all mankind, with the exception of occasional abnormal freaks, will become totally hairless and toothless—when liquid food only will be consumed, the dentist and the barber relegated to the limbo of forgotten public servants, and men and women reassume the appearance and innocence, if not the helplessness and other characteristics of extreme infancy, with its exemption from the agonies of toothache and of being talked to death. In the meantime, while patiently awaiting that blissful epoch of toothless gums and capillary poverty, men and women are advised to comb their hair occasionally, keep their teeth clean, and patronize the dentist as usual—only taking care to avoid the tooth carpenter, who is abroad in the land seeking diligently whom he may ruin somebody's incisors, canines and masticators. Among the most thoroughly trained, most skillful and best patronized of Worcester's practical dentists is Dr. F. H. Kendrick, a native of Rowe, Franklin County, and a graduate of the Pennsylvania Dental College at Philadelphia, class of '85. He subsequently practiced for a year at Middletown, Conn., and then removed to Worcester, establishing himself on the east side of Main street, between the common and Franklin square. Three years ago he secured and occupied his present beautifully appointed quarters—suite 3, Knowles building, consisting of commodious and brilliantly lighted reception and operating rooms and private office, all overlooking Main street, with neat and completely equipped work-room attached, where the mechanical operations are carried on—the most delicate and important part of the practical dentist's work, though the least trying to the nerves of patient and operator, as many of those who submit their mouths to his skillful manipulations (ordinarily great hulking men) make as much fuss as though they expected to suffer death or at least the amputation of a limb. Dr. Kendrick is prepared with all the latest approved appliances of his profession, thoroughly understands his work in all its branches, and can guarantee 'satisfaction in every instance, from the removal of a loose milk tooth to the extraction of a full set, upper and lower, and their substitution with perfect fitting, comfortable, pretty and serviceable artificial teeth. In the delicate specialties of filling with gold and crown work he has no superior, and invites comparison of samples and prices. An experienced coadjutor assists him in attending his large and growing *clientele*. Nitrous oxide gas, electricity and ether are administered when advisable, if desired.

THE EYRIE.

J. G. Bieberbach, Sole Proprietor—Summer Pleasure Resort—East Shore of Lake
Quinsigamond, Town of Shrewsbury.

The attractions of Lake Quinsigamond are of the most delightful character, embracing all that
can please the eye of varied landscape — gentle knoll and verdant vale, cultivated glebe and
blooming bower, rustic village and city spire, broad vistas of fertile meadow, towering forest and
clustering copse, distant blue mountain ranges that bound the horizon, and, stretching away to
the north and south, the glistening waters lying mirror-like between emerald shores and dotted
here and there with snowy sail, dancing row-boat or toy steamer, laden with light-hearted youths
and maidens, fathers, mothers and children, whose only thought is enjoyment, the whole scene
o'erspread by sapphire skies and the ambient air filled with the elixir of life. It is not many
years since access to this charming region was made easy by the construction of a grand approach
—Southeastern-boulevard — broad, smooth and level, which, skirting the lake, penetrates the
superb new Lake View Park, from the highest point of which may be obtained one of the most
entrancing of New England views. The most popular means of reaching the lake, however, is
by rail. The cars, running at frequent intervals, are crowded all day and late into the night
during the pleasant days of spring, summer and early fall by pleasure seekers, who make the
most of the opportunities for recreation afforded by land and water, well-behaved people of all
classes standing upon a footing of absolute equality, so far as public accommodations go. Special
privileges are, however, accorded people of means through private enterprise, several handsome
summer hotels having been erected in the vicinity of the lake. Prominent and popular among
these is "The Eyrie," built in 1882, and managed up to July, 1889, by Mr. Tom Rice, who
then sold out his interest to Mr. J. G. Bieberbach and retired. The Eyrie is an ornate four-story
frame structure, 50 feet square, beautifully finished in natural woods and crowned by a lookout
from which, with a glass or the naked eye, may be obtained a magnificent view in all directions
for a distance of twenty miles. The house, surrounded by broad verandas, stands on the eastern
or Shrewsbury shore, at an elevation of ninety feet above the water, which ripples at the foot of
the hill and is easily reached by paths. The interior is in keeping with the prospect, richly
fitted up, provided with all modern conveniences — telephone, electric lights and bells, baths,
etc. There are also spacious parlors, and a large, lofty, bright and airy dining-room, while
thirty-two beautiful sleeping rooms are set apart for guests, the whole establishment newly
decorated and finished with all the requirements of a luxurious home, including a splendid grand
piano. Out doors, five acres of grounds are attached to the hotel, two and a half acres of which
are tastefully laid out in flower gardens, shrubbery, terraces and romantic walks, with steamboat
landing in front. The subsistence department is abundantly supplied with every procurable, substantial and luxury, and the *cuisine* is perfect. Tourists and summer visitors will find here every
pleasure and attention they could desire, at moderate rates. Mr. J. G. Bieberbach, the owner
of the property, is a German by birth, a resident of Worcester for twenty-eight years and largely
interested in brewing and bottling. His son and business manager, the popular host of The
Eyrie, is a native of Roxbury, and a wide-awake, enterprising, public-spirited business man,
courteous and obliging.

OLIVER P. SHATTUCK,

Manufacturer of Havana and Domestic Cigars and Wholesale Dealer in Tobacco,
Pipes and Cigars—No. 369 Main Street.

This is a leading representative house in its line, controlling a flourishing trade that covers not
only Worcester city and county, but all of Central Massachusetts and a portion of Connecticut,

distributing immense quantities of superior
goods to retailers on favorable terms. Mr.
Oliver P. Shattuck established himself here
in this branch of business in 1869, and by
upright methods, close application and the
exercise of tact and capacity has succeeded
in making for himself an enviable place
among the city's most enterprising merchants.
His store at No. 369 Main street is a very
attractive one, 20 x 50 feet, and fully stocked
with samples of all goods he handles, but
gives no idea of the volume of his sales, as
orders from the trade are filled direct from
the factory and importing house. He
handles all grades of Havana and domestic
cigars, chewing and smoking tobaccos, pipes
and smokers' articles. Sustaining close

relations with the famous New York cigar manufacturing house of I. Henry & Son, he is general agent for their choicest products, among which may be named the celebrated "We Three" and "O. P. S. La Norma" brands, the latter made expressly for him, and unsurpassed for good qualities by any cigar on the market. Mr. Shattuck is a native of Belvedere, Vt., whence he removed to Worcester in 1853. For some years prior to embarking in business on his own account he was associated with his brothers. Public spirited, enterprising and genial, he has served the public four years in the Common Council—a part of the time as president. He is a Free Mason, an Odd Fellow, a Knight of Pythias, and highly esteemed by a wide circle of personal friends.

THE WIRE GOODS COMPANY,

Arthur W. Parmalee, President and Manager—Manufacturers of Wire Chains, Awning Hinges, and Wire Articles of All Kinds—No. 20 Union Street.

Wire is susceptible of ready and easy manipulation, and is capable of being applied to more varied uses, probably, than any other material known to the mechanic arts, ranging through all the ramifications of industry from the making of a pin to the construction and equipment of a steamship. A visit to the works of the Wire Goods Company, No. 20 Union street, and observation of the processes and products, would be of more value to the student of mechanics than the perusal of a volume upon that subject. This company, incorporated under the laws of Massachusetts in 1883, with $25,000 capital, Mr. Arthur W. Parmalee president and manager, has its office and warerooms at the place indicated, connected with which is one of the two factories, the whole domiciled in a substantial brick building of

AUTOMATIC BLIND AWNING FIXTURES.

four stories, 150 feet front by 60 feet deep. On Prescott street is the branch factory, also of brick, one-story, 80 x 500 feet. Both are equipped throughout with the latest and best improved appliances, the most noticeable of which is a line of ingenious special machinery for making wire chain, a specialty in which this company excels and of which the output is simply immense, more particularly of the new wire sash chain, so flexible that kinking is impossible. This chain is indorsed by builders and carpenters at sight, and is rapidly superseding all other devices employed for the same purpose. This, however, is but one item of the company's products, which embrace all goods in which wire is the sole or principal component — patent awning hinges, steel door-mats, coat and hat hooks, staples, and an interminable catalogue of minor articles, all in constant and increasing demand and supplied to the trade everywhere at moderate prices and on reasonable terms. A flourishing trade is being built up in Great Britain and on the continent of Europe. Mr. Parmalee, who has entire control of the works, is a wide-awake, enterprising, successful business man, always at his post. He enjoys the respect and confidence of the mercantile community in an unusual degree. The company gives employment to about 200 hands.

BAY STATE LAUNDRY.

William H. Balcom, Proprietor—No. 17 Church Street.

Worcester is unquestionably a center of culture of the best kind, as may be readily seen by even a cursory observer who notes the quiet behavior, courtesy and neatness of the people. Cleanliness of person and apparel is a matter of course and of habit, as are good manners and morality. There are numerous laundries scattered about the city, all of which seem to enjoy a fair share of prosperity, and deservedly, but few, if any, are more liberally patronized by the best class of citizens than the famous Bay State, established by Mr. Wm. H. Balcom six years ago. In 1885 Mr. Balcom purchased the Waldo street laundry, removed the entire plant to the commodious premises No. 17 Church street, where, provided with a superb equipment of Empire laundry machinery, steam power, steam dryers, etc., assisted by skilled hands, he does a vast amount of superior work in his line for city and suburban patrons, keeping several wagons and collecting and delivering garments without extra charge. Mr. Balcom is a Massachusetts man by birth, enterprising and progressive, and a prominent Odd Fellow. He is ably seconded in the management by Mrs. A. B. Jackson, formerly of the Waldo street laundry.

GEORGE P. KENDRICK & CO.,

Livery, Feed and Boarding Stables—Nos. 12 and 14 Trumbull Street.

This establishment ranks with the largest and is said to be in many respects the most complete livery and boarding stable in Central Massachusetts. The building, of brick, 50 x 120 feet, four stories in height, is well lighted and ventilated, thoroughly drained and kept as clean as care and solicitude for the health of the horse can make it, and is in all respects a model that it would be well for some others to pattern after. As a result of the pains lavished, the animals housed here are always fat, sleek and in good spirits, and it is a pleasure to drive them. The same remarks, with proper modifications, apply to the vehicles of the firm, which are stylish, nice and bright. Messrs. George P., George A. and Edward H. Kendrick are experienced livery men, who devote their attention exclusively to their business, which accounts for their success. They own and keep for hire sixty horses, some of them blooded animals and all of them creditable roadsters, and an equal number of fine double and single carriages, coupes, hacks and buggies. Those in want of a good turnout for pleasure or business driving or for any other purpose will find it here. The firm also have superior facilities for feeding and boarding horses by the meal, day, week, month or year at moderate rates, and guarantee the very best attention.   .

GEORGE KINGSTON,

Building Contractor, Room 46½ Knowles Building. John P. Kingston, Architect, Room 47 Knowles Building, No. 518 Main Street.

The numerous fine manufacturing, mercantile and office blocks erected within the past few years indicate that Worcester is gradually awaking to modern requirements in architecture, and

is on the way to a development in this respect that will eventually make the hitherto conservative old " Heart of the Commonwealth " one of the most beautiful and substantial of New England cities. The best materials are readily obtainable in abundance; labor, both skilled and unskilled, is plentiful and reasonably cheap, and her master builders are unsurpassed for energy, good taste and technical and practical knowledge of their profession, which is at once exacting and thoroughly appreciated by the thoughful and progressive in all ranks of life. Among those who are making for themselves a solid and enduring reputation is Mr. George Kingston, who came hither from New Brunswick thirteen years ago and engaged in business for himself in 1883. He soon made his mark, and each season has brought him an increased number of valuable contracts, among the most recent and important of which were the Wood block on Belmont street, and the Healy block (shown in our engraving) on Jackson street — handsome, substantial and costly brick structures that will long attest the professional and mechanical skill involved in their planning and construction. These, however, are but two examples out of many that bear witness to his capacity. Mr. Kingston's office is in room 46½ Knowles building, No. 518 Main street, where he will be pleased to see those who contemplate building improvements of any kind. He employs this season thirty-five or forty expert workmen, controls all necessary facilities, and is prepared to execute speedily and in superior style contracts for construction of any kind. Mr. Kingston's brother, John P., an accomplished and successful carpenter and draughtsman for nineteen years, who has had charge of some of the best buildings in the State, occupies the adjoining office, room 47, and will give prompt and skillful attention to those requiring plans, specifications and estimates. These offices, though on the sixth floor, are quickly and easily reached by means of an elevator that plies constantly during business hours.

THE TOWN OF SPENCER.

SPENCER, settled about 1740 and incorporated April, 1753, forms an almost exact parallelogram four miles wide from east to west, eight miles long from north to south, and containing about thirty-two square miles of territory, bounded on the north by Oakham and Paxton, on the south by Charlton, on the east by Leicester and Paxton, and on the west by Brookfield and North Brookfield. The surface is somewhat hilly, though fertile vales abound, and is well watered by Seven-mile river, Turkey-hill brook, and numerous reservoirs and ponds, the largest of which, Moose pond, situated in the center of the town, is eighty acres in extent, fed by natural springs, and stocked with fine pickerel. Spencer Center is connected with the Boston & Albany by a branch railroad two miles and a quarter in length. Population, per census of 1890, 8,686. The industries of Spencer, though limited in number, are of much importance as regards extent, and embrace the manufacture of machinery, leather, boots and shoes, wire goods, woolen yarns and textiles, packing boxes, etc.

BACON & SIBLEY,

Manufacturers of Men's, Boy's and Youths' Boots and Shoes.

The above-named firm, composed of Messrs. A. B. Bacon and E. F. Sibley, was formed more than six years ago—February, 1885—and has built up a very large and prosperous business, based upon liberal and upright dealing and the production of first-class goods. The factory building proper is a substantial frame structure of four stories, basement and attic, 30x80 feet, with three-story addition, 30x 40 feet, the whole warmed by steam and thoroughly well equipped in all departments. One hundred superior workmen are employed, and the output of men's, boy's and youths' kip, veal calf,  grain, buff and split pegged and standard screw boots and shoes averages about fifty dozen pairs daily—hand work for the most part, though a fine complement of improved cutting, lasting and other machinery, driven by a thirty-horse-power steam engine, is utilized. The footwear made here is unsurpassed for quality of material, workmanship, style and finish, and is designed more especially for the use of farmers and others whose avocations expose them much to the weather. Jobbers through the west and south supply the trade in those sections, and discriminating consumers are eager buyers when they have once tested the fit and the endurance of the Bacon & Sibley boot or shoe. The firm maintain an office and salesroom at No. 131 Summer street, Boston.

J. GREEN & CO.,

Manufacturers of Boots and Shoes—No. 271 Main Street.

This is the oldest shoe manufacturing concern in Spencer, founded in the memorable year

1812—seventy-nine years ago—by the noted Josiah Green, the successful pioneer of the trade

in this vicinity, the first, in fact, who permanently established himself here in this branch of business. After a long and prosperous career Mr. Green passed away in 1876, and the management devolved upon his sons about 1853. They continued thus until 1884, when the present firm of J. Green & Co. was organized by Mr. Charles H. Green, under whose capable direction the house has flourished as never before. The factory, a substantial old-style frame building of four stories, 40x60 feet, is provided with all modern conveniences and appliances, including steam heating apparatus, automatic sprinklers as a safeguard against fire, and a full complement of late improved shoe manufacturing machinery of the best kind, the whole operated by a fine fifty-horse-power steam engine. One hundred and seventy-five hands are employed in all departments, a portion of whom live in

JOSIAH GREEN.

tenement houses owned by the firm near the factory. The goods made here embrace superior styles of medium grade boots and shoes for men, women, boys, girls and children, and command ready sale wherever offered, principally in the west and northwest. In point of material and workmanship these goods are unexcelled. The output averages about sixty cases per diem.

ISAAC PROUTY & CO.,

Manufacturers of High Grade Boots and Shoes—Established 1820—Boston Office, Nos. 105 to 111 Summer Street.

This is the most extensive boot and shoe manufacturing concern in Worcester county, and one of the largest in the United States, its ramifications reaching every nook and corner of the country, and exerting an immense influence upon the trade at large. Yet the house had a very humble and unpretentious origin, when in 1820 Isaac Prouty, the founder, established himself here as the village shoemaker, opening a small shop in his own house, employing one or two journeymen, and executing orders by hand for his customers, mostly farmers and their families. But Mr. Prouty was an enterprising man as well as a superior practical workman, and as his patronage grew he increased his facilities. After a time he took a step which must have surprised his slow-going competitors: he built a three-story frame shop 30x60 feet, introduced such labor-saving devices as had then been perfected, augmented his working force, and engaged in

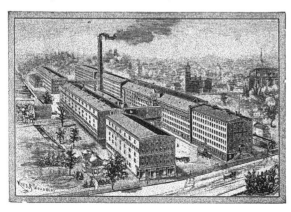

manufacturing to some extent for the trade. His venture proved successful; orders multiplied, and ere long he found it necessary to again enlarge, when he built what remains to this day the front of the "big shop," a frame structure of four stories, 42x104 feet. Since then the additions under his own and his sons' administrations have been frequent, large and costly, the plant and grounds now comprising some five acres. Our engraving gives a general idea of the buildings, principally of brick. The famous "big shop" has grown from its original dimensions to 42

x485 feet, the additions being of brick, six stories in height. The warehouse proper, of brick, 60x400 feet, is six stories high, and connected therewith is an addition, also brick, 60x300 feet. Throughout the establishment is lighted by electricity generated on the premises and protected against danger from fire by a complete system of automatic sprinklers, hydrants and escapes. The machinery equipment is superb and complete, comprising every late improved device of demonstrated value, all driven by steam power and manipulated by skilled and experienced workmen, of whom from 1000 to 1200 are employed. In all departments the best order prevails; neatness and cleanliness are taught by precept and example, and Prouty & Co.'s great factory is a recognized model for all aspiring competitors. The output of this establishment averages 300 cases of boots and from 1800 to 2200 pairs of shoes daily, annual sales varying little from $2,000,000 The goods comprise strictly high grades of men's, youths' and boys' calf, kip and grain thick split mining and Hungarian boots and shoes, together with women's, misses' and children's calf, kip, buff and split shoes in every style, shape and size, which are handled by the trade everywhere and are special favorites among the farmers, lumbermen and miners of the eastern, western, middle and northwestern States and territories, though they are fast making for themselves a market in the south and southwest.

Isaac Prouty closed his earthly career in 1872, previous to which time his sons, Lewis W. and George P., became associated with him as partners. Lewis W. died also in 1872, since which time the remaining brothers, George P., Charles N. and Jason W., have conducted the business under the old firm name, adopted in 1856. The Boston office and salesrooms are situated at Nos. 105 to 111 Summer street.

BACON, YOUNG & CO.,

Manufacturers of Boots and Shoes for Men's, Boys' and Youths' Wear—Main Street.

This house, while not so old as some of its local competitors, ranks with the best in point of substantial character, progressive spirit, liberality and business enterprise. It was established in 1881 by Bacon, Kent & Co., the present firm succeeding in 1888, and being composed of Messrs. I. L. Prouty, J. E. Bacon and M. A. Young, individually and collectively gentlemen of great experience, undoubted capacity, and lofty social and business standing and all connected as partners with the concern since its inception. The factory is of brick, five stories in height, 40x 85 feet, heated by steam throughout,  and equipped in all departments with the newest and most perfect machinery and appliances, including every new invention and improvement of practical value, all driven by a model twenty-five-horse-power steam engine. From one hundred to two hundred skilled hands are employed as required by the state of trade, and vast quantities of superior footwear are produced for the western and southern markets principally, the leading specialties embracing superior lines of fine and heavy kip, heavy kip and split, split, grain and miners', buff, calf and grain boots and shoes for men, boys and youths. The goods, well and carefully made from selected stock, bear favorable comparison with those of the same class made anywhere, and are steadily and surely extending the fame of the house.

E. JONES & CO.

Manufacturers of Men's, Boys', Youths' and Children's Heavy, Fine Kip, Veal Calf, Split and Miners' Boots and Shoes—Factory, Spencer; Boston Office, No. 103 Bedford Street.

Prominent among the leading representatives of Spencer's principal industry stands the great shoe manufacturing concern of E. Jones & Co. This house was founded in 1841 by the late Asa T. Jones. The style changed to A. T. & E. Jones on the admission of Mr. Erastus Jones in 1846. The senior member retired and Mr. H. P. Starr became associated with Erastus Jones in 1862. Mr. F. E. Dunton entered the firm in 1872, and during the year 1889 Mr. Starr withdrew, the firm now consisting of Messrs. Erastus Jones and F. E. Dunton, the former a native of Spencer, an enterprising, public-spirited citizen and president of both the Spencer National and Spencer Savings banks. E. Jones & Co's plant comprises the factory proper of three stories and basement, 38x80 feet, with 36x54 feet L, connected with which is a large four-story warehouse 40x60 feet—all frame buildings, heated by steam, fitted up with automatic sprinklers, and equipped in the best manner with all modern improved shoe machinery adapted to the profitable production of the firm's specialties, driven by a twenty-five-horse-power steam engine. Two hundred hands find steady and remunerative employment here, and the output, unsurpassed for excellence of material, style and workmanship, averages six hundred dozen pairs per week of heavy, fine kip, veal calf, split and miners' boots and shoes for men's, boys', youths' and children's wear. These goods, standard favorites with the trade and consumers, find eager demand in the Boston, New York and western markets. E. Jones & Co.'s Boston office is at No. 103 Bedford street.

MASSASOIT HOUSE.

Leighton & Goodrich, Proprietors—Main Street.

The old Massasoit was never in its palmiest days more popular than the rehabilitated Massasoit, erected upon the same site in 1888, now conducted by Messrs. Leighton & Goodrich,

who took charge in December, 1890. Standing alone upon a commanding elevation off Main street, the building is an ornate modern frame structure of four stories, 100 x 150 feet, with French roof and all appropriate architectural embellishments. A beautiful lawn extends to the street, and the approaches only suggest the hospitality and comfort that await the guest. The interior arrangements are in keeping. Two elegantly furnished public parlors, two handsomely appointed reading-rooms, two commodious dining-rooms, a grand dancing hall, large billiard-room and fine office occupy the ground floor, while up stairs are situated the eighty sleeping apartments, arranged singly and *en suite*, richly furnished, cosy, neat and comfortable. The table is only lavishly supplied with every substantial and delicacy in season. The establishment is heated by steam, provided with electric annunciators, lighted throughout by gas, and is in all respects a model hotel, presided over by two genial and liberal hosts, one of whom, Mr. Leighton, was for four years manager of the Whitney House, Westboro, a native of Upton, a Freemason, an Oddfellow, a war veteran and a G. A. R. man. His associate, Mr. Goodrich, was born in Stafford, Conn., and is a pleasant, obliging young gentleman.

DUSTIN & CLARK,

Manufacturers of Boot and Shoe Machinery, Shafting and Loom Work—No. 11 Wall Street.

Every few months the attention of the trade is challenged by the appearance in the market of some novelty for the simplification and expediting of processes in the shoe-making industry. There are, however, certain standard devices of proved value for which there is a steady demand, and it is in the construction of these that the firm of Dustin & Clark excels. This house was established at No. 11 Wall street, Spencer, about seven years ago, and has made for itself a national reputation for the excellence of its specialties, which embrace a general line of first-class shoe manufacturing machinery, such as hand and power stamping and boning apparatus, wax thread stitching machines, Varney's pegging machines, Dwyer's patent heel trimmer, etc., together with shafting, loom work and general jobbing, including skillful repairs of leather-splitting and other appliances pertaining to the shoe factory. They also give prompt and careful attention to steam, hot water and gas-fitting for the trade and all who require such work. Remarkable skill, accuracy and effectiveness characterize all machines made here. Messrs. Dustin & Clark's shops are located in the one-and-a-half-story frame building, 45 x 30 feet, at the above number, and are fully equipped with all requisite facilities—lathes, planers, drills, etc. —driven by a ten-horse-power steam engine. The firm confidently refers to its hundreds of patrons in all parts of the Union. Mr. Dustin was born in New Hampshire, Mr. Clark in England: both are experienced and competent practical workmen, and they employ a capable force of assistants.

FITCHBURG.

THE town of Fitchburg (named for John Fitch, an influential resident and one of the committee who secured favorable action by the General Court) was originally a part of Lunenburg. The act of incorporation was finally passed and approved by Governor Francis Bernard, February 3, 1764. Territorially the town is four and a-half by six and a-half miles in extent, hilly, stony, and poorly adapted to agriculture, though constant labor for generations has accomplished wonders, the census of 1885 crediting the town with 209 farms, 3,676 acres under cultivation, 5,850 acres of pasture, 5,134 acres of woodland, and farm products valued at $294,558. The north branch of the Nashua river traverses the southern portion of the town, and along its banks and upon the adjacent hills is built the busy and flourishing

CITY OF FITCHBURG.

It is unnecessary for our purpose to follow the history of Fitchburg as a town from 1764 to its incorporation as a city in 1873. The story differs little from that of a score of other towns in this part of the State ; the people bore their part in the revolution and the establishment of the State and the nation, planted and reaped, built houses for themselves, erected mills and factories, married and reared families, served their country in time of need, and in all things proved a model community, waxing strong in numbers and wealth and in the accompaniments of modern civilization—moral and intellectual culture, art and refinement.

The city extends for a mile or more along the valley of the North branch, which forms the business center, interspersed here and there with homes for the most part erected long ago, the principal residence districts lying back from the river and on the hillsides and summits. There are several neat and well-kept parks—the upper and lower commons and Monument park—all situated on Main street, the first near the western extremity, the second opposite the Union railway station, and the third in front of the court-house, nearly midway between the others. In its center is a massive and tasteful soldiers' monument of granite surmounted by three bronze statues and guarded by four brass cannon. This is the most accessible and most popular of Fitchburg's parks, but will soon be rivaled by the upper common. Near the eastern terminus of the street railway is the new and extensive Fitchburg park, formerly the grounds of the Worcester North Agricultural society.

Primarily Fitchburg was indebted to the North branch for the establishment of manufactures in her midst, but the stream long since proved inadequate to the demand for power and was for the most part abandoned for that purpose, steam being substituted. The scenery in the vicinity is very fine, and extensive and delightful prospects are commanded from the summits of Pearl and Roll-

9

SOLDIERS' MONUMENT AND COURT HOUSE.

FITCHBURG RAILROAD DEPOT.

stone hills, the former northwest, the latter southwest of the city. Pearl hill, the loftiest of the two, is precipitous on one side, and composed of a peculiar variety of micaceous rock of little practical value, while Rollstone is a stratified mass of the choicest granite, which is quarried in large and increasing quantities for building and monumental purposes at home and throughout this and adjoining States.

The manufacture of woolen goods at this point had its inception in 1793, the production of hardware and tools in 1838. The Putnam Machine Company, founded about 1858, was the first to engage in that industry, now represented here by several extensive establishments of world-wide reputation. Paper, chairs, furniture, woodenware and many other useful commodities swell the industrial output to vast dimensions.

WALLACE LIBRARY AND ART BUILDING.

The Fitchburg railroad, affording direct communication with Boston and Worcester, was opened for traffic in 1845, the Cheshire and Vermont & Massachusetts railroad not long afterward, and, with their connections, have contributed vastly to the development of the region and the advancement of the city. The water-works, of ample capacity, were put in operation in 1872.

Fitchburg shares with Worcester the honor of dispensing law and justice to the county, having its branch county offices and courts.

FITCHBURG STEAM ENGINE CO.

Frederick Fosdick, President; William E. Sheldon, Treasurer; William J. Clifford,
Secretary; Charles Fosdick, Superintendent—Manufacturers of Steam Engines
and Boilers,—Water Street.

President Frederick Fosdick is a practical engineer, machinist and inventor of long and
varied experience, formerly employed by the Haskins Steam Engine Company of this city, established in 1870. On the failure of that company in 1876 there was organized and incorporated
the Fitchburg Steam Engine Company, capital $40,000, which purchased the former company's
plant and made a gratifying success where there had been only failure—a success with
merit for its corner-stone and industry, enterprise and upright dealing as its foundations. In
this instance at least the expected happened, and the prosperity that has crowned the company's
labors might have been safely predicted from its inception. It seems a pity that Fitchburg
should lose so valuable and influential and industrial a concern, but so it is, and a lack of elbow-
room is the cause. As above intimated, this company upon its establishment occupied the shops
of its predecessor, the Haskins company—three floors of a four-story brick building, 40x130

feet, on Water street, thoroughly equipped, the machinery driven by a 40-horse-power engine
of their own construction. This arrangement did well enough for some years, but as the demand for their work increased they found themselves more and more crowded; expansion in
any direction was impracticable, and it became necessary to look elsewhere. An eligible site
was finally secured at Gardner, plans perfected, work begun, and in July the works will be removed to the fine new shops at that point, a substantial two-story-and-basement brick structure, 70x150 feet, fitted up with every convenience, including new and improved machinery and
tools, and connected with the main railway line by means of a spur track for convenience in
handling materials, fuel and finished product. The corporation will retain the name—Fitchburg Steam Engine Company—which has earned an excellent reputation, and President Fosdick
will continue for the present to reside here. He, in conjunction with Charles Fosdick and William E. Sheldon, are proprietors of the Willard Screen Plate Company of Leominster.

The engine company's present works are well fitted up and of great capacity, the concern
employing sixty-five men and paying out in wages about $35,000 per annum. The engines
made by the company go to every part of the world, the demand for these engines being especially great in the United States, Canada, Germany and Holland. These engines embrace
the latest improvements (many of which are special and peculiar to this company, being
patented) in high and low speed steam motors, horizontal, vertical, automatic, cut-off, "Cross"
or twin and tandem compound condensing, portable, semi-portable, stationary and marine—the
latter of reversible pattern for tug boats and yachts. The horizontal twin compound condensing engine illustrated herewith is an example of simplicity and mechanical skill, as is the special.

electric light engine constructed here in high or low speed styles, economical, reliable, and fitted with a positive, simple and effective patent governor.

We have exhausted the space allowed, and still have not been able to go into particulars as we would wish. Those interested will be supplied with all desired information upon application to the company, who will forward illustrated catalogues, printed technical descriptions and price-lists to any responsible address in the world.

FITCHBURG HOTEL.

F. W. Judkins, Proprietor; J. E. Alexander and T. J. Sullivan, Clerks—Main Street.

The Fitchburg Hotel, erected about forty years ago, passed into the hands of Mr. Judkins in 1886. The building is of brick, the main structure four stories and wing three stories in height, containing in all one hundred and ten airy and spacious sleeping apartments, handsome parlors, reception, dining, billiard and bath-rooms, barber shop, etc., the office fitted up with pneumatic annunciators, telephones and all conveniences—the whole house being newly furnished, equipped, decorated and renovated from cellar to attic in 1889. Those who have enjoyed the hospitality of this house under the present management require no special invitation

to return, and those who have not should not fail to do so, as the house is conveniently situated, guests are conveyed free to and from all trains, and the *menage* is first-class in all respects—inviting accommodations, clean and tidy rooms, restful beds, a table that cannot be surpassed, superb service and moderate charges. A good many fastidious citizens board here in preference to housekeeping, and this is not to be wondered at when one has made the acquaintance of Mine Host Judkins, and his polite and obliging clerks, Messrs. J. E. Alexander and T. J. Sullivan. Mr. Judkins is a native of Lewiston, Maine, and though this is his first venture in the business, he is rapidly becoming one of the most successful and popular bonifaces in the country.

PARKHILL MANUFACTURING COMPANY.

John Parkhill, President; Arthur H. Lowe, Treasurer; Office, Circle Street.

This manufacturing enterprise was founded in 1880. The company began business in a four-story building, 48x150 feet in dimensions, operating at the start thirty looms. The works produce the celebrated "*Toile du Nord*" fabric, fine ginghams and dress goods. The history of this house since its inception has been a record of continual success and prosperity, due mainly to the remarkable excellence of the product, coupled with the high order of commercial enterprise and practical experience of the gentlemen at the head of the management. The enviable reputation gained by the company's brands are unequaled by reason of their excellence, and needs no better illustration than the frequent necessity for increasing the capacity of the works. Commencing with thirty looms, the company has added from time to time new buildings replete with new improved methods for conducting the business and as recently as August, 1889, this company purchased the Clegh mill (manufacturers of fine dress goods) located at No. 204 River street, thereby adding materially to their already large facilities for the manufacture of these special lines of goods. So that now the company owns and operates three factories known as mills A, B, and C, embracing 1,517 looms, and employment is furnished to 850 oper. atives; the products of the mills reaching the enormous quantity of a million and a-half yards monthly. The product of these works is sold through Denny, Poor & Co., of New York city, and reaches the great west through Chicago agencies. A perfect system prevails in every de. partment of this extensive business. Its managers are practically experienced men in their line, and give their personal attention to every important detail of the manufacture, so as to insure the very best results in placing the goods upon the market.

F. A. BENNETT.

Boarding, Livery and Sale Stable—No. 21 Snow Street, near Main.

Mr. Bennett, a native of Ashburnham, established himself here in the livery and sale stable business in 1883. That he has succeeded is evidenced by the fact that his is now the most extensive

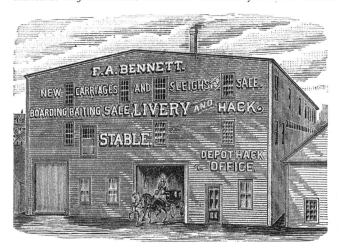

and most largely patronized stable in the city, a commodious and handsome three-story addition having been erected last summer, constructed on the new plan, with carriage repository on the ground floor and stables above, thus insuring excellent ventilation, while the drainage and general sanitary arrangements are about perfect. Here are kept more than eighty horses—his own and boarders —and a large number and great variety of vehicles, including single and double carriages, buggies, light road wagons, hacks, and sleighs of every style. Ten experienced hostlers, drivers and other assistants are employed, and his patronage is extremely liberal, not only from residents but from commercial travelers, pleasure tourists and others, who find here at all times just the kind of animals and vehicles they want at reasonable prices. Mr. Bennett also makes a specialty of buying and selling horses and new and second. hand carriages of all kinds, carrying a large stock of each, besides boarding horses and storing conveyances for regular and transient patrons on reasonable terms.

SIMONDS MANUFACTURING COMPANY.

Main Street, Fitchburg, Mass.

This pioneer industrial concern has a reputation second to none in its line in America. It was founded in 1832 by Mr. Abel Simonds. In 1864 the firm of Simonds Bros. & Co. was formed, and in 1868 the Simonds Manufacturing Co. was incorporated, since which time the business has very largely developed. Works are now maintained in Chicago, Ill., and San Francisco, Cal., as well as in this city, but in this sketch mention shall be made particularly of the Fitch. burg factory. This comprises two buildings, one of which is four stories in height, with two L's, while the other is a two-story brick building 44x100 feet in dimensions. The total floor space is almost one acre in area. Employment is there given to 175 men, and the elaborate and costly plant is run by two steam engines of 150 and 75 horse-power respectively.

Among the specialties manufactured special mention should be made of circular saws—solid tooth and inserted point—crescent ground cross-cut saws, gang, mill, mulay and drag saws, band saws, planing machine knives, leather-splitting knives, etc., all of which are too well and favorably known to render detailed description necessary.

The process, machinery and saw are protected by letters patent granted in 1874, 1875, 1877, 1878, 1881, 1882 and 1885. This saw has an unequaled reputation for efficiency and durability, and is preferred by practical millmen throughout the United States. All the productions of this company are made from carefully selected material, and no imperfect goods are knowingly allowed to leave the works, so strict is the inspection. Having unsurpassed facilities, the company is in a position to quote fair prices.

The president, Mr. Daniel Simonds, and the treasurer, Mr. H. F. Cogshall, are both well known business men, prominently identified with the advancement of the best interests of this section.

AMERICAN HOUSE.

George H. Cole & Son, Proprietors, Main Street, Nearly Opposite Union Depot, Fitchburg, Mass.

A conspicuous landmark in the rise and progress of this city is the well-known and popular hostelry, the American House, which was opened to the public in 1846. "The American" is in all respects one of the leading hotels in Fitchburg, has a frontage of 160 feet on Main street, an average depth of 100 feet, and is four stories high. In its architectural construction it is somewhat irregular but withal quite unique and attractive. The building contains 100 rooms, well lighted and ventilated and equipped with all improvements and conveniences conducive to the comfort of guests, including gas light, electric bells, hot and cold water, bath-rooms, sanitary appliances, telephone connection. The entire building is finely furnished and perfect in its appointments. The dining-room is well lighted and pleasant, fronting Blossom street, and has a seating capacity to accommodate 125 guests at one time. Some twenty-five persons are employed in dispensing the comforts of the house, and the *cuisine*, in charge of a competent *chef*, is unexcelled. A livery stable is connected with the house, and hacks attend upon the arrival and departure of all trains for the free transportation of guests and their luggage to and from the hotel. The reading-room is large, airy and well lighted; two public parlors are provided with piano and other modern social luxuries. Traveling-men's sampling rooms are also a notable feature of this modern establishment. In short nothing is wanting to make up what constitutes a first-class hostelry in modern metropolitan equipment. The genial hosts, Mr. Geo. H. Cole and his son Mr. W. A. Cole, are eminently fitted for the conduct of their business, and since assuming control of this famous house in October, 1886, they have added many valuable and necessary improvements to the establishment. They were formerly in the hotel business for eleven years or more at Leominster, Mass., and sustain an enviable reputation for efficiency in this important department of our commercial and social system. The rates are $2.00 and $2.50 per day—remarkably moderate, considering the excellent fare and superior accommodations provided. Mr. Geo. H. Barrett presides at the office during the day-time, and is thoroughly posted on the requirements of his responsible position. He is assisted by Mr. Ernest Kendall, who has charge of the office during the night. Billiard and refreshment rooms are conveniently located in the building, and perfect order and discipline prevails in every department of this model house.

FITCHBURG COTTON MILL.

B. M. Pitts, Proprietor—Manufacturer of Cotton Warps,—No. 527 Main Street.

The Fitchburg cotton mill was erected in 1867 by the late H. W. Pitts, under whose capable direction it was run successfully until his death in December, 1881, when his son, Mr. B. M. Pitts, for ten years superintendent, assumed the proprietorship and management. The plant comprises five buildings, the mill proper being of brick, four stories, 50x100 feet, containing a very fine equipment of modern machinery and 3,100 spindles, the whole driven by combined steam and water power. Sixty hands are employed, and the capacity is 40,000 pounds of cotton warp per month, the product going for the most part to certain Boston carpet mills requiring high-grade warps.

Mr. Pitts is a thoroughly practical man in his specialties, and gives his personal attention to the execution of all orders. Perfect system prevails throughout, and the best results are attained without jar or friction.

C. H. BROWN & CO.,

Manufacturers of the "Brown" Automatic Cut-off Steam Engine — Works, Main Street.

The Brown automatic engine, simple in principle and construction, built in the most perfect and workmanlike manner, easily managed and attractive in style, meets exactly the wants of a

vast number of mill-owners and manufacturers. Provided with an infallible cut-off attachment, strong, durable and reliable, especial attention has been directed to preventing or overcoming the effects of expansion and contraction while providing for proper adjustment and lubrication—

with what success is attested by its fast increasing sale. This engine was awarded the first prize, a gold medal, at the Paris exposition of 1889, in competition with the world. They also received the leading awards at Philadelphia, New York, Boston, Cincinnati, New Orleans and wherever exhibited. The unobstructed operation of the valves alone commends it to favorable consideration. This concern was established in 1868 by Mr. C. H. Brown, an accomplished mechanic and inventor of note, previously a member of the Putnam Machine Company and originator of the Putnam engine. His sons, C. H., junior, and F. E., subsequently became associated with him, and, being theoretical and practical masters of mechanics as , applied to engine and machinery construction, have proved of great assistance in bringing their house to the front. Up to a recent period the firm has confined its attention to the ordinary styles, but is now building compound engines, and solicits orders for cross, tandem or any other kind of any capacity. The works are domiciled in a modern two-and-a-half-story brick structure 50x162 feet, on Main street, fitted up with the latest and best appliances, and at present give employment to seventy-five skilled workmen, turning out a large number of complete engines, of an average value of $3,000, annually. These engines are provided with the Brown gridiron sliding valve, and are shipped to every State in the Union, to France, to Belgium, to Brazil and elsewhere.

BURLEIGH ROCK DRILL COMPANY.

John Burney, President; C. R. Burleigh, Treasurer—Manufacturers of Rock Drills, Air Compressors and Ice Machines—No. 129 Main Street.

ROCK DRILL MOUNTED FOR SURFACE WORK.

The Rock drill shown in our first cut is but one form of a machine that has performed no small part in some of the most daring and successful engineering achievements of modern times. Its first use upon a large scale—and, be it said, ere it had been developed to anything like its present degree of perfection—was in the construction of the Union Pacific railway, when it was extensively employed in the deepest cuts and most difficult tunnels of that road. It has since played an important part in railroad construction and quarrying, not only in this country but all over the world, and is everywhere conceded the palm of superiority. Among the many grand undertakings accomplished in great part by the agency of this remarkable device the Hoosac tunnel, nearly five miles in length, is worthy of mention. It is needless to say that the machine in some form is in universal use. The Panama and Nicaragua canal companies have had a large number built to aid in their work of "mingling the waters of the Atlantic and Pacific," and the manufacturers are kept busy filling orders for shipment to miners and railroad builders in the west, the south, the southwest, Mexico, Central and South America and more remote portions of the globe. The air compressors and ice machines supplied by this company are also of the highest order as regards principle, construction and effectiveness. The air compressor in particular is of incalculable service in conducting underground operations where for any reason the introduction of steam is impracticable.

The late Charles Burleigh invented the first successful steam drill, upon which he procured the necessary patents, and subsequently organized the Burleigh Rock Drill Company, incorporated in 1867, capital $120,000. After his death Mr. John Burney, formerly of the Putnam Machine Company, and lately of the Union Machine Company, was promoted to the presidency, Mr. Charles R. Burleigh continuing to act as treasurer. President Burney and Treasurer Burleigh, with Messrs. M. H. Curley, J. Q. Wright, and D. A. Carey, compose the board of directors of the Burleigh Rock Drill Company, whose office is at No. 129 Main street, Fitchburg. This company owns no manufacturing plant, experience and practical knowledge of the machine building business having taught the managers that it is more economical and less troublesome to have their work done by contract with competent and responsible machinists. Sales vary from $120,000 to $150,000 per annum. All required information is supplied upon application by letter or otherwise, and correspondence is invited from all interested n this class of machinery.

AIR COMPRESSOR.

PUTNAM MACHINE COMPANY'S WORKS.

PUTNAM MACHINE COMPANY.

Charles F. Putnam, President; Salmon W. Putnam, Vice-President; Henry O. Putnam, Treasurer; George E. Putnam, General Superintendent—Offices Corner of Main and Putnam Streets, Fitchburg, Mass.

The history of the Putnam Machine Company embraces the first efforts at metal-working established in Fitchburg, when, in 1836, J. and S. W. Putnam began business for themselves. The company was incorporated in 1858 by D. W. Putnam, who was chosen president and business agent, which position he held until his death in 1872. The present works, located at the corner of Main and Putnam streets—the main machine shop building being 625 feet deep, by a frontage of 45 feet on Main street with seven large L's, foundries, etc.—were erected in 1866, and cover an area of fifteen acres, the entire plant being provided with the most approved modern machines and appliances for the expeditious and efficient execution of this class of work. In the production of railroad machine tools, steam engines, etc., this company has enjoyed the reputation, well sustained, of being one of the first-class builders of the world; and, although since its inception great improvements have been made in this line, it has been this company's constant endeavor to manufacture only such as at the time justly entitled them to their world-wide reputation. In 1866 the Putnam Tool Company (S. W. Putnam Sons) was consolidated with the Putnam Machine Company, and all the valuable patents and improvements in railroad machine tools, etc., built by that company became a part of the product of the Putnam Machine Company. By this consolidation, the additon of a new iron foundry 150x60 feet in dimensions, additional railroad turnouts, iron cranes, steam engines of greater power, replacing the older machinery throughout the works with the latest and most improved, now finds this establishment one of the most extensive and best equipped in the United States, with facilities for greater production than ever before in its history. A partial list of the products of this great industry will doubtless interest the reader. The company, however, publish a comprehensive illustrated catalogue, which is designed to give the fullest possible information upon the subject. As far as the limited space allows in this work, it may be noted that this company manufacture railroad machine tools and special metal-working machinery, steam engines, wood-planers, water wheels, mill work, shafting, radial drills, shaping machines, etc., engine lathes, iron planers, upright drills, transverse drills, hydrostatic presses, milling machines, gear cutters, bolt cutters, pulley lathes, car axle lathes, slotting machines, nut tapping machines, boring machines, pattern lathes, car wheel boxes, etc. Upon all of which the highest award was given this company by the United States Centennial Commission, at the international exhibition in Philadelphia in 1876. The location of this company's works affords them the very best shipment facilities, being on the direct line of the Fitchburg, Boston, Hoosac Tunnel and Western, Old Colony, and other important railroad connections. They have unsurpassed advantages for prompt and easy communication to all parts of the United States and foreign countries and for obtaining in Fitchburg the lowest possible through freight rates on bills of landing. Much more could be said of this great enterprise, both as to its facilities and honorable record.

The *personnel* of this company comprise gentlemen of superior commercial ability and practical knowledge of the mechanical arts. The phenomenal success of the enterprise attests the truth of these statements. Their social standing also is of the highest order in this enlightened community by reason of the deep interest always displayed by the Messrs. Putnam in all that tends to advance the public welfare of this city and the social condition of their army of employees.

FITCHBURG DUCK MILLS.

Samuel A. Clough, Treasurer; Thomas H. Clark, Agent—Manufacturers of High Grade Cotton Duck—Factory at South Fitchburg.

The Fitchburg duck mills were erected in 1830 by George Blackburn, who also built the mills now owned and occupied by the Fitchburg Worsted Company and the Wheelwright Paper Company, which were sold after Mr. Blackburn's death; by his daughter, Mrs. Harriett F. Nevins, who, however, reserved the duck mill, which has been run in her interest since the death of her father. The premises comprise the main mill building, four stories, 40x100 feet, and a two-story addition, 40x40 feet; a two-and-a-half story machine building 30x40 feet, picker and boiler house—all brick—with commodious frame storage sheds adjacent. The machinery outfit includes fifteen revolving flat cards, 3,400 spindles and forty-four looms, driven by a 150-horse-power turbine, and 100 hands are constantly employed, the product averaging 3000 pounds per diem of superior cotton ducks, the specialties embracing the best grades of belting, hose and sail ducks, which are distributed throughout the United States and the southern republics through the principal office, No. 78 Chauncey street, Boston, presided over by Treasurer Samuel A. Clough.

F. S. LOVELL MACHINE COMPANY.

F. S. Lovell — Manufacturer of Lever-Set Circular Saw-Mills — Dealer in Portable Steam Engines, Boilers and Water Wheels, and Saw-Mill Outfits—No. 87 Boutelle Street.

Mr. F. S. Lovell is an experienced and successful machinist, formerly located on Wilson street, whence he removed to No. 87 Boutelle street in 1885. In 1887, after the death of Mr.

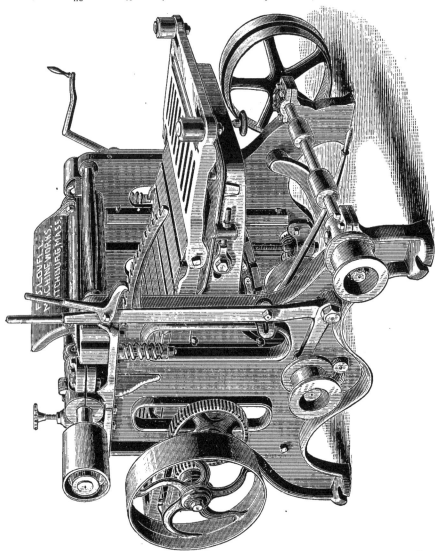

C. M. Flint, the famous saw-mill inventor and builder, Mr. Lovell bought the business from the executors and has continued to improve the construction until now he has the most accurate set and the best dogging device applied to any mill in the market, and he will continue to manufacture a full line of this class of machinery under more favorable auspices and with better results than attended the labors of the founder, Mr. Flint. The Flint patent mill and a new board and timber planer are illustrated herewith. Early in January Mr. Lovell completed and shipped to Colon McKenzie of Ellsworth, Me., one of these mills—the largest single saw-mill ever constructed in Massachusetts, and perhaps the largest ever made in New England — capable of cutting a log five feet in diameter and fifty-five long and of sawing from 20,000 to 50,000 feet of lumber per day. In addition to saw-mill machinery Mr. Lovell manufactures quite a line of gingham machinery, such as spoolers, quillers, beaming appliances, loom temples, etc., and also does much fine work in the construction of electric light and plating dynamos, under contract

for J. W. Colburn of this city. He is, besides, an extensive dealer in water-wheels, circular saws, mill supplies, engines, boilers, etc., and is general agent for T. M. Nagle of Erie, Pa., manufacturer of portable, stationary, agricultural and vertical engines and boilers. Mr. Lovell is an agreeable gentleman and a master machinist, having learned his trade at Worcester, where he spent his youth and was educated, going afterward to Clinton, where for seven years he was superintendent of the J. B. Parker Machine Company's works. His shops on Boutelle street occupy a one-story frame building 40 x 125 feet, are fitted up with steam power, electric lights, iron and wood-working machinery, furnishing employment to from fifteen to twenty-five skilled workmen. The leading specialties embrace the Flint patent lever-set circular saw-mill and saw-mill machinery in general, the output averaging about twenty-five complete mills per annum.

CHAS. A. PRIEST LUMBER COMPANY.

Factory and Yards, Rollstone Street; Office 45 Rollstone Street.

Among the representative establishments engaged in the lumber business in Fitchburg special mention may be made of this one, founded in 1878 by Mr. Charles A. Priest, who conducted it with extraordinary success until his death, in 1887. His widow, Mrs. Emily Priest, and his son, Mr. George H. Priest, succeeded to the business and continued to run it under the above firm designation. The son's practical experience in connection with his father's conduct of this business eminently fitted him for the successful management of this important industry. The plant and yards cover fully an acre in area. The factory and workshops comprise several buildings completely equipped with the most approved modern machinery; a force of thirty-five skilled workmen are here employed, and the product is in every respect first-class, and largely in demand among contractors and builders at home and abroad, consisting of Michigan, Canada and Northern lumber, laths, clapboards, pine and cedar shingles, in which this house deal extensively. This firm also manufactures doors, sash, blinds, glazed windows, window frames, window and picture glass, mouldings, brackets, blinds, trimmings, etc. A leading feature of this firm's business is stair building and wood turning. All kinds of builders finish and packing boxes are made to order at short notice. School furniture is a leading specialty, of which a very large and deversified stock is constantly carried. Both steam and water power are utilized in propelling the machinery. The factory and yards being located adjacent to railroad facilities, this firm possess superior advantages for promptness in receiving and shipping.

Mr. Geo. H. Priest is a native of Hillsboro, N. H., where his father resided prior to embarking in business here. The family is well and favorably recognized in social as well as business circles in this portion of New England. It is a gratifying reflection to the friends and patrons of this reputable house that the widow of a worthy citizen and enterprising business man is a member of a prosperous manufacturing establishment.

A. D. WAYMOTH & CO.,

Manufacturers of Variety Wood-Turning Lathes—Newton Place.

The Waymoth self-centering and self-adjusting variety wood-turning lathe is so well-known to and its advantages so well appreciated by woodworkers in this and other countries as to render a technical description of the machine as a whole unnecessary. It is not out of place, however, to call attention to recent important improvements, among them an arrangement whereby all side motion occasioned by the continual wear of tail-stock and middle-piece may be taken up, thus enabling the operator to keep his lathe firm as the slides wear. The accompanying cut illustrates this. The new patent rougher bed permits the use of a nine-inch instead of a two-inch knife, as hitherto; the swing head is operated by a rack and gear, which supplant the stud and crank, doing away with the troublesome dead center. The lathe is so constructed that all wear

can be readily taken up and any mechanic can run it. The new patent rougher knife holder and adjustable front tool-holder are entirely satisfactory and guaranteed to save from $75 to $100 a year in the time and labor of setting tools as compared with the old style. These lathes, which practically have no rivals, were awarded gold medals by the American Institute fair, at the New Orleans Cotton Centennial Exposition, by the Cincinnati Industrial Exposition of 1880, and highest premiums wherever exhibited. They are sold at remarkably low figures. Mr. A. D. Waymoth began the building of lathes in Fitchburg as long ago as 1857, not one turning lathe having been made here prior to that time; not only being the pioneer here, but the first to manufacture lathes of this class in the world. In 1875 he admitted his son, Charles W., to a copartnership under the present style of A. D. Waymoth & Co. The shops on Newton place are 40 x 100 feet in area, fitted up with steam power, planers, engine lathes, upright and horizontal drills and all necessary appurtenances, and gives employment to six superior mechanics, who turn out 100 lathes per annum, valued at $175 to $200 each and shipped all over the United States, a few being exported, for the most part to Germany. All required information is supplied on application. They have already manufactured and sold over 3500 of these lathes.

GEO. J. D'ALLAIRD, .

Shirt Manufacturer—Jackson Avenue, Jacksonville.

If enterprise, industry, tact and liberality ever deserved recognition and success, they certainly do in the case of Mr. D'Allaird. A shirt-cutter by trade, but familiar with every department of that industry, he came from Troy, N. Y., to Leominster in 1889 with the expectation of finding employment as a journeyman, in which he was disappointed. Among strangers, destitute of money or influence, he in July of the year named obtained a sewing machine on the installment plan and sat down, single-handed, to solve the problem of shelter and daily bread. But his product was of superior quality and found ready sale, and ere long he had three hands in his employ and under his immediate supervision in a large room on Jackson avenue. His progress from that point was comparatively rapid and easy. His present factory, erected last year — frame, 24 x 76 feet—cost $1200, and its equipment $2000 more, the latter including forty sewing machines of the best kind, several improved button-holers, a twenty-horse-power steam engine, a dynamo and an abundance of incandescent electric lights. He employs from seventy to 100 hands, as the state of the market requires, pays about $800 a week in wages — the best, on the average, known to the trade—makes a leading specialty of Domet flannel shirts, and when running full force turns out eighty dozen daily, worth $4.50 per dozen. These goods, which rank with the best made, are supplied to the trade through Boston jobbers. Mr. D'Allaird trained all of his help himself, from cutters to engineer, and has reduced shirt manufacturing to an exact science as regards materials, facilities and results.

FITCHBURG MANUFACTURING COMPANY.

Samuel E. Crocker, President; Adams Crocker, Agent and Treasurer—Manufacturers of Fine Ginghams,—West Fitchburg.

The Fitchburg Manufacturing Company, incorporated with $20,000 capital in January, 1890, purchased the old Battie mill property, tore down and rebuilt a part, remodeled and altered a part, and have as the result a practically new plant, comprising two brick mills respectively three stories 40x110 feet, and two stories 60x90 feet; a two-story frame storehouse 30x110 feet; a one-story brick cloth-room 30x30 feet; a one-and-a-half-story frame tank-room 30x30 feet, commodious dye-house, machine-shop, etc. The mills contain 180 looms, driven by steam and water power, and when in full operation will employ 150 hands. The work of rebuilding, and equipment was completed and the mills started last August. The stock since accumulated was placed on the market last spring by Deering, Milliken & Co., selling agents, New York, and it is expected that they will at once establish the reputation of the Fitchburg Manufacturing Company, as they are extra fine fabrics in original styles.

Messrs. Samuel E. and Adams Crocker, president and treasurer, are both experienced business men.

FITCHBURG FILE WORKS.

F. C. and W. E. Culley, Proprietors—Manufacturers of Hand-cut Files—Works and Office, Newton Place.

The late Eli Culley, father of F. C. and W. E. Culley, began the manufacture of files on a small scale at North Weymouth in 1864, removing in 1868 to the city of Fitchburg, where he built up a flourishing business. Dying in April, 1890, his sons succeeded to the management and have greatly increased facilities and enlarged transactions, introducing improved modern methods in all departments, mechanical and commercial. The works, situated in a commodious building in Newton place, occupy space 100x60 feet, two and one-half stories high, connected with which is a grinding room at the rear. The equipment of machinery and special tools is first-class and comprehensive, and from forty to fifty experienced and competent workmen are regularly employed, turning out a superior grade of hand-cut files of all sizes, shapes and degrees of fineness, suitable for every conceivable purpose. These goods rank with the best and most popular on the market, and are sold by the trade throughout New England, the Middle States and the South. These are the oldest file works in this part of the country; their output has an established reputation, and the course of the concern is such as to secure and retain the confidence of all interested in this particular class of implements.

ORSWELL MILLS.

W. N. Orswell, President; W. F. Stiles, Treasurer—Manufacturers of Cotton Yarns, —River Street, West Fitchburg.

Cotton yarn is a staple product for which there is at all times a good market, and among the most extensive manufacturers are the Orswell Mills, established and incorporated in 1886 and owning the largest plant of the kind in the State outside of Fall River and New Bedford. The capital stock of the company, of which the heaviest owner is Mr. C. T. Crocker, is $100,000. Mr. W. M. Orswell, the president, is a native of Rhode Island, a practical spinner, and has been long identified with the cotton yarn industry in various parts of New England.

As they now stand the mills represent an investment of about a half million dollars and comprise an immense four-story brick structure, 80x351 feet, fitted up with seven enormous boilers 72 inches by 20 feet each, engines aggregating 1000 horse-power, 24,000 spindles for spinning and 6000 for twisting, ten sets of cards and all modern improvements in methods and appliances. About 220 operatives are employed, and the output, embracing cotton yarns from No. 20 to 50, single-twisted and warp, will average 30,000 pounds per week, at an aggregate value of $360,000. Hitherto every pound of these yarns has been consumed by some of the twenty-five cotton mills who are regular customers, but the plant and buildings are about to be enlarged for the accommodation of 10,000 additional spindles, and the work will be pushed to early consummation, when the company hopes to keep up with its orders. Situated on River street convenient to the railroad, and provided with superior facilities in all departments, the Orswell mills is one of the most prosperous and desirable manufacturing properties in this part of Massachusetts.

EZEKIEL DAVIS,

Manufacturer of Paper Mill Bars and Bed Plates, Wood and Leather Working Knives—Phillips' Brook, West Fitchburg.

Manufacturers of paper are interested in securing for their mills the very best procurable appliances. The same rule holds good with planing mills, consequently these classes of industrial representatives will be more than ordinarily interested in this article. The paper mill bars and bed plates made by Mr. Ezekiel Davis of West Fitchburg have been practically tested for the past decade in the mills of this and adjoining States, and have rendered uniform satisfaction, as have his rag cutter and trimming knives and his machine knives for use in planing and moulding mills, logwood, veneer, shingle and leather-splitting knives. Only the finest material and most expert workmanship enter into the construction of these devices as made by Mr. Davis, and his reputation is established upon an enduring basis. His shop on Phillips' brook is of stone, one story in height, 35x125 feet, contains a comprehensive equipment of appropriate tools and machinery, and gives employment to a number of competent workmen. Orders are promptly filled and satisfaction guaranteed.

Mr. Davis, born in New Hampshire, came to Fitchburg in 1853—nearly thirty-eight years ago. For twenty years he was employed in a responsible capacity by the Whitman & Miles Manufacturing Company, then established himself in business on his own account. He is a courteous gentleman and upright man.

BEOLI MILLS.

James Phillips, Jr., Proprietor; James Pierce, Superintendent—Manufacturers of Worsted Goods—West Fitchburg; P. O. Address, Fitchburg.

The Boeli worsted mills, situated on River street, West Fitchburg, were completed and started in April, 1871. The buildings are all of brick, and comprise the mill proper, two stories, 60x300 feet; weave shed, one story, 65x200 feet; second weave shed, three stories, 35x100 feet, with 35x70 foot L, dry-house 50x115 feet; burling-room, sorting-room, picker-room, two stock-rooms and boiler house, the whole lighted by electricity and protected by a system of automatic sprinklers. A description of the machinery and appliances would be tedious; suffice it to say that it includes 150 broad looms and that engines aggregating 300 horse-power and a 35-horse-power breast wheel, taking water from the north branch of the Nashua river, are required to drive the pickers, cards, looms, etc. Four hundred people are employed about the premises, and the output averages about 600,000 yards of fine worsted suitings annually, of the value of $1,200,000. The quality of these goods makes them very popular with the merchant tailoring trade especially. They were awarded a gold medal at the Philadelphia centennial exposition of 1876 for "worsted suitings unsurpassed for quality and beauty of style." Messrs. Oelbermann, Dommerick & Co., of New York are the selling agents, and the New York, New England and western trade are the principal purchasers. James Phillips, jr., is proprietor of this superb plant.

THE TOWN OF CLINTON.

CLINTON, originally a part of Lancaster, was incorporated as a town in March, 1850. In area it covers 4,907 acres, and owes its early settlement to the fine water power afforded by the north branch of the Nashua and South Meadow brook, which, uniting here, form the Nashua river. The falls of the latter stream were especially inviting, and here John Prescott erected and completed in 1654 the first grist mill west of the Sudbury river—the germ from which sprang her present varied industries. Horn comb making was introduced at the beginning of this century, and a cotton mill was erected in 1809. The Lancaster Cotton Company was incorporated in 1821, and was succeeded in 1838 by the Clinton Company, of which H. N. and E. B. Bigelow were the ruling spirits. The latter perfected his Brussels carpet loom in 1849, and the brothers then started for themselves. The Worcester & Nashua railroad was opened November 5, 1847. The town (then called Clintonville) was incorporated in March, 1850; population about 3,000. From that time growth was rapid and substantial. The village is provided with water works, gas and electric lights, and contains a population of 10,379.

BIGELOW CARPET COMPANY.

James H. Beal, President; Charles F. Fairbanks, Treasurer; C. B. Bigelow, Manufacturers' Agent; William B. Kendall, Selling Agent; E. W. Burdett, Paymaster—Manufacturers of Wilton, Axminster and Brussels Carpets and Worsted and Woolen Yarns—Cor. South and Main Streets.

The Bigelow Carpet Company ranks with the most famous representatives of that important industry in this country. The enterprise had its inception in 1849, when E. B. and H. N. Bigelow and H. P. Fairbanks began on a modest scale the manufacture of carpets in Clinton. Mr. E. B. Bigelow constructed the first power carpet loom in the world, continued to improve upon that class of machinery, and may be fairly pronounced the founder of the carpet industry at this point. The present company, backed by ample capital, which has been increased from time to time, was incorporated in 1854. With the growth of trade and increase of demand the facilities of manufacture have been steadily augmented until at this time these are among the largest works of the kind in the United States, comprising several one and four-story brick buildings that cover 460,000 square feet of ground. The equipment of machinery and appliances includes every improved device of value, together with all necessary conveniences in the various departments of carding, combing, spinning, twisting, dyeing and weaving. Three 200-horse-power steam engines drive the machinery, and from 1100 to 1200 hands are employed, many of whom live in tenements belonging to the company. Every part of carpet-making is carried on here, from the preparation of the wool for yarns and worsteds, through the processes of combing, carding, spinning, dyeing and weaving, up to the time the goods are ready for market. Designing is a specialty, the company employing its own artists, and the original patterns of Wiltons, Axminsters and Brussels carpets made here compete successfully with the products of any similar mills in this country. The company also makes yarns in great variety for the trade at large.

J. B. PARKER MACHINE COMPANY,

Manufacturers of the Bancroft Mule, the Clinton Yarn Twister, and All Kinds of Carpet Machinery — Model and Pattern Makers — A. C. Dakin, President; C. C. Murdock, Treasurer—Sterling Street, near Depot.

The accompanying cut represents the J. B. Parker Machine Company's Clinton yarn twister

10

made to run in one, two or four sections, according to the number of spindles, each section

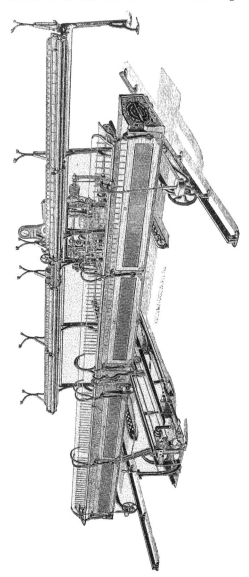

running entirely independent of the others, the whole machine being operated with one belt. Different kinds of yarn can be twisted at the same time, and a different twist put into each section. One section of the twister only need be run to twist a small quantity of yarn, and in doffing, or when the yarn breaks, only one section need be stopped at a time. Drums are provided for twisting from jack spools, or a creel suitable for two, three or four-ply yarns, or all, as may be desired. The spindle is an improved one, with a superior bearing, in an adjustable spindle stand. Looping and knotting attachments are put on when required. The stocking yarn twister has an automatic clock attachment, which stops each section by itself, when the necessary number of yards for a skein are wound onto the spool. This clock can be set so as to make the skeins contain anywhere from 50 to 500 yards. Attention is also invited to the same company's Bancroft improved woolen mule. The main features of this machine are the same as heretofore, viz: a steel race shaft instead of a race belt, and flexible iron chains instead of ropes, which, together with a great many improvements which have been made from time to time, to give strength where it is required and insure perfect work, renders it as near a perfect mule for spinning all kinds of yarn, from the coarsest to the finest, as can be made. Among recent improvements of value is the new builder, the improved spindle with a straight foot, and an attachment for running the spindles the other way, for making left-handed twist, without changing the bands. Every part of the machine is built in the most thorough and substantial manner, and there being no ropes or belts to wear out, the outlay for repairs is very small. Satisfaction is guaranteed. They also make to order a great variety of other ingenious labor and time-saving devices for the use of woolen and carpet manufacturers, together with working models and patterns for machinery of all kinds. These works were founded in 1853 by J. B. Parker & Co., and have always enjoyed a high reputation for the character and extent of their products. The present company was incorporated in 1875, capital $45,000. All of the officers named above are natives of Massachusetts and practical workmen. They are all connected also with the Clinton Foundry Company, and President Dakin is a director of the First National Bank of Clinton. The company's shops are situated in the large two-story brick building, 35 x 100 feet, on Sterling street near the railroad depot, of which they occupy one floor and an L 35 x 70 feet, the whole fitted up with the best iron-working appliances and a twenty-five horse-power steam engine. In all fifty expert mechanics and assistants are employed, and a flourishing business is transacted, the output going wherever woolen textiles, and especially carpets, are made. ¶

CLINTON WIRE CLOTH COMPANY.

James H. Beal, President; Charles F. Fairbanks, Secretary and Treasurer; Charles Swinscoe, Manager; H. J. Brown, Superintendent—Manufacturers of Power Loom Wire Cloth, Galvanized Hex. Nettings, "Clinton" Wire Lath, Perforated Metals, etc.—Sterling St., near Depot; Branches: Boston, New York, Chicago.

The Clinton Wire Cloth Company, incorporated in 1856, commenced operations on a small scale, but its affairs were wisely managed from the start, and now, after thirty-four years of almost uninterrupted prosperity, the works, representing an investment of $600,000, are easily the largest, most complete and most valuable of the kind on the globe, comprising eight distinct one, two and three-story brick mills, covering 200,000 square feet of ground, with a massive eight-story tower, 185 feet tall, in front. The equipment is in keeping with the buildings, comprising the best and latest improved wire-working and perforating machinery in great variety, driven by four steam engines aggregating 400 horse-power. From 400 to 500 people find employment here, and the output is enormous in volume and value, comprising every description of wire cloth and nettings, such as bolting mills, fanning mills, malt kiln, threshing machines, cheese safes, flax sieves, meal sieves, riddle bottoms, coal screens, flour sieves, milk strainers, rag dusters, coffee roasters, foundry riddles, oat sieves, sand screens, cotton dryers, fruit dryers, ore screens, wool dryers, cotton dusters, putty sieves, locomotive stacks, Clinton painted window screen cloths, Clinton galvanized wire cloth, Clinton patent twist warp wire lath, brass and copper wire cloth, Clinton patent galvanized fencing, tin-plated wire cloth, Clinton galvanized hex. nettings, perforated metals, poultry netting, croquet and lawn tennis netting, etc., which are handled in vast quantities and find a ready market everywhere in this and foreign countries. The principal office of the company is at the mills, Sterling street, Clinton. Branch offices and salesrooms are located at No. 199 Washington street, Boston; No. 76 Beekman street, New York, and No. 137 Lake street, Chicago.

THE LANCASTER MILLS.

W. R. Robeson, President; Harcourt Amory, Treasurer; G. W. Weeks, Agent; George P. Taylor, Superintendent; J. A. Morgan, Paymaster —Manufacturers of Ginghams—Green Street.

The Lancaster gingham mills date from 1845, and may be said to have "grown up with the country." The present company was incorporated in 1844 with $800,000 capital. At that time the plant contained 240 looms, three water wheels of 225 combined horse-power, and a 225-horse-power steam engine, and employed 900 hands, producing 400,000 yards of goods annually. The development since then has been wonderful, as is shown by the fact that the buildings, all brick, furnish seventeen acres of floor space—one floor alone being four acres in area. There are 2800 looms driven by improved turbine water wheels supplying 900 horse-power and steam engines of 1560 horse-power; 2000 operatives earn a livelihood on the premises, and last year the output aggregated 28,000,000 yards, which were disposed of in the American markets. Ginghams alone are produced, and the goods are of the best grades. The officers are named in our caption, and are representative citizens. Agent Weeks, who has held that position for twelve years, is a director of the First National Bank.

THE TOWN OF MILFORD.

MILFORD, formerly a part of Mendon, was organized as the "Easterly Precinct" of that town January 18, 1742, and incorporated under its present name April 11, 1780 ; population at that time, 750. It was a farming community, with only one grist and one sawmill and two or three small private fulling mills for the finishing of home-made woolens. There were eight school districts in 1784 ; now there are seventeen common schools and a high school, with a combined attendance of nearly or quite 2000. The town library was established in 1858. The town of Hopedale was set apart from Milford territory in 1886, and carried with it about 1300 of the population, which by last years' census numbers 8,769.

MILFORD PINK GRANITE COMPANY.

I. F. Woodbury, President; George E. Leighton, Secretary; A. W. Eames, Treasurer—Quarrymen—Office, East Main Street; Boston Office, No. 164 Devonshire Street.

BOSTON PUBLIC LIBRARY BUILDING.

The celebrated pink granite found in this vicinity is justly regarded with favor by architects and builders who have had practical experience with it. The stone is worked as easily and economically as any other good granite, is susceptible of a very high polish, and in appearance is exceedingly attractive, the faint pink tint having a charming effect. Some of the finest new buildings in the State—notably the Boston public library and the Elliott church at Newton—are constructed of the superb material furnished by this company, and it is fast coming into general use. The leading quarriers of this stone are the Milford Pink Granite Company, who own fifty acres of choice quarry land near Milford village, with office on East Main street. Their equipment of machinery, derricks and steam power is complete, and they give employment to from two hundred and fifty to three hundred hands, including quarrymen, granite cutters, laborers, etc. A spur track from the Boston & Albany railroad (Milford branch) connects the quarries with the main line, and all necessary facilities are provided for handling the output with dispatch. Sales are steadily increasing, and shipments are being made to principal points in New England and the Middle Atlantic States.

President Woodbury and Secretary Leighton compose the famous Boston firm of building contractors, Woodbury & Leighton. Treasurer Eames is a resident of Ashland, but is present at the office and quarries, superintending operations, almost daily. The company was organized in 1887 and incorporated the next year. They furnished the cut granite for the Boston library building, shown in our cut, and are prepared to fill orders to any extent for Milford pink granite. Correspondence is invited, estimates made, and contracts solicited. This company was the recipient of the highest award from the Massachusetts Charitable Mechanics Association, at its last exposition, for beauty and fineness of granite. The company's Boston office is at No. 164 Devonshire street.

C. A. SUMNER,

Manufacturer of Shoe Racks, Shoe Trees, Boot Trees, Crimping Forms, Brakes and Screws—Nos. 185 and 187 Central Street.

Of the numerous devices employed in the boot and shoe industry none are in greater or more constant request than properly made racks, trees, crimping forms, brakes and screws. One of the few successful establishments devoted to supplying these articles to the trade is located in Milford, Mass., Nos. 185 and 187 Central street, and was founded in 1868 by E. Mann & Howard, who were succeeded by E. Mann. In 1879 Mr. C. A. Sumner bought the plant, and in 1881 bought and added the business of S. Jefferds of Milford, made various improvements in buildings and appliances, put new life and new ideas into the business, and has since conducted it upon correct methods, the result being that he enjoys an excellent reputation and a prosperous trade that embraces the entire United States and Great Britain. His factory, fitted up with late improved machinery and all requisite appliances, is situated on Central street, and occupies one floor 40x70 feet, with attic above of the same dimensions, with

which are connected spacious stock and storage rooms. From eight to twelve expert workmen are employed, and the output is very large and valuable. Herewith is printed a cut exhibiting Mr. Sumner's shoe rack for factory use, which commends itself at a glance. His other products are of a like recognized grade of excellence as regards design and workmanship.

HOTEL WILLIAM.

J. H. Matthews, Proprietor—Main Street.

This hotel is conveniently situated with reference to the business centre of the village and all points of interest, and is in all respects one of the best and most attractive hostelries

in southeastern Worcester. The building an ornate four-story brick structure 50x110 feet, was erected in 1886 and first occupied in 1887, and is consequently new and modern in all its appointments, containing on the ground floor a handsome office, reading-room, pool and billiard rooms, sumptuous parlors, and large and lofty dining-room, while up stairs are forty commodious, airy and tastefully furnished sleeping apartments, each connected with the office by means of electric annunciators and speaking tubes. Steam heat, gas and electric lights still further contribute to the ease and comfort of guests, while a neat barber-shop and livery stable in connection will be appreciated. A free omnibus conveys guests to and from departing and arriving trains. As to the table, suffice it to say that every substantial and luxury in season is provided in abundance, temptingly prepared by a skilful *chef*, and served by tidy and courteous waiters. Rates very reasonable—$2.00 to $2.50 per day.

Mine Host Matthews is a native of New Hampshire, and for twenty years has been managing hotels in that State, Vermont and Massachusetts. Elderly, polite, kindly and hospitable, he is the *beau ideal* of a good landlord.

JOHN F. HASKELL,

Livery, Boarding, Teaming and Exchange Stable—Central Street.

A properly conducted public stable is a universally recognized convenience, and is almost always well supported by the community in which it is located. Such a one is that of Mr. John F. Haskell, on Central street, Milford. It was established in 1882 by Amasa L. Smith, to whom Mr. A. Smith succeeded in 1888. In 1889 Mr. J. F. Haskell succeeded to the property and stock. He has made many improvements, and the stables are now of the first-class. The building is a two-story frame, 60x120 feet, well fitted up and thoroughly drained, provided with a large number of stalls, storage for carriages, feed, etc. He keeps twenty-five horses of his own for hire, and has besides a considerable number of regular and transient boarders, single feeds being provided when desired. He has also thirty vehicles of all kinds, among them several elegant double and single carriages and buggies, and is prepared to furnish turnouts for pleasure driving or business purposes whenever required. He has six men in his employ, of whom several are skillful and careful drivers, well acquainted with the country for many miles around. A specialty is made of teaming and jobbing, and parties having hauling to do cannot entrust it to better hands.

Mr. Haskell is a native of Pawtucket, R. I., and was for several years engaged in the teaming hereabouts previous to his present venture. He is industrious, courteous and enterprising, and is building up a large and prosperous business.

IRVING E. JONES,

Manufacturer jof Builders' Trimmings, Store and Office Fixtures, Cabinet Work, etc.—Eastman's Steam Mill, Central Street.

Mr. Jones is a skilled practical wood-worker, a native of Milford, and, previous to becoming proprietor of this mill in 1890, was for several years superintendent for his predecessor. The plant comprises a two-story frame building 35x60 feet, fitted up with appropriate sawing, planing, turning and other woodworking machinery, driven by steam power. A competent force of expert mechanics is employed, and a very considerable amount of fine store and office fixtures, builders' trimmings, cabinet and other intricate and artistic woodwork is produced, pattern-making of the highest order forming a notable specialty. Mr. Jones has a large and growing patronage from builders, joiners, foundrymen and others in this and adjoining New England States. His methods are upright and straightforward; accuracy and promptitude characterize the execution of all orders, and the greatest care is taken to render unvarying satisfaction.

MANSION HOUSE.

Hapgood & Mayhew, Proprietors—Main Street.

The Mansion House, established in 1872 by Lewis Fisher, is the leading hotel of Milford, and one of the best of its class in the State, being a modern four-story frame structure, of hospitable and attractive appearance, 100 feet front by 150 feet deep, with broad shady piazzas in front and at the sides. On the ground floor front are the office, reading-room, parlors for the use of the public, etc , in the center a spacious, lofty and inviting dining hall, and at the rear the pantries and kitchen. Up stairs are the private parlors and sixty tastily furnished, cosy, well-lighted and comfortable sleeping apartments, arranged singly and *ensuite*, while the house is supplied throughout with hot and cold water, steam heat, gas and all desir-  able conveniences. The table is first-class, as are all the appointments, and tourists and travelers on business or for pleasure will find a stay here enjoyable, a shady square in front affording coolness and a pleasant strolling ground in summer. A large and well-kept stable in the rear is well equipped with horses and vehicles for hire, and private turnouts are boarded on reasonable terms. A specialty is made of catering to the wants of commercial travelers.

Mr. S. E. Hapgood is a native of Maine, Mr. J. S. Mayhew was born in Milford.

T. N. SHERMAN & CO.,

Quarriers of and Dealers in Granite and Building Stone—Quarries, Cedar Street, Milford ; Office, Braggsville.

The pink granite quarries of this vicinity are of great extent and value, while the output steadily grows in popularity with builders, architects and those who contemplate the erection of public and private edifices of all kinds. Among the leading producers is the firm of T. N. Sherman & Co., established in 1882, who own thirty-five acres of quarries, all equipments for quarrying stone, employ from twenty to thirty men, and ship heavily to all points in this and adjoining States, doing a steadily increasing business.

Mr. Sherman is an enterprising, progressive and successful business man, well and favorably known to the building trade. Orders are promptly and carefully filled to any extent. Mr. M. T. Philp is a partner with Mr. Sherman, and has had large experience in the granite business.

F. W. MANN,

Machinist—Light and Heavy Machine Jobbing, Manufacturer of Special Machinery and Tools to Order, Shafting, Pulleys, Hangers and Gearing—Mann's. Patent Bone Cutter—Dealer in Steam and Gas Piping—No. 70 Central Street.

These shops were originally started in 1877 by a Mr. Willard, who retired in 1880, when Craig & Severance became proprietors. Chapman & Mann purchased the plant in 1886, and

Mr. Chapman withdrew in 1887, since which time Mr. F. W. Mann has successfully managed the business alone. The works comprise a three-story frame building 30x40 feet, provided with a complete outfit of iron-working machinery and a powerful electric motor. Eight skilled workmen earn a livelihood in the several departments and the output is quite large, embracing every description of light and heavy machine jobbing, the construction of special machinery and tools to order, and the building of Mann's patent bone-cutter for poultry food. This latter device, which is faithfully represented by the above engraving, meets fully the requirements of poultry-raisers for an implement that will rapidly reduce beef-bones direct from the market to the form of poultry food.

Mr. E. L. Willis, the leading photographer of Milford, brought to Mr. Mann's notice the long-felt want among poultry men for a hand machine to grind up fresh bones, and showed how every machine then manufactured was entirely impracticable for that purpose. In accordance with this, Mr. Mann and his foreman, Mr. Clarence Farrington, invented and built a machine which was constructed upon the principle of cutting or planing the bones instead of grinding or crushing them. It was a venture to put sharp steel knives in a machine against the hard flinty bones, but the inventors saw there was no other way that offered hopes of success. The first machine, although very imperfect, proved conclusively that the knives would not break and that they would remain sharp for six or eight weeks of constant use. It also proved that the machine would not clog. With such marked encouragement, Mr. Mann placed his shop and his private capital at the disposal of the bone-cutter invention. By the aid of Mr. Farrington he was able after scores of alterations and improvements extending from September, 1888, to June, 1890, to bring on to the market a thoroughly practical and reliable machine for reducing green bones, meat and gristle by hand power to poultry food. The machines were sold in numbers during the time of their improvement, and in this way a practical and tested machine was produced. The important and final change was made during May, 1890, since which time hundreds have been sold and no cause for further alteration found necessary. Three sizes of power machines and five styles for hand driving are built. Patented June 15, '86, Aug. 20, '89; Canada, patented June 12, 1890. It has been awarded a diploma by the Attleboro Agricultural Association, a certificate of merit by the Bay State Agricultural Society, two Toronto (Canada,) bronze medals and diplomas, and a bronze medal from the Massachusetts Charitable Mechanics Association, Boston, with numerous marks of approval from other sources.

Mr. Mann was born at Norfolk, Mass. He received a four years' course at Cornell University and graduated as a mechanical engineer, class of '78.

HOPEDALE.

HOPEDALE is the newest of Worcester's galaxy of towns, incorporated April 7, 1886 ; area, 3,547 acres ; population, 1176. It was formerly a part of Mendon. Mill river supplies excellent water power. The town owes its existence to the "Hopedale Community," a body of religious total abstainers who undertook to live and prosper according to the gospel of Christianity as they understood it. Ebenezer D. Draper was president in 1856 ; the treasurers' report for the preceding year showed a deficit, and it was decided to wind up the affairs of the community. Messrs. Ebenezer D. and George Draper then took control of the property, and, being enterprising, energetic, public-spirited and liberal business men, soon changed the course of things and made a prosperous and successful manufacturing village of what had been a humdrum hamlet of unpractical cranks.

GEORGE DRAPER & SONS,

Manufacturers of Cotton Mill Machinery—Selling Agents for the Hopedale Machine Co., the Dutcher Temple Co., the Hopedale Machine Screw Co., and the Elastic Goods Co.—Works and Office, Hopedale.

The industries of Hopedale have been built up during the last fifty years by the Draper family and their associates, now represented by the firm of Geo. Draper & Sons and the various companies they are interested in.

This family has been connected with the development, improvement and manufacture of cotton machinery for the last seventy-five years. The present standing of the firm in the manufacturing world is due largely to the enterprise and ability of the late George Draper. The business of the firm is peculiar in the respect that it sells or manufactures no products not covered by patents, and for years it has had an exclusive field in several lines of cotton machinery. Some of the improvements introduced have been of extraordinary value to the manufacturing public, and have been sold in enormous quantities. The latter fact is best shown by the records, which tell that in the last twenty years George Draper & Sons have sold eight million spindles, seven million spinning rings, four million separators. They are chiefly known as the introducers of the Rabbeth spindle, the Sawyer spindle, and the double adjustable spinning ring. The list of inventions brought into use by them, however, if given in its entirety, would be tedious from length. The Hopedale Machine Company manufactures a large proportion of the machinery sold by George Draper & Sons, and has a large, well-equipped plant, producing twister warpers, spoolers, reels and other cotton machines, and never make anything but the best. This is a Massachusetts corporation, with $400,000 capital stock. The Dutcher Temple Company is the result of the association of the late Warren W. Dutcher with Hopedale parties as far back as 1856. This company manufactures loom temples of all varieties and special machine work. The works are fitted up in an unexcelled manner, and the products control their field. George Draper & Sons are the selling agents. The Hopedale Machine Screw Company is but a few years old, but has taken a leading position in the production of machine screws and special turned work. It does business with the principal electrical companies, and uses special patented automatic machinery. The Hopedale Elastic Goods Company has a large plant filled with the most modern machinery, and produces all sorts of silk and cotton elastic fabrics, shoe gorings, etc. The present company was incorporated this year—1891.

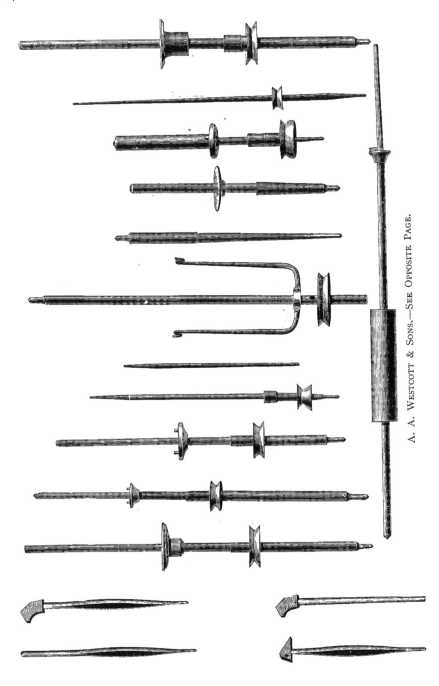

A. A. WESTCOTT & SONS.—SEE OPPOSITE PAGE.

A. A. WESTCOTT & SONS,

Manufacturers of Spindles, Steps, Bolsters, Shuttle Irons, etc., of Every Description.

Spinners generally do not require to be reminded of the importance of procuring the best appliances that human skill and ingenuity can devise, for in their business serious losses often result from apparently trifling causes. Once informed where the best is procurable, self-interest will indicate the course to pursue. Mr. A. A. Westcott, who has had nearly forty years' practical experience in the selection of material and the manufacture of spinners' requisites of the more delicate kind, established a business on his own account at North Scituate, R. I., in 1869, and soon secured an encouraging patronage, but there were some obstacles to contend with at that point, and in 1871, having purchased a mill-site and water privilege about a mile distant from Hopedale village, he erected a branch shop there, continuing the North Scituate establishment until 1874, when he removed and consolidated his business at Hopedale. Considerable additions and improvements have since been made; and his works and appurtenances are now quite extensive, the buildings, three in number, respectively 30 x 150 and 25 x 25 feet, being of stone and brick, an adjoining brick structure 20 x 40 feet containing a boiler and 60-horse-power steam engine. The river at this point has an eight or nine-foot fall, and additional power is obtained from that source when required. Mr. Westcott in 1882 admitted to copartnership his sons, Augustus W. and Wilmarth A., when the present style was adopted. A younger son — David — entered the firm in January, 1889. The firm employ from thirty to fifty expert and experienced mechanics, and every article made on the premises is of the highest order. Messrs. A. A. Westcott & Sons' specialties embrace only the choicest grades of ring, mule, spooler, twister, winder, silk and other varieties of spindles, steps and bolsters, shuttle irons, etc. Attention is also given to repairs of these devices, and satisfaction is guaranteed patrons in every instance. One of the best evidences of the skill and reliability of this concern is found in the fact that all the Sawyer and Rabbeth spindles handled by George Draper & Sons are made here.

THE TOWN OF WINCHENDON.

ASHBURNHAM, Winchendon and Royalston are the three northern towns of Worcester county, bordering upon New Hampshire. Winchendon, in the center, has an area of about thirty-six square miles, Gardner and Templeton forming her southern boundary. The surface is hilly and rocky, and Miller's

river, the principal stream, winds its mazy course for some fifteen miles within the town.

June 14, 1764, the town, previously called Ipswich Canada, was incorporated under its present name. Agriculture is only moderately profitable.   The manufacture of woodenware is the leading industry, and is carried on upon a colossal scale.   But there are other important interests, such as the construction of machinery, the making of hardware, the weaving of cotton and woolen goods, etc. Of banks there are two—the Winchendon National Bank, capital $150,000, and the Winchendon Savings Bank, chartered 1854.

Winchendon is connected with "the rest of mankind" by the Cheshire, the Ware River, the Monadnock, and the Worcester division of the Fitchburg railroads.

MORTON E. CONVERSE & CO.,

Manufacturers of Reed Furniture and Toys.

This firm, composed of Messrs. Morton E. and Alfred C. Converse, enjoys a wide and well-earned reputation for enterprise and business ability, as well as for upright methods and liberality.

Theirs is the largest manufactory of wood toys in the world.   Both partners are natives of New Hampshire and richly endowed with energy, industry and ingenuity, those ruling characteristics of the genuine Yankee. The house was founded by Mason & Converse, who in 1878 began making toys in a small way at Waterville, a suburb of Winchendon, subsequently removing to the present location.   In 1883 the style was changed to the Converse Toy and Woodware Company, and finally, in 1885, the present style was adopted—Morton E. Converse & Co. The works occupy three adjoining frame buildings—two each 40 x 100 feet, one of these three, the other of four stories, connected by bridges and shafting for the transmission of power—and one building about 50 x 60 feet, three stories; adjoining there are two frame warehouses, each about 28 x 80 feet; also a brick boiler and engine-house, a fifty-horse-power steam engine driving a complement of the most approved machinery for their business, including numerous unique manufacturing devices not found elsewhere, the firm owning the patents and controlling their construction.   The working force ranges from 150 to 200, many of whom are mechanics of rare skill and ingenuity. Messrs. Morton E. Converse & Co. manufacture a comprehensive line of rattan and reed chairs in standard and orginal styles that embraces all the popular goods of that kind, besides a constant succession of novelties, especially in children's reed goods, children's furniture, toys, toy trunks and toy military drums.   These goods are made in various material and style; drums in embossed gold, brass or nickel-plated, drums with fancy cord, hook and sling complete in six sizes; Prussian rod drums in six sizes; children's blackboards in a variety of styles; children's games, children's furniture, children's and dolls' chairs and swings, children's wash sets, folding tables and chairs, dolls' bedsteads and cribs.   They are also manufacturers of the celebrated bean bag game of Faba Baga, made under special patent owned by this firm.   Catalogues and price-lists—the former fully illustrated by engravings — are mailed to the trade on application. The New York store is at No. 21 Park place; Willard & McKee, selling agents.

THE HIGHLANDS.

A Family Home for the Treatment of Nervous and Mental Diseases — Founded by Dr. Ira Russell; Dr. Frederick W. Russell, Proprietor.

This home for nervous and mental invalids was instituted in 1875 by the late Dr. Ira Russell, an ex-army surgeon, an acknowledged authority on the troubles indicated, widely known to, and of high rank in, his profession. His theory — and it has worked to a charm in actual practice — was to allow the patient the comforts of home life and the greatest possible liberty compatible with security. His experiments were carefully noted and .the results indorsed by physicians and philanthropists all over the civilized globe, and thus The Highlands became famous. His son, Dr. Frederick W. Russell, was his father's assistant from the first; and upon the founder's death succeeded to the responsibilities and cares of the management. Dr. Russell has made the diseases named his special study from early manhood, has written much and well upon the subject, and is a celebrated and accepted authority. The home is beautifully situated upon an eminence that commands a magnificent view of the Miller's river valley, the town of Winchendon, and a grand mountain range that embraces the far-famed Wachusett and Monadnock. The buildings are very handsome, and, like the surroundings, cheerful and bright, tending to banish gloomy thoughts and depression of spirit. The furnishings are in keeping, while the appliances for entertainment and amusement include a piano-room, billiard-room, bowling saloon, croquet and tennis courts, etc. Ample stables are provided, and patients may have their own private equipages whenever desired. We regret that our. space. forbids going into particulars, but those interested are referred to Dr. Russell, who will cheerfully furnish any desired information. Letters of inquiry should be addressed to Winchendon.

PIPER & BOSWORTH,

Manufacturers of Electric Axes, Hammers, Hatchets, etc.—Piper's Grove.

This is a bran new enterprise, established in September last, and gives promise from the start of unusual success, since the goods made are in universal demand for domestic purposes, cheap, useful and durable, and cannot fail to sell "like hot cakes." The works include a two-story frame machine-shop 24 x 60 feet, and one-story foundry 18 x 25 feet, also frame. Mr. Piper's residence is near by.   The machinery plant is complete and is driven by a fifty-horse-power steam engine, power being obtained from the same source to operate the dynamos of the village electric light plant.   At their works a competent force of hands is employed, and they are producing large quantities of specialties for the New England and western markets. The "electric" ax and hatchet are ingenious combinations of cast-iron and steel and are really valuable additions to household economy, as are the hammers, ice-picks and non-heating stove-hooks made here. Another specialty is the improved carpenter's saw-clamp, which sells at sight. Prompt attention is given to orders for the filing, setting and jointing of saws, the work done in the best manner and returned by express or otherwise as directed.

ALVIN STREETER,

Manufacturer of Improved Woodworking Machinery—Front Street.

Mr. Alvin Streeter ranks with the most successful and famous inventors, improvers and constructors of woodworking machinery, and his product in one form or another is found working satisfactorily in nearly every prominent planing mill, carriage, sash, blind, door and woodenware factory in America.   Mr. Streeter has had long experience in this branch of manufacturing, and for some years was at the head of a similar concern at Marlboro, removing to and establishing himself in Winchendon in 1874.   Here he occupies one floor, 25 x 45 feet, fronting on Front street, employs eight skilled mechanics and a splendid equipment of modern iron and steel-working machinery, and manufactures a choice line of woodworking devices, designed or improved to the point of perfection by himself, embracing machinery for the use of manufacturers of butter tubs, fish kits, pail handles, clothes-pins, wood spoons, oval and nest boxes, wooden measures, etc., his leading specialties comprising improved cylinder planers, upright horizontal boring machines, clothes-pin and pail-handle lathes (the latter provided with improved twist bits for boring pail-handles, spool-blocks, and for similar work).   The improved panel or surface cylinder planer shown in our first cut is adapted to all kinds of work from one-sixteenth of an inch to eight inches thick, planing smooth. It is made with reversible feed, from the best iron and steel, and can be regulated by means of cone pulleys to any desired speed, while the appliances for changing the thickness (raising and lowering bed) are novel and unequaled for accuracy and convenience. Every machine is finished in the best style, belted up, tested and put in complete running order previous to shipment. The cylinders are of cast steel and can be safely driven at a speed of 4000 or 4500 revolutions per minute. There are seven sizes, from twelve to twenty-four inches wide and weighing from 500 to 1400 pounds, ranging from $150 to $325 in price.   Of planers not provided with the reversible feed eleven sizes, twelve to twenty-four inches wide, are made — prices $135 to $450. Pressure bars are attached to the above

planers for—eighteen inches, $25; twenty inches, $28; twenty-four inches, $35.   In addition to the machines already referred to Mr. Streeter

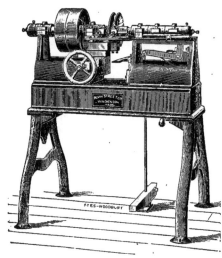

builds a superior buzz planer, sixteen inches wide; price, $200. Our second cut shows Streeter's improved horizontal boring machine; price, $110. The upright boring machine, of the same general excellence, is sold at the same price. Our third cut presents a view of Streeter's improved tub or pail bottom cutter, which commends itself at sight to all interested in this· class of machinery. It is simple in form, strong, substantial and accurate, and of remarkable capacity, cutting round heads of every description and turning out pail bottoms at the rate of 5500 in ten hours. Mr. Streeter also manufactures a wonderful automatic pail-handle lathe that will turn ready for use 30,000 to 40,000 handles per day. Price, $375. The machinery named above forms only a portion of Mr. · Streeter's specialties, which include a full line of the latest and best appliances for the making of tubs, pails, cane and wood-seat chairs, etc. Catalogue and price-list sent on application. Mr. Streeter, a native of Fitzwilliam, N. H., is a practical machinist and works at the bench daily besides managing a large and growing business.

G. N. GOODSPEED,

Manufacturer of Woodworking Machinery — No. 2 Front Street.

Parties interested in woodworking will consult their own interest by calling upon or communicating with Mr. G. N. Goodspeed, who for the past forty-one years has been engaged in designing, improving and constructing devices for that purpose, his specialties covering a wide range and embracing tub, pail, chair, bobbin and spool machinery, pony planers, back-knife gauge lathes, cylinder stave saws, Stimpson's dovetail machines, etc., of the most approved style and effectiveness. Provided with a comprehensive plant accumulated through a career of many years in this particular branch of industry, Mr. Goodspeed's facilities are first-class and he is enabled to respond without loss of time to any demand made upon him. Superior material, workmanship, accuracy and finish marks every machine built here, while prices are as low as any legitimate builder can afford. This concern was founded in 1849 by Robinson & Goodspeed. In 1851 Goodspeed & Wyman became proprietors, and since 1878 Mr. Goodspeed has managed it alone. The works comprise a two-story building 40 x 120 feet, with 30 x 50-foot blacksmith shop, office, storehouse, dry-house, etc., the whole equipped with all requisite machinery and tools and ample water-power for all the skilled workmen that can be employed. The output is large and valuable, going to all quarters of the globe.

WILLIAM MURDOCK,

Manufacturer of Cotton and Woolen Mill Spools—River Street.

This machine shop, erected by Colonel Murdock in 1831, was the first ever established in Winchendon, has been conducted by the original proprietor during a period of sixty years, and is widely celebrated for the manufacture of superior spools and bobbins for the use of cotton and woolen manufacturers. The bobbin still generally used in the Lawrence and many other representative mills is Mr. Murdock's own invention and manufactured exclusively under his supervision. The machine-shop, situated on River street, is a substantial and convenient frame building of three and-a-half stories, 30 x 65 feet, and is fitted up with a comprehensive equipment of improved machinery, driven by water power. From eight to ten skilled mechanics are kept busy, and the quantities of bobbins and spools turned out are very large, the concern working steadily on orders from mill owners all over the country. Colonel Murdock was born and has passed his whole life in Winchendon, where he is universally known and respected l y all classes.

WM. BROWN'S SONS,

Manufacturers of and Dealers in Pails and Packages for Jelly, Lard, Oysters, Confectionery, etc.—Bullardville.

The late William Brown established these works about 1878, and developed his facilities and trade until at the time of his death, three years ago, he was one of the largest manufacturers of wooden packages in this vicinity. His sons succeeded him in business, and being energetic, enterprising, practical workmen and trained business men, are fast increasing the reputation and adding to the productive capacity of the works — which, by the way, were destroyed by fire last year and entirely rebuilt upon a much more extensive scale than before, besides being completely refitted with modern machinery and appliances of the best kind. The plant is situated upon a tributary of Miller's river, about a mile from the junction of the two streams, the factories comprising three substantial new one-story frame buildings, one of which is a saw-mill 40 x 50 feet, the others the shops, each 32 x 96 feet. Adjoining are the warehouse and office. They buy timber as it stands in the neighborhood, do their own logging, saw their own lumber, and, in a word, control every step of their business, from the forest to the market. They have a steam engine of 100-horse-power, 110-horse water-power, employ eighty hands, and ship annually $50,000 worth of superior pails and packages, principally to New York, Philadelphia, Baltimore, Cincinnati, St. Louis and Chicago packers of jellies, confectionery, oysters, lard, fish, pickles and similar goods. Their output, ranging from a quart oyster pail to a nine-gallon barrel, is of the best quality as regards material and workmanship, and there is ready demand for all they can produce with present facilities—that is, about 2000 pieces daily.

TOWN OF LEOMINSTER.

LEOMINSTER was set aside from the town of Lancaster and incorporated July 4, 1740. The area is 18,602 acres of hill and meadow and fertile valley, full of variety and natural beauty. It is an elevated and delightful region and contains some of the best farming and grass lands in northern Worcester. The educational advantages are excellent, and a fine public library is maintained. Aside from agricultural pursuits there are a number of flourishing industries in the town, the manufacture of combs, shell goods, paper, boots and shoes, leather, leather board, pianos and piano cases, childrens' carriages, toys and games, furniture, shirts, and machinery being the most important. Population, 7,266.

UNION DESK COMPANY.

Arthur B. Curtis, President; A. Frank Curtis, Treasurer; Wm. F. Smith, Superintendent—Manufacturers of Roll Top Desks, Library Tables, Shoe Sample Cases, and General Office Furniture—Factory, Leominster; Salesrooms, No. 104 Sudbury Street, Boston.

The furnishing of a business office nowadays is a serious matter, demanding an appreciation of art, good taste, and the expenditure of considerable money. Among the most important adjuncts are one or more handsome new-style roll-top desks and a library table or two. The roll-top

desk has been developed of late years until, as now constructed by the Union Desk Company, it is a veritable cabinet of conveniences provided with appropriate and handy places for everything required in the management of a mercantile or business house.

This company—Arthur B. Curtis, president; A. Frank Curtis, treasurer; Wm. F. Smith, Superintendent—was organized in 1889, capital, $25,000, the same gentlemen having been in business as copartners for five years previously. The factory at Leominster is a model establishment, domiciled in a fine two-story building 60x125 feet, and equipped with the latest and best improved woodworking machinery, driven by a forty-horse-power steam engine. Thirty skilled hands are kept constantly busy, and a vast amount of very superior work is done, the product embracing the superb roll-top desks already referred to, in various sizes and styles, a beautiful line of library tables, general office furniture of every description, cases for the display of shoe samples, etc., all of which are supplied to the trade on favorable terms. The salesrooms and principal office of the company are at No. 104 Sudbury street, Boston, where all orders will receive immediate attention. Buyers from a distance visiting Boston are invited to call and judge of the merits of these goods.

LEOMINSTER HOTEL.

George S. Jones, Proprietor—Livery in Rear of Hotel on Central Street, Head of Main Street.

One of the most complete and attractive hotels in the interior of Massachusetts is the Leominster, situated at the intersection of Central and Main streets, near Monument square. The

building is four stories in height, with four stores on the ground floor, office, parlors, billiard-room, dining-room, etc., on the second floor, and fifty sleeping apartments above, the whole newly and handsomely furnished, provided with all obtainable modern conveniences, neat, clean and inviting. The accommodations, table and service are first-class, the service unexceptionable, and rates quite reasonable. Connected with the house is a well appointed livery stable, where fine teams and vehicles may be had at any hour. The Leominster is a favorite with commercial travelers, for whose comfort and convenience the arrangements are of the best.

Mine Host Jones, a native of New Hampshire, was for twelve years previous to coming here engaged in the hadware business at Fitchburg. His original venture in Leominster was the establishment of a tinware factory, which was burned in July, 1873, entailing a loss of $10,000, whereupon he erected this hotel upon the same site in 1875. He is a popular boniface and enjoys a large patronage. He went to Boston after erecting this hotel and kept hotel in Boston and Lynn, Mass., and other places He is well qualified for keeping a first-class hotel, experienced and obliging.

MONOOSNOCK MILL.

Edward M. Rockwell—Manufacturer of Woolen Yarns—Leominster.

Mr. Rockwell erected the Monoosnock mill in 1876, and for some years manufactured fine cassimeres and fancy worsteds in large quantities; but, that branch of his business ceasing to make profitable returns, he removed his looms, filled their places with additional carding and spinning appliances, and devoted his attention exclusively to the production of woolen yarns for the use of hosiery and textile manufacturers. His plant comprises the brick mill building proper, of four stories, 50x100 feet; a three-story L, 40x100 feet, commodious picker-house, dye-house, ware-house, office, etc. The present outfit (which is soon to be largely reinforced) comprises ten sets of cards and sufficient spindles to spin all the wool they can prepare, the whole driven by water power from Monoosnock brook, a fine 100-horse-power engine being held in reserve. One hundred and seventy-five people are now regularly employed, and the number will be greatly increased the present year. The output, averaging over $200,000 per annum in value, is disposed of to the trade throughout New England, a good deal of it going also to New York and Pennsylvania mills, from whom the demand grows steadily.

LEOMINSTER WORSTED COMPANY.

Incorporated December 1, 1891—Nahum Harwood, President; W. H. Chase, Treasurer —Manufacturers of Fancy Worsted Suitings.

Massachusetts is the principal center of the woolen industry of this country, and its repre-

sentatives are found in all parts of the State. For reasons not necessary to state the establishment of new woolen mills has become rare of late years, one of the most recent ventures being
that of the Leominster Worsted Company, whose plant dates from 1886, and comprises the
main structure, of brick, two stories, 52x150 feet, containing thirty-two broad looms, with carding, spinning and finishing machinery to match, with L 52x64 feet for engine and boiler and
storage; dye-house 25x30 feet, also of brick, and two capacious frame warehouses, the machinery, including a 100-light dynamo, is driven by a sixty-horse-power steam engine, and the mill is
brilliantly illuminated throughout by electricity, employing ninety hands, and last year produced
200,000 yards of superior suitings in the best and most acceptable material, styles and finish—
goods that are unexcelled in their class and find ready sale to the trade all over the United
States. The senior member, Mr. William Roger, is Scotch by birth; Mr. W. H. Chase is a
native of New Hampshire. Both are practical, experienced woolen manufacturers and capable
business men.

VALPEY & ANTHONY SHOE COMPANY.

H. R. Valpey, President; J. W. Brophy, Secretary; J. S. Anthony, Treasurer—Manufacturers of Fine Boots and Shoes—Mechanic Street—Office 89 Bedford Street,
Boston.

Next to cotton manufacturing the shoe industry is the most important in Massachusetts, the
census of 1885 showing that there was then nearly $34,500,000 invested in it—a total which
has doubtless been greatly increased since that time. Among the most reputable and prosperous representatives of this interest is the Valpey & Anthony Shoe Company, established at Lynn
in 1868. The venture was so successful that the managers cast about for a suitable place to
start a branch factory, their choice falling upon Leominster, where in 1887 they began the erection of a commodious four-story and basement building, which was completed and occupied
in the same year, the company as now constituted being incorporated in 1888, with $50,000
nominal capital. The four great floors of the Leominster shops, each 35x120 feet, are fitted up
and equipped with a view to the best results; 110 skilled operatives are employed, and the output, large and of immense value, consists of fine goods only, special attention being given to
the highest grades of boots and shoes in attractive and popular styles for ladies' wear.
    The salesrooms are in Boston, where is also handled the product of the Lynn factory, and
where Messrs. Valpey and Anthony reside. Mr. George W. Standley is superintendent of the
Leominster branch.

WESTBOROUGH.

THE town of Westborough, formerly a portion of Marlborough and then
known as Chauncy in honor of the second president of Harvard, was incorporated in 1717; area 16,182 acres (since reduced by cessions to 11,000 or
12,000 acres); population, twenty-five families and six unmarried men. The land
is hilly, romantic and fertile, and one of the loveliest inland sheets of water in the
State forms a principal feature of the landscape—Lake Chauncy. In this town
are situated the State Reform School and the Lyman School for boys, and the
common school privileges are ample. Present population about 5,230. The
principal industries embrace the manufacture of boots and shoes, straw goods,
bicycles, brick, tile and sewer pipe, wood and paper boxes, wagons, carriages,
sleighs, leather, machinery, etc. The village of Westborough is thirteen miles
east of Worcester, on the Boston & Albany railroad.

WHITNEY HOUSE.

U. Searles, Proprietor; Walter J. Taft, Clerk—West Main Street.

Westboro has reason to pride itself upon its principal hotel, the Whitney House, built by
Christopher Whitney, and occupied in 1882 by a Mr. Reid, who retired after a career of four
years and was succeeded by Mr. C. Whitney. Mr. Whitney, however, finding that his other

business engagements were of such importance as to demand the whole of his time, in 1886 disposed of his interest to Mr. H. Leighton, and was in turn superseded by Mr. U. Searles in April of 1890. The present proprietor has had considerable experience in this branch of business, and has already succeeded in spreading abroad the reputation of the Whitney, besides attracting a large and desirable share of local patronage. The building is of brick, substantial and ornate, four stories in height, 80x110 feet; the ground floor occupied by several stores. The office is up one flight and is flanked by the reading-room, parlors, and spacious dining-room capable of

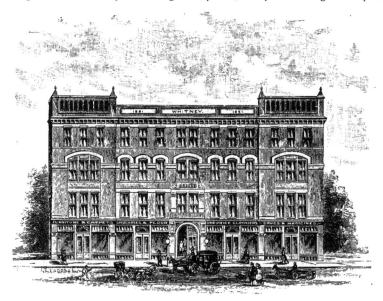

seating one hundred and ten guests at a time. The third and fourth stories are set apart for sleeping-rooms, handsomely furnished, neat, airy, well lighted, provided with all conveniences, including steam heat throughout the house. There are enough of these desirable apartments to accommodate seventy-five people in comfort. The table is bountifully supplied with the choicest of everything edible, the *cuisine* is first-class and the attendance unexceptionable. In a word, nothing is left undone by Mr. Searles to please his guests—a task that is shared by the urbane and obliging clerk, Mr. Walter J. Taft. Terms are reasonable, and the house is headquarters for visitors to Westboro, whether intent upon business or pleasure. Free conveyance is provided for guests to and from all trains.

THE TOWN OF MILLBURY.

MILLBURY, formerly a part of the town of Sutton, was incorporated June 11, 1813. Bounded on the north by Worcester, on the south by Sutton, on the east by Grafton, and on the west by Auburn and Oxford, the area of the town is 10,106 acres. The ponds, or miniature lakes, are peculiar for the purity of their waters and for the abundance of small but delicious fishes that inhabit their depths. These lakes also feed the numerous mill streams, which in turn empty into the Blackstone river, which winds and twists through many a crooked mile until it mingles its flood with Narragansett bay at Providence.

Wilkinsonville is situated on the Blackstone river and N. Y. P. & B. railroad, about three miles south of Millbury center or Armory Village.

WHITNEY & MOLT,

Manufacturers of Compound Indigo-Blue Dye and Dyers of Wool, Cotton and Yarn
in all Shades of Indigo, Millbury.

Dyeing is an art of which few besides those directly engaged in it have any accurate knowledge. We see and admire results, but with the actual processes by which they are produced we are unfamiliar. There are several reasons for this, two of the most important being that contact with dyestuffs is unpleasant and avoided by mankind for the most part, and second, that the secrets of the trade are guarded with the utmost jealousy, because they are acquired at great expense of time, labor and money and are entirely too valuable to squander upon an unappreciative public. Massachusetts, being the principal American seat of textile manufactures, is of course the great center of the dyeing industry, where it finds its best rewards and is brought to the greatest perfection. Of those who have achieved distinction for skill in this art we know of none more deserving of notice than the Millbury firm of Whitney & Molt, established in 1875. Their premises consist of an L-shaped two-story frame building fifty feet wide, eighty-five feet long on one front and one hundred feet on the other, containing twelve coloring vats and sixteen dyestuff grinders, the latter driven by a forty-horse-power steam engine, supplemented by water-power when required. The working force numbers five, and vast quantities of wool, cotton and yarn are dyed to order for consumption in Massachusetts, New Hampshire and Vermont mills. The leading specialty, however, is the manufacture of their own incomparable compound indigo-blue dye, much of which is consumed on the premises, but by far the larger portion is disposed of to the trade and shipped to dyers and cloth manufacturers elsewhere. It is pronounced on all hands the best and cheapest blue dye known.

Mr. Levi L. Whitney was born in Princeton, Mass., Mr. Molt in Germany. Both are practical and competent dyers.

D. T. DUDLEY & SON,

Manufacturers of Shuttles and Shuttle Irons for Broad, Cassimere, Satinet, Silk and
Cotton Power and Hand Looms, Wilkinsonville.

When textile manufacturing had secured a firm footing in New England it was not long ere a number of auxiliary industries were established, one of the most important of which was the making of shuttles and kindred loom appliances. In 1825 Jefferson Bellows engaged in this business at Farnumsville and in the course of time built up a first-class reputation and an excellent trade with mill-owners throughout this region—a reputation and trade which have remained with the concern and steadily increased during the years that have since elapsed. Mr. Bellows' successors in their chronological order were: Ruggles & Fowler, Fowler, Pratt & King, Sumner Pratt & Co., Wilkinsonville Shuttle Company, Chase & Dudley, Chase & Wilder, Wilder & Co., and finally D. T. Dudley & Son, the present proprietors, who assumed the management in 1867, and whose progressive methods have resulted in making it one of the most extensive and valuable plants of the kind in the country, running constantly on orders and shipping to all principal points in the United States, Canada, Mexico and South America, their shuttles and shuttle irons for looms of every description ranking with the best made anywhere. The plant comprises two substantial two-and-a-half-story frame buildings, respectively 40x100 and 25x50 feet, with which are connected a commodious storehouse and other appurtenances. The outfit of machinery, special tools, etc., is complete, and twenty expert mechanics are regularly employed. Mr. D. T. Dudley, the senior member of the present firm, embarked in this business in the year 1836 at Wilkinsonville, and has been continuously engaged therein, with the exception of a few years, ever since, and may therefore be considered one of the oldest persons in his line in this State, and at the ripe age of seventy-three years is still actively engaged in his factory every day in the year.

OAKHAM.

THE town of Oakham, situated in the western half of Worcester county, is almost the geographical center of the State. The land, though hilly, is productive, but there are no considerable streams. Originally known as the "West wing of Rutland" it was made a precinct in 1759, and incorporated under the present name as a town June 11, 1762. Manufactures comprise lumber, baskets, agricultural implements, wood furnaces, wire goods, and flavoring extracts. Remote from the busy world and until recently deprived of railroad communication, the town is not growing in population or wealth, the census of 1890 crediting it with only 738 residents.

S. M. SARGEANT,

Manufacturer of and Wholesale and Retail Dealer in Flavoring Extracts, Essences, Jamaica Ginger, Tinctures, Perfumes, etc.—Oakham, Mass.

Mr. S. M. Sargeant of Oakham is widely and favorably known, personally and through his meritorious preparations, not only throughout this county and State but all over the country. He began the manufacture of flavoring extracts and similar commodities in 1865, has adhered to the best processes and highest standards, and has consequently built up a permanent, extended and flourishing trade, his goods finding and retaining favor with that large and steadily increasing class of housekeepers and others who place quality above cheapness, buy only the purest and strongest, and rejoice in satisfactory results for the time and money expended. For many years Mr. Sargeant has personally visited and publicly displayed his extracts, etc., in the principal cities and villages of the State; he has constantly upon the road in this and adjacent counties two splendidly-appointed four-horse wagons to supply the retail trade, and ships heavily to wholesalers and all over the eastern, middle, southern and western States. Mr. Sargeant's laboratory at Oakham, erected the past year, is a tasteful and commodious three-story frame building 20x40 feet, equipped with the latest improved apparatus and appliances suited to his requirements. He employs ten assistants, uses only the choicest fresh materials, and produces large quantities of the finest extracts of lemon, vanilla, orange, almond, rose, Jamaica ginger, wintergreen, peppermint, spearmint, etc., together with tincture of rhubarb, bay rum and cologne. As before said, these goods are unexcelled for quality; they are sold at comparatively low prices, and dealers need have no fear of their being returned because of any fault.

WEBSTER.

WEBSTER owes its origin as a manufacturing point to Messrs. Samuel Slater and Bela Tiffany, who began here, in 1813, the spinning of cotton yarns, adding to that, during the war of 1812, the weaving of broadcloth. The town was incorporated in 1832. Webster, situated on the line of the Norwich & Worcester railroad, sixteen miles south of the latter city, is in the center of the southern tier of towns and has a population of 7015.

JOHN CHASE & SONS,

Manufacturers of Woolen Worsteds, Men's Suitings, Cheviots, etc.—Chaseville; P. O. Address, Webster.

These mills rank with the largest and most famous of the kind in New England. A portion of the present structure was erected in 1860 by the late John Chase, who subsequently admitted to copartnership his sons, one of whom, Mr. Frederick F. Chase, is the present sole proprietor, retaining the honored style under which the establishment originally won its reputation. The mills were in 1878 and 1882 enlarged to their present capacity. The buildings, constructed entirely of stone, consist of the principal mill, four stories, 42x300 feet; the weaving shed, one story 100x160 feet; the picking and spinning mill, three stories, 34x100 feet; warehouse, one story, 30x200 feet; picker and engine-room, 32x165 feet; dye-house, 32x55 feet; second dye-house, two stories, 28x76 feet; burling-room, 28x68 feet; stock-room, 30x65 feet, and boiler-house, 42x60 feet. The equipment of new improved machinery is first-class and includes twenty sets of cards, 16,000 spindles and 102 broad looms. Three hundred and seventy-five operatives are employed, and the output, enormous in quantity and value, comprising the best grades of woolen and worsted fabrics, suitings, cheviots, etc., is distributed to all parts of the United States through Boston and New York selling agents. These mills form quite an industrial village of themselves, eligibly situated in the midst of spacious and well-kept grounds.

The machinery is driven by a combination of steam and water—a 150-horse-power Corliss engine and two monster Humphrey turbine wheels.

CHASE MILL NO. 2.

This mill, producing the same variety of goods and situated at North Oxford, comprises two-three-story stone buildings, respectively 60x110 and 45x90 feet, one-story and basement, boiler and engine-house 25x95 feet, frame one-story and basement warehouse 35x100 feet, and furnishes employment to 175 hands, with eight sets and forty looms. The annual output of the two mills averages about $1,500,000, being distributed throughout the United States.

THE STEVENS LINEN COMPANY.

M. T. Stevens, President; H. S. Shaw, Treasurer—Mauufacturers of Linen Crash—' Dudley; P. O. Address, Webster.

These mills probably took their rise in the embargo of 1809 and subsequent events that led up to our second war with England; at any rate the original plant—since entirely rebuilt and vastly enlarged—was established in 1812 by the Dudley Mill Company, which, under various administrations, continued to own and operate the property until 1864, when H. H. Stevens became the purchaser. Great improvements and additions were made under his management, which lasted for twenty-one years, when the present company, capital $350,000, was incorporated and assumed control, the present president being a brother of the preceding proprietor. The buildings are of stone, built in the most substantial manner, handsomely finished, perfectly lighted and ventilated, and comprise two great mills, one of five stories, 70x207 feet, the other of three stories, 36x110 feet. A description of the machinery would not interest the general reader, but some idea of its extent may be gained from the statement that one 375-horse-power Corliss and one 175-horse-power Woodruff & Beach engine and three turbine wheels aggregating 180-horse-power are required to drive it. Four hundred operatives are steadily employed at good wages and pensioned when retired by old age, injury or declining health—a provision that has long distinguished the management of these mills and that enables them to secure the best possible help, an earnest rivalry existing among the working people of the district to secure place and preferment in the linen mills. The output is exclusively of coarse crash of the best grades, and is simply enormous in volume, selling agents being maintained in New York and Boston for the distribution of the goods to the trade east, north, south and west.

THE TOWN OF ATHOL.

THE town of Athol is bounded on the north by Royalston, on the south and southeast by Petersham, on the east by Philipston, and on the west by Franklin county. It is quite irregular in form, watered by Miller's river and its tributaries, is noted for fine scenery, and as originally surveyed in 1732 contained an area of thirty-six square miles, now greatly reduced by the rearrangement of township lines and the erection of Philipston out of Athol's ancient territory. The town was long known as " Pequoig on Miller's river," but was incorporated March 6, 1762, under the present name. The population of Athol shows a steady and healthy increase, thus : 1790, 848 ; 1840, 1591 ; 1860, 2,604 ; 1870, 3,517 ; 1880, 4,307 ; 1885, 4,758 ; 1890, 6,318. In educational matters Athol is fully abreast of the times. A high school was established in 1856, and many of the most active and useful young men of the town are its graduates. The grammar and graded schools are also of the highest order for thoroughness and efficiency. The Athol Library Association was organized December, 1878, but was merged in the Free Public Library, April, 1882.

Athol's transportation facilities are quite satisfactory, and consist of the Vermont & Massachusetts railroad, running east and west (a part of the Fitchburg system), and the Springfield, Athol & Northeastern, of the Boston & Albany system.

The Worcester Northwest Agricultural and Mechanical Society owns extensive grounds and substantial buildings adjacent to the village, where annual fairs are held. Of banks there are three—the Miller's River National (opened September 12, 1854, as the Miller's River State Bank, and rechartered under the National banking law January 12, 1865), capital $150,000, reserve fund $100,000; the Athol National Bank, opened September 15, 1874, capital $100,000; and the Athol Savings Bank, chartered 1867.

The industries of Athol are varied and important, embracing the manufacture of silk, woolen and leather goods, boots and shoes, woodenware, building materials, furniture, chairs, etc. The press is represented by two excellent weekly newspapers—the *Worcester West Chronicle* and the *Athol Transcript.* The latter was established in January, 1871, by Lucien Lord, then postmaster of Athol, and Edward F. Jones, an expert printer. Its first editor was Dr. V. O. Taylor. After one or two changes of ownership it passed into the control of its present proprietors, Mr. Lord and Mr. W. L. Hill. The latter has been its sole editor and manager about nineteen years, and has made it what it now is—one of the ablest and most influential and prosperous weekly papers in Massachusetts. It is an eight-page, 48-column paper, and covers the local field thoroughly, with an advertising patronage that sufficiently attests its popularity. Connected with the *Transcript* office is a large, splendidly equipped printing office, which enjoys the highest reputation for its work. The whole establishment is a model one, reflecting the greatest credit upon its managers and upon the community of which it is a leading institution.

HILL & GREENE,

Manufacturers of Ladies', Misses' and Children's Dongola, Goat and Grain Shoes —Office, No. 105 Summer Street, Boston.

This firm is composed of Messrs. C. S. Hill and F. D. Greene of Boston, and Eli G. Greene of Athol, and W. L. Hyde (special partner) of Salem. Mr. Mat Regers is superintendent of the Athol factory, which was opened and commenced operations February 11, 1889. The factory here is an immense frame structure 40x120 feet with 22x36-foot L, three and a-half stories in height throughout. It is entirely new, erected by the company for the purpose, and is admirably arranged in every department, heated by steam, lighted by gas and numerous windows, fitted up with automatic sprinklers and fire alarm, and in all respects is a model establishment. Great care was exercised in the selection of the equipment, which includes all the latest and best improved devices applicable to the class of work to be performed. Ample power is obtained from Mill brook, which at this point has an abrupt fall down the hillside. Two hundred and fifty operatives are employed, and the output averages about twelve cases per day of high grade dongola, goat and grain shoes for ladies,' misses' and children's wear. The excellence of the goods is evidenced by the widespread demand throughout the south and west and on the Pacific slope.

ATHOL SHOE COMPANY.

F. W. Breed—Manufacturer of Ladies' and Misses' Fine and Medium Shoes—Athol Center; Office, No. 286 Devonshire Street, Boston.

Mr. F. W. Breed ranks with the most extensive and reputable of American shoe manufacturers, and conducts large factories at East Rochester, N. H., and Rochester, N. H. The Athol factory, erected in 1887, is run under the name of the Athol Shoe Company to distinguish it from the other enterprises of Mr. Breed, who, a prominent and popular citizen of Lynn, exercises general supervision of his various interests from this point. The Athol factory is of brick, three stories, 50x150 feet, complete in all details, provided with fire alarm, automatic sprinklers and fire escapes. The machinery, of which a superb complement is used, is of the latest approved pattern and driven by water power from Mill brook, a fine steam engine being held in reserve for use in case of accident or failure of water supply. From 250 to 300 hands are employed, dependent upon the season and the state of trade, and have made nearly 3000 pairs per day of ladies' shoes, which were disposed of to dealers through the Boston office, No. 286 Devonshire street, where the wants of buyers receive prompt attention.

NORFOLK COUNTY.

THE territory forming Norfolk was formerly a part (the greater part) of Suffolk county, but by act of the General Court dated June 20, 1793, all of Suffolk with the exception of the towns of Boston and Chelsea was erected into a new county, and incorporated under the name of Norfolk. Subsequently the towns of Hingham and Hull were detached from Norfolk and annexed to Plymouth county. Agriculture—the wresting of a frugal livelihood from a reluctant soil—was the principal industry of the white inhabitants for several generations. The first permanent settlement was made at Dedham by order of the General Court dated September 3, 1635, the name authoritatively conferred a year later, and in a few years most of the inhabitants of Watertown, settled five years earlier, had abandoned their homes for the more fertile and attractive lands in the new town. Naturally Dedham became the county seat of Norfolk when that county came into existence. Dedham's first trouble arose from an embarrassment of riches in land, which was gradually disposed of by the creation of new towns, thirteen of which and portions of four more were hewn out of her original territory. The county is well watered, traversed by a dozen main line and branch railroads, and the seat of diversified and important industries. Population—census of 1890—118,911.

THE TOWN OF FRANKLIN.

THERE is an unexplained mystery about the naming of Franklin. The town, previously known as the Westerly part of Wrentham, applied for incorpora-

OLD UNIVERSALIST CHURCH, FRANKLIN.

tion as Exeter, and is so named in the original charter, but when the General

Court passed the act, March 1778, the name of Franklin was substituted, by whom is not known, but probably by some ardent admirer of the printer philosopher, who was at the time ambassador to France and had but recently completed negotiations with the king of that country of a highly advantageous nature to the American Colonies, then engaged in the revolutionary struggle. Years afterward Franklin, in recognition of the compliment, presented the town with 116 volumes to found a library. Franklin contains 27.6 square miles (17,602 1-2 acres) of hill, dale and water. The village is 27 1-4 miles southwest of Boston, and is a bustling, enterprising place, the site of numerous extensive factories and the home of an intelligent, courteous and prosperous people. Much of Franklin's prosperity of late years is referable to the Ray family, whose enterprise is proverbial and whose influence is felt in finance, manufacturing, commerce and railroad building. More particular reference to this remarkable family will be found in the subjoined articles descriptive of their business interests. The water power of the town, derived from Uncas, Pepolatic and Kingsbury's ponds, Mine brook and Mill river, is ample, and is discharged into the Charles river, which skirts Franklin on the north.

FRANKLIN NATIONAL BANK.

James P. Ray, President; M. Farnum, Cashier—Capital Stock, $200,000—Banking House, Over Post Office, Main Street.

The Franklin National dates from 1865, and was chartered under the Federal banking law, to supersede the Franklin State Bank, incorporated with $100,000 in 1850. Under its present

auspices the institution has proved a most valuable and important auxiliary to the business interests of the village and surrounding country, being conducted upon a conservatively liberal basis that assures first-class service to the community and all proper encouragement to industry.

RESIDENCES OF J. G. AND J. P. RAY,

The banking rooms are neat and commodious, conveniently situated on the second floor over the post office on Main street, and special attention is given to deposits, loans, collections, exchange, discounts, etc.   President James P. Ray is so well known in this and adjoining States that his name is sufficient guarantee of any enterprise in which he is engaged.   The board of directors embraces other familiar and popular names, such as Joseph G. Ray, A. H. Morse, O. J. Rathbun, A. D. Thayer, James F. Ray and D. K. Ray—all representative business men.

THE CITY MILLS COMPANY.

James P. Ray, President; Joseph G. Ray, Treasurer; W. H. Sweatt, Superintendent —Manufacturers of Felt Goods.

The City mills, representing an investment of $96,000, were erected by Messrs. J. P. & J. G. Ray in 1881, and comprise two stone buildings respectively 30x60 feet and 30x40 feet in area. The outfit of improved felting machinery is complete; a large number of hands earn a livelihood in the works, and the output is very heavy.   The City Mills Company dates from the establishment of the plant in 1881.

The history of the Ray family and its connections in this part of the country is a record of effort and achievement of which those interested may well be proud.   Many years ago Colonel Joseph Ray established a cotton mill in this place, but reverses overtook him, and after a heroic struggle he was forced to give up and retire.   His son, James P., a born business man, started upon his career at the age of seventeen with a total ready capital of seven dollars.   At different times he has had associated with him all of his brothers, but of late only the youngest, Joseph G., and Oscar J. Rathbun, have taken an active part in some of the various enterprises of which he is the master spirit.   The Messrs. Ray now own or control Ray's Woolen Company, the City Mills Company, the Franklin Cotton Company, the Franklin National Bank, the Putnam (Conn.) Manufacturing Company, the Massachusetts division and most of the Rhode Island division of the Franklin and Valley Falls railroad, and are the owners of the Woonsocket & Pascoag railroad, now approaching completion.   Their Woonsocket interests include the ownership of the Ballou, Bartlett, Jenckesville and Lyman mills and a majority of the Citizens' National Bank stock.   They are also large stockholders in numerous other industrial ventures. Among their daily products are 700 "comfortables" or bed-spreads (a commodity which James P. Ray first offered and failed to sell in Boston in 1840, and afterward disposed of in Providence), 10,000 yards of batting, one ton of carpet lining, and vast quantities of other goods. On textiles alone they have constantly running 1200 cotton looms, 100 cassimere looms and 100 satinet looms.

Mr. James P. Ray's original seven dollars has yielded decidedly handsome returns.   His individual holdings comprise several elegant brick blocks on Main street, many houses and lots in different parts of the village, and valuable real estate in this and other States.   Personally he is an agreeable and popular gentleman who commands the respect and confidence of all classes, as is shown by the fact that he has been elected to and served creditably in both branches of the State Legislature.

THE NORFOLK WOOLEN COMPANY.

W. F. Ray, President and Treasurer—Manufacturers of and Dealers in Wool Substitutes—Franklin, Norfork, Bellingham and Mendon.

The Norfolk Woolen Company (succeeding the private concern of W. F. Ray, established in 1882), was incorporated in 1887 with $30,000 capital, and owns or controls mills at Unionville (a suburb of Franklin), Norfolk, Bellingham and Mendon, their output of shoddy, wool waste and wool extracts averaging about 650 tons per annum, all of which is taken for consumption by manufacturers of woolen goods in New England, New York and Pennsylvania.   The carding mill recently erected at Norfolk by this company is a substantial frame structure of two stories, 28x119 feet, with which is connected an older mill of one, two and three stories and about the same dimensions.   Four pickers and twenty-two cards are required here, and thirty men are employed on the premises, besides a large number of people in the sorting and grading departments at Boston and Franklin.   The Franklin mill at Unionville is a two-story frame building, fitted up with one picker and two garnet machines.   The Bellingham mill is of wood and brick, two stories, 25x60 feet, contains two pickers and eight cards, and employs six operatives.   The Mendon mill is of brick, contains two pickers and seven cards, and employs eight hands.   The products of these mills are of the highest grade, and the company does a flourishing business, one of their greatest advantages being found in the fact that their works are eligibly situated upon excellent mill streams that usually supply an abundance of water the year round, thus enabling them to economize very much in the matter of power.

RAY'S WOOLEN COMPANY.

James P. Ray, Edgar K. Ray, Joseph G. Ray, Oscar J. Rathbun—Manufacturers of Cassimeres, Satinets and Shoddy—Mills at Franklin and North Bellingham.

Ray's Woolen Company, composed of the above-named prominent and capable business men, ranks with the largest producers of woolen fabrics in this part of New England. The capital invested in this particular industry by the firm aggregates $300,000, and the mills are three in number—a shoddy mill and a cassimere mill at Franklin, and a satinet mill and printing works at North Bellingham.

THE SHODDY MILL

And appurtenances, erected in 1874, comprises one two-story brick building, 30 x 60 feet; one one-story brick, 50x100 feet; one two-story frame, 30x60 feet, and one one-story frame, 30x100 feet. Eight pickers and twenty-five carding machine, form a part of the equipment, thirty-eight hands work here, and the output averages 23,000 pounds per week, a portion of which is consumed in the company's own mills, and the remainder disposed of to the trade.

THE SATINET MILL,

Built in 1876, consists of a two-story brick structure, 50x300, and a one-story frame, 50x130 feet. The machinery outfit includes all late and valuable improvements; 130 hands are employed, and the product of medium grade union cassimeres averages 260,000 pieces per annum, sold principally in the western markets.

THE SATINET PLANT,

Situated at North Bellingham, is in fact two mills, each three stories in height, one partly of stone and partly of brick, with basement 38x100 feet; the other entirely of stone and of the same dimensions, and each is equipped with four mules and forty-two looms. A brick one-story print shop, 50x150 feet, containing three machines, adjoins the mills. One hundred and twelve operatives are employed in the mills and twenty in the print works, and the product averages 1,200,000 yards of superior satinets annually. Messrs. James P. and Joseph G. Ray and Oscar J. Rathbun are associated in other business enterprises, mention of which is made in the article on the City Mills Company.

FRANKLIN COTTON COMPANY.

William F. Draper, President—Manufacturers of Grain Bags, Twine, etc.—Unionville.

This company, incorporated in 1883, capital $50,000, is one of the numerous corporations controlled by Messrs. J. P. Ray and Oscar J. Rathbun. The mills are of stone, 50x120 feet, two stories in height, fitted up in the best manner with improved special machinery, give employment to many people, and turn out goods of the average value of over $40,000 per annum. The grain bags and bagging, towels, cotton twine, etc., made here are in general request and the demand steady and increasing.

F. B. RAY,

Ray Fabric Company—Manufacturers of Felt, Patent Woven and Knit Horse Blankets, Patent Knit Mops, Fabrics and Linings—Unionville.

The felt and knit goods mills now under consideration were built many years ago by F. B. Ray, who assumed sole proprietorship upon the dissolution of the original firm of Ray Brothers, of which he became a partner with Joseph G. and James P. Ray. The mill buildings, three in number, are of stone, frame and brick, 30x100, 30x60 and 30x40 feet, fully equipped with felting and knitting machinery driven by steam and water. Fifty hands earn a livelihood here, and great quantities of horse blankets, mops, linings and kindred goods are produced and supplied to the trade throughout the country.

This was the first shoddy manufacturing mill ever erected in the United States. In fact the town of Franklin is largely indebted to Mr. F. B. Ray for his enterprise in starting and establishing new industries and in inducing and assisting others to establish manufactories in this section. Not only was he a member of the old firm of Ray Brothers, one of the earliest manufacturing firms of this part of the State, but he was the first to utilize old material and wool substitutes in the manufacture of goods in this country, and can fairly claim to be the pioneer of that industry on this side of the Atlantic. He was also the first maker of knit goods and felt in this town. He was originally in partnership with his brothers in the manufacture of twine, yarn, batting and shoddy. He is now located at Unionville, and his goods are in such great demand that he is. putting in new and improved machinery from abroad. He is also connected as director with the Norfolk Woolen Company and the Franklin Cotton Company.

FRANKLIN KNITTING COMPANY.

A. D. Thayer, Proprietor—Manufacturer of Glove and Boot Linings, Jersey Cloths, etc.

Mr. A. D. Thayer, proprietor of the Franklin Knitting Company, is related by marriage to both the Thayer and Ray families, leading citizens, manufacturers, and financiers of this vicinity, and is himself prominent in business circles. In 1884 Mr. Thayer erected the knitting mills and established the business under its present style, with cash capital invested to the amount of $35,000. How successful the enterprise has proven is shown by its magnitude to-day, occupying two buildings, 40x120 and 40x80 feet respectively, fitted up with all requisite appliances, including twenty-eight Crane circular knitting machines, employing thirty-five hands, and producing an average of 2,250 square yards of fabric per diem. Sales range from $80,000 to $100,000 per annum, but if driven to their full capacity $125,000 worth of knit goods could be made in the same period. These fabrics—fleece and plush linings for rubber boots and gloves and popular grades of jersey cloth—find a ready market at remunerative prices.

O. F. METCALF & SONS,

Dealers in Hay, Grain, Flour, Oats and Mill Feed, Lumber and Builders' Supplies— Manufacturers of Packing Boxes and Cases—Woodworkers and Jobbers.

Old-established business houses are as plentiful as new ones in this portion of the old Bay State, and, in the estimation of many, a good deal more respectable. The concern named in our caption furnishes a case in point. It was founded about fifty years ago by E. L. and O. F. Metcalf, and, strange to say, the latter is still at its head, now as senior partner, having associated with him his sons N. F. and Frank Metcalf and W. M. Fisher, the last-named acting as general manager. The premises comprise three two-story frame building—grain mill 30x40 feet, saw mill 20x30 feet, and woodworking shops 60x150 feet, all well equipped and together furnishing employment to twenty men. The firm deal largely in flour, grain, hay and mill feed, doing considerable grinding, and are also extensive handlers of lumber and builders' supplies at wholesale and retail, executing promptly, besides, all orders for shop work and jobbing. Transactions amount to 25,000 bushels of grain, 1,500,000 feet of lumber, and 800,000 packing boxes and cases annually—the latter a specialty made expressly for the various straw goods manufacturers of the village and vicinity. Transactions aggregate about $100,000 a year.

WAITE'S FELTING MILLS.

E. Waite, Agent—Manufacturers of Graduated Pads and Polishing Felts—Rubber Linings of All Kinds a Specialty.

The felting mills erected in 1884 by Mr. Enoch Waite form an important and interesting feature of Franklin's industries. The building is an unpretending two-story frame structure 56x 125 feet, equipped with steam power and all late improvements in felting machinery, gives employment to forty hands, and turns out 2000 pounds of car journal and saddle felts, skirt goods and boot linings daily, or $50,000 worth per annum. These goods are in steady request, and are sent to New York from the factory, and thence distributed to all parts of the country. Mr. Waite, the originator of this enterprise, was born in England, coming to this country when quite young. For more than thirty years he has been connected in one capacity or another with the manufacture of felt and identified with some of the largest mills in the neighborhood of Franklin, and is consequently thoroughly conversant with the business in all its branches. In addition to managing the Waite felting mills he is interested in the Rockville felt mills and the Norfolk paper mills.

TOWN OF FOXBOROUGH.

FOXBOROUGH, named for the Right Honorable Charles James Fox, the eminent English statesman and friend of America, was formed out of parts of Wrentham, Walpole, Stoughton (now Canton), and Stoughtonham (now Sharon) the act of incorporation passing the General Court June 10, 1778. Foxborough is a lively interior town and a busy place. More than a hundred years ago it was a center of some commercial importance, and at the time of the Revolution supplied the Continental army with many cannon, shot and shell. The old foundry is still in operation and is described further along.

FOXBORO FOUNDRY AND MACHINE COMPANY.

**H. C. Williams, President; Benjamin F. Boyden, 2d, Treasurer and Manager—
Manufacturers of the Foxboro Hot Water Heater, etc.**

A lingering flavor of patriotic reminiscence attaches to the works of the Foxboro Foundry and Machine Company, which were originally established in 1781, the darkest hour of the revolutionary period, for the purpose of casting cannon, solid shot and shells for the use of the Continental army. It is a singular fact that whereas hundreds of New England foundries have since sprung into existence, failed and been forgotten, the Foxboro works have never been shut down, save for repairs or improvement, since the day, one hundred and ten years ago, they were first fired up. The plant was leased in 1878 by Mr. H. C. Williams, a skilled practical foundryman, who ran it for account of himself and the Otis Carey estate, owners, until 1888, when the present company, capital, $20,000, was incorporated, with Mr. Williams as president and B. F. Boyden, 2d, secretary and treasurer. The buildings, all frame, comprise a one-story foundry, 60x120 feet, a two-story-and-basement machine shop, 40x80 feet, with a fifteen-horse-power engine below ground; setting-up shop 40x 60, pattern shop 40x60, and sand-house 40x40 feet, all one story, besides several warehouses. The machinery, which consists of the usual foundry and machine shop equipment, is driven about ten months each year by a twenty-five-horse-power wheel, taking water from Wading river. The force of molders and machinists employed averages about forty, and the annual value of output varies from $40,000 to $50,000, specialties being made of presses, stampers, flats and pressing jacks for straw goods manufacturers, furnaces and hot water heating apparatus. The straw goods appliances are supplied to the trade all over the country; the furnaces are sold in Boston, and the heating apparatus is shipped to Boston, New York and Philadelphia. Since January, 1890, Mr. Boyden has had the active management of the business, and under his control it has largely increased in extent. Mr. Jarvis Williams retains his position as superintendent of the machine shop, which he has held for many years past. The Foxboro Foundry and Machine Company's Boston office is at No. 74 Tremont street.

TOWN OF WRENTHAM.

WRENTHAM (Indian name, Wollomonopoag) dates back to October 17, 1673, at which time an act of the General Court was passed setting her apart from Dedham and conferring upon her the powers and privileges of a separate town. Subsequently the town was subdivided into four precincts, each of which eventually became distinct towns, viz: Wrentham, Franklin, Norfolk and Bellingham. Wrentham lies in the extreme southwest corner of Norfolk county, and, besides being a delightful place of residence, is the seat of several important industries. South Wrentham is a lively village in the same town.

CROOK BROTHERS,

Manufacturers of Woolen Yarns of All Kinds—South Wrentham.

The manufacture of pure woolen yarns is one of the most useful and important of industries, but in this country is handicapped to a certain extent by unfavorable conditions of an artificial nature; notwithstanding which there are still a few moderately prosperous mills at various points, a notable example being that of Crook Brothers, South Wrentham. The concern was originally established at Central Falls by the late Henry Crook, who subsequently removed, first to Attleboro, and subsequently, seventeen years ago, to South Wrentham. Nine years ago he died, and was succeeded in business by his sons S. W. and A. W., practical spinners, brought up under their father's instructions. The mill is a two-story frame structure with attic, 50x70 feet, with engine and boiler-room and packing-house attached. The machinery equipment is first-class, embracing all useful modern improvements, and eight skilled hands are employed. The yarns made here are of the best quality according to grade, and are readily disposed of to the trade, the firm finding its principal and most profitable market in the New England States. Sales average 1300 pounds of custom-made yarns in all grades daily, the average value of which is fifty cents per pound. Crook Brothers also own and cultivate a sixty-acre farm near the mill.

MEDWAY.

THE town of Medway, originally that part of Medfield north and west of the Charles river, was incorporated October 25, 1713. The territory comprises fiften square miles and is watered by the Charles river. Population, about 3000. Medway village, East Medway, West Medway and Rockville are the post offices. Careyville is situated two or three miles south of Rockville, and the N. Y. & N. E. railroad passes through both places.

CHARLES C. CAPRON.

Manufacturer of Woolen Yarns—Mill on Charles River, Medway.

This mill, formerly known as the Sanford mill, was purchased in September last, by Mr. Charles C. Capron, who is also the owner of two similar establishments at Uxbridge. Mr. Capron's son, John L., an experienced and energetic young man, is the capable resident super-intendent, and both father and son already manifest an active interest in the local affairs of the town, its progress and improvement. The mill is a handsome and substantial modern four-story brick structure, 55x150 feet, advantageously situated on the bank of the Charles river, and is splendidly equipped throughout with five sets of the latest improved carding, spinning and twisting, weaving, finishing and dyeing machinery, driven by an 80-horse-power turbine wheel and a steam engine of like power. Twenty-five operatives work in the various departments, and the capacity of the plant is 5,000 to 10,000 pounds per week of all-wool yarns in all grades for the use of woolen cloth, stocking and carpet manufacturers. The product is readily taken by the trade here in New England, New York and Pennsylvania. Orders for specialties are filled at short notice.

SYLVESTER A. GREENWOOD,

Manufacturer of Packing Boxes for the Boot, Shoe and Straw Goods Trade—Careyville.

Careyville is situated on the line of the New York & New England railroad, in the town of Bellingham, Norfolk county, and occupies a particularly favorable position with reference to the packing case industry, having direct communication by rail with Boston, Woonsocket, Port-land and other points as well as with neighboring manufacturing villages.

In 1885 Messrs. Hunter and Greenwood began the business of making and supplying wooden boxes for the trade, and were quite successful, but Mr. Hunter retired last July, his in-terest reverting by purchase to Mr. Greenwood, a native of the village, a competent mechanic and enterprising citizen. His factory, erected in 1886, is a commodious frame structure of two stories, 60x120 feet, fitted up with all requisite woodworking machinery, driven by a 40-horse-power engine, the boiler also supplying steam for warming the building. Sixteen men are kept steadily hammering away to fill orders, and during the past year worked up 1,500,000 feet of lumber, producing $25,000 worth of packing bokes in various styles, which were disposed of to boot and shoe and straw goods manufacturers in this State and Rhode Island, many of them going to Howard penitentiary and still greater quantities in Medway and adjacent places. Mr. Greenwood's facilities are first-class, and he is prepared to execute orders in his line at short notice and at moderate prices. His shop adjoins the railroad station.

TAFT, M'KEAN & CO.,

Manufacturers of Satinets, Careyville—Macintosh, Green & Co., Selling Agents, No. 56 Franklin Street, Boston; No. 59 Leonard Street, New York.

C. H. Cutler & Co. established this business in 1868. Moses Taft, Esq., of Uxbridge (who has since sold his interest to his son, Mr. L. H. Taft) William A. McKean and A. E. Bullard organized a copartnership and bought the plant in 1880. They have made many improvements in the buildings and equipment, and it stands to-day a valuable and productive property —a handsome and substantial three-story frame structure with basement, the appurtenances comprising a separate finishing room, office, brick boiler and engine house, outhouses, etc., a 75-horse-power wheel driven by the current of the Charles river and a 140-horse-power engine supplying an abundance of motive power. The machinery outfit includes eight sets of woolen cards, eighty looms, and all requisite dyeing and finishing appliances. One hundred operatives find employment here, and the product averages in value $150,000 per annum, the well-known standard Careyville satinets forming the leading specialty, though large quantities of heavy coatings and union cassimeres are turned out. The village of Careyville, on the N. Y. & N. E. railroad, consists principally of the mill buildings, a number of neat cottages for the help, and the elegant houses of Messrs. McKean and Bullard, resident partners and big-hearted, public-spirited gentlemen.

ADDITIONAL SPENCER.

SPENCER WIRE COMPANY.

Richard Sugden, President and Treasurer; H. W. Goddard, Secretary—Manufacturers of Iron and Bessemer Steel Wire—Wire Village.

The Spencer Wire Company's plant at Wire Village, three miles distant from Spencer Center, was founded forty-two years ago by Messrs. Richard Sugden and Nathaniel Meyrick. The present company, capital stock $75,000, was organized in 1878. The premises comprise four commodious frame mill buildings along the Quabaug, a rapid stream with a hundred-foot fall. The product is very large and of the highest grade, comprising iron and Bessemer steel wires of every gauge and description, and is in steady and increasing demand.

President Sugden is an Englishman by birth, and an experienced practical wire manufacturer. He is also an influential and respected citizen, treasurer of the Spencer Gas Company, a director of the Spencer National Bank, and recently erected the finest brick business block on Main street in that village, to which he also presented the Sugden Library building.

E. E. STONE & CO.,

Wholesale and Retail Dealers in Lumber, Window Frames, Sash, Blinds, Doors, Mouldings, etc—Wall St.

The planing mill and lumber yard now under consideration were established many years ago by a Mr. Temple, who afterward disposed of his interest to Barnes & Mullett. Messrs. Mullett & Stone formed a copartnership in 1862, and three years later Mr. E. E. Stone became sole proprietor. Barnes & Horr purchased in 1885, but soon resold to Stone & Prouty, Mr. Prouty subsequently retiring and Mr. Stone succeeding under the present style of E. E. Stone & Co. The planing mill, situated on Wall street opposite the railroad depot, is a three-story frame building, 40x60 feet, heated by steam, lighted by gas, and equipped with a fine complement of improved woodworking machinery. Ample storage yards are attached, and a modern dry-house of 50,000 feet capacity completes the plant. Ten competent workmen are employed, and great quantities of superior doors, sash, blinds, mouldings, window frames and inside finish are made here to order or carried in stock for the trade. Parties in want of any of the materials named, or of dressed lumber, builders' finish, etc., will find it to their interest to inspect Stone & Co.'s facilities, stock and prices. Mr. Stone is a practical mechanic and thoroughgoing business man of high standing.

˙ BRISTOL COUNTY.

BRISTOL COUNTY is one of the two extreme southern counties of the State, Plymouth being the other and forming the eastern boundary, Norfolk county lying north, Buzzard's Bay south, and Newport, Bristol and Providence counties, Rhode Island, west. The county was incorporated under the present name, and the town of the same name made the seat of justice in 1685, and so continued until the rectification of the colony boundaries in 1746, when the towns of Bristol, Barrington, Warren and Little Compton were awarded to Rhode Island and the present name was adopted. Taunton became and remained the sole county-seat, where all courts were held, until 1828, when New Bedford, then an important whaling, commercial and shipbuilding port with more than 6000 inhabitants, was made a half shire village, suitable buildings being erected, officials provided, and a share of the court business transferred to that place. The State boundary was again adjusted in 1860, when Bristol county parted with Pawtucket and a part of Seekonk, obtaining in return that portion of Tiverton which adjoins Fall River. The city of Fall River was made a third shire town in 1877, and now has the finest court-house and public buildings in the county, where is transacted the bulk of the legal business of the Bristol courts. The population of the county in 1780 was little more than 26,000 ; in 1870 it was 102,886 ; in 1890, 186,403. The three cities contain, by the last census, inhabitants as follows : Taunton, 25,389 ; New Bedford, 40,705 ; Fall River, 74,351. The towns number twenty, and stand in alphabetical order : Acushnet, Attleborough, North Attleborough, Berkley, Dartmouth, Dighton, Easton, Fairhaven, Fall River, Freetown, Mansfield, New Bedford, Norton, Raynham, Rehoboth, Seeconk, Somerset, Swansea, Taunton and Westport. The early history of the county relates principally to Indian troubles, and, besides being confused and in some respects apochryphal, is too voluminous and inconsequential for repetition here. Those fond of that kind of reading can find all the pioneer annals, quaint spelling and preposterous Indian names they desire upon the library shelves all over New England. The first white settlements were planted in the county by detachments from Plymouth about 1637, and Taunton was incorporated in 1639, nineteen years after the landing of the pilgrims. ˙

FALL RIVER.

THE original settlement occurred in 1656, and the incorporation of Fall River town in 1803. The name was adopted in deference to the outlet of the Watuppa lakes, a rapid and turbulent stream supplying a vast water power, previously known to the Indians as Quequechan (Falling Water), but rechristened by the whites in consonance with its natural characteristics. This stream drains the lakes referred to—a series of deep ponds some six miles in length lying three and a-half miles distant from Mount Hope bay, a superb harbor now overlooked by the flourishing city, one of the most important cotton manufacturing centers in the United States. On the opposite or northwest side the city is

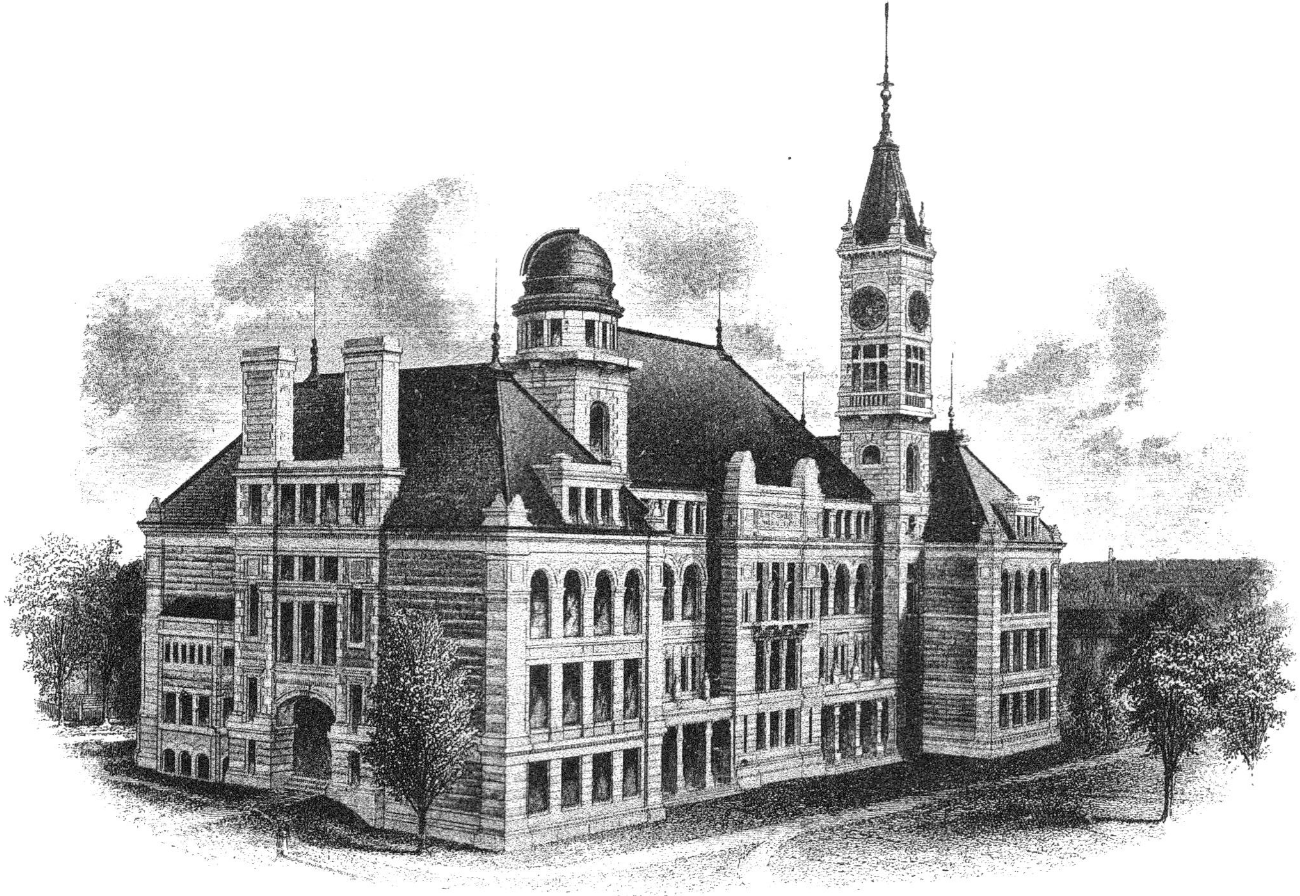

DUFREE HIGH SCHOOL.—FALL RIVER,

washed by the noble Taunton river, into which the waters of Fall River finally empty. The shore of the bay is rather bold and precipitous, but at a distance of half a mile becomes a gradually rising plateau which extends to the lakes already mentioned, the latter supplying an unfailing abundance of water, which is largely utilized for industrial purposes, though the steam engine is the main reliance for power of late years. It is claimed by those who have studied the subject that the climate of Fall River is moderate and quite uniform, the extreme rigors of winter and the enfeebling heats of summer being alike unknown, and that consequently the healthfulness of the locality is unsurpassed by that of any other on the North Atlantic coast. An almost constant refreshing breeze and cool nights in summer make Fall River a delightful place of residence—a fact that is recognized and appreciated by many wealthy residents whose homes are designed and constructed with reference to the enjoyment of life at all seasons, and who seldom seek the sea-shore resorts save for temporary change of scene and society.

Fall River was incorporated as a city in the year 1854, from which time until 1870 her progress and growth, more particularly in the matter of population, was more marked for substantial worth than for rapidity, but in the year last named began a rush to secure the desirable mill-sites and other advantages of the vicinity, the making of public and private improvements, the erection of factories, etc., all of which tended to the attraction of permanent dwellers, with the result that in 1880 the city boasted 48,961 residents, in 1885 56,870, and in 1890, as shown by the recent census, 74,351—a gain of about 47,000 in twenty years, or nearly 150 per cent.

The prosperity of Fall River is based upon cotton manufacturing and its collateral industries. Twenty-odd millions of dollars are invested in the mills here, which employ an aggregate of 25,000 hands in all departments and pay $6,500,000 annually in wages. The profits in this business are fair, but for 1890 were not so large as in the preceding year, owing to various causes, among them an advance in the price of raw material, extensive and costly repairs, a dull market for the last half of the year, and a two weeks shut-down, which, by the way, failed of favorable effect upon quotations. Mr. F. O. Dodge furnishes the following figures, showing the capital stock and dividends of thirty mills for the twelve months ending November 10, 1890 :

	Dividend Per cent.	Capital stock.	Amount.		Dividend Per cent.	Capital stock.	Amount.
American,	4	$800,000	$32,000	Metacomet,	1 1-2	$288,000	$4,320
Barnard,	6	330,000	19,800	Narraganset,	6 1-2	400,000	26,000
Border City,	8	1,000,000	80,000	Osborne,	6	600,000	36,000
Barnaby,	6	400,000	24,000	Pocasset,	8	800,000	64,000
Bourne,	12	400,000	48,000	Ric'd Borden,	6	800,000	48,000
Chace,	7 1-2	500,000	37,500	Robeson,	7 1-2	260,000	19,500
Crescent,	4	500,000	20,000	Sagamore,	6 1-2	900,000	58,500
Conanicut,	6	120,000	7,200	Shove,	6 1-2	550,000	35,750
Davol,	8	300,000	24,000	Slade,	5	450,000	27,500
Flint,	9	580,000	52,200	Stafford,	9 1-2	400,000	38,000
Globe yarn,	8	900,000	72,000	Tecumseh	6 1-2	500,000	32,500
Granite,	1	400,000	76,000	Troy,	14	300,000	42,000
Hargraves,	9	400,000	24,000	Union,	14	700,000	105,000
King Philip,	6	1,000,000	60,000	Wampanoag,	9 1-2	750,000	71,250
Laurel Lake,	1-2	400,000	38,000	Weetamoe,	4	550,000	22,000
Merchants'		800,000	64,000				
Mechanics'	9 1-2	750,000	41,000	Totals,		$18,778,000	$1,414,270

Average, 7.55 per cent., against 9.37 per cent. for 1889. The mills showing the largest falling off were the Merchants', American, Wampanoag, Seaconnet, Linen, Sagamore and Flint, while those paying increased dividends were the Crescent, Pocasset, Stafford and Border City.   The mills of Fall River produce every grade and description of cotton cloths, yarns and kindred goods made on this side of the Atlantic, in vast and steadily increasing quantities.   Among the other notable and important industries developed and fostered in large part by

POST OFFICE.—FALL RIVER.

the cotton interest may be mentioned the manufacture of boilers, engines, ma_ chinery of all kinds, loom reeds and harnesses, hats, shoes, etc., while the hand_ ling of coal for mill, railway and domestic consumption, mill supplies, food pro_ ducts, etc., involve millions of capital and the employment of thousands of people.

Banking facilities for all classes are excellent, there being seven National banks with $2,150,000 aggregate capital, two co-operative and three savings banks. Transportation facilities are also ample, there being direct railroad lines to Boston, Providence, New Bedford and Newport, with daily steamers to New York and to Providence. Extensive wharves and docks along the water front afford all requisite conveniences for handling freight and passengers, while the coal companies and cotton mills own and control docks for the accommodation of their own business. The fire and police departments are organized and managed on liberal and enlightened principles. The former is numerous and efficient; the latter strong in numbers, under perfect discipline, provided with the latest improved apparatus and appliances, and thoroughly reliable under all circumstances, having at command inexhaustible supplies of water and further aided by a sprinkler system, operated automatically, with which the mills are equipped.

The public school system, like that of other Massachusetts cities, is hardly susceptible of improvement,—the city owning forty-two school-houses; average attendance, 1889, 7,264, or 71 per cent. of the entire enrollment. In this connection mention should be made of the B. M. C. Durfee high school, the gift of Mrs. Mary B. Young and a memorial to her deceased son Bradford Matthew Charloner Durfee. We have not space for a detailed description, but will state that the building, three and a-half stories in height, is of granite, is 253 feet in length, of an average width of seventy-five feet, and is ornamented with two towers, one containing a clock and chime of bells, the other an observatory fitted with telescope and other appropriate apparatus. Twelve commodious class-rooms, a chemical laboratory, a chemical lecture-hall, masters' room, reception room, mechanical drawing room, gymnasium, industrial science room, and exhibition hall that will seat 1,400 spectators are provided. The generous donor added to her beneficence an endowment fund $50,000. This is the handsomest edifice in the city, which contains also a $250,000 custom-house and post office, a fine court-house, city hall and numerous other public buildings, besides many costly and imposing church structures, massive business blocks and mills. The public library is a conspicuous feature for many reasons, not the least of which is the noble collection of over 30,000 volumes upon its shelves.

Street railways, electric lights and general intelligence and courtesy add much to the attractiveness of the city.

NARRAGANSETT MILLS.

Edward S. Adams, President; James Waring, Clerk and Treasurer—Manufacturers of Cotton Cloth—N. Main Street.

This company was incorporated with capital stock to the amount of $400,000 in 1871. The board of directors meets annually the last week in October, and is composed of President Adams, Clerk and Treasurer Waring, George W. Nowell and George H. Hawes of Fall River; John H. Thompson of Providence, and Abraham Steinau of New York. The company's buildings, situated on North Main street, comprise the mill proper, six stories, 73 x 298 feet, with two-story L, 32 x 106 feet; two-story cloth house, 57 x 78 feet, and storage warehouse of one story, 66 x 150 feet. Superintendent John Harrison has under his direction 325 hands, whose aggregate wages average $2,500 per week. The machinery outfit includes all modern improvements, and consists in part of 38,000 spindles and 948 looms, all driven by a splendid 1000-horse-power triple expansion steam engine. To run the engine and machinery requires the consumption of 3,000 tons of coal and 3,500 gallons of oil annually; the materials used comprise 4,800 bales of cotton and 50,000 pounds of starch, and 12,000,000 yards of superior goods for home and foreign trade are produced.

DR. WM. B. SOLOMON,

Botanical Medical Institute for the treatment of Chronic Diseases — Office and Residence, No. 157 N. Main Street.

A good many years ago Dr. James M. Solomon of Attleboro, Mass., invited the opposition, criticism and scorn of the medical fraternity by devoting himself to the study of certain special-

ties in chronic complaints, including throat and lung troubles, female difficulties, impurities of the blood, liver and kidney irregularities, debility, etc. His success as an investigator was phenomenal, and the remedies he discovered have long since taken their place among the most reliable standard vegetable curatives known. The doctor long enjoyed the fame and favor resulting from his well-directed labors, and, dying, left a worthy successor in his son, Dr. Wm. B. Solomon, trained from boyhood under his father's personal instruction, a graduate of the medical department of Columbia College, New York, and of the New York College of Physicians and Surgeons, and himself an enthusiastic investigator. After some years' active practice and unremitting study and experiment, the younger Dr. Solomon removed to Providence, R. I., where he achieved wonerful success, but the field finally became too narrow for a physician of his reputation and capacity, and he finally removed in May, 1890, to Fall River, establishing his Botanical Medical Institute and laboratory at No. 157 North Main street, where provided with spacious and elegant reception and consultation rooms, ample stocks of the choicest foreign and American medicinal roots, herbs, barks, gums, leaves and blossoms, a superb-

ly appointed laboratory and appurtenances and an intelligent corps of competent assistants — in a word, with every conceivable intellectual, material, physical and mechanical aid—the doctor is prepared to diagnose and treat successfully every form of disease known to the profession, giving, however, special attention to the chronic afflictions indicated in our reference to his father and exemplar. All the medicines he prescribes are prepared direct from the original materials under his own supervision, and are consequently of definite known strength and efficacy. The standard medicines of which he is sole proprietor and manufacturer include Dr. Wm. B. Solomon's vegetable antiseptic tablets for catarrh, bronchitis, hay fever, asthma, influenza, etc.; Dr. Wm. B. Solomon's anti-catarrhal pills; Dr. Wm. B. Solomon's anodyne pills for diarrhea, dysentery and summer complaint; Dr. Wm. B. Solomon's blood syrup, for humors, skin diseases, liver and kidney complaints, general debility, etc.; Dr. Wm. B. Solomon's herbal female pills, and Dr. Wm. B. Solomon's vegetable spermatorrhœa pills. He is also proprietor and sole manufacturer of Dr. Wm. B. Solomon's catarrh cure, harmless salve, cough balsam, fever drops, rheumatic destroyer, India plants (for female complaints — a radical cure), gum liniment, laxative cordial, great appetite medicine, and king of pain cures. Dr. Solomon is an earnest, studious, conscientious and extremely progressive physician, with whom the treatment of the ills that flesh is heir to is neither a pastime nor an experiment, as his phenomenal success attests. He stands high in his profession and the community, and deserves the material prosperity and mental equipoise which he enjoys.

FLYNN BOILER WORKS.

Daniel Flynn — Manufacturer of Flynn's Upright Tubular Boilers — Marine, Locomotive and Stationary Boilers, Tanks, Gas Holders and Heaters — Sheet Iron Work of All Kinds—No. 10 Pond Street.

The world is promised a perfected electric engine that will generate its own power—sometime, and probably the promise will eventually be made good, but in the meantime the steam engine will not be abandoned, and while it survives its indispensable auxiliary and source of power, the steam boiler, will continue in request. A vast amount of ingenuity and experiment have been expended upon the boiler, and it has been brought to a point of perfection and efficiency never dreamed of by Watt or Fulton. Practically speaking, every new boiler·made is an improvement in some respect over the last, even when constructed on the same general lines, in the same shop, by the same mechanics. The skillful boiler-maker is known by the success that attends his work and the patronage influenced thereby. Judged by this standard, Mr. Daniel Flynn ranks with the best. He is the inventor of Flynn's famous upright tubular boiler, which has triumphed in all tests, and in 1882 established works at No. 10 Pond street, this city, for the purpose of manufacturing on a large scale. His shops are abundantly provided with all requisite tools, machinery and appliances. Employing expert workmen only, Mr. Flynn is prepared to execute in the best manner and without delay all orders for marine, locomotive and stationary boilers in new or standard styles, tanks, gas-holders, heaters, and sheet-iron work of every description. Prompt attention is given to repairs in his line. All work done by him is fully warranted, and he does a flourishing business in Fall River and throughout New England.

LAUREL LAKE MILLS.

John P. Slade, President; Abbott E. Slade, Clerk and Treasurer — Manufacturers of Print Cloths and Wide Goods—Broadway.

The Laurel Lake Mills Company, incorporated with $400,000 capital stock in 1881, is one of the most prosperous enterprises in this vicinity, investment considered, the stock being quoted at par and yielding a dividend of 12 per cent. for 1889 — a result, however, which is not so very surprising when it is remembered that the directory is composed of such able and experienced manufacturers as President John P. Slade, S. H. Miller, John B. Whitaker, Prelet D. Conant, Leonard N. Slade and George W. Nowell of Fall River; J. Frank Howland of Boston; James E. Easterbrook of Swansea, and A. E. Slade of Fall River. The mills, situated on Broadway, are of granite, and comprise the main building of five stories, 93 x 244 feet; a three-story picker-house, 51 x 74 feet; a one-story boiler-house, 40 x 58 feet, and a one-story warehouse, 72 x 130 feet. The mill, of which Horace W. Tinkham is superintendent, is fitted up with 35,008 spindles, 880 looms, three steam engines of 800 aggregate horse-power, and all requisite accessories, and gives employment to 365 hands, whose aggregate weekly pay averages $2,400. The annual output is about 13,000,000 yards of print cloths and wide cotton goods for the home market and export, and the consumption of materials and supplies amounts to 4,500 bales of cotton, 40,000 pounds starch, 3,000 gallons of oil and 3,000 tons of coal.

THE MELLEN HOUSE.

G. H. Bowker & Co., Proprietors—Corner of North Main and Franklin Streets.

The Mellen is a truly superb hotel—a magnificent five-story granite, brick and brownstone pile, at once an oranment to the city and a monument to the taste of the architect and the liberality of the projectors. The imposing exterior is, however, but an imperfect index to the interior, where oriental splendor in subdued form combines western elegance and convenience in ministry to the ease and comfort of the inmates and the pleasure of transient visitors, who obtain here a glimpse of what ample means allied to artistic taste may accomplish for the traveler and the permanent guest. A broad and lofty corridor with mosaic floor of marble and walls of hardwood panels leads from the main entrance to the beautifully appointed and commodious office. To the left of the main corridor is the spacious and handsomely equipped billiard hall, to the right of the office a broad and ornate stairway leads to the main corridor of the second floor, and still further to the right is the entrance to the grand dining-hall, capable of seating two hundred people and fitted up in the most attractive style, with antique fireplace and hardwood floor in mosaic design. Returning to the corridor, we find on the left the great public reception-room, sumptuously furnished and fitted with rich hangings and costly carpets, carved tables, luxurious chairs and consoles, rare pictures and a splendid square grand piano. Six equally elegant private parlors are found conveniently distributed upon the various floors, and in addition each of the twenty *suites* of rooms provided for family occupancy has its own separate parlor in the appointments of which cost has been the least consideration. Sixty large and inviting rooms, fitted and furnished to correspond with the rest of the house, are reserved for the accommodation of such guests as are unaccompanied by wives and children. Of course every conceivable provision in the way of toilet rooms, baths, electric lights, watchmen, safeguards against fire and its perils, steam heat, proper ventilation, etc., is made, and the weary stranger who hands over his grip and inscribes his name upon the Mellen's register may retire in the assurance of absolute safety. A fine 60-horse-power steam engine in the basement drives the dynamo and runs the elevators; the house is flooded with light when required, and the necessity of tiresome journeys up and down stairs is dispensed with. Reading and smoking rooms, sample-room, barber-shop and four private dining-rooms for the use of families and parties are also among the attractions.

Messrs. G. H. Bowker & Co., the lessees, are experienced and popular hotel men, proprietors besides of the Hotel Hamilton at Holyoke and the Winthrop Hotel at Meriden, Conn. The firm is composed of Messrs. G. H. and J. H. Bowker, born and reared at Charlestown, N. H. Their first venture in the rôle of hosts was made twelve years ago when they opened the Windsor Hotel at Holyoke, and two years ago took the management of the Hotel Hamilton in that city, which is at present managed by G. H. Bowker & Co. They succeeded so well that five years later they opened the Winthrop at Meriden, Conn., and in 1888 took charge of the Mellen. They study to please and satisfy the traveling and hotel-patronizing public, and, measuring their success by the prosperity that has attended their several enterprises, it is great indeed.

HARGRAVES MANUFACTURING COMPANY.

Reuben Hargraves, Thomas Hargraves - - Manufacturers of Soaps, Refined Tallow, Ground Scraps, Ground Bone, Glue Substitute, etc.---Packers of Tripe, Pigs' Feet and Lambs' Tongues — Neatsfoot Oil — Opp. Stafford Mills, Off Pleasant Street.

Among the largest producers of soaps of various kinds in New England is the Hargraves Manufacturing Company of Fall River, established in 1850 and now managed by Messrs. Reuben and Thomas Hargraves. The works, situated opposite the Stafford mills, off Pleasant street, occupy fifteen two-story frame buildings averaging 30 x 40 feet in dimensions, and are fitted up with the best obtainable machinery and appliances, including soap presses and crushers of large capacity, bone-grinders, four immense steam tanks, three vast soap kettles, one enormous tallow and grease kettle, one glue tank, four box tanks, two stamping machines, etc., a powerful steam engine and two 50-horse power boilers being also provided. Three single and one double teams are employed in the delivery and shipping department. The company are also extensive dealers in tallow, ordinary and steam refined (the latter for mill purposes), greases, neatsfoot and palm oils, glue substitute for calico printers, fresh and pickled tripe, pigs' feet, lambs' tongues, etc., total annual sales of all commodities averaging $200,000 per annum. The ground bone fertilizer made here is claimed to be equal to the most celebrated commercial fertilizers on the market for general use and much cheaper than most others. This preparation of ground bone is employed and indorsed by many of the most progressive farmers in this and adjoining States. The Hargraves Manufacturing Company issue a beautifully illustrated almanac, filled with interesting and instructive reading, especially valuable to the intelligent, progressive farmer.

CHARLES KIRBY & CO.,

Livery, Hack and Boarding Stable   No. 14 Rock Street.

These stables — by all odds the largest, finest and most perfectly appointed in Fall River, were originally established in 1857 — more than thirty-three years ago — by the late Charles S. Kirby, to whom Charles Kirby & Co. eventually succeeded. The building is a massive stone structure of two stories, 50 x 200 feet, with entrance at No. 14 Rock street. Here is kept a superb livery stock, comprising fifty-five horses and ninety vehicles of all kinds suited to the business, and parties in want of elegant carriages for calling or pleasure driving in city or country, backs for carrying passengers to and from the depots, weddings, balls, funerals, etc., hearses, buggies, saddle horses or any of the conveniences of a first-class livery stable can be accommodated here on reasonable terms. Especial attention is given to boarding horses for private owners, and those of transient patrons are carefully looked after. Twelve assistants — hostlers, drivers, etc. — are employed here. A feature of the output is a magnificent $1,800 hearse and team of splendid coal-black horses.

KILBURN, LINCOLN & CO.,

Machinists—Manufacturers of Cotton Looms and Shafting—Canal, Corner Annawan Street.

The old and world-renowned firm of Kilburn, Lincoln & Co. was established in 1844. Its contributions in the way of improved machinery to the development of the cotton manufacturing and other industries is now matter of history. In 1868 the firm became incorporated, and a new era of usefulness and prosperity was inaugurated. The present officers are: President, Andrew Luscomb; clerk and treasurer, Leontine Lincoln; directors, Andrew Luscomb, Chas. H. Dring, Leontine Lincoln and Charles P. Dring. There are no stockholders outside these families. The works of the company, situated at Canal and Annawan streets, are very extensive, the buildings of granite, substantial and commodious, and comprising the machine shops, two stories in height, 50x200 feet; the foundry, one story, 80x138 feet, and three two story warehouses and pattern shops, each 30x100 feet. It would be impossible to describe, in the limits to which we are confined, the machinery and facilities of this plant, but the whole may be summed up in a few words it comprises everything needed in all departments, and every appliance is of the newest and most perfect improved pattern. The same rule applies to the working force, which numbers 200 skilled machinists, pattern-makers and molders.

The company's leading specialties embrace the construction of improved cotton and silk-weaving machinery, shafting, hangers, pulleys and water wheels, in all of which they excel, doing an immense business. Their new high-speed loom is a mechanical wonder, as experienced cotton manufacturers will attest when informed that at the Seaconnet mills, this city, last year, 926 of these looms made 14,229,210 yards of cloth in 301 days of ten hours an average of 114.10 yards per loom per day.

CONGDON, CARPENTER & CO.,

Wholesale Dealers in Iron, Steel, Tin Plates and Metals, Heavy Hardware, Blacksmiths' Supplies, Carriage Woodwork and Trimmings - Nos. 50 and 52 Pocasset Street--Herbert Field, Manager.

The great house of Congdon, Carpenter & Co., of Providence, R. I., of which the above-named concern is a branch, was established in 1874 and is noted throughout New England for the extent of its business and the fairness and liberality that characterizes its transactions. The Fall River establishment occupies the three-story brick building Nos. 50 and 52 Pocasset street, forty feet front by sixty feet deep, and is under the immediate personal management of Mr. Herbert Field, a courteous, enterprising and successful business man, selected by his principals because of his special qualifications to represent them here. Five clerks and assistants are employed, and orders receive instant attention, whether large or small. An immense and carefully assorted stock is shown in all departments, comprising merchant iron and steel in all desirable grades, tin plates and metals, heavy hardware, blacksmiths' supplies, carriage woodwork and trimmings, and kindred commodities in endless variety. Especial attention is given to the wants of the trade and favorable terms guaranteed.

OSBORN MILLS.

Weaver Osborn, President; Joseph Healy, Clerk and Treasurer Manufacturers of Print Cloths, Lawns and Wide Goods Tower Street.

The Osborn Mills rank with the largest producers of fine cottons in this country. The company was incorporated in 1871, with Weaver Osborn at its head and $600,000 capital stock. The present board of directors annual meeting the last Tuesday in April is composed of the president, the clerk and treasurer (both named above), John C. Milne, Edward E. Hathaway, Benjamin Hall, James M. Osborn and Frank S. Stevens. The mill buildings, situated on Tower street, are very extensive and comprise two distinct plants. Mill No. 1 is a massive and ornate granite pile, comprising the mill itself, of six stories, 74x318 feet, connected with which is the picker-house, four stories, 40x90 feet, and one-story boiler-house, 41x61 feet. Mill No. 2 is of brick, six stories, 75x240 feet, with three-story picker-house, 42x75 feet, and two-story cloth-house, 41x69 feet. Together the mills contain 70,200 spindles and 1,848 looms, driven by three improved steam engines, aggregating 1,700 horse-power, and give employment to 800 hands whose weekly wages average $5,800. The annual consumption of cotton is 8,000 bales, of starch 87,000 pounds, of oil 75,000 gallons, of coal 6,500 tons, and the average output 19,500,000 yards of high grade print cloths, lawns and wide goods, the sale of which is confined principally to the United States.

journeys up and down stairs is dispensed with. Reading and smoking rooms, sample-room, barber-shop and four private dining-rooms for the use of families and parties are also among the attractions.

Messrs. G. H. Bowker & Co., the lessees, are experienced and popular hotel men, proprietors besides of the Hotel Hamilton at Holyoke and the Winthrop Hotel at Meriden, Conn. The firm is composed of Messrs. G. H. and J. H. Bowker, born and reared at Charlestown, N. H. Their first venture in the rolé of hosts was made twelve years ago, when they opened the Windsor Hotel at Holyoke, and two years ago took the management of the Hotél Hamilton in that city, which is at present managed by G. H. Bowker & Co. They succeeded so well that five years later they opened the Winthrop at Meriden, Conn., and in 1888 took charge of the Mellen. They study to please and satisfy the traveling and hotel-patronizing public, and, measuring their success by the prosperity that has attended their several enterprises, it is great indeed.

HARGRAVES MANUFACTURING COMPANY.

Reuben Hargraves, Thomas Hargraves — Manufacturers of Soaps, Refined Tallow, Ground Scraps, Ground Bone, Glue Substitute, etc.—Packers of Tripe, Pigs' Feet and Lambs' Tongues — Neatsfoot Oil — Opp. Stafford Mills, Off Pleasant Street.

Among the largest producers of soaps of various kinds in New England is the Hargraves Manufacturing Company of Fall River, established in 1850 and now managed by Messrs. Reuben and Thomas Hargraves.

The works, situated opposite the Stafford mills, off Pleasant street, occupy fifteen two-story frame buildings averaging 30 x 40 feet in dimensions, and are fitted up with the best obtainable machinery and appliances, including soap presses and crushers of large capacity, bone-grinders, four immense steam tanks, three vast soap kettles, one enormous tallow and grease kettle, one glue tank, four box tanks, two stamping machines, etc., a powerful steam engine and two 50-horse-power boilers being also provided. Three single and one double teams are employed in the delivery and shipping department. The company are also extensive dealers in tallow, ordinary and steam refined (the latter for mill purposes), grease, neatsfoot and palm oils, glue substitute for calico printers, fresh and pickled tripe, pigs' feet, lambs' tongues, etc., total annual sales of all commodities averaging $200,000 per annum. The ground bone fertilizer made here is claimed to be equal to the most celebrated commercial fertilizers on the market for general use and much cheaper than most others. This preparation of ground bone is employed and indorsed by many of the most progressive farmers in this and adjoining States. The Hargraves Manufacturing Company issue a beautifully illustrated almanac, filled with interesting and instructive reading, especially valuable to the intelligent, progressive farmer.

CHARLES KIRBY & CO.,

Livery, Hack and Boarding Stable—No. 14 Rock Street.

These stables — by all odds the largest, finest and most perfectly appointed in Fall River, were originally established in 1857 — more than thirty-three years ago — by the late Charles S. Kirby, to whom Charles Kirby & Co. eventually succeeded. The building is a massive stone structure of two stories, 50 x 200 feet, with entrance at No. 14 Rock street. Here is kept a superb livery stock, comprising fifty-five horses and ninety vehicles of all kinds suited to the business, and parties in want of elegant carriages for calling or pleasure driving in city or country, hacks for carrying passengers to and from the depots, weddings, balls, funerals, etc., hearses, buggies, saddle horses or any of the conveniences of a first-class livery stable can be accommodated here on reasonable terms. Especial attention is given to boarding horses for private owners, and those of transient patrons are carefully looked after. Twelve assistants — hostlers, drivers, etc. — are employed here. A feature of the output is a magnificent $1,800 hearse and team of splendid coal-black horses.

KILBURN, LINCOLN & CO.,

Machinists—Manufacturers of Cotton Looms and Shafting—Canal, Corner Annawan Street.

The old and world-renowned firm of Kilburn, Lincoln & Co. was established in 1844. Its contributions in the way of improved machinery to the development of the cotton manufacturing and other industries is now matter of history. In 1868 the firm became incorporated, and a new era of usefulness and prosperity was inaugurated. The present officers are: President, Andrew Luscomb; clerk and treasurer, Leontine Lincoln; directors, Andrew Luscomb, Chas. H. Dring, Leontine Lincoln and Charles P. Dring. There are no stockholders outside these families. The works of the company, situated at Canal and Annawan streets, are very extensive, the buildings of granite, substantial and commodious, and comprising the machine shops, two stories in height, 50x200 feet; the foundry, one story, 80x138 feet, and three two story warehouses and pattern shops, each 30x100 feet. It would be impossible to describe, in the limits to which we are confined, the machinery and facilities of this plant, but the whole may be summed up in a few words—it comprises everything needed in all departments, and every appliance is of the newest and most perfect improved pattern. The same rule applies to the working force, which numbers 200 skilled machinists, pattern-makers and molders.

The company's leading specialties embrace the construction of improved cotton and silk-weaving machinery, shafting, hangers, pulleys and water wheels, in all of which they excel, doing an immense business. Their new high-speed loom is a mechanical wonder, as experienced cotton manufacturers will attest when informed that at the Seaconnet mills, this city, last year, 926 of these looms made 14,229,219 yards of cloth in 301 days of ten hours—an average of 114.10 yards per loom per day.

CONGDON, CARPENTER & CO.,

Wholesale Dealers in Iron, Steel, Tin Plates and Metals, Heavy Hardware, Blacksmiths' Supplies, Carriage Woodwork and Trimmings—Nos. 50 and 52 Pocasset Street—Herbert Field, Manager.

The great house of Congdon, Carpenter & Co., of Providence, R. I., of which the above-named concern is a branch, was established in 1874 and is noted throughout New England for the extent of its business and the fairness and liberality that characterizes its transactions. The Fall River establishment occupies the three-story brick building Nos. 50 and 52 Pocasset street, forty feet front by sixty feet deep, and is under the immediate personal management of Mr. Herbert Field, a courteous, enterprising and successful business man, selected by his principals because of his special qualifications to represent them here. Five clerks and assistants are employed, and orders receive instant attention, whether large or small. An immense and carefully assorted stock is shown in all departments, comprising merchant iron and steel in all desirable grades, tin plates and metals, heavy hardware, blacksmiths' supplies, carriage woodwork and trimmings, and kindred commodities in endless variety. Especial attention is given to the wants of the trade and favorable terms guaranteed.

OSBORN MILLS.

Weaver Osborn, President; Joseph Healy, Clerk and Treasurer—Manufacturers of Print Cloths, Lawns and Wide Goods—Tower Street.

The Osborn Mills rank with the largest producers of fine cottons in this country. The company was incorporated in 1871, with weaver Osborn at its head and $600,000 capital stock. The present board of directors—annual meeting the last Tuesday in April—is composed of the president, the clerk and treasurer (both named above), John C. Milne, Edward E. Hathaway, Benjamin Hall, James M. Osborn and Frank S. Stevens. The mill buildings, situated on Tower street, are very extensive and comprise two distinct plants. Mill No. 1 is a massive and ornate granite pile, comprising the mill itself, of six stories, 74x318 feet, connected with which is the picker-house, four stories, 40x90 feet, and one-story boiler-house, 41x61 feet. Mill No. 2 is of brick, six stories, 75x240 feet, with three-story picker-house, 42x75 feet, and two-story cloth-house, 41x69 feet. Together the mills contain 70,200 spindles and 1,848 looms, driven by three improved steam engines, aggregating 1,700 horse-power, and give employment to 800 hands whose weekly wages average $5,800. The annual consumption of cotton is 8000 bales, of starch 87,000 pounds, of oil 75,000 gallons, of coal 6,500 tons, and the average output 19,500,000 yards of high grade print cloths, lawns and wide goods, the sale of which is confined principally to the United States.

N. U. LYON,

Manufacturer of Lyons' Extracts. Essences of all Kinds. Blacking, Blueing and Inks
—Sole Proprietor of Davis' Inflammatory Extirpator—Agent for Mrs. Sabin's
Cough Syrup and Mrs. Dinsmore's Cough and Croup Balsam—No. 115 Bay
Street.

More than thirty-five years ago—in 1855—Mr. N. U. Lyon entered into the manufacture, on a
small scale, of pure essences and extracts, gradually extending his field of experiment and research and adding to the list of his products as means and opportunity permitted. He is now
one of the most famous New England chemists in his particular line, and his flavoring extracts,
essences, blacking, blueing and inks are celebrated all over the east. He is, in addition, sole
proprietor of that world-renowned remedy for nervous and muscular inflammation, Davis' Inflammatory Extirpator—an instant and unfailing relief and cure for headache, earache, toothache,
sprains, burns, etc.—and general agent for Mrs. Sabin's Cough Syrup, and Mrs. Dinsmore's
Cough and Croup Balsam—home medicaments familiar to and appreciated all over the United
States.

Mr. Lyon's laboratory—his own property—is a substantial two-story frame building 30x48
feet, fitted up with appropriate machinery and apparatus. He employs a sufficient number of
assistants and one team, and does a flourishing and beneficient business.

BORDEN & REMINGTON.

Wholesale Drug and Chemical Manufacturers; Painters' and Masons' Supplies,
Corn, Wheat and Potato Starch, Akron Drain and Sewer Pipe, Lubricating Oils,
etc.—Corner Pond and Annawan Streets.

This firm, successors to R. K. Remington, is composed of Messrs. Charles F. Borden and
Edward B. Remington. They have commodious premises—a two-story frame building, 45x150
feet—at the intersection of Pond and Annawan streets, where is shown an immense stock of the
commodities named in our caption, which are delivered to local consumers or shipped to buyers at
other points at lowest quotations and on favorable terms. Their leading specialties are drugs, chemicals and lubricating oils, but they give prompt attention to orders for manufacturers', painters'
and masons' supplies, Akron drain and sewer pipe, and the best grades of starch of the different varieties, being sole Bristol county agents for the National Starch Manufacturing Company
of Covington, Ky., whose principal office is in New York, representing all leading American
starch manufacturers.

WYOMING MILLS.

C. C. Rounseville, President; W. W. Howland, Treasurer—Manufacturers of Cotton Twines, Carpet Warps, Rope and Wickings—Chase Street, Near Bay.

The Wyoming mill was erected by the late Augustus Chase in 1842, and has long been
known as one of the principal New England representatives of the cordage and carpet warp
industry. The present company was organized and incorporated last year (1890), with
$60,000 capital stock, purchased, remodeled and refitted the premises, and is already doing an
immense business. The mill building, a substantial three-story granite structure 60x270 feet,
fronts Chase street, near Bay, and with adjoining outbuildings and appurtenances constitutes a
very valuable property. The equipment, mostly new, is complete and of the most improved
kind, and is driven by a 240-horse-power steam engine. The employé number 130, and the
output is extremely large, comprising every description of cotton twines and rope, carpet warp
and lamp wickings, which are supplied to the trade all over the United States and exported to
Europe, Central and South America and other countries. The leading specialty is cotton twine
of all kinds, and in these the product of the Wyoming mills is unexcelled. The board of directors is composed of such well-known and reputable gentlemen as C. C. Rounseville, president,
Joseph Slack, A. L. Chase, Isaac W. Howland, and W. W. Howland, treasurer.

NARRAGANSET STABLE.

W. H. Stone—Livery and Boarding Stable—West Bank Street.

This stable was built in 1873, and Mr. Stone has made it one of Fall River's popular institutions. The structure, comfortable and substantial, is of brick, two stories in height, 60x120

feet, well drained and ventilated, provided with all requisite modern sanitary arrangements and conveniences, dry, neat and clean. The regular livery outfit comprises forty horses and the same number of vehicles of all classes—fine carriages, hacks, buggies, etc. In addition to the livery horses, however, there are generally about forty boarders, the property of residents. Every convenience is provided for the proper feeding of physicians' teams and their prompt delivery when wanted, the stables, fitted up with telephone, being open all night. Calls from hotels and depots are met with equal celerity, and a specialty is made of supplying elegant carriages, buggies and teams for pleasure driving, weddings, balls, funerals, etc. Rates are reasonable.

TAUNTON.

THE present city of Taunton marks the site of the first white settlement within the existing limits of Bristol county. It is not known who were the hardy pioneers who planted here their frontier homes and dared the perils of the wilderness and of Indian hatred. The date is fixed as 1639—nineteen years after the landing at Plymouth—but the advance guard of civilization that spread its tents here was not composed of Plymouth men. We have neither space nor inclination to enter upon a detailed account of early events hereabout ; suffice it to say that the region, previously called Cohannet, had the name Taunton conferred upon it by the General Court, March 3, 1640. No formal act of incorporation of the town was ever passed. The bounds of the territory were fixed by the celebrated Miles Standish and John Brown, June 19, 1640, but it was subsequently much enlarged by additions, most of which were lost by cessions to new towns, so that when the city was incorporated on the first Monday of January, 1865, the territory was (and is) both attenuated and awkward in shape, over ten miles in extreme length and varying from two to nine miles in width, principally level, fertile, and watered by numerous ponds and streams of greater or less importance. Geographically, Taunton is situated in the northeasterly part of Bristol county, and is bounded by Norton on the northwest, by Easton on the northeast, by Raynham, Middleborough and Lakeville on the east, by Berkley and Dighton on the south, and by Rehoboth on the west. The Mill, Taunton and Three-mile rivers are the principal water courses. The Taunton rises in Plymouth county and meets the tides at East Taunton, to which lighters ascend and from which they return with freights. Weir village, however, is the port of Taunton, to which light-draught freighters, colliers and similar craft ascend, and where a considerable shipping trade is done. The river empties into Mount Hope bay, seventeen miles below, and is famous for its herring fisheries. Taunton was formerly the sole county seat of Bristol county, but that honor is now shared by Fall River and New Bedford. Population, 1865—the year of incorporation—16,205 ; 1890, 25,389. The city is provided with Holly water-works, well equipped and efficient fire and police departments, level, well-kept streets, handsome public buildings, schools, etc., and is in many respects the equal of larger and more pretentious places in the comforts and conveniences of life.

The model high-school building, of which we present a view, was completed in 1885, and is situated on Washington street, the lot, 279 feet in length, extending to North Pleasant and Grove streets. The basement walls are of bluestone, the superstructure of brick with brownstone trimmings. The edifice has an extreme length of 170½ feet, the central section three stories, 77 feet front and 62 feet wide, while the wings are each of two and a-half stories, 46½ feet front by 88 feet wide, projecting thirteen feet beyond the central section in front and rear.   There are three front entrances to the second story, and under the stairways leading thereto are the entrances to the basement, which, extending under the entire building, is paved with brick, and contains, besides the coal storage, heating apparatus, chemical laboratory, janitor's room, etc., two spacious recreation rooms — one in each wing — thoroughly ventilated, clean and dry.   The sewage, drainage and ventilation are perfect throughout.   On the main floor are two large school-rooms, each 44½ x 60 feet and 16 feet high ; four recitation rooms—two adjoining each large room, each 25 x 28 feet and thirteen feet high ; an apparatus room, 18 x 21 feet — with an adjoining dark room for chemicals ; two hat and cloak rooms, each 17 x 19 feet (each divided into two

HIGH SCHOOL.—TAUNTON.

apartments) ; two teachers' rooms, each 10 x 17 feet, with adjoining closets and toilet rooms ; an entrance hall, 12 x 77 feet, extending lengthwise through the central section of the building, with adjacent vestibules.   Two spacious flights of stairs—one from the vestibule at each end of the main entrance hall, lead to the upper story.   Under each of these is a stairway leading to the basement.   The upper story of the central section contains an assembly room 38 x 77 feet in floor space (exclusive of the very large stage), and 17 feet in height ; also several adjacent small rooms.   The attic rooms in the wings correspond in floor space to the rooms below them.   They are intended mainly for the use of the evening drawing school.   The windows are sufficient in size and number to admit an abundance of well-distributed light.   Those for the school-rooms (including the recitation-rooms) extend from 4 feet above the floors to the ceilings.   The light is admitted from the left and rear of the pupils, when they are sitting at their desks.   The building is warmed by means of steam upon the latest improved principle.

Of churches there are many; the hotels and places of amusement are sufficient in number and of ample capacity ; a most valuable public library is maintained ; the Old Colony Historical Society has its headquarters here, and

every facility is afforded for the intellectual and moral development and entertainment of young and old, as well as for the aid of the poor by the Associated
Charities. The business center and residence districts are substantially and
handsomely built, and the suburbs are embellished by many palatial homes.
Street car lines traverse the city in all directions, and the transportation question
in the city is solved so far as those interested are concerned, while two lines of
railroad furnish connection with " the rest of the world."

The industries of Taunton are extensive and diversified, and embrace the
manufacture of machinery of various kinds ; silver and britannia ware ; fire brick,
tiles, cement, etc. ; cotton fabrics and yarns ; stoves, ranges and furnaces ; electrical supplies and apparatus ; lumber, windows, doors, inside finish, and minor
articles in great variety. The building of locomotive engines was at one time a
leading interest, but has declined of late years, the construction of printing
presses taking its place.

REED & BARTON,

Henry G. Reed, President; George Brabrook, Treasurer; F. L. Fish, Clerk—Manufacturers of Sterling Silver and Electro Plate—No. 48 Britannia Street, Taunton
Mass.—Salesrooms, No. 37 Union Square, New York.

This concern has a history of which we are sure a brief resumé will interest all and instruct
not a few of our readers. In 1824 Isaac Babbitt began making britannia ware by hand and
with the crudest appliances in a small shop near the present City square, soon afterward forming
a copartnership with a practical mechanic named William W. Crossman. The two leased a
room and power on Spring street, and ere the close of the year named succeeded in producing
the first finished britannia ware ever made on this side of the Atlantic. The original rolls used
by the pioneer firm in making plates, teapots, etc., are still exhibited to visitors at Reed & Barton's office, and as compared with the superb machinery now employed for similar purposes are
about as effective as the stage coach of those days alongside a vestibule train of palace sleepers.
The devices served their purpose, however, and in 1827 the enterprising partners were enabled
to build for themselves a new brick factory. The next year Messrs. William Allen West and
Zephaniah A. Leonard became associated with Mr. Crossman under the style of Crossman,

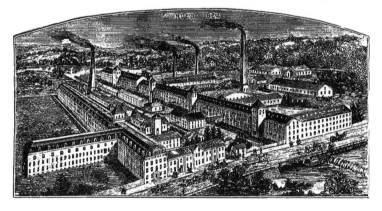

West & Leonard, Mr. Babbitt remaining with the new firm in the capacity of metallurgist.
About the same time Henry G. Reed and Charles E. Barton entered the works as apprentices.
The firm prospered, and soon had all they could do to supply the demand for tea and coffee
pots, urns and britannia table ware. In 1830, with a view of increasing facilities and obtaining
more economical power, the firm erected a much larger brick factory on the west bank of Mill
river, in what is now known as Britanniaville, and organized the Taunton Britannia Manufacturing Company : and after a few years the company closed up the business and paid all their
debts, leaving their equipment in the hands of Reed & Barton, who in the meantime

had become expert workmen. They were also industrious and capable, and at once formed a copartnership and went to work, with small capital and in a modest way, to recover the ground lost by their former employers, which, thanks to indomitable energy and first-class business capacity, they were enabled to do. After two years Mr. Gustavus Leonard became associated with them, under the style of Leonard, Reed & Barton, and after a time the firm was enabled to purchase the buildings and plant. In 1840 they were awarded a gold medal for the best exhibit of britannia ware at the American Institute fair, New York. Mr. Leonard died in 1845, when the style was changed to Reed & Barton, and Henry H. Fish was admitted. In 1859 George Brabrook, an old and faithful employé, was made a member of the firm, which continued without further change until the death of Mr. Barton in 1867, when the surviving members purchased his interest, retaining the old name and style. Mr. Fish died in 1882, and was succeeded by his sons, George H. and Frank L. In 1888, for convenience and the segregation of the various interests, an act of incorporation was procured under the style of Reed & Barton; capital stock, $600,000.

From time to time new buildings have been erected, the mechanical appliances multiplied, facilities in all departments increased, greater numbers of operatives employed, and the productive capacity augmented in every way, until now these works are unquestionably among the largest in the United States and turn out great quantities of fine sterling silver and electro-plate, while design and quality are unsurpassed by any rival in America or Europe. The goods are handled by all leading dealers in the world. It is unnecessary to describe the works, which are shown in our engraving. They cover about eight acres of land.

UNION STOVE LINING COMPANY.

G. A. Lincoln, Treasurer—Manufacturers of Fire Brick Linings for Stoves, Ranges, Furnaces, etc.—Corner Fifth and West Water Streets, Weir Village.

Messrs. G. A. Lincoln, E. N. Goff and Nathan W. Welch established this company in 1882. The premises, situated at the corner of Fifth and West Water streets, Weir Village, comprise a great one-and-three-story frame structure, 60x240 feet, with L's respectively 28x60, 30x34 and 30x30 feet, connected with which is a 25x80-foot clay storage house—all wood; a fire-proof-moulding-room 22x40 feet, barns, sheds, etc., with ample yards attached. The appliances are complete, from eighteen to twenty-five hands are employed, and the output of stove, range and furnace linings varies from 300 to 400 sets daily. These goods, which are of the best quality and sold at lowest living prices, are delivered free on board cars or vessels at Taunton for shipment, mostly to Boston and New England cities and to Philadelphia, the central west and the Pacific slope, though orders are filled at any time for foundrymen, repairers and jobbers. About 1000 tons of fire clay is consumed annually. Large stocks are carried, and catalogues and price lists furnished on application.

ELIZABETH POOLE MILLS.

William C. Lovering, President; Albert E. Swasey, Treasurer—Manufacturers of Cotton Flannels—Adams Street.

The Elizabeth Poole Mills (named in honor of the English lady who is credited with having patronized and assisted the early settlers of Taunton) were incorporated in 1877; capital stock, $75,000. The plant, situated on the bank of Mill river at the foot of Adams street, comprises buildings of brick, one and two stories in height, with spacious appurtenances, the whole covering about two acres of land. The equipment is first-class and includes 8,896 spindles, 240 looms and a duplex Harris-Corliss steam engine of 250 horse-power. The number of operatives is about 175, and the output of high-grade cotton flannels varies from 8,000 to 12,000 yards daily. These goods are sold readily, and distributed all over the United States and the hot countries south of us through the usual channels—New York and Boston jobbers.

NEW ENGLAND STOVE COMPANY.

L. B. West, Treasurer; W. H. Lindsey, Manager—Manufacturers of Stoves, Ranges and Hollow Ware—Wales Street.

In 1845 Deacon Lemuel Leonard erected a small foundry below and near the present Whittenton mills site on Mill river, where he embarked in the casting of stoves and small hollow ware. After a few years he admitted to a copartnership his son, Lemuel M., and the works were enlarged. The good deacon died in 1858, and the son succeeded to the sole proprietor-ship, remaining on Mill river and prospering until 1865, when he erected and occupied a large foundry on Wales street, where he continued to transact a flourishing business up to the time of his death in 1876. The Leonard Co-operative Foundry Company was organized in 1877; capital, $25,000; John Eddy, president; Henry G. Leonard, treasurer. After one year L. B. West was made president and remained so until last February, when the New England Stove Company was organized by Messrs. West and Lindsey, who took entire control as treasurer and manager respectively. Mr. West is well known to the commercial world as head of L. B. West & Co. and the West Silver Company, and Mr. Lindsey is an experienced practical stove manu-facturer. The works on Wales street consist of the brick foundry building, 55 x 135 feet, with L 55 x 65 feet, and several frame storehouses, sheds, etc., the whole covering ground more than two acres in extent. The establishment is well equipped throughout with all desirable appliances, including a fifty-horse-power steam engine, and gives employment to from thirty to fifty skilled molders, mounters, etc., the annual capacity being about $100,000 worth of finished goods, embracing full lines of stoves, ranges, furnaces and hollow ware. Among the leading specialties may be named the "Rockford" parlor stove and the "Montello" range, which have no superiors.

WEST SILVER COMPANY.

Successors to F. B. Rogers Silver Co. — L. B. West, Treasurer — Manufacturers of Hollow Ware, Spoons, Forks, Knives, Ladles, Cutlery, etc.—Winthrop Street.

The West Silver Company — unincorporated — is composed of Messrs. W. H. Phillips, presi-dent of the Taunton Crucible Company, treasurer of the Taunton Iron Works, and a director of

the Taunton Street Railway Company; Lewis Williams, a director of the Dighton Furnace Company and of the Staples Coal Company; L. B. West, of L. B. West & Co., hardware mer-chants, treasurer; Lemuel C. Porter, designer and foreman of the works, and E. W. Porter, superintendent. This company in 1887 bought the plant of the world-famous F. B. Rogers Silver Company, and assumed the management, with the result that the business has grown and continues to grow rapidly, annual sales exceeding $100,000 in value, while territorially the field of operations covers the entire United States, Canada, Mexico, the West Indies and South and Central America. Constantly bringing out new designs of artistic merit, and manufacturing only the best of silver-plated table-ware — tea and coffee sets, spoons, knives, forks, cutlery, etc., together with silver-plated, nickel, silver flat ware in extra, double and triple-plated grades — which is sold at reasonable prices, the outlook for indefinite extension of the business seems very bright. The premises on Winthrop street, in the form of a hollow square, are four stories in height and seventy feet long on each front, fitted up with steam power, and divided into foundry, electro-plating, stamping, finishing and engraving departments, each complete in itself and distinct from the others. In all seventy hands are employed, and the output is very large. Mr. L. B. West was treasurer and E. W. Porter superintendent of the F. B. Rogers Silver Company, incorporated, of which J. F. Montgomery was president.

BRISTOL COUNTY SAVINGS BANK.

Joseph E. Wilbar, President; William H. Fox, Vice President; Alfred C. Place, Treasurer and Clerk of Corporation—No. 35 Broadway.

The Bristol County Savings Bank was incorporated March 2, 1846; Silas Sheperd was president from May 9, 1846, to January, 1882, since which time Mr. Joseph E. Wilbar has officiated in that capacity; George B. Atwood was the first treasurer, Charles H. Atwood second treasurer, and Alfred C. Place succeeded to that position in January, 1881, acting also as clerk of the corporation. Messrs. Alfred B. Sproat and Chester E. Walker are respectively first and second clerks, William H. Fox vice-president. The board of trustees is composed of leading business men, as follows: Ezra Davol, Charles Foster, Wm. H. Fox, Everett D. Godfrey, Timothy Gordon, R. Henry Hall, Thomas J. Lothrop, Francis L. Morse, Charles H. Paull, Silas D. Presbrey, E. Maltby Reed, Zacheus Sherman, Joseph E. Wilbar and Philander Williams. Board of investment—Ezra Davol, Wm. H. Fox, Silas D. Presbrey, Zacheus Sherman and Joseph E. Wilbar. From its inception the Bristol County Savings Bank has held a leading place among the fiduciary trusts of Massachusetts, and has rendered immeasurable service to all classes of the community while enjoying exceptional prosperity as a corporation. The appended statement, copied from the books March 29, 1891, shows the present condition of the institution:

LIABILITIES.		ASSETS.	
Deposits	$3,680,011.54	Public funds	$815,000 00
Interest	92,186 49	Loans on public funds	1,000 00
Profit and loss	105 87	Bank stock	370,500 00
Guaranty fund	135,000 00	Loans on bank stock	1,300 00
		Railroad bonds	485,000 00
		Real-estate for banking purposes	25,000 00
		Loans on real-estate	1,098,435 00
		Loans on personal security	917,200 00
		Loans to cities, towns, etc	146,000 00
		Loans on bank books	4,530 00
		Deposits in banks on interest	38,880 98
		Current expenses	3,245 77
		Cash on hand	1,212 15
Total	$3,907,303.90	Total	$3,907,303 90

The bank occupies one-half of the fine two-story brick building No. 35 Broadway, which stands back from the street, the other half containing the Taunton free public library. The bank has recently rebuilt its vault and put in a new safe, and the security offered for its funds is second to none in the country.

DIGHTON ROCK PANTS COMPANY.

P. H. Corr, H. A. Cushman, Proprietors; McElroy & Cushman, General Agents—Manufacturers of Clothing—Winthrop Street.

A celebrated feature of the Taunton river is the so-called Dighton rock in the town of Dighton, a large gneiss boulder that projects above water at low tide and exhibits upon its face a series of rude hieroglyphics, which may have been the work of the Norsemen who visited the North American coast in the eleventh century, though it was more probably executed by some idle native savage. It was in commemoration of this rock that the Dighton Rock Pants Company, established in August, 1890, was named by the proprietors, Messrs. P. H. Corr and H. A. Cushman—the latter of McElroy & Cushman, the well-known Main street clothing merchants, who are general agents of the company. The pants company's factory is situated in the West Silver Manufacturing Company's building on Winthrop street, occupying the upper floors, where are employed from thirty to thirty-five designers, cutters and operatives, the latter provided with improved sewing machines in abundance. Here the company is kept busy on orders from all parts of the country, and some export, for clothing in great quantities and of every description, their specialties embracing full lines of men's custom pants at prices from $3.50 to $6.50, suits, overcoats, ulsters, reefers, club, band and military uniforms, boating, yachting and tennis suits, etc., of superior material, excellent fit and first-class workmanship, all of which, by reason of their peculiar facilities, they are enabled to furnish at prices about twenty-five per cent. lower than are ordinarily paid. Mr. P. H. Corr, the senior partner, is a well-known citizen, prominent in many manufacturing and commercial enterprises.

M'ELROY & CUSHMAN,

Hatters, Custom Tailors and Clothiers—Mason's Block, Main Street.

The firm of McElroy & Cushman was established in 1874. Occupying one of the handsomest and most commodious stores on Main street, fitted up with all modern attractions and improvements, plate glass front, electric lights, cash carrier system, etc., they have a courteous and competent corps of assistants. The stock of ready-made clothing and men's furnishings is carefully selected and comprehensive, embracing the latest styles and choicest goods at low prices. Their hat salesmen will delight in exhibiting the very newest Paris, London and New York wrinkles in male head-gear from the most celebrated manufacturers, while, a little further along, may be seen the largest, most varied and seductive line of fine imported woolens ever shown in Taunton. Orders for outer garments of any kind for men's wear will be executed with dispatch and in a style equal to that of the most noted fashionable tailor in Gotham or the Hub, and at lower prices. Mr. McElroy is a Vermonter, Mr. Cushman a native of New Bedford. The latter has resided here for many years, and served under the old flag in the civil war for four years.

ELDRIDGE & CO.,

Manufacturers of Superior White Metal and Silver-Plated Coffin Plates, Hinges, Lining Tacks, etc.

For many years the name of Eldridge has been familiar to all jobbers of undertaker's hardware, and the funeral directors have for a long time recognized the value of their goods. The business was established in 1848 by Eli Eldridge, on West Britannia street; later, his son Eli H., who was making a similar line in another place, united his business to his father's under the present name of Eldridge & Co. Upon the death of Eli Eldridge, in 1875, his grandson, John H., became a member of the firm, and in 1890 another grandson, Albert S., was admitted to the company. There has been a constant increase of business from year to year, their goods going to all parts of the United States and Canada, and a few to South America. Eldridge & Co.'s works, situated on Eldridge street, were erected in 1882, and consist of a two-and-a-half-story frame building, thirty-two feet front and ninety feet deep, fitted up with a twenty-horse-power engine, a forty-horse-power boiler, large and superior power presses, rolling mill, electroplating apparatus and other necessary machinery, and furnishes employment for twenty to thirty skilled workmen. The specialties made here are coffin and casket name plates, hinges, lining tacks, etc. All the goods are made from superior metals, and finished in the best possible manner. Their goods are unsurpassed for finish and style. They sell to the jobbing trade only, and all orders are shipped at short notice to the extent of stock on hand, or as soon as manufactured. Their goods are kept in stock by all the leading jobbers.

J. C. SPROAT,

Manufacturer of Boxes and Nail Casks—Dealer in Box Boards and Boxes in Shooks for Shipment—Mill and Yards at the Weir.

James Sproat, a well-known lawyer and former town clerk of Taunton, established this industry in 1837, subsequently admitting to copartnership therein his son, James H. The elder Mr. Sproat died in 1857, whereupon the son succeeded to and managed the business until his death last year, when the property and the direction of affairs passed to his son, J. C., the present capable and enterprising proprietor, who, brought up in the office and shops, is intimately acquainted with all details, besides being an affable and popular gentleman personally. As an indication of his amiability and kindly disposition and the regard in which he is held by those who know him best, it may be stated here that he still has in his employ several men who, beginning with the grandfather, have worked uninterruptedly for three generations of Sproats, all liberal and considerate employers. The original mill was built at the Weir. Later another was started opposite the village green at the Center, but was burned in 1848, after which the Weir factory was enlarged and operations concentrated there. In September, 1883, a fire occurred which destroyed the entire plant, but it was reconstructed, completely refitted with new and improved machinery and appliances, and again started up within three months, the brick shops covering ground 70 x 100 feet in area, with spacious yards and all necessary appurtenances. The equipment includes a steam engine, three box-board and three box-fitting saws, heading machine, planer, etc.; twenty-six men form a full complement of employes, and the output is very large, though the mills are seldom run to their utmost capacity, transactions last year aggregating 50,000 finished boxes and kegs for the local trade and over 1,000,000 feet of box-boards in shooks for shipment by water direct from the wharf to New York. If necessary, production could easily be increased 100 per cent., and Mr. Sproat anticipates running to his full capacity ere long, as the demand steadily increases.

PHŒNIX MANUFACTURING COMPANY.

Arthur Pickering, President; H. D. Atwood, Treasurer; H. C. Atwood, Secretary—
Manufacturers of Pure Ceylon Plumbago Crucibles—West Water Street.

Previous to 1844 no crucibles were made in the United States. That year Messrs. Charles R.
Atwood and Charles R. Vickery of Taunton undertook the manufacture of these indispensable
adjuncts to metallurgy and the mechanical arts, and succeeded so well that in 1851 the Legislature incorporated the Phœnix Manufacturing Company; C. R. Vickery, president; C. R.

Atwood, agent; H. D. Atwood, secretary; J. P. Crane, clerk. Prior to that time, however, in
1846, the silver medal of the Franklin Institute of Pennsylvania had been awarded the company
—a distinction again conferred in 1852, the Maryland Institute awarding a silver medal the
same year. The great bronze medal of the New York World's Exhibition of 1853 followed, and
since then substantial and enduring tokens of recognition have rewarded the company whenever
and wherever it has entered into competition with its rivals or would-be rivals. It is true that
its trade has been confined principally to New England, the Atlantic and Middle States, but
that was because of the greater demand east of the Mississippi and the unprofitableness of the
far western market; notwithstanding which, the Phœnix crucibles have been tested and unquali-
fiedly indorsed by many prominent western smelters. The works, which employ twenty-five
men and a 100-horse-power steam engine, are situated on West Water street, and occupy, with
their appurtenances, tenements for help, etc., about three acres of land. The machinery equipment, peculiar and of special design, is comprehensive and costly, and so effective that, with the
aid of so small a working force — twenty-five — the company is enabled to put upon the market
about 2,000,000 perfect crucibles, valued at $75,000, per annum. Président Pickering is a
resident of Boston and prominent in political circles. Treasurer H. D. Atwood and Secretary H.
C. Atwood live in Taunton and manage the business. The central western agents are: M. M.
Buck & Co., St. Louis; C. D. Colson, Chicago; Post & Co., Cincinnati.

H. L. CUSHMAN & CO.,

Manufacturers of Papier-Mache Shoe and Tufting Buttons—No. 24 Court Street.

Among the smaller manufactured articles in every-day use by all classes of people, none are
of greater or more abiding importance than are buttons — buttons for under and outer garments,
buttons for shoes, buttons for gloves, buttons for decoration and ornament—buttons for every conceivable purpose; buttons of silk, of wool, of cotton, of linen; buttons of gold, of silver, of
nickel, of brass and of iron; buttons of pearl, of ivory, of bone, of horn; buttons of glass, of
stone, of wood; buttons of composition, and finally, buttons of papier-maché—the latter among
the most durable and economical, and especially adapted to exposure and rough usage, as in the
finishing of shoes, the upholstering of furniture, and for similar purposes. Among the most
extensive manufacturers of papier-maché buttons in this country is the firm of H. L. Cushman &
Co.—H. L. and David B. Cushman—established in 1882 and occupying one floor (7000 square
feet) of the Anthony & Cushman Company's mill, entrance No. 24 Court street, conveniently
divided into well-appointed office, storage wareroom, factory and japanning department. The
machinery, driven by steam, is specially designed for the purpose and of the most perfect character, enabling the firm, with twenty-four button machines and thirty operatives, to produce

700 great gross—84,000 gross—per day, in all sizes and styles, which are supplied to the trade all over this continent. Mr. David B. Cushman, who was agent of the Anthony & Cushman corporation, tack manufacturers, looks after the buying and selling operations and general management of the factory of H. L. Cushman & Co., while Horatio L. has charge of the financial department of the concern.

STRANGE'S MACHINE WORKS.

Emerson C. Strange — Manufacturer of Cast Steel Cylinder Saws, Improved Hogshead, Barrel, Nail Keg, Tub and Pail Machinery and Improved Box Board Machines, Combination Foot Lathes, Patent Combination Vise and Drill, etc.— No. 36 Washington Street.

Strange's Machine Works of Taunton was one of the pioneers in this particular industry, having been engaged in it since 1827, when the works were established by Elias Strange, father of

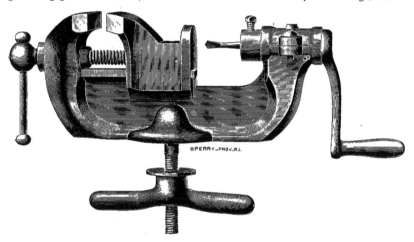

the present proprietor, who, in time, after some changes, succeeded to the business in 1885 under the present title. The works, which occupy all of the three-story frame building, 60 x 80 feet, at No. 36 Washington street, are equipped in the best manner with steam power and all requisite iron, steel and woodworking machinery and special tools, while a sufficient force of skilled mechanics is employed to fill all orders promptly, whether for delivery in the United States and Canada or for export to other countries. The specialties made here embrace the latest perfected improvements in cooperage machinery, together with boxboard machines, combination foot lathes, improved iron tackle blocks, and, latest and among the most ingenious and useful of all, E. C. Strange's patent combination vise and drill for the use of mechanics, amateurs, jewelers and others to whom a handy tool of the kind is of importance. It is made of the best materials and in four sizes and styles, ranging in weight from 27 inches to 22 pounds, and in price from $1 to $7. Attachments extra. Complete catalogues are sent on application.

HARRUB STABLE.

John A. MacDonald, Manager—Broadway.

George Harrub established this stable twenty-five or thirty years ago, and managed it successfully until Mr. John A. MacDonald took charge in 1882. Under the latter's administration the enterprise has continued to maintain its place as the largest, best appointed and most popular concern of the kind in Taunton. The stable, situated on Broadway and approached through the arch, is of stone, 60x130 feet in area, and has fifty stalls, office with telephone, harness and robe rooms, waiting-room, etc., under the same roof, and adjoining are two commodious carriage houses. A large stock of fine horses and carriages are kept for hire, and the best attention is given to animals kept at board. Any kind of team and vehicle is furnished at short notice at reasonable rates, and a specialty is made of supplying hacks for funerals, weddings, parades, excursions and the transfer of passengers.

S. A. WILDE MANUFACTURING COMPANY.

S. A. Wilde, Randall Dean—Manufacturers of Superior Heavy Polished Tin Ware—
Wholesale Dealers in Kitchen Furnishing Goods, Patent Siphon Oil Cans and
" Patent Tea Kettle Steamers "—No. 24 Court Street.

The S. A. Wilde Manufacturing Company is a comparatively new enterprise, having been
established in October, 1889, but is already a pronounced and expanding success, transactions
from July 1, 1890, to January 1,
1891, aggregating over $37,000
—say at the rate of $75,000 per
annum, which is ample evidence
that Messrs. Wilde and Dean
not only know how to do it,
but do it. The factory occupies
the Old American Screw Company's mill just off Court street
—one great floor, 7000 square
feet in area — and is fitted up
with the latest and most approved new machinery adapted
to their purposes, including rolling, stamping, cutting, drawing,
wiring and polishing devices driven by steam, retinning vats, and,
in a word, every conceivable facility, implement and appliance that
will contribute to the excellence and rapidity of the work done by the twenty-five skilled
mechanics employed. The output includes every description of superior heavy polished tin ware,
and the goods are extremely popular with New England and western buyers and consumers, one
of their new specialties — the improved cream pail — receiving the instant indorsement of every
farmer and dairyman who has examined it. The firm are also wholesale dealers in kitchen
furnishing goods, patent siphon oil cans, the " patent tea kettle steamers," etc., and agents for
the Eustis Manufacturing Company of New York, whose " Puritan " cookers and house furnishing specialties are favorably known everywhere. Messrs. Wilde and Dean are wide-awake,
energetic young men, and have taken the right course to reach the top round of business fame.

WHITTENTON MANUFACTURING COMPANY.

Wm. C. Lovering, President; Charles Lovering, Treasurer; Henry M. Lovering,
Agent—Manufacturers of Ginghams, Dress Goods, Fancy Shirtings, Cottonades
and Stripes—Whittenton.

The village of Whittenton, situated on Mill river in the town of Taunton, owes its origin,
industrially, to James Leonard, who began the manufacture of bar iron in 1656 and in 1670
erected a forge on the west bank of Mill river. These works remained in the Leonard family
until 1805, when Crocker, Bush & Richmond established a nail factory above the bridge, to
which in 1807 they added another story and began spinning cotton yarn, which was woven into
cloth by neighboring farmers' families. The combined yarn and nail mill was destroyed by fire
in 1811, but rebuilt, three stories and an attic in height, 30x70 feet, and the spinning of yarn
resumed. Some years later about forty Slater looms were added to the equipment, and it is
said that this was the first American mill to make good cloth by water power. In 1824 the
Whittenton mills were incorporated with the Taunton Manufacturing Company, and in 1831-32
a new stone mill was built, the property remaining under the control of the Taunton Manufacturing Company until 1835, when the Whittenton Manufacturing Company succeeded to the
ownership. In 1835 Mr. Willard Lovering took charge as agent, and, after devising and developing sundry improvements in the manufacture of cotton cloth, became joint proprietor. In
1858 Mr. Lovering and his sons purchased the Whittenton Company's franchise outright, and
in 1875 Mr. Lovering, senior, retired, when the concern was reorganized on a basis of $600,000
capital stock: William C. Lovering, president; Charles Lovering, treasurer; Henry M. Lovering, agent.

As it now stands the plant comprises about twenty-five two, three and four-story brick and
stone buildings (twelve acres of floorage), surrounded by fifteen acres of yards and eighty acres
of streets and tenements. A railroad station on the land affords all necessary conveniences for
travelers to and from Taunton city and other points. That the passenger traffic is a considerable item will be understood when it is stated that the 1200 mill hands and their families reside
upon the premises. The mill is fitted up in the very best manner, the equipment consisting in
part of 42,000 spindles and 1,455 looms, driven by two turbines and seven Corliss engines, the
latter supplying 1500 horse-power. The output of high-grade ginghams, dress goods, fancy
shirtings, cottonades and stripes averages nearly 60,000 yards daily, and is distributed throughout the United States and other American countries.

CHAS. HEWITT & CO.,

Manufacturers of Fine Calf and Buff Shoes—No. 34 Court Street—Boston Office, No. 120 Summer Street.

This firm is composed of Messrs. Charles Hewitt and Albert B. Witherell, the first-named formerly of Leach & Hewitt, shoe manufacturers at Raynham, from which concern he retired in 1885 and formed the present copartnership with Mr. Witherell, an experienced practical cutter, familiar with all details of factory management. Their establishment, fitted up and started in February, 1885, is an extensive one, the principal building being of brick, two stories, 40x135 feet, in addition to which they occupy the two upper floors, each 40x45 feet, of the adjoining three-story structure fronting on Court street. Here, provided with a comprehensive plant of modern improved machinery, steam power and all facilities, and employing about sixty hands, the house produces about 100 cases (twenty-four pairs to the case) weekly, of cheap and medium buff and calf bals, button and congress gaiters, Oxfords, etc., for men's, youths' and boys' wear. These goods are sold principally in the New England and Middle States to jobbers through the Boston office, No. 120 Summer street.

SWEET & TUCKER,

Steam, Gas and Water Fitters, Repairers and Jobbers—Dealers in Steam Pipe and Fitters' Supplies—No. 26 Cohannet Street.

This firm, established April 1, 1891, is composed of Messrs. I. H. Sweet, a native of Taunton, a machinist, engineer and brass finisher of long experience and great skill, formerly connected with several of the most reputable houses here, and G. W. Tucker, who learned his trade with the old concern of H. R. Barker & Co. of Lowell, and remained in their employ for a long time. He has been a resident of Taunton during the past five years, and was with L. W. Cooper for awhile.

Sweet & Tucker's shops and salesroom are situated in the two-story brick building No. 26 Cohannet street, which they have fitted up in a convenient manner with requisite machinery and tools, and where they employ a competent force of expert workmen in their specialty of steam, gas and water piping and fitting, repairing and jobbing, giving prompt and careful attention to all calls for their services, either in the city or any part of this and adjoining States. They guarantee satisfaction in all cases. Those who contemplate building or introducing gas, steam, hot or cold water and steam heating are advised to communicate with Messrs. Sweet & Tucker, who also carry large stocks of goods in their line for the convenience of the trade.

TAUNTON COPPER MANUFACTURING COMPANY.

George M. Woodward, President; H. F. Bassett, Treasurer—Refiners of Copper—Manufacturers of Yellow Metal Sheathing, Sheet Copper and Brass and Copper —West Water Street, Near Third.

The above-named company, incorporated in 1831, long stood at the head of the American copper manufacturing industry, and still transacts a very large business, which, now that there is a prospect of the revival of American shipbuilding, it is hoped will again expand to something like its former proportions. The works, situated on West Water street, near Third, cover one and a-half acres and comprise a completely equipped copper refinery, copper rolling-mill, yellow metal mixing department, yellow metal rolling-mill, and appropriate workshops fitted up with elaborate and costly machinery, the latter driven by steam engines aggregating 900-horse-power. There are now employed in all capacities about the premises one hundred and twenty workmen, so that it will be seen that the plant is by no means idle. The leading specialties include the refining of impure copper brought direct from the mines; the rolling and finishing of sheet copper for smiths' use in all sizes and thicknesses and for all purposes; the mixing and rolling of yellow metal into sheathing for the bottoms of marine craft, and the making of cut copper nails of every description.

President Woodward is a prominent citizen, identified with banking interests. Treasurer Bassett is a practical machinist, mechanical engineer and business man, a graduate of the shops and office of the Taunton Locomotive Works. After three years' practical experience as superintendent of the Taunton water-works, he embarked in the foundry and machine shop business in Wisconsin, but sold out to accept his present position. He is also a director of the Locomotive Works corporation and an enterprising, energetic and successful young man.

TAUNTON NICKEL PLATING COMPANY.

J. M. Evans, Proprietor—Water Street.

The decorative arts have crept quietly and unobtrusively into the homes of the people, and to such an all-pervading extent that the commonest every-day household implements are more or less tinged with the beautiful, either in form, color or ornamentation. The very stove, the range, poker and tongs have imparted to them an additional luster by the action of the electric fluid upon metallic salts brought in contact through the medium of water with the parts it is desired to so enrich, and the brightness of the kitchen and the fireside is greatly enhanced thereby, nickel being the favorite metal for that purpose, and for obvious reasons. In 1880 Mr. J. M. Evans, then a prosperous grocer, concluded that one of Taunton's pressing industrial wants was a first-class nickel-plating concern, and at once set about supplying it. The success he has met with may be measured by the extent of last year's business, which aggregated nearly $20,000. His establish- ment on West Water street, Weir village, is a one-and-a-half-story frame building, 35x125 feet, thoroughly equipped in all respects with battery, vats and all appliances, and furnishes employ- ment to twenty-five workmen under the supervision of an expert. His patronage is mostly of a local character, the great stove, range, and hardware manufacturers being his best customers, and most of his work being confined to the plating of stove and range trimmings, but he is pre- pared to execute orders for every description of nickel-plating at reasonable prices. Mr. Evans has served in the Legislature and in both branches of the city government, is a Freemason, a vet- eran of the civil war, and a member of the G. A. R., besides being a popular citizen. He owns 400 feet of river front and wharf, and transacts a good business in the loading and unloading of coal, iron and clay vessels.

NEW PROCESS TWIST DRILL COMPANY.

B. L. Dwinnell, President; Peter H. Corr, Treasurer—Manufacturers of Hot-Forged Straight Lip Increase Twist and Bit-Stock Drills—No. 34 Court Street.

The success that has attended the New Process Twist Drill Company is a signal proof, if one were needed, that the best is not only the cheapest, but will inevitably win its way, under ordinarily fair conditions, into general confidence. Only five years ago—in 1886—this company was incorporated, capital stock $15,600, and already controls a great and fast-increasing trade all over this continent and Europe, actual trial having demonstrated the immeasurable superior-

ity of its goods over those of all rival manufacturers. Neither time, experiment, labor or expense have been spared to attain perfection, and results are all that the most sanguine could have hoped for. These drills, besides possessing all the best qualities of others, incorporate many advantages hitherto unknown. By the new process the drill, made of the best imported steel, is hot-forged, not milled; the mild center—a characteristic of all bar steel—is thoroughly incor-

porated with the mass by the forging process, whereby the point and cutting lip are made much tougher and firmer than by any of the older processes. "The proof o' the puddin' is the eatin' o' 't," and the evidence of the New Process Twist Drill Company's improved method is found in the fact that every year since operations commenced has witnessed an increase of facilities to meet augmented demand for a grade of drills that no other house can supply. The shops now occupied at No. 34 Court street are two in number, frame, 40 x 60 and 40 x 100 feet respectively, fitted up with steam power and appropriate machinery, such as power hammers, lathes, planers, forges, rolling and grinding machines, milling machines for small drills, etc., and giving employment to about fifty expert tool-makers. Here are made complete lines of twist drills for every conceivable purpose, jewelers' sets, steel sockets for taper shank drills, steel sleeves, and black walnut cases for drills, jewelers' chucks and sockets. Sales for last year exceeded $60,000. The officers of the company are well-known citizens. President Dwinnell is Taun- ton's leading homœopathic physician, and Treasurer Corr is an extensive dealer in cotton, cot- ton waste and paper stock. Owing to the steady increase of the business, the company intend to double the productive capacity at the end of next year.

PRESBREY STOVE LINING COMPANY,

Manufacturers of Fire Brick and Stove Linings—Dealers in Fire Clay, Fire Cement, Kaolin, Fire Sand, etc.—No. 212 Somerset Avenue.

The Presbrey Stove Lining Company, incorporated in 1866, capital $28,000, was organized to succeed William and Albert Presbrey, who had been for forty years engaged in the same industry, occupying two small sheds on the opposite side of the street from the present works. These latter are the largest of the kind in the United States, embracing three and three-fourths acres of land, skirted on the east side for 600 feet by the Old Colony railroad, thus facilitating the delivery of materials and fuel and the shipment of products. About two acres are covered with connecting frame buildings as follows: Stove lining shop, 36x172 feet; mix-

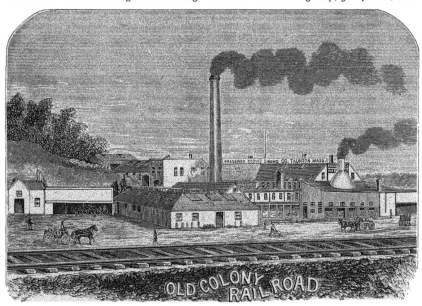

ing room, 35x100 feet; molding shop, 30x90 feet; unburnt stove lining storage room, 40x86 feet—each two stories in height; two three-story packing houses, respectively 32x100 and 30x 60 feet; two drying-rooms, respectively 30x100 and 15x90 feet, fitted up with stoves, etc.; cement sheds, 25x50 feet, and stable, 25x90 feet. The office, tastefully fitted up, is of two stories, 20x40 feet. The equipment consists in part of an outfit of mixing machinery, a 50-horse-power steam engine, and three two-story kilns in which are combined all late practical improvements. The storage house for molds is especially worthy of mention, being fire-proof, 36 1-2 x 60 feet, with capacity for more than 20,000 molds. About seventy-five men and boys are employed, and the output, enormous in volume and value, comprising every description of fire brick and stove linings, fire clay, fire cement, kaolin, fire sand, etc., is distributed all over the United States and exported to other countries. Any shape or size of fire brick is made promptly to order from pattern, and all goods are supplied at lowest ruling prices.

Mr. Harry T. Root, a representative Providence stove and range man, is president of this company. Mr. B. C. Pierce, a practical and experienced fire-clay worker, is treasurer and superintendent. Mr. James T. Maher, the wealthy plumber and real estate dealer; William Miller, and D. A. Trefethen, the well-known brass founder, are members of the board of directors.

REED, BARTON & COMPANY.

William Reed, President; E. S. Barton, Agent; Waldo Reed, Treasurer— Manufacturers of Silver-Plated Ware—Court Street.

The old firm of Reed & Barton of Britanniaville enjoyed a world-wide fame for the excellence of its wares and the extent of its trade. In 1886 a copartnership was arranged between Messrs.

Waldo Reed and E. S. Barton (the latter a son of Mr. Chas. E. Barton, deceased, of Reed & Barton), and they began the manufacture of silver-plated ware in Taunton. Having demonstrated the feasibility of continuing the industry upon a different scale, the brothers-in-law—for such they are—determined to organize a stock company, which they did in 1889, with $50,000 capital, Mr. Reed's father, Wm. Reed, Esq., accepting the presidency, while Mr. Barton's mother became a principal stockholder. The factory, occupying three floors (9,000 square feet) of the American Screw Company's old works on Court street and several adjoining buildings, is divided into foundry, moulding, rolling, stamping, cutting, engraving and electro-plating departments, each complete in itself, and all combined making a perfectly appointed establishment of fine productive capacity, employing the best skill in abundance and turning out artistic and meritorious goods in great quantities and much variety, though a leading specialty is made of high-grade silver-plated hollow-ware in novel and original styles. The goods are sold direct to the jobbing and retail trade, east, west, north and south, to whom catalogues and price-lists are furnished on application.

FRENCH & WINSLOW,

Manufacturers of Fire Brick and Stove Linings; Dealers in Fire Clay, Fire Cement, Fire Sand and Kaolin—Weir Village.

Messrs. Seth C. French and Albert H. Winslow formed their present copartnership twenty-one years ago, and have been quite successful, their transactions averaging about $15,000 a year. They have access to an abundance of the best materials; their works are conveniently located on the line of the Old Colony railroad, and their buildings are well appointed and commodious, being four in number, each one and a-half stories in height and 30x250, 35x65, 30x 48 and 30x40 feet in area respectively. The mixing and molding appliances are of the best, as are the kilns, which are also of large capacity. The working force numbers sixteen, and the output of fire brick and stove linings is shipped to manufacturers and repairers of stoves, furnaces, etc., in New York and Boston, while their fire clay, fire cement, fire sand and kaolin are distributed to the trade generally. Orders filled at short notice.

WILLIAMS STOVE LINING COMPANY.

J. G. & J. S. Williams—Manufacturers of Stove Linings and Fire Bricks—Dealers in Fire Clay, Fire Sand, Fire Cement, etc.—Weir Village.

The works of the above-named company, located at Weir Village, on the banks of the Taunton river, were founded in 1846 by the late J. R. Williams, father of the present proprietors, but have repeatedly been enlarged and improved during the forty-five years of their existence until now they are quite extensive, comprising five two-story frame buildings, viz: Molding and drying departments, 40x150 feet; mixing department, 35x75 feet; clay shed, 100x60 feet; packing department, 40x80 feet, and kiln department, 40x75 feet; also 22,500 square feet of floor surface for manufactured stock. The machinery outfit is complete, and a large number of skilled operatives are employed in the manufacture of stove linings and fire bricks. The reputation which this company's goods have gained has created a constantly increasing demand from all parts of the United States and Canada.

The elder Mr. Williams died last year, whereupon the property reverted to his sons, both brought up to the business from boyhood, a calling, in fact, with which the Williams family has been identified for generations. Mr. J. S. Williams, one of the most capable fire clay manipulators living, is superintendent of the establishment.

TAUNTON STOVE LINING COMPANY.

A. W. and W. N. Parker—Manufacturers of Fire Brick and Stove Linings— Corner Somerset Ave. and Highland Street.

Messrs. A. W. and W. N. Parker are natives of Maine, whence they removed to Taunton more than thirty-five years ago. Here they learned the practical part of their trade, and by untiring industry and economy succeeded in establishing themselves as manufacturers in 1864, adopting the style which they have since retained—Taunton Stove Lining Company. Their extensive and well-appointed works at Highland street and Somerset avenue comprise several commodious frame buildings, the molding-house being one and a-half stories in height, 30x100 feet, and the packing-house two stories, 35x200 feet. Connected are two large kilns, and the best improved appliances are provided in all departments, the twenty-two employés turning out $40,000 worth of fire brick and stove linings annually, most of which are sold to the trade in New England and New York State. Orders are filled at short notice and satisfactorily. Mr. A. W. Parker is treasurer. Address, Taunton.

CITY HOTEL.

Floyd Travis, Proprietor; G. S. Harrington, Clerk—Corner Broadway and City Square, Opposite the Green.

The City Hotel was erected many years ago, has always been conducted on liberal lines, and is in some respects the best as well as among the most favorably known and most largely patronized hostelries in the interior of Massachusetts. The present proprietor, Mr. Floyd Travis, who assumed control January 1, 1886, had a large previous hotel experience in New

York, and by close attention to the wants and comfort of the traveling public and regular guests has made the house more popular than ever before, his legion of old friends and acquaintances making it a point not only to stop with him themselves when here but to commend him and his house to others coming this way, so that probably in all its history the City Hotel has never prospered as it has under his administration or catered to so many desirable guests.

The engraving printed here shows the main facade, ornamented with lofty tower, piazzas, etc. The structure is of brick, three and a-half stories in height, 125 feet front, 260 feet deep, and stands at the corner of Broadway and City Square, facing the latter and immediately opposite the famous "Green." Within, the house more than carries out the promise of the exterior, having on the ground floor a spacious and handsome office, with telephone and telegraph office attached, large and well-lighted reading-room, commodious and well-appointed sample room for the use of commercial tourists, public and private parlors, billiard-room, bar and barber-shop. On the second floor are the capacious, airy and splendidly equipped dining-room, ladies' parlor, etc., while on that and the upper floors are 102 daintily furnished, sweet, clean and inviting sleeping apartments, arranged singly and en suite to accommodate solitary inmates or families as required. Throughout the house is fitted up with steam heat, hot and cold water, baths, gas and electric lights, and, in a word, all modern improvements. Of the table and service it is sufficient to say that they are unsurpassed by those of any hotel between Boston and New York, and equaled by few even in those metropolitan cities. Rates are reasonable, and nothing is left undone to please the most fastidious and exacting.

☞ Mr. Travis is also proprietor of the popular Menauhant Hotel, Menauhant, Cape Cod, one of the most delightful of seaside resorts, to which the attention of seekers for refreshing ocean breezes, salt baths and luxurious living is directed.

TAUNTON STONE AND EARTHEN WARE POTTERY.

F. T. Wright & Son—Manufacturers of Stone and Earthern Ware,—No. 26 Presbrey Court.

These works were founded a long time ago by the late F. T. Wright, whose son Solon became associated with him in business about 1867. In 1872 the old plant was destroyed by fire, and the present commodious modern pottery erected on the same site. The senior Mr. Wright died in 1882.

The workshops are all frame and three stories in height, the main building 45x100 feet, with three spacious L's, for the accommodation of the workmen, ten in number. All improved facilities, including a ten-horse-power steam engine, are provided, a thirty-horse-power boiler supplying steam for heating purposes. Adjoining are three capacious kilns—two for the burning of stoneware and one for earthenware. All the clay consumed is brought from New Jersey along the coast and up the Taunton river by means of sailing craft, and the product, which is large and of superior quality, is sold direct from the factory to the trade and consumers, principally in Massachusetts, New Hampshire, Rhode Island and Connecticut. There are but four potteries in Massachusetts.

Mr. Wright is a well-known and popular citizen, takes some interest in political matters, but has never held or sought office.

A. G. WILLIAMS & CO.,

Dealers in All Kinds of Lumber, Doors, Sash, Blinds, Etc.—Yards, Ingell St., near
Weir Junction; Factory, No. 62 Weir Street.

This house was founded many years ago by Abiatha and A. K. Williams, who were succeeded by George B. Williams, and he, after fifteen years, in 1887 transferred the management

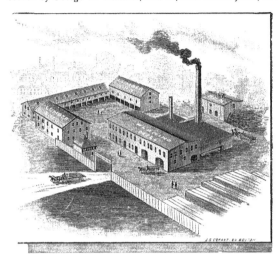

to his sons A. G., George B.,
jr., C. K., and A. B. Williams.
The plant comprises a very large
two-story brick saw and planing-mill at No. 62 Weir street,
provided with all necessary machinery, and a lumber-yard two
acres in extent on Ingell street;
Weir Junction, where are stored
great quantities of carefully
selected northern, western and
Canadian pine and other varieties of lumber for all purposes,
including liberal supplies of
dimension timber, shingles, lath,
etc. The mill is the same erected by F. L. Newcomb, pur-
chased several years ago, and is
utilized in the manufacture of
doors, sash, blinds, frames,
mouldings, dressed stuff for interior and exterior finish, and
general wood-work to order.
Twenty men are employed in all,
and the firm transacts a large

business, principally with local builders. The members were all born in Taunton and are favorably known to the entire community. Their lumber-yard is a portion of the old Williams
homestead and has been in the family for seventy-five years.

BRISTOL COUNTY NATIONAL BANK.

S. L. Cushman, President; H. H. Townsend, Cashier—City Square.

This influential and powerful fiduciary trust dates its inception from 1832, when the Bristol
County Bank was incorporated as a representative of the State banking system, and a worthy
example it proved of what that system was capable of developing. After an honorable career
of thirty-three years the Bristol County was reorganized in 1865 and chartered under the
National banking act; capital stock, half a million dollars. How well it has served the business public under old and new auspices is attested by the confidence it has always enjoyed.
President S. L. Cushman, promoted several years ago from the cashier's desk, has been connected with this institution for about twenty-two years. Among the directors we find the well-
known names of S. N. Staples and Joseph E. Wilbar, Oliver Ames and Philander Williams.
The appended statement to the Comptroller of the Currency shows the condition of the Bristol
County National at the close of business December 19, 1890:

RESOURCES.		LIABILITIES.	
Loans and discounts..................	$826,204 90	Capital stock paid in ··· ·················	$500,000 00
U. S. Bonds to secure circulation······	105,000 00	Surplus fund · ······················· ·	200,000 00
Stocks, securities, claims, etc······	114,921 58	Undivided profits ········ ··· ·······	24,019 62
Due from approved reserve agents······	64,115 62	National Bank notes outstanding ········	94,500 00
Banking house, furniture and fixtures··	10,000 00	Dividends unpaid ············· ········	815 00
Current expenses and taxes paid·······	1,280 00	Individual deposits subject to check·····	329,023 85
Checks and other cash items···········	885 49	Demand certificates of deposit,·········	5,637 17
Bills of other banks ·····················	27,174 00	Due to other National Banks··· ·········	43,500 61
Fractional paper currency, nickels and			
cents ········ ·······················	1,089 68		
Specie ·············· ···············	31,000 00		
Legal tender notes ··· ············· · ...	12,000 00		
Redemption fund with U. S. treasurer (5			
per cent. of circulation)····'·········	4,725 00		
Total····· ·····················$1,198,396 25		Total··········· ·················$1,198,396 25	

SANDERS & BUFFINGTON,

Wholesale and Retail Lumber, Doors, Sashes, Blinds, Builder's Hardware, etc.—
Wholesale Yard, Weir Junction; Retail Yard and Office, No. 68 Weir Street.

Messrs. Sanders & Buffington are the most extensive of Taunton's dealers in lumber, builder's finish and hardware, and conduct a very large and steadily increasing business. Their
wholesale yards at the Weir Junction cover a good deal of ground and are always heavily
stocked with choice Maine, western and southern pine, spruce, hemlock, whitewood, birch,
etc., in the rough. Large orders are filled there and shipped to any point in this and adjoining
States, the yards being connected by a spur with the main railway lines. Their office is at No.
68 Weir street, adjoining the retail yard and sheds, where are shown a great variety of dressed
lumber, matched flooring, clapboards, lath, shingles, doors, sashes, blinds, frames, and inside
finish. The building at this point is one and a-half stories in height, quite commodious, and
affords storage for immense stocks. Buyers will find here a fine assortment from which to make
selections, and prices just right.

Mr. Sanders, born at Raynham, has lived in Taunton since early infancy. Mr. Buffington
is a native of Somerset, and has resided here for twenty-five years. Both are well and favorably
known in business circles.

TAUNTON IRON WORKS.

Manufacturers of and Dealers in Ranges, Stoves, Furnaces, Hollowware, etc.—Works
at Weir Village; Showrooms, Nos. 104 and 106 Pearl Street, Boston.

The Taunton Iron Works Company was organized and incorporated in the year 1854 by Enoch
King of Raynham and Wm. L. Hathaway of North Dighton as a corporation. In 1889 Captain
William H. Phillips bought the property, and, retaining the former corporate character, resumed
operations on a large scale as the Taunton Iron Works, having retained the services of the former
experienced and competent manager, Mr. Wm. H. Swanton, a practical stove manufacturer and
energetic business man. The plant, covering about ten acres of land at Weir Village, comprises
eleven frame buildings, consisting of the well-equipped foundry, machine shop and polishing department, mounting department, four store-houses, two sand houses and stables. Some idea of the
quantity and value of the output may be drawn from the number of molders, mounters, finishers,
packers, clerks, teamsters, etc., employed—one hundred in all. The specialties embrace a great
variety of superior heating and cooking stoves, ranges (among the latter the favorite "New Tariff"
and "Quaker"), furnaces in several styles, and hollowware of every description. The showrooms,
commodious and inviting, are situated at Nos. 104 and 106 Pearl street, Boston. Captain
Phillips first saw the light in Pawtucket, R. I., but was reared in Taunton, where he is well
known and highly respected. He took to the sea at the age of fourteen, commanded a vessel
belonging to his father when but eighteen, and continued in the coasting trade until his business
interests ashore required his undivided attention; he settled in Taunton, engaging in the coal
business in 1854. In 1857 he formed a copartnership with S. N. Staples, under the style of
Staples & Phillips, which recently closed up its accounts and retired. Captain Phillips has for
many years been prominent in every movement, political, social and religious, that commended
itself to his judgment as calculated to advance the material and moral interests of Taunton. He
was a prime mover in procuring the city charter, and a member of the first council thereunder.
An enthusiastic Republican since the formation of the party, he has also distinguished himself
among those who contend for the absolute prohibition of the liquor traffic, and in that cause his
name is a tower of strength here, all over the Commonwealth, and throughout the Union. He
is also an earnest and consistent member of the Methodist Episcopal church, and has contributed largely of his means for its extension.

OSCAR G. THOMAS,

Manufacturer of Stoves, Ranges, Plows, Stable Fixtures, Cast Iron Thresholds,
Funnel Irons, etc.—Castings to Order—Nos. 99 to 107 W. Water St., Weir Village.

This is the oldest of Taunton's existing iron foundries, established away back in the last
century by Crocker & Richmond. After several changes of ownership it passed into the hands
of the widely-known Samson Perkins, who died in 1873, when the property reverted by
inheritance to Mr. Oscar G. Thomas, a son of Mr. Perkins' only surviving daughter. Mr.
Thomas is ably assisted in the management by his father-in-law, Mr. Joseph Wright, an experi-

enced iron-master, long connected with the now defunct Union Furnace Company. The works, situated in Weir Village, front 300 feet on West Water street and comprise a number of substantial and commodious two and three-story brick and frame buildings, completely fitted up for foundry and machine shop purposes, with steam power and all requisite appliances, and giving employment to a large number of hands, as' may be supposed from the volume of products, aggregating an annual value of $80,000 or more. The products are varied, the leading specialties comprising a line of stoves of which the universally known "Premium," "Grand" and "Herald Grand" ranges and parlor stoves are types, while a general assortment of light iron castings are made, including plows of many kinds, stable fixtures, thresholds,

funnel irons, etc. Castings of all kinds are made to order. Mr. Thomas' market is for the most part in New England, but he ships largely to Chicago and other western points.

In this age of culture and scientific research, what wonder that some of it should be developed in the manufacture of stoves and ranges? The "Herald," a strictly new and first-class range in every particular, embodies in its construction all the valuable and modern improvements of the times, with many not found in any other—a double-top, large and capacious oven, so heated and ventilated that all the gases and odors generated in cooking pass off into the flues, thereby guaranteeing a pure, sweet oven, preventing shrinkage in weight of food cooked. Durable and attractive in appearance. The dealer who has the good fortune to secure the sale of this range has a right to consider himself on the road to honorable success in his line of business.

D. ARTHUR BURT & CO.,

Taunton Monumental Works—Manufacturers of Memorial, Cemetery, Marble, Freestone, Granite and other Stonecutter Work—No. 84 Weir Street.

From time immemorial it has been the desire of surviving relatives, friends and admirers of the dead to perpetuate in imperishable stone their names, virtues and deeds, and it is doubtless to this impulse, immediate or remote, that the world is indebted for its greatest and most enduring examples of monumental art, with which is closely allied architecture and collateral pursuits. For obvious reasons New England is the principal center of monument construction on this continent, and among its most notable representatives in south-eastern Massachusetts is

the firm of D. Arthur Burt & Co., of Taunton, with workshops and warerooms, 42 x 105 feet, at No. 84 Weir street and 10,000 square feet of yard space adjoining. Here are shown many very fine examples of mortuary art in the form of monuments, tombs, headstones, etc., in imported and domestic granite and marble, and the facilities for designing and executing this class of work, together with ornamental carving and general sculpture, are unsurpassed, the firm controlling a very large and select patronage in this and adjacent States. This concern was founded by the late Samuel Warren in 1844. In May, 1846, D. A. Burt, senior, entered Mr. Warren's employ as an apprentice, and a year later went to Boston, where in the studio of Alpheus Cary (a celebrated monumentalist of the time) he studied for six years, mastering both the artistic and the practical branches of his profession. He then returned to Taunton and established himself in business on a small scale opposite the court-house. His originality, artistic skill and enterprise soon attracted notice, however; he did an excellent and growing business, and in 1856 he bought out and succeeded Mr. Warren at the present location. In 1860 the plant was considerably enlarged, and in 1864 the buildings were burned to the ground by a fire that originated next door. In 1865 the present warerooms and shops—said to be the finest in New England—were erected. Mr. R. L. King, an accomplished artist, was admitted to a copartnership about the same time. He died in 1877, and D. Arthur Burt succeeded to the sole proprietorship, his father accepting the superintendency and assisting by advice and otherwise in the further development of the business. In 1881 Mr. Edward W. Ellis of Fairhaven was admitted, and the firm of D. Arthur Burt & Co. was established.

While devoting their best talents to designing and constructing the higher grades of public and private monuments, mortuary sculpture and ornamental carving in stone, the firm willingly accept commissions for every description of cemetery embellishment and improvement, which is executed in unexceptionable style and on reasonable terms. Orders by mail, telegraph or telephone receive prompt attention.

CANOE RIVER MILLS.

J. C. & A. R. Sharp, Proprietors—John P. Sharp, Jr., Treasurer and Agent—Manufacturers of Cotton Yarns—Chandler Avenue.

The Canoe River mills were established in '1875' and add not a little to the industrial importance of Taunton. The mill building, situated on Chandler avenue, is of brick, three stories in height, 75x242 feet, with brick boiler and engine-house adjoining, containing a fine 600-horse-power Harris-Corliss engine and boilers of ample capacity for both power and heating. The mill equipment is complete and of the latest improved style, consisting in part of 21,000 spindles. Employing 150 operatives, the mill produces on an average 18,000 pounds weekly of superior cotton yarns in the various numbers required for weaving and knitting, etc. The firm also own and operate another mill of large capacity at North Scituate. They find ready sale for all the yarns they can produce, and ship to consumers all over New England and adjoining States.

Messrs. John C. and A. R. Sharp are much respected citizens, and John C. Sharp, jr., who acts in the capacity of treasurer and agent, is a bright and successful young business man.

WEBSTER FILE WORKS.

Charles Webster—Manufacturer of Hand-cut Files of all Kinds—Court Street.

The file in some form is an indispensable necessity to the mechanic, most of whom are obliged to keep at hand an assortment that includes a great variety of sizes and grades of fineness. When we consider the vast number of men employed in the machine, blacksmith, wood-working and other shops in all the cities and villages of New England, and then remember that in the best files each ridge is made by a separate blow with hammer and chisel, it does not appear wonderful after all that the file market is never overstocked, for the demand is always equal to the supply of the better grades, and few care to buy any other —all consumers tacitly agreeing that in this article at least "the best is the cheapest," saving time, labor and money.

For many years one of the most famous of American file manufacturers was the late Joseph Webster of Taunton. During a quarter of a century he did a flourishing business, which at his death, in 1888, he turned over to his son Charles. The latter, brought up a practical file-maker, a bright, energetic young man, is following closely in the footsteps of his worthy progenitor, ex- cept that he is perhaps more enterprising and more desirous of expansion. His works occupy one floor, 25x75 feet, of the Amer- ican Screw Company's old mill on Court street, are fitted up with steam power and all requisite conveniences, and give employment to fourteen skilled workmen. The premises are arranged as office and salesroom, packing room, forging and hardening shops, and are easily accessible. While the output is large, stock does not accumulate, there being ready sale for the entire product, which goes direct to consumers, principally in New England. Old files are recut equal to new.

DIGHTON.

THERE is no certainty that the alleged early Norse discoverers ever entered the Taunton river (notwithstanding the sculptured stone), nor that Verazzano, the Florentine, sent any exploring parties up from his quiet harbor at Newport in 1524; so it may be accepted as an historical fact that the first white men who ever gazed across its placid waters were those who, with Winslow and Hopkins, made their way through the wilderness from Plymouth to visit the great chief Massasoit, on Narragansett bay, in the month of July, 1621. They found the country adjacent to the river bearing evidences of having been thickly popu- lated by the Indians, who four years previously were almost extirpated by a mysterious plague—perhaps small-pox or yellow fever—that swept the coast from the mouth of the Penobscot to Narragansett three years before the landing of the Pilgrims. The territory now composing the town of Dighton, four miles square, was purchased of King Philip, in 1672, by Taunton parties, and added to that town under the name of the South Purchase or precinct. Three square miles were afterward sold to Swansea. The first actual settlement occurred after

King Philip's war. The act of incorporation was passed and approved in 1712. Dighton took an active and patriotic part in the revolutionary struggle, and subsequently became interested in shipbuilding, which industry was disastrously affected by the war of 1812, in which many Dighton soldiers and sailors served with credit. Shipbuilding was resumed with the return of peace. Two cotton mills were erected in North Dighton about the same time, and the town of Wellington was carved out of Dighton in 1814.

The first successful attempt at silk culture in Massachusetts was made at Dighton. The first cotton mill in the town was built on Three-mile river in 1809, the second on the same stream in 1810. The manufacture of paper was begun in 1850 at North Dighton. The making of iron from bog ore, and the manufacture of gas pipe, stoves, tacks, white lead, stove linings, furniture, etc., were later industries, as were saw and grist-milling, fulling, color-grinding, and sash, door and blind-making. Population, 1890, 1889. The Old Colony railroad, following the course of the Taunton river, skirts the town from south to north.

DIGHTON STOVE LINING COMPANY.

Cyrus Talbot, President; William Z. Whitmarsh, Treasurer; G. C. Francis, Agent— Manufacturers of Stove and Range Linings—Dighton, Mass.

This company was established in 1876 by Messrs. G. C. Francis, George Horton, Stephen H. Pierce and John Hinds, but reorganized and incorporated with the officers above named and $25,000 capital stock in 1882. The site of the works, directly opposite the celebrated Dighton rock and immediately upon the bank of the Taunton river, with fifteen feet of water at the wharf and but a few miles from Mount Hope Bay, is in all respects a most desirable one and has for generations been utilized for manufacturing purposes. Access is easy by both rail and river, the supplies of New Jersey and Long Island fire clay being delivered by sailing vessels. The Jersey clay is pronounced the best in the world, and the Dighton Stove Lining Company consumes immense quantities of it. The company's plant comprises the factory proper, a three-story frame structure, 70 x 150 feet, several storehouses, sheds and office of wood, and a fire-proof brick pattern-house, covering in all about two acres. The machinery consists of a series of crushers and grinding wheels driven by a twenty-horse-power steam engine, the moulding, handling, drying, etc., being performed by hand. From fifteen to twenty-five skilled workmen are employed, and the output, which embraces every description of stove, range and furnace linings to the value of $20,000 per annum, is shipped to all parts of the Union, more especially to the stove manufacturing centres of the middle and western States.

L. LINCOLN & CO.,

Manufacturers of Rope and Linen Roll Papers, Colored Pattern, Plated Ware and Cop Tube Papers—North Dighton, Mass.

This plant is situated upon one of the oldest and best manufacturing sites in the town of Dighton, adjacent to the river and but a few miles from the city of Taunton, a branch of the Old Colony railroad connecting North Dighton with Taunton and Boston to the northeast and Fall River and Newport to the southwest. Here, in 1806, were erected the Dighton Manufacturing Company's cotton mills, the same company subsequently adding to its works a foundry and machine shop for the construction of cotton-spinning and cotton-weaving machinery. These shops were in 1843 leased to T. S. Dunlap, who converted them into a woolen mill, occupied it for a few years, and then removed, when Messrs. C. M. & L. Lincoln leased and fitted up the premises as a paper mill. C. M. Lincoln died in 1856; the style was soon after changed to L. Lincoln, and later to L. Lincoln & Co. In 1881 the mills were destroyed by fire and rebuilt, the present plant consisting of several brick and stone structures covering an acre and a-half of land on Three-Mile river, and well equipped with machinery driven by two turbine wheels and a 150-horse-power steam engine. From twenty-five to thirty hands are employed, and the output varies from four to five tons daily of hardware and plated-ware, wrapping, rope and linen roll, pattern and cop tube papers of the best grades. The firm, consisting of Lorenzo Lincoln, his nephews, Edward L. and J. M. Lincoln, and J. Philbrick, ship directly from the mills, and transact a business of about $70,000 per annum.

NORTH DIGHTON CO-OPERATIVE STOVE COMPANY.

Frank K. Chase, President; Charles H. Evans, Treasurer; Wm. B. Hathaway, Corp. Clerk and Agent—Manufacturers of Ranges and Parlor Stoves — North Dighton, Mass.

The North Dighton Co-operative Stove Company is composed of practical workmen and business men, and was incorporated in 1886. The works, situated near the railroad station, cover about an acre, and comprise the foundry, 50 x 80, and finishing shop, two stories, 70 x 50 feet, a storehouse and office, two stories, 35 x 50 feet, and necessary

outbuildings and appurtenances. The outfit of machinery and appliances, like the buildings, are almost new, a fine steam engine supplying the requisite power. About forty skilled workmen are employed, and the average output is 3,200 ranges and from 400 to 500 parlor stoves annually, which are distributed to the trade east, west, north and south. Catalogues, prices and terms are mailed to all applicants, and every facility afforded buyers. While making a general line of ranges and stoves, this company's specialties are of the highest order and embrace the renowned "Oak Grand" ranges in four sizes; the "Live Oak" in four sizes; the "White Oak" in four sizes; the "Oak Leaf" in four sizes, the "Prize Oak" parlor stove in two sizes (Nos. 12 and 14), and "Oak Leaf Air Tight" in three sizes, and they invite the attention of dealers to these goods particularly.

BRADFORD YARN MILL.

R. T., E. and H. E. Grant, Proprietors—Manufacturers of Yarns—East Brookfield.

The Bradford mill has now been in operation under the management of Messrs. Grant for six years or more, and the yarns made here have achieved a national reputation. The plant comprises a three-story brick building, 35x50 feet, fitted up with two sets of cards, three mules and a complete equipment of auxiliary machinery and appliances, the whole driven by steam power. Fourteen hands are employed, and the output is quite large, most of it being readily disposed of to manufacturers of woolen goods in the eastern States.

Messrs. R. T. and H. E. Grant reside here and have immediate charge of the mill and business, while the third brother, Mr. E. Grant, lives in Connecticut; all are practical yarn manufacturers, and energetic, enterprising, successful business men.

ATTLEBOROUGH.

THE Indian title to the territory out of which has since been carved a part of Rehoboth, Seekonk, Attleborough, and Cumberland (R. I.) was purchased in 1661 by Captain Thomas Willett on behalf of Plymouth Colony from Wamsutta, son of Massasoit and elder brother of Metacomet (afterward distinguished as King Philip). The land—then called the North Purchase—was subsequently cut up into fifty-acre tracts and divided by lot among original and incoming settlers. In October, 1694, the town of Attleborough (named for Attleborough, Norfolk county, England) was incorporated, and then contained about eighty square miles. There was a good deal of bloodshed within the limits of the town during King Philip's war. The people distinguished themselves for patriotism in the Revolution, showed proper spirit in the second war with England, and poured out physical and financial aid without stint in the war for the Union. Cumberland was separated from Attleborough in 1745. North Attleborough was separated from the original town and incorporated by special act of the General Court July 30, 1888. By the census of 1890 the old town has a population of 7,575 ; total assessed valuation, $4,026,335. There are in the town six post-offices—Attleboro, West Attleboro, South Attleboro, Briggs's Corner, Dodgeville and Hebronville ; one National bank, one savings and loan association ; one opera-house ; eight Protestant and two Roman Catholic churches ; free public library ; high, grammar, intermediate and primary schools housed in fine, commodious, well lighted, well heated, and well ventilated buildings ; two daily and one weekly newspapers ; gas and electric light plant ; complete water-works ; an excellent fire department. The Old Colony railroad bisects the town ; an electric railway extends from Attleboro via North Attleboro to Plainville in Norfolk county, and two others are projected, respectively from Attleboro to Pawtucket, R. I., and from North Attleboro via South Attleboro to Pawtucket. The town contains the usual secret and beneficiary societies, trade organizations, etc.

The distinguishing industry of Attleboro is the manufacture of jewelry, and is said to have had its origin here in the unpretentious labors of a solitary French worker in the precious metals—perhaps a discharged soldier of the Franco-American contingent of the revolutionary army—who settled here in 1780. Even his name is forgotten, but the seeds he planted have brought forth abundant fruit, and Attleborough, after a century of growth and development in this direction, is now one of the most important jewelry manufacturing centers in the world. In connection therewith the construction of jewelers' machinery has reached a wonderful degree of perfection here, and Attleboro artisans are kept busy supplying home and foreign customers with both appliances and products. Electrical supplies and apparatus are also made in considerable quantities.

ATTLEBORO DYE WORKS.

R. Wolfenden & Sons—Dyers and Bleachers of Woolen and Worsted Yarns, Braids, Tapes, Hosiery, etc.—Rear of No. 88 County St.; P. O. Address, Lock Box 753.

Mr. R. Wolfenden, an experienced practical dyer, established the Attleboro dye works in 1868, and ten years later admitted to copartnership his sons, John W. and Oscar. At the founder's death the sons became proprietors, retaining the former style, R. Wolfenden & Sons. The works, situated in rear of No. 88 County street, are quite extensive, comprising a two-story frame dye-house, several outbuildings, yards, etc., utilized for dyeing and bleaching purposes. From fifteen to twenty hands are employed in the various departments, and the machinery and appliances are driven by several small engines supplied with steam from an 85-horse-power boiler. The specialties embrace the dyeing and bleaching of woolen and worsted yarns for all purposes, braids, tapes, hosiery, etc., and the product is of the most satisfactory kind, as is evidenced by the amount of business done—$30,000 to $40,000 a year. Particular attention is given to first-class work, and all orders are promptly executed.

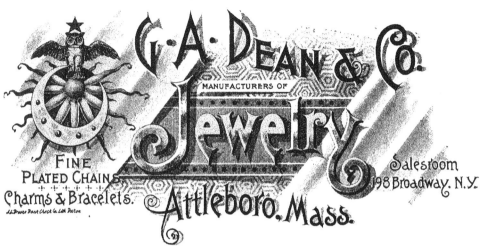

Mr. G. A. Dean embarked in the manufacture of jewelry at this point in 1856. The present style, G. A. Dean & Co., was adopted in 1884. On the whole it has been a very successful house from the start, and has built up a most enviable reputation with the trade everywhere. The factory occupies two spacious floors of the Bates' building No. 1, a large four-story frame structure on the railroad, and is fitted up with all modern improved machinery and appliances, steam power, etc., about seventy-five hands being required to keep up with orders from jobbers and to fill those sent in by a corps of active salesmen in various parts of the country. A vast quantity of elegant goods in tasty forms is produced, the leading specialties comprising fine roll plated chains, charms, lockets, bracelets, etc. New designs are being brought out at all seasons, and the trade when in search of novelties will make no mistake in sending their inquiries direct to G. A. Dean & Co.'s factory or to the salesroom, No. 198 Broadway, New York.

W. H. WILMARTH & CO.,

(E. B. Bullock), Manufacturing Jewelers — Robinson Building, Corner Union Street and Bailey Avenue.

Messrs. L. and W. Wilmarth established the house of Wilmarth Bros. in 1872, but afterward retired in favor of W. H. Wilmarth & Co., who finally sold out in May, 1890, to E. B. Bullock. The salesroom and office are in room 11, No. 176 Broadway, New York. The Attleboro factory is situated in the four-story brick Robinson building No. 3, Union street, corner of Bailey avenue, occupying three floors each 45 x 80 feet and employing from 160 to 175 expert operatives. The machinery plant is complete in all departments, including steam power, rolling mills, presses, etc., a noticeable feature being the electro-plating apparatus, which is of the latest and most approved style. The goods made here embrace very full lines of stylish rolled gold jewelry of all kinds and in all grades, but the leading specialties, upon which the concern's reputation principally rests, comprise a superb variety of lever and separable sleeve and collar buttons, curb, rope, Geneva and fancy link ladies' and gents' chains, etc., in the best quality electro rolled plate. New designs are being constantly brought out, and the jobbing and notion trade is supplied with an uninterrupted succession of novelties through the firm's travelers. Fifteen hundred styles of buttons are made here constantly, three hundred old being discarded and three hundred new and popular styles substituted each year — that is, about one fresh novelty for each working day. The "Dandy," the "Daisy" and the "Crescent," three of the most popular styles of collar buttons ever sold to the people at large in this country, Europe, Australia, Central and South America, are manufactured by this house at the rate of one hundred gross each—300 gross in all—daily. Of the millions of stone settings used in the ornamentation of sleeve and collar buttons, at least nine-tenths are prepared on the premises by skilled lapidaries, thus effecting a saving of more than one-half in cost to manufacturer, dealer and consumer, and placing the richest gems in reach of all classes. By a process peculiarly his own, Mr. Bullock has these handsome brilliants made from glass canes. Buyers visiting New York are invited to visit the new salesroom, room 11, No. 176 Broadway, and inspect stock and prices. Sales for last year footed up $260,000. The trade of this house extends to Europe, Australia and Central and South America, where it is widely and favorably known.

SLADE & WHIPPLE,

Gold and Silver Refiners, Assayers, Smelters, Dealers in Crucibles, Chemicals and Acids—Taunton Branch Railroad, near Pleasant Street.

Messrs. William L. Slade and Frank C. Whipple, experienced practical metallurgists, formed a copartnership in September, 1890, and succeeded to the old firm of Barber & Burlingame, established ten years previously. The smelting and refining works, situated beside the Taunton branch railroad near Pleasant street, consist of a two-story frame building 40 x 60 feet, with additions and outbuildings, the whole provided with the requisite machinery and apparatus and a ten-horse-power steam engine. Here, with the assistance of several workmen, Messrs. Slade and Whipple are kept busy in their specialties of smelting, refining and assaying and the preparation of fine gold, silver and copper for the jewelry and silverware trade of Attleboro, Taunton and other places in this vicinity, whom they also supply with sand and black lead crucibles, ammonia, nitric, sulphuric and muriatic acids, etc. They manufacture 50,000 pounds of blue vitriol per year, and do a business of $40,000 or $50,000 annually.

J. T. INMAN & CO.,

Manufacturing Jewelers—Robinson Building No. 1, Railroad Street.

Lindsey & Inman established this house in 1882, and continued in business together until 1890, when Mr. Lindsey retired, and for several months Mr. Inman continued alone. A new copartnership was then formed between Messrs. J. T. Inman and James McNerney under the style of J. T. Inman & Co. The factory occupies one floor of the four-story brick Robinson building No. 1, on Railroad street, contains the usual plant

of rolling, stamping and pressing machinery and steam power, and furnishes employment for ten to fifteen hands. The output, valued at from $12,000 to $15,000 per annum, comprises a general line of solid gold and rolled plate jewelry, the leading specialties consisting of lockets and charms in gold, silver and plate. They sell to jobbers everywhere. The accompanying cuts represent a few patterns of their solid gold lockets.

STREETER BROS.,

Manufacturing Jewelers—Wilmarth Building, No. 18 County Street.

Messrs. Henry A. and John F. Streeter established this house about 1866, and during their career have introduced scores of popular novelties besides building up a prosperous trade with jobbers and exporters east, west and south. Their present specialties comprise a superb line of high grade rolled gold and plated vest, guard, matinee and opera chains in elegant designs and of beautiful workmanship, of which they dispose of $18,000 or $20,000 worth annually. Their factory, situated on the second and third floors of the Wilmarth three-story frame building, No. 18 County street, is 7,200 square feet in area, and thoroughly equipped in all respects. They employ from thirty-five to forty-five hands.

SMITH ELECTRIC COMPANY.

Earl B. Smith—Manufacturing Electrician, Sixth Street, Near County.

In 1886 Messrs. H. E. Swift and H. C. Blackinton began the manufacture of electrical appliances, but later sold out to Mr. Earl B. Smith, who continues the business under the style of the Smith Electric Company. He is junior partner in the firm of Smith, Carpenter & Co., manufacturers of coffin and casket trimmings, but travels in the interest of his electrical business.

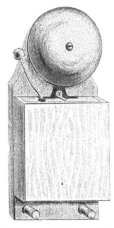 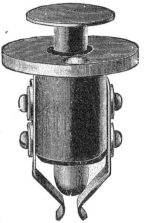

The works occupy a two-story frame building, 26x50 feet, on Sixth street near County, and are fitted up with a complete equipment of iron, steel, brass, nickel and wood-working machinery and special tools, a ten-horse-power steam engine and the usual apparatus for experimenting and testing. Mr. Smith, who is an accomplished practical electrician, has general charge, assisted by twelve or fifteen expert workmen. The specialties made here embrace a full line of newly improved electric bells, gas lighting keys, nickel press buttons, door pushes, floor pushes, spark coils, etc., of beautiful design and superior workmanship. These goods, which are fast becoming indispensable to builders and house-owners, are supplied to the jobbing trade in quantities to suit and at reasonable prices. They are just now introducing the Smith "rosette cut-out," made either in porcelain, moulded mica or wood. This is used for incandescent lamps and is the most valuable article of its kind ever placed upon the market.

A. BUSHEE & CO.,

Manufacturers of Jewelry—No. 19 County Street.

Messrs. Albert and Charles A. Bushee have been engaged in the manufacture of rolled plate and fine-gilt goods for many years and have an established reputation under the firm-name of A. Bushee & Co. They were the originators and are still among the largest producers of separable sleeve and collar buttons, and turn out besides full lines of standard plate jewelry and novelties, employing from fifty to seventy-five people and doing a business of $100,000 to $150,000 per annum with jobbers everywhere. Their factory is situated on the ground floor, 35x100 feet, with wing 20x25 feet, of the three-story frame building No. 19 County street, where they control the best facilities in the way of machinery, apparatus and steam power.

HORTON, ANGELL & CO.,

Manufacturing Jewelers—Bushee Building, No. 19 County Street.

The house of Horton, Angell & Co. dates from 1869, and was established by the late E. J. Horton, B. J. Angell and G. M. Horton. Mr. E. S. Horton succeeded his brother on the latter's death in June, 1880; Messrs. Angell and G. M. Horton subsequently retired, and Messrs. H. A. Clark, M. E. Rowe and T. S. Carpenter were admitted in 1887. Mr. Carpenter manages the New York and western trade, and Mr. Clark looks after the interests of the concern in Boston and Providence. The principal office is at No. 276 Broadway, New York, where complete lines of samples are kept in stock and orders received for shipment from the factory. The latter is located in the Bushee building, No. 19 County street, a three-story frame structure designed and erected expressly for the purpose, and of which two 40x85-foot floors are occupied by Horton, Angell & Co.'s 125 work people and machinery plant, which includes all modern improved appliances, steam power, etc. Besides manufacturing the original separable sleeve and collar buttons and studs in great quantities, the firm produce many styles of patent buttons, together with general lines of special initial buttons, scarf pins, etc., in rolled gold plate and gold front. All goods made here are guaranteed as represented, and jobbers and exporters find greater difficulty in supplying the demand than in making sales.

RICHARDS MANUFACTURING COMPANY.

Philip Brady, President; Frank R. Grimes, Treasurer and Manager—Manufacturers and Jobbers of Gold and Rolled Plate Jewelry. Rooms 18 and 19, Horton Block, Park Street.

The Richards Manufacturing Company is exerting a very perceptible and valuable influence in developing and extending the jewelry interests of Attleboro. Occupying for office and salesroom the handsome and commodious suite 18 and 19 Horton block, Park street, and maintaining intimate relations with representative manufacturers, the company has superior advantages for executing orders from the trade for every description of standard goods and also for the designing and making of novelties in gold and rolled plate, besides doing a general jobbing business. Their last year's transactions more than doubled any previous year. Orders for jewelry, in any degree of fineness and to any extent, are filled promptly and on reasonable terms. Selection packages will be sent to any responsible dealer on request.

P. E. WITHERELL,

Manufacturer of Patent Enamel Collar Buttons, Spiral Wire Studs, etc.—West St., Near Farmers' Station.

Hayward & Carpenter founded this concern about eighteen years ago. Mr. Carpenter subsequently retired, when the firm of Hayward & Witherell succeeded, Mr. P. E. Witherell becoming sole proprietor in 1886. His factory, employing twelve or fifteen hands and fitted up with special machinery and steam power, occupies the upper floor of the Electric Light Company's building on West street, near Farmers' station, a three-story structure 40x120 feet. Mr. Witherell controls valuable patents on enameling processes in connection with the manufacture of collar buttons and spiral wire studs, of which goods he makes specialties. The buttons especially are handsome, very strong and durable, have rolled gold-plate fronts, and all parts that come in contact with the linen or flesh are enameled, and consequently will not wear away, corrode and destroy the border of the button holes, or poison the flesh, as do the metallic surfaces of the ordinary plated buttons. These are made in great and pleasing variety, as are the studs. Mr. Witherell has entire control of the United States for these patents, and in consequence of the great demand has added improved tools and machinery and devotes his entire attention to their manufacture. All orders from the jobbing, export and notion trade promptly attended to.

C. E. STREETER & CO.,

Manufacturers of Regalia and Ribbon Badges, Emblematical Charms, Badges, Cuff Buttons, etc.— Suite 17 Horton Block, Park St.

This house—which, by the way, now consists of Mr. Charles E. Streeter alone—was established in 1889, and is already famous throughout the length and breadth of the land for the excellent taste and superior material and workmanship that distinguish its productions. The leading specialties comprise full lines of regalia and ribbon badges in regulation styles, but in addition he manufactures an infinitely varied line of charms, badges, cuff and lapel buttons, pins, etc., emblematical of the various orders and societies—Freemasons, Odd Fellows, Good Templars, Knights of Pythias, A. O. U. W.; Knights of Honor, Grand Army of the Republic, Knights of Labor, Red Men, Sons of Veterans Brotherhood of Locomotive Engineers, Elks, Foresters, Locomotive Firemen, United Order American Mechanics and many others. Any kind or style of badge is made to order at short notice, and catalogues mailed to applicants.

W. & S. BLACKINTON,

Manufacturers of Jewelry—Specialties, Fine Gold-Plated Chains and Lockets— Bates Building, between Mill and Capron Streets; New York Office, Nos. 14 and 16 Maiden Lane.

This house, composed of Messrs. William Blackinton, Samuel Blackinton and Lewis Blackinton, was founded in 1868 and ranks with the most prominent and prosperous representatives of an industry which of late years has developed to vast proportions, involving the employment of millions of capital and thousands of operatives. The works, where may be found at all times from 175 to 200 busy workers, occupy one floor of the great four-story Bates frame building, recently enlarged expressly for the purpose, so that Messrs. Blackinton's premises are now 40x 250 feet in area, perfectly lighted by electricity, and the most comprehensively equipped jewelry factory in the United States, the outfit of hand, foot and power presses, stamps, rolling machinery, etc., embracing all that is new and valuable in the way of improved appliances, a fine steam engine supplying the needed power. This firm manufacture specialties of rolled gold chains and lockets, gold and rolled gold bracelets, and sterling silver chain bracelets, sterling silver chatelaines, and similar goods, which are disposed of in all parts of the country, a number of competent salesmen being kept on the road, and exported in considerable quantities through jobbers. The New York office and salesroom are located at Nos. 14 and 16 Maiden lane. Transactions average $250,000 a year.

SHORT, NERNEY & CO.

Manufacturing Jewelers—Bates Building, No. 13 Mill Street.

This house, established 1876, is composed of Messrs. M. B. Short, Peter Nerney and J. J. Horton, experienced practical men who devote their undivided attention to their business and have consequently made it a success. Occupying one entire floor of the big four-story Bates building, No. 13 Mill street, they have a complete outfit of improved machinery, steam power and electro-plating apparatus, employ seventy-five hands, and produce from $70,000 to $80,000 worth of novelties in rolled gold and plated jewelry per annum, making specialties of fine rolled gold chains and similar goods. This house makes the only absolutely seamless wire chain on the market, nothing but seamless stock being used from bar to swivel and including both. The ordinary so-called seamless chain is made differently, and is not, therefore, strictly speaking, a seamless chain. Short, Nerney & Co.'s "Acme" line of goods is well known to the trade and popular with the public. They supply jobbers and notion dealers all over the continent.

R. B. MACDONALD,

Manufacturing Jeweler—Bates Building, No. 1 Railroad Avenue.

Mr. Robert B. Macdonald has been in business here for the past twelve or thirteen years, and is well and favorably known to the jobbing trade by his tasty and exceedingly salable goods, with which they are supplied by Mr. William A. Macdonald, the popular salesman. These comprise beautiful lines of high-grade rolled gold and plated scarf and lace pins, brooches, chains and bracelets, sterling silver combs, hair pins and ornaments. The factory, commodious and well equipped with all requisite appliances, including jig-sawing machinery for fancy work, is situated on the ground floor of Bates' building, No. 1 Railroad avenue, employs from ten to twelve hands, and produces $18,000 or $20,000 worth of goods per annum.

146

BRIGGS HOUSE.

Seth R. Briggs, Proprietor—No. 19 S. Main Street.

Mr. Seth R. Briggs is one of Attleboro's most popular citizens, chief constable of the town, ex-governor and secretary of the American Protective League, treasurer of the Royal Society of Good Fellows (Attleboro assembly No. 138), clerk of Union Endowment (No. 17), member of supreme lodge of United Order of Pilgrim Fathers, captain of the Fire Police, and prominent in other orders and societies of a beneficent character. Eight years ago he purchased the property No. 19 South Main street, remodeled, refitted and furnished it throughout, and opened the establishment with himself as host, ably seconded and assisted by his amiable, cheery and capable wife. The house came at once into public favor; its patrons and citizens generally conferred upon it the name of the new owner, and out of deference to their evident wishes the name Briggs House was given to it. The house is a substantial four-story frame structure, and with recent improvements presents a neat and attractive exterior. On the ground floor is the commodious office, connected with which are a well-appointed reading-room, a large billiard and pool-room, and two dining-halls — one public that will seat one hundred guests, the other private and smaller. On the second floor are the parlors, public and private, the family living rooms, etc., and on the third and fourth floors are thirty-six cosy, comfortable, airy and well-lighted sleeping rooms, tastily furnished and upholstered and provided with all conveniences, including hot and cold water, toilet and bath rooms. The lighting and heating are all that could be desired, and the table and service first-class. Rates are reasonable, and special terms are made for commercial and theatrical people. The Briggs House is located near the mercantile and manufacturing center, convenient to the railroad station, electric street cars, opera-house, post office, etc., and has in connection a large and well-kept livery and boarding stable.

BATES OPERA HOUSE.

Joseph M. Bates, Proprietor; Joseph G. Hutchinson, Manager—Park Square.

Though Mr. Bates is unquestionably Attleboro's most enterprising and progressive citizen and has successfully labored for many years in developing the material interests of the town, he probably never conferred upon the people a greater beneficence than when, in 1885, he erected the opera-house that bears his name. The building is of brick, seventy feet front on Park square, and forms a part of the Bates block. The main entrance is broad and lofty, with ample lobby. The body of the auditorium—dress circle, parquette and orchestra—has seating capacity for one thousand spectators, and there are four elegant private boxes. The whole interior is sumptuously fitted and finished and artistically decorated, and the chairs are richly upholstered. The stage, on a level with the ground floor, is sixty feet wide, forty-two feet deep, and forty feet high; the proscenium opening thirty and one-half feet wide by thirty feet high; the flats seventeen feet, and twenty-eight full sets of scenery are provided. At the wings and in rear of the stage are sixteen dressing rooms and an orchestra room, fitted up with gas and water; in front a magnificent drop curtain. In a word, the appointments are of the highest order and complete in all details, even to the providing of hose throughout the house and over the stage as a safe-guard against fire. Those who should know pronounce Attleboro and her opera-house the best one or two-night stand in New England. There is no question regarding the perfection of the lighting, heating and ventilating arrangements. The season lasts from September to June. Directors of dramatic and concert troupes should address Manager Hutchinson.

BATES BUTTON COMPANY,

Manufacturers of Ladies' and Gentlemen's Cuff and Collar Buttons—Bates Building, No. 13 Mill Street.

The Costello patent lever cuff and collar buttons are so well known and in such universal favor with the trade and consumers as to require neither description nor commendation, as they are unrivaled for neatness, convenience, strength and durability, while the plating is so heavy and perfect that only an expert can distinguish the goods from genuine gold even after long service. Costello & Co. began manufacturing in 1886, but retired in 1889, when Joseph M. Bates bought the plant and patents, and has since continued the business as the Bates Button Company, how successfully may be judged from the fact that $80,000 worth of goods were sold last year, and from forty to sixty hands are regularly employed upon this class of work alone. The factory occupies a portion of the great Bates building—four-story frame—near the railroad, with entrance at No. 13 Mill street, and is fitted up with special machinery of the most ingenious kind, steam power and all facilities.

OPERA HOUSE HOTEL AND CAFÉ.

Joseph M. Bates, Owner; Everett W. Eddy, Manager — Opera House Block, Park Square.

Mr. J. M. Bates, who is president of the First National Bank, proprietor of the Bates Button Company, head of the firm of Bates & Bacon, and owner of several of Attleboro's largest manufacturing buildings, also erected the opera-house on Park square, and in 1885 fitted up a portion of the second floor for the purpose and leased it under the title of the Park Square Café. It is evident that the enterprise prospered, as in 1889 the establishment was remodeled, the upper floors converted into sleeping apartments, the office and café removed to the ground floor, elegantly refitted and handsomely appointed, and reopened in December as the Opera House Hotel and Café. Mr. Everett W. Eddy, a most agreeable boniface, is manager and host. Adjoining the office are the tasty cigar, confectionery and soda water stands, and opening therefrom the spacious, lofty, tastily decorated and inviting dining hall and café, where delicious meals are served from 6 a. m. to 10 p. m., either a la carte or at fixed prices, in order to accommodate both transient and regular guests. Board is furnished by the day or week, and special rates accorded commercial and dramatic tourisits. Public and private parlors are provided, and sixteen delightful chambers up stairs invite to repose. The house is lighted by electric lights, heated by steam, fitted with hot and cold water service, and a telephone in the office ministers to the convenience of patrons. The opera-house and post office are in the same building, and electric street cars pass the doors. Mr. Eddy makes a specialty of catering for social reunions, parties, balls and banquets.

JOHN ANTHONY,

Manufacturer of Chains and Bracelets—Bank Street, near Park.

Mr. Anthony first embarked in business on his own account in 1884, when he established a factory at North Attleboro. Three years later he removed to Attleboro as a more central and otherwise advantageous location, and has since occupied the upper floor, 18 x 50 feet, of the two-story frame structure on Bank street near Park, where, employing eight or ten hands and a complete outfit of appropriate machinery—the latter driven by a two-horse-power electric motor, —he devotes his undivided attention to the manufacture of neck and vest chains and bracelets in novel and elegant designs and great variety, dealing exclusively with Massachusetts and Rhode Island manufacturers, who readily take his entire output. A specialty is made of the manufacture of aluminum chains and of chains of combined red gold and aluminum.

C. S. SMITH & BROTHER,

Electro-Platers—Bates Building No. 1.

Short & Nerney established these electro-plating works in 1868. They were succeeded by Nerney & Lincoln, and in 1888 Messrs. C. S. Smith & Brother became proprietors, the firm being composed of Messrs. Charles S. and Harvey L. Smith, practical and experienced electroplaters. The works, situated in the basement of the three-story frame Bates building No. 1, 40 x 40 feet, are thoroughly equipped with steam power, dynamos and other requisite apparatus, and give employment to eight or ten men, who are kept busily engaged infilling orders for work demanded by local jewelry manufacturers. The plating executed here is of the best quality, and the house has an established reputation.

FIRST NATIONAL BANK.

J. M. Bates, President; Homer M. Daggett, Cashier — Sturdy Building, No. 27 Park Street.

It is not too much to say that, taking all conditions into consideration, the First National Bank of Attleboro has a record such as few similar institutions can boast. Incorporated March, 1875, with $100,000 capital stock, nearly if not quite every industrial and mercantile concern in the town can attest from direct knowledge the courtesy and liberal conservatism of its administration and the readiness ever exhibited to accommodate and encourage public and private enterprise of a deserving character. This course may be accounted for upon several hypotheses, but the most reasonable one that occurs to us is that the officers and directors are all immediately interested in the permanent prosperity of Attleboro and have never hesitated to exert their influence and advance their money for its upbuilding. As above stated, the president is Mr. Joseph M. Bates, president also of the Bates Button Company, head of the firm of Bates & Bacon, owner of the Bates Opera-house, the Opera-house Hotel and Café, and of several immense factory buildings; the other directors Messrs. William M. Fisher, of Wm. M. Fisher & Co., manufacturing jewelers; George A. Dean, of George A. Dean & Co., manufacturing jewelers; Benjamin S. Freeman; James H. Sturdy; James J. Horton, of Short, Nerney & Co., manufacturing jewelers; Clarence L. Watson, of Watson, Newell & Co., manufacturing jewelers; and Albert A. Bushee, of Bushee & Co., manufacturing jewelers. The appended sworn statement to the Comptroller of the Currency shows the condition of the First National Bank at the close of Business May 4, 1891:

RESOURCES.		LIABILITIES.	
Loans and discounts,	$350,928 74	Capital stock paid in	$100,000 00
U. S. bonds to secure circulation	25,000 00	Surplus fund	20,000 00
Due from approved reserve agents	45,902 05	Undivided profits	15,352 22
Due from other National banks	1,268 56	National bank notes outstanding	22,500 00
Banking house, furniture and fixtures	800 00	Dividends unpaid	27 00
Other real estate and mortgages owned	1,500 00	Individual deposits subject to check	273,496 36
Current expenses and taxes paid	504 c8	Demand certificates of deposit,	15,415 42
Premiums on U. S. bonds	3,000 00	Due to other National banks	1,834 59
Checks and other cash items	350 82		
Bills of other banks	1,710 00		
Specie	8,836 34		
Legal tender notes	2,700 00		
U. S. certificates of deposit for legal-tenders	5 000 00		
Redemption fund with U. S. treasurer (5 per cent. of circulation)	1,125 00		
Total	$448,625 59	Total	$448,625 59

The banking-house, neatly and conveniently arranged and fitted, is situated on the second floor of the Sturdy building, No. 27 Park street, where those having business with the institution will receive prompt and polite attention. Discount day, Monday.

M. E. CLEMONS,

Manufacturer of Electrical Supplies—Electric Light Co.'s Building, West Street, near Farmers' Station.

The Dillon Manufacturing Company fitted up these works in 1889, but were soon afterward succeeded by Mr. Maynard E. Clemons, with Mr. Homer M. Daggett as special partner. Located on an upper floor of the Electric Light Company's building, West street, provided with a complete equipment of late improved machinery and tools, steam power, etc., and employing about fifteen expert mechanics under his own supervision, Mr. Clemons — a practical electrician of high repute—is prepared to undertake and execute in the most perfect manner any required work in his line, which embraces the manufacture of electric apparatus generally, incandescent appliances, switches, cut-outs, sockets, rosettes, hanger boards, etc., together with devices of various kinds for operating electric railways, making a leading specialty of the construction and equipment of such lines. The company is now building and has the contract for furnishing complete electric roads as follows: Attleboro & Pawtucket; North Attleboro & Pawtucket; Pawtucket & Providence, and Providence & Bullock's Point — in all about thirty-five miles, to be known when completed as the Inter-State electric railway. The jewelry manufacturers hereabout are largely interested in this enterprise, and there is little doubt that the work will be finished and the line in full operation in the spring of 1892. It is intended that every possible improvement in tracks, cars and motive power shall be incorporated, and it is safe to say that the work could not have been committed to more capable hands. Mr. Clemons is a young man of rare ingenuity and skill, thoroughly posted in the latest advances pertaining to his profession.

F. H. SADLER & CO.,

Manufacturing Jewelers—Robinson Building No. 1, Railroad Street.

F. H. Sadler & Co. was established nearly eight years ago. The factory, employing from twenty-five to forty operatives, occupies one floor of the large four-story brick Robinson building No. 1, situated on Railroad street, and is completely equipped for the manufacture of such specialties as bracelets, scarf, lace and stick pins, necklaces, spiral bracelets, studs, drops, etc., in gold, silver and rolled gold plate, and sold to the jobbing trade. The feature of this establishment is the mounting of "Borneo Diamonds," of which this house are the sole importers and have made it known so popularly all over the United States and Canada, Central and South America, as well as in Australia, on account of their immense sales of these goods. Their trade mark, "Borneo Diamonds," is registered and protected and guarantees to the purchaser the nearest, most brilliant and perfect imitation of the pure diamond ever attempted. No exception taken. They are mounted into studs, scarf pins, pins and ear drops, in solid gold and rolled gold plate, and none are genuine without the cards being stamped with the trade mark "Borneo Diamonds." The manufacturers are prepared to send a selection of these famed goods to all responsible parties upon request by addressing F. H. Sadler & Co., Attleboro, Mass.

A. H. BABCOCK,

Manufacturer of Paper Boxes — West Street, near Farmer's Station.

Probably Mr. Hartford S. Babcock, who established this house many years ago, foresaw the wonderful development of Attleboro's jewelry industry and the demand that must arise for his products; at any rate events have fully justified the wisdom of his selection of a location, for he lived to see his unpretentious little paper box shop expand to large proportions and take its place among the useful and important establishments of the place. His son, Abbott H., succeeded to the proprietorship and control early in 1890, and has added much to the value and effectiveness of the plant, which now comprises two frame buildings, one of three stories, 30 x 60 feet, being utilized as a factory, the other, of two stories, 20 x 45 feet, containing the office, storage warerooms, etc. The equipment includes all the latest improved facilities in machinery and appliances; eight or ten operatives are employed, and the output of paper boxes of every description is valued at from $12,000 to $15,000 a year, the leading specialties comprising full lines of neat jewelry and confectionery boxes, boxes for packing plate, cartoons, boxes for braids, etc. Mr. Babcock has a large local patronage and ships to Boston, Pawtucket, North Attleboro and many surrounding points.

WILMARTH, HOLMES & CO.,

Manufacturers of Rolled Gold Plate Jewelry—Bates Building No. 1, Railroad Street.

This firm is composed of Messrs. W. H. Wilmarth and Chas. F. Holmes. Mr. Wilmarth was formerly senior member of W. H. Wilmarth and Co., founded in 1872, and which was sold out to E. B. Bullock, Mr. Wilmarth forming a copartnership with Mr. Holmes and making a new start last year. The new establishment is domiciled on the spacious first floor of the immense four-story frame Bates building No. 1, Railroad street, where, provided with all requisite machinery and facilities and employing fifteen or twenty hands, the firm confidently expect to do a large business from the start, the outlook for a liberal patronage being very bright and orders from jobbers coming in rapidly. The line of specialties embraces every description of rolled gold plate jewelry — lace, bar and scarf pins, brooches, bracelets, collar and sleeve buttons, ear drops, hoops and pendants, chains, etc.

BATES & BACON,

Manufacturers of Watch Cases and Jewelry—Bates Building, No. 13 Mill Street.

This is an old-established house, of which Mr. J. M. Bates has been sole proprietor since May 28, 1890. The factory, occupying a portion of the monster four-story frame Bates building, situated near the Old Colony railroad between Mill and Capron streets, is a commodious one, splendidly equipped throughout with the latest improved machinery, steam power, etc., and gives employment to from seventy-five to one hundred hands, many of whom are experts. For a long time the house made fine gold plated bracelets its leading specialty, but of late has devoted greater attention to the manufacture of full and complete lines of gold and filled watch-cases in all grades to fit all American movements. This is the only house in this vicinity which manufactures watch-cases, and the magnitude of the undertaking may be imagined from the fact that Mr. Bates had invested more than $75,000 in special machinery and tools for the purpose before a single case was made. The firm's watch-case specialties embrace the "B. & B." "Favorite," "Peer," "Gem," "Orient" and "Puritan." They also make full lines, in o and 6 sizes, of satin-finished cases, cases with raised gold ornaments, and stone-ornamented cases. Of these goods the Providence *Manufacturing Jeweler* of July 14, 1891, says: "The new line of o and 6-size cases made by Bates & Bacon are in reality some of the handsomest goods in this line ever produced. The designs on these cases having raised gold and stone ornamentations are exquisitely beautiful, and their finish is of a character found only on the best and most expensive work of this class. With goods containing so many meritorious features, it is not to be wondered at that the prospects for the biggest business ever done in any one season at the factory is making itself manifest."

Mr. J. M. Bates, sole proprietor, owns several large buildings in this village, furnishing factory accommodations and steam power for about thirty jewelry manufacturing concerns. In this particular he has done more than any other individual to encourage and build up the industry, develop the material interests of the Attleboroughs, and extend their fame throughout this country, the southern latitudes and Europe.

PARK HOTEL.

M. A. Davenport, Proprietor; W. B. Arnold, Clerk—Nos. 40 and 42 Park Street.

The Park Hotel was originally opened in 1871 or 1872. In 1874 Mr. Frederick A. Newell (who is still owner) purchased the property of J. G. Ryder and leased it to Isaac Potter. A Mr. P. H. Roberts subsequently became host, and was succeeded by Mr. M. A. Davenport, who retired after three years, but resumed the management in 1890. The Park Hotel is a handsome and substantial modern three-story frame building with a frontage of seventy-five feet, facing an ample yard, and a depth of 100 feet. It is situated on the principal thoroughfare near the post office, banks, railroad stations and opera-house, and the electric cars pass every few minutes; on the ground floor are the office, reading and sample rooms, billiard room and barber-shop, and the commodious dining-room and parlors; upstairs are forty neat, clean and comfortable sleeping apartments. The house was recently refitted, refurnished, renovated and provided with new steam heating apparatus, electric bells, telephone, bath-rooms, etc., and is first-class in all respects, as are the tables and service. A well-appointed livery stable at the rear will furnish horses and carriages at moderate rates.

Mine Host Davenport is fat, genial, liberal and obliging, the very *beau ideal* of a landlord, whose well-rounded cheeks and jovial *embonpoint* augur well for the stranger within his gates.

C. A. WETHERELL & CO.,

Manufacturing Jewelers—No. 104 North Main Street.

This firm, composed of Messrs. Charles A. Wetherell and William Nerney, established in 1885, commands excellent facilities for manufacturing economically, occupying as it does the second floor, 40 x 90 feet, at No. 104 North Main street, on the bank of the Bungay river, from which an abundance of power is obtained by means of a turbine wheel. The outfit of machinery is of the highest order; from fifteen to twenty hands are furnished employment, and from $15,000 to $20,000 worth of goods are made annually and distributed through jobbers to notion and fancy goods dealers all over the country. The specialties comprise all the latest novelties in ladies' rolled plate ornaments—lace, bar and jersey pins, bracelets, necklaces, bangles, drops, etc.

ELLIS, LIVSEY & CO.,

Manufacturers of Ladies' and Gents' Chains from C. R. Smith Seamless Wire, Ladies' Charms and Lockets, Swivel Spring Rings, and Chain Bars in Rolled Plate — Bates' Building No. 1, Mill Street.

This is a new concern, established in November, 1890, by Messrs. F. M. Ellis and G. W. Livsey, young, enterprising and competent business men. Mr. Ellis, a practical jeweler, has immediate supervision of the mechanical department and office, while Mr. Livsey, an experienced and successful salesman, travels with full lines of samples, which embrace the latest popular novelties in standard seamless wire chains for ladies and gentlemen, ladies' charms and lockets, swivel spring rings, chain bars and kindred rolled gold plate specialties. The factory, provided with the best improved machinery and tools, steam power, etc., and employing from ten to fifteen hands, is situated in the roomy and well-lighted basement of Bates' building No. 1 on Mill street, and is capable of turning out $15,000 worth of goods per annum.

THE D. F. BRIGGS COMPANY,

Manufacturing Jewelers — Bates' Building, Corner Union Street and Bailey Avenue.

Mr. D. F. Briggs was the founder of this house, having established himself here in 1887. He was extraordinarily successful in originating novelties and extending his business connections, and in 1890 Messrs. Tappan, Berry & Co. bought him out. The company is at present composed of C. H. Tappan, W. C. Tappan, James Hume and W. F. Briggs. The factory, occupying two floors each 60 x 125 feet, of the Bates four-story frame building, corner of Union street and Bailey avenue, is not only very capacious but splendidly equipped with the latest improved and most effective appliances, including hand, foot and power presses, dies, draw benches, rolling mills, electro-plating apparatus and everything desirable in an establishment of the kind. Over 100 skilled operatives are employed, and the output is valued at rather more than $100,000 per annum. It is handled by the jewelry and fancy goods trade all over the United States and exported to Canada, Mexico, Central and South America. This house devotes much attention to vest chains, of which it makes more than 2,000 varieties, besides producing an endless assortment of novelties, etc.

VANIER & SLATERLY,

Plumbers, Gas and Steam Fitters, Tin, Copper and Sheet Iron Workers—Robinson's Building, Mill Street.

In July, 1889, Messrs. George R. Vanier and Michael J. Slaterly, both expert practical mechanics, formed a copartnership for the prosecution of a general plumbing, steam and gas fitting, tin, copper and sheet-iron-working business. Their shop, 25 x 40 feet in dimensions and fitted up with the best special tools, occupies the basement of the three-story brick Robinson building on Mill street and gives employment to eight or ten hands in the several departments. Equal and prompt attention is given to orders for work in either of their lines, and those who have had occasion to require their services unite in praise of the work done and the promptitude and liberality of the firm, who have a large and growing patronage among manufacturers, builders and householders in this and surrounding villages, besides carrying large stocks of tin, sheet-iron and copper ware, plumbers' supplies, gas fixtures and kindred commodities, which are sold at lowest prices. Both members of the firm had ten years' active experience at the bench and in the store before starting for themselves.

NORTH ATTLEBOROUGH.

THE town of North Attleborough is an outgrowth of Attleborough, and the same historical resumé applies to both. The extraordinary growth of the northern half of the old town, and that desire for independence that seems implanted in the nature of all Americans, led to the setting up and incorporation of the new town, which was carried into effect by act of the Legislature approved July 30, 1888. Population, 1890, 6,727; assessed valuation, $3,708,678. The town contains two post-offices, Attleboro' and Attleboro' Falls; one National and one savings bank, and one savings and loan association; board of trade; grammar, high, intermediate and primary schools in handsome modern buildings; public library; one daily newspaper; telegraph and telephone offices; gas and electric light plants; water-works; fire department; opera-house; seven Protestant and one Roman Catholic churches, and the usual secret and other societies and organizations. Communication is had with the outside world by means of the Old Colony railroad. An electric railway extends to Attleboro' and Plainville, and another is about to be built to Pawtucket. The leading industry here, as at Attleboro', is the manufacture cf jewelry, vast quantities of which are shipped to New York and other principal markets.

E. V. JENNEY,

Manufacturing Jeweler—Richards' Building, Elm Street.

Mr. Jenney is the successor of C. W. Chase & Co., who started the house in 1881. His factory, 40x60 feet, is situated on the upper floor of the two-story stone Richards building on Elm street, and contains all requisite appliances and adjuncts, steam power, etc. Ten or twelve men are employed, and a general line of jewelry is made for the jobbing and notion trade, the leading specialties comprising an immense variety of fire gilt and plated rings with imitation settings—diamonds, emeralds, rubies, sapphires, pearls, etc.

J. O. COPELAND & CO.,

Manufacturers of Jewelers' Findings, etc—Whiting's Building, No. 128 Broad St.

Not the least curious or important of the numerous industries domiciled in Whiting's great building on Broad street is the factory of J. O. Copeland & Co., established 1888 and located on the ground floor, 30x40 feet, of the L. Under the style of J. O. Copeland & Co. Mr. C. employs about a dozen competent operatives and a fine complement of machinery in the manufacture jewelers' findings of various kinds, including metallic shot, twist wire, twist wire rings, silver and rolled plate wires, jewelers' gold, etc., his sales to manufacturing and commercial jewelers averaging nearly or quite $12,000 a year. His products are of the best quality and satisfactory in all respects.

HEALY BROTHERS,

Manufacturers of Ladies' and Gentlemen's Novelties in Rolled Plate and Sterling Silver Chains, Charms and Trimmings—Totten's Building, East Street.

Messrs. John T. and James H. Healy commenced the business of manufacturing about nine years ago, and have been very successful, making for themselves a high reputation and an enviable place in the trade. Their factory is quite spacious—the lower floor, 40x100 feet, of the Totten building on East street—and equipped in the best manner with improved machinery, special tools and steam power. Employing from thirty to forty-five operatives, including many experts, they sell to jobbers through their own travelers between $40,000 and $50,000 worth of finished goods annually, their specialties embracing a comprehensive line of ladies' and gentlemen's rolled plate and sterling silver novelties in chains, chain trimmings, charms, etc., of artistic design and fine quality—goods such as the wealthy as well as the poor are proud to wear.

SANDLAND, CAPRON & CO.,

Manufacturers of Rolled Gold Plate and Sterling Silver Jewelry—Union Power Company's Building, No. 14 Chestnut St.; New York Office, No. 176 Broadway.

This firm dates from the centennial year of the republic, 1876, and is composed of Messrs. Thomas G. Sandland, Henry E. Capron and Ira Richards, Mr. J. R. Palmer having charge of the New York office, No. 176 Broadway. The factory, thoroughly equipped in all departments and employing from forty to forty-five hands, occupies the upper floor, 60x100 feet, in area, of the Union Power Company's building, No. 14 Chestnut street. The concern manufactures a magnificent line of specialties in rolled gold plate and sterling silver, including all late and attractive styles of bracelets, bangles, ladies' sets, drops, lace and jersey pins, hair ornaments, etc., placing upon the market an unfailing succession of tasty novelties of their own design and giving particular attention to new ideas in gentlemen's scarf pins—a class of work in which they excel. Sandland, Capron & Co.'s wide-awake travelers are constantly on the move among the jobbers and wholesales dealers, but buyers visiting New York are invited to inspect the stock at the salesroom No. 176 Broadway.

J. G. CHEEVER & CO.,

Manufacturing Jewelers—Whiting's Building, No. 130 Broad Street.

Whiting's great three-story stone building, No. 130 Broad street, is a hive of industry such as is seldom found outside the large cities. Among the tenants, occupying one floor of an upper story 35x130 feet in area, is the above-named firm, established some years ago and composed of Messrs. James G. Cheever, H. E. Bailey and A. E. Bailey. The concern is well equipped with all the late improvements in machinery and appliances, steam power and adjuncts, employs about forty practical jewelers, and turns out large quantities of stylish and tasty goods in rolled gold plate, making leading specialties of chains- in all styles and bringing out a constant succession of elegant and attractive novelties. Their trade extends to all parts of the country and is principally with jobbers and wholesale dealers in jewelry and notions.

F. L. SHEPARDSON & CO.,

Manufacturing Jewelers—No. 67 East Street.

Messrs. Frank L. and Isaac Shepardson formed their present copartnership about sixteen years ago, and under the style of F. L. Shepardson & Co., and have established an excellent reputation and flourishing trade with the retail trade in jewelry throughout the United States, to whom the firm's courteous and obliging salesmen and beautiful goods are familiar. The leading specialties are ladies' and gents' vest chains in infinite variety of styles commanding admiration and ready sale wherever shown. The factory, No. 67 East street, is a two-story-and-basement building, 26 x 40 feet square, with detached L containing boiler and twenty-horse-power steam engine for driving the machinery, the latter embracing the newest and most approved devices in all departments. Forty hands are employed, and the output is quite large and of great aggregate value, comprising, in addition to the popular chains already referred to, a general line of art jewelry in rolled gold plate—brooches, drops, pins of all kinds, sleeve links, collar and cuff buttons and personal ornaments in constantly varying styles.

THE WALCOTT MANUFACTURING COMPANY.

J. E. Walcott, President and Treasurer—Manufacturers of Jewelers' Machinery and Tools—Draper Building, No. 68 Broad Street.

The Walcott Manufacturing Company was formed in 1889 for the purpose of supplying the jewelry interest with improved appliances. The machine shop—one of the finest in the country in the matter of appointments—is situated upon the immense 40 x 165-foot ground floor of the Draper three-story frame building No. 68 Broad street. As yet the firm is only in the early stages of development—is making a business reputation as it were — and is not, of course, running to anything like its full capacity, but a sufficient number of skilled mechanics are employed to execute orders as received, and others will be engaged as needed. Small machine work of any kind is contracted for and built in the best style, but the specialties comprise the latest and most perfect devices and special tools for jewelers' use, including double-acting power presses, both cam and crank, for gang tools, whereby thirty per cent. of stock is saved in cutting over the old style, together with all sizes and styles of single and double-acting power, foot, screw, hand and sub presses, etc., with any automatic feed required, either roll, ratchet, finger, or Walcott's patent positive, straight-line, angular, vertical, horizontal or reversible feed that is warranted to feed practically to the one-thousandth part of an inch, and is used on planers as well as presses. They also build chain, setting, bead, ball button, cap and cartridge machinery with many new improvements; edging and trimming lathes; wire-drawing, straightening and cutting machines with automatic roll or slide feed, whereby any lengths can be accurately cut. They also have patterns and designs for many machines not mentioned here. The machinery made here is of the highest order of merit, and the house is steadily gaining the confidence and patronage of the trade all over the United States.

AUGUST SCHILLING,

Manufacturer of Fancy Gold, Gold Plate and Silver Chains—Draper's Building, No. 68 Broad St.

Mr. Schilling, who started in business on his own account in 1890, occupies one floor of the Draper building, No. 68 Broad street, has a fine plant of improved special machinery and appliances, with steam power, and turns out large quantities of fancy chains of all sizes and kinds in gold, gold plate and silver, making specialties of the smaller and more intricate patterns. His products are taken principally by manufacturing jewelers, though wholesale and retail dealers handle considerable quantities.

O. M. DRAPER,

Manufacturer of Rolled Plate, Fire Gilt and Nickel Chains—Richards' Building, Elm Street; New York Office, No. 18 Cortland Street; Chicago Office, No. 155 State Street.

The jewelry and notion trade are no strangers to Mr. Draper's goods, as he is among the old and reliable manufacturers through whose industry and enterprise the rolled gold interest has been developed. He began here in 1862, and on a small scale, but by close application to business and experiment has not only contributed much to perfecting processes and products, but built up a reputation and market that embraces every commercial center between the Atlantic and the Pacific. Mr. Draper's premises comprise one floor, 35 x 200 feet, of the Richards' three-story frame building on Elm street, and are fitted up with a complete plant of improved machinery and steam power. Ninety hands on an average are steadily employed, the output being distributed to jobbers everywhere through travelers and through the salesrooms, room 14, No. 18 Cortlandt street, New York, and No. 155 State street, Chicago. The goods consist of superb lines of rolled plate, fire gilt and nickel chains, charms, swivels, etc., in late styles and embracing all popular novelties.

T. E. HANCOCK & CO.,

Wholesale and Retail Dealers in Groceries, Crockery, Furniture, Wall Papers, Window Shades, Carpets, Flour, Grain, etc. — Corner Washington Street and Richards Avenue and No. 5 Anawan Block.

This house was founded in July, 1870, by Mr. T. E. Hancock, who continued to manage the same with success until about two years ago, when he sold out to his son, Mr. George A. Hancock, under whose competent direction the business is prosecuted under the former style but on a much larger scale than before. Mr. Hancock, junior, is one of North Attleboro's most enterprising business men, and, with H. M. Daggett, jr., established the North Attleboro Electric Light Company, whose works supply light for Attleboro, North Attleboro and Plainville, and power for operating the Attleboro & North Attleboro street railway. Of that corporation Mr. Hancock was president for two years, and is still a large stockholder. Mr. Hancock's commercial enterprises are conducted in a comprehensive and characteristically energetic manner. His principal warerooms are situated at the corner of Washington street and Richards avenue, requiring for their accommodation the entire building, 40 x 110 feet, three stories and basement. Here are shown immense stocks of choice groceries and shelf goods, crockery and glassware, lamps, flour, grain, etc., the upper floors being devoted to the largest and finest display of furniture in all styles and grades ever seen in North Attleboro. The most extensive dealer in flour and grain hereabout, he buys in car-load lots at the west for spot cash, and in breadstuffs as well as in the other commodities named is prepared to quote the very lowest prices. The elegant storeroom No. 5 Anawan block, appropriately named "The Only" carpet store, is full of attractions for housekeepers, as here is seen the finest exhibit of imported and domestic carpets, rugs, oil cloths, window shades, wall papers, pictures and picture frames, solid and plated silverware, etc., in the town. For the convenience of those interested, a portion of this store is set aside for the sale of dry and oil paints and colors, oils, window and plate glass, putty and painters' supplies generally. The trade and the public will find here everything they require in this line.

INTERNATIONAL HOUSE.

Henry Kern, Proprietor — Nos. 150 and 152 Washington Street.

The International, established eleven years ago by Mr. Henry Kern, and still conducted by him, is the principal hotel now open in North Attleboro. The building is of wood, three stories in height, sixty feet front on Washington street, contains a neat office and reading-room, parlors, dining-room, and twenty spacious, clean, neatly furnished and comfortable sleeping rooms, and is provided with hot and cold water, baths, steam heat, gas and electric lights, etc., with a telephone in the office. The post office, opera-house and railroad station are near by, and electric cars for Attleboro, Wrentham and other points pass within a short distance. The accommodations are first-class, and the table unsurpassed. Permanent boarders and transient guests alike receive the best of attention on reasonable terms, and special rates are made for commercial and theatrical patrons. North Attleboro voted to go dry this year, so there is no bar. The International market, adjacent to the hotel, is a new enterprise started last spring by Mr. Kern, and is kept fully stocked with choice meats, poultry, game, fruits, Swiss and American cheese, butter, eggs and sausages.

H. F. BARROWS & CO.,

Makers of Fine Quality Plated Chain — Division Street, Corner Broad — Samples at
No. 1½ Maiden Lane, New York.

Mr. H. F. Barrows, now president of the North Attleboro National Bank, established this
house in 1853. The present style was adopted in 1856, and on the retirement of Mr. Barrows,
senior, his sons, Henry F., jr., and Ira, succeeded to the proprietorship. Ira Barrows resides in
New York and manages the office and salesrooms at No. 1½ Maiden lane, while Mr. H. F.
Barrows, jr., lives in North Attleboro and has personal supervision of the factory — one of the
most extensive and productive in the country, as is shown by the fact that 125 skilled and
unskilled operatives are employed in the various departments, the plant of machinery, etc.,
driven by a fifty-horse-power steam engine, being housed in a frame building of one story, 30 x
125 feet, at the corner of Broad and Division streets. The firm devote exclusive attention to
the manufacture of fine quality rolled gold-plated chains for ladies' and gentlemen's wear, of
which they produce an infinite variety of every description, bringing out a constant succession of
novelties in styles and designs. Their goods, which are unsurpassed for beauty and excellence,
are handled by the jobbing trade, sold by dealers and worn by all classes of people in this
country, besides being exported largely to the Spanish-American republics and Canada.

BRISTOL CIGAR COMPANY.

Frank O. Coombs, Bernard W. Wunder — Manufacturers, Wholesale and Retail
Dealers in Fine Cigars, Tobacco, Smokers' Articles, etc.—No. 5 Anawan Block.

Mr. Bernard W. Wunder, who established himself here two years ago last spring, is an
experienced and skillful practical cigar-maker and energetic, enterprising business man, who
also gives his many customers pleasant business calls at different times during the year. March
14 last he formed a copartnership with Mr. Frank O. Coombs, a wide-awake, capable and progressive man, and formerly a partner in the firm of Frank Mauser & Co., silversmiths, No. 30
Union square, New York. Mr. Coombs will in the future devote his undivided efforts to the advancement of the new firm's interests, and his wide acquaintance, industry and popularity augur
well for a prosperous career. The Bristol cigar store occupies the capacious store No. 5 Anawan
block, in the heart of the business district, is elegantly fitted up and heavily stocked with choice
goods, embracing the best and most popular grades of fine imported, Key West and domestic
cigars, smoking and chewing tobacco, pipes and smokers' articles of every description, which
are offered to the trade and consumers in large or small quantities at prices as low as can be
quoted in Boston or New York for similar grades. They also employ several superior workmen
and manufacture certain favorite brands of their own, among which the "Bristol," "American
Eagle" and "Henry Clay" are especially worthy the attention of fastidious smokers. The
Bristol Cigar Company has a flourishing and rapidly increasing trade in this and adjoining States,
and leaves nothing undone to merit the confidence of dealers and consumers.

NORTH ATTLEBOROUGH NATIONAL BANK.

Henry F. Barrows, President ; Edward R. Price, Cashier—No. 144 Washington St.

First and last this institution has a history that covers a period of more than half a century.
Originally incorporated as a State bank in 1836, it continued to do business as the Attleborough
Bank until 1865, when a reorganization was effected and a charter secured as the Attleborough
National Bank. Upon the expiration of that charter, in 1885, a second reorganization took
place and the name was changed to the North Attleborough National Bank, for the reason that
it was situated in the northern part of the township, since set apart as North Attleborough. The
oldest surviving officer is Cashier Price, who entered the old Attleborough Bank as a clerk
many years ago and has a long and enviable record of faithful and capable service both in this
institution and the Attleborough Savings Bank, of which he is treasurer. The following named
prominent business men are directors of the North Attleborough National Bank: Henry F. Barrows, president; Joseph L. Sweet, of R. F. Simmons & Co., manufacturing jewelers, Attleborough Falls; Roswell Blackinton, of R. Blackinton & Co., manufacturing jewelers, North
Attleborough; Wm. H. Wade, of Wade, Davis & Co., manufacturing jewelers, Plainville;
Edwin Whiting; Handel N. Daggett, treasurer of the Gold Medal Braid Company, Attleborough Falls; E. R. Price, cashier; Frank M. Whiting, of F. M. Whiting & Co., manufacturers of silverware; Samuel E. Fisher, of S. E. Fisher & Co., manufacturing jewelers,
North Attleborough; J. D. Lincoln, of Lincoln, Bacon & Co., manufacturing jewelers, Plainville. The North Attleborough National, capital stock $150,000, surplus fund $30,000, oc-

cupies handsome apartments on the second floor of the three-story brick Bank building, No. 144 Washington street, where a general banking business is transacted and where special, prompt and courteous attention is given to deposits, loans, discounts, exchange and collections. The appended report of May 4, 1891, shows the sound condition of the institution:

RESOURCES.		LIABILITIES.	
Loans and discounts..............	$478,045 28	Capital stock paid in.....................	$150,000 00
U. S. bonds to secure circulation........	37,500 00	Surplus fund............................	30,000 00
Stocks, securities, claims, etc........	54,916 67	Undivided profits..................... ..	30,984 37
Due from approved reserve agents.......	39,624 88	National bank notes outstanding........	33,750 00
Due from other National banks....	7,824 20	Individual deposits subject to check....	393,213 74
Banking house, furniture and fixtures....	15,791 65	Demand certificates of deposit.........	10,835 90
Current expenses and taxes paid........	2,209 26	Due to other National banks............	15,947 87
Premiums on U. S. bonds................	7,683 12	Due to State banks and bankers........	1,960 67
Checks and other cash items............	759 30		
Bills of other banks.....................	2,312 00		
Fractional paper currency, nickels and cents.............................. .	686 39		
Specie..............................	9,147 30		
Legal-tender notes.....................	8,000 00		
Redemption fund with U. S. Treasurer (5 per cent. of circulation).....	1,687 50		
Due from U. S. Treasurer, other than 5 per cent. redemption fund	500 00		
Total........ .. ..$666,692 55		Total..... ....$666,692 55	

A. H. BLISS & CO.,

Manufacturers of Cable and Machine Chain—Draper Building, No. 68 Broad St.

A. H. Bliss & Co. established themselves here in 1888. Mr. Bliss, the present sole proprietor, is an experienced practical chain manufacturer and has contributed not a little toward bringing the art to the wonderful perfection it has attained. His factory, situated upon the upper floor of the Draper building, No. 68 Broad street, is one of the best equipped in the world, much of the machinery being of special design and construction and all driven by steam. His specialties include high class cable and machine chains in rolled gold, silver, German silver and brass — vest, guard, and locket chains, chains for ladies and gentlemen, eye-glass chains, curb chains, etc.—which are disposed of to manufacturing jewelers, jobbers, wholesale jewelers and the notion trade.

BUGBEE & NILES,

Manufacturers of Solid Gold Jewelry and Imitation Diamond Work—Whiting's Building, No. 130 Broad Street; New York, No. 176 Broadway; Chicago, No. 155 State Street.

This house, one of the most widely and favorably known in the trade, was founded in 1860 by C. E. Smith, to whom Bugbee & Niles (Samuel H. Bugbee and Gardner H. Niles) succeeded in 1888. The factory is a splendidly appointed one, containing everything adapted to the business, including much that is of a special nature, and is situated upon an upper floor of Whiting's great three-story stone building, No. 130 Broad street. Here are employed from thirty to forty hands, not a few of whom are expert jewelers, and all are kept busy on orders from jobbers for the superior goods made, which embrace full lines of solid gold jewelry in rings, bracelets, bangles, necklaces, lace, scarf and bar pins, drops, studs, etc., of exquisite design and finish, with and without imitation stones. The house is represented in New York by F. P. Scofield, No. 176 Broadway; in Chicago by H. L. Joseph, No. 155 State street.

C. E. SANDLAND & CO.,

Manufacturers of Silver Jewelry and Novelties in Silver — Draper Building, No. 68 Broad Street.

Mr. Charles E. Sandland, a son of Thomas G. Sandland of Sandland, Capron & Co., was formerly a traveling jewelry salesman and later general manager of the Bay State Silver Company (now Curtis & Wilkinson). On the first of July last he bought out J. E. Draper & Co.—established in 1883 — and started in business for himself under the style of C. E. Sandland &

Co. He occupies the first floor, 40 x 165 feet, of the three-story frame Draper building No. 68 Broad street, equipped with steam power and a complete outfit of fine improved machinery, employs from thirty-five to forty people in the various departments, and, when necessary, can produce more than $50,000 worth of goods per annum, his specialties embracing every description of sterling silver jewelry and novelties in silver, of exquisite design and elegant workmanship—solid goods of substantial service and value, such as rings, chains, hair pins and ornaments, thimbles, napkin rings, bonbon boxes, pocket match safes and small fancy articles generally in silver. New York office and salesroom, No. 23 John street.

THE ATTLEBOROUGH SAVINGS BANK.

Abiel Codding, President; George A. Dean, Vice-President; Edward R. Price, Treasurer—Bank Building, No. 144 Washington St.

The Attleborough Savings Bank is one of the most honored and reliable representatives of a fiduciary system which, in the solid benefits it has conferred, more especially upon the industrious and economical poor, has never been equaled in the history of banking. Organized and incorporated in 1860, extraordinary caution has marked its entire career, and while it has paid its depositors hundreds of thousands in interest and dividends, not one of its patrons has ever lost a penny through any fault of the management. Nor has it been found necessary at any time to take advantage of a stay law or in any way to delay payment of deposits when called for. The board of trustees is composed of sound and conservative business men, as follows: Abiel Codding (president), Randolph Knapp, J. R. Bronson, J. H. Sturdy, Joseph E. Pond, S. E. Fisher, J. D. Lincoln, Fred. E. Sturdy, B. S. Freeman, Jos. G. Borden, George A. Dean, Edward R. Price (treasurer, cashier of North Attleborough National Bank), A. E. Codding, B. Porter, jr., E. I. Franklin and J. L. Sweet. The offices, occupied jointly with the North Attleborough National Bank, are situated on the second floor of the Bank building, No. 144 Washington street, and are commodious and handsomely appointed. Substantially the same rules govern this as other savings banks in Massachusetts, and depositors have the same rights and privileges. The subjoined statement shows the condition of the bank at the close of business April 23, 1891:

LIABILITIES.		RESOURCES.	
Deposits	925,277 48	Real estate loans	433,474 85
Guaranty fund	35,400 00	Personal "	308,125 00
Surplus earnings	20,205 61	Public funds	106,500 00
Interest	19,704 98	R. R. bonds and loans on same	88,000 00
		Bank stock	12,300 00
		Real estate	29,273 67
		Deposits in banks	21,653 11
		Expense	1,261 44
Total	$1,000,588 07	Total	$1,000,588 07

DEMAREST & BRADY,

Manufacturers of Fine Plated Jewelry — Whiting's Building, No. 128 Broad Street.

G. Demarest & Co. began the manufacture of jewelry at Plainville eighteen to twenty years ago. The subsequent changes in style were first to Demarest & Fisher, then to Demarest & Packard, and finally to Demarest & Brady — George Demarest and Bernard B. Brady — who removed to North Attleboro and now occupy one floor 35 x 115 feet in the great Whiting building No. 128 Broad street, where they have a well-appointed factory and employ from twenty-five to-forty work people in the manufacture of fine rolled gold plate commodities, making specialties of cuff pins, sleeve links, lace, bar, jersey, cuff and scarf pins, brooches, bangles, ear drops, chains, etc. These goods, to the value of $40,000 to $50,000 per annum, are disposed of by salesmen to eastern and western jobbers, and by them distributed to the jewelry and notion trade everywhere.

R. BLACKINTON & CO.,

Manufacturers of Solid Gold, Silver and Plated Jewelry—Whitney Building, No. 32 Chestnut Street; New York Office, No. 182 Broadway.

The firm of R. Blackinton & Co. is one of the old reliables, established about 1862, and is composed of Messrs. Roswell Blackinton and Walter Ballou, the senior member a director of the

North Attleboro National Bank and prominent in business and social circles. Mr. Ballou, a thorough practical jeweler, looks after the factory. The office and salesroom are situated at No. 182 Broadway, New York, where buyers visiting the city are invited to call and examine a superb line of samples that embraces all the late popular novelties in solid gold, silver and plated jewelry in every grade and style, suited to the wants of all markets and both sexes. The factory occupies one- floor, 60x200 feet, of the big three-story Whitney brick building, No. 32 Chestnut street, and is thoroughly fitted up with the newest and most effective machinery and appliances, the firm giving employment to about 100 skilled and unskilled operatives, and dealing for the most part with eastern, western and southern jobbers. In response to a growing demand, Messrs. Blackinton & Co. are making more silver novelties than heretofore.

E. S. CARGILL.

Grist and Planing Mill—Dealer in Grain, Meal, Feed, Lumber and Building Materials—Nos. 10, 12, 11 and 13 Chestnut Street.

Mr. Cargill has been engaged in business here for twenty years, is one of the most liberal and public-spirited of North Attleboro's citizens, popular with all classes and known personally to almost if not quite every resident. His grist mill and grain warehouse, Nos. 10 and 12 Chestnut street, comprise a three-story frame building, 40x60 feet, thoroughly equipped with

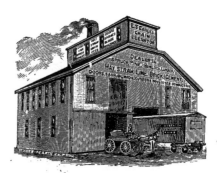

milling and grain handling machinery, with commodious yards, outbuildings, etc., in connection. A spur track enters the building. On the opposite side of the street is the new planing, sawing and moulding mill, and the lumber-yard is near the Old Colony railroad depot. A fifty-horse-power steam engine drives both mills, and from thirty to forty men are employed in all, so it may safely be presumed that a flourishing business is done. Most of the corn, cornmeal, cracked corn and mixed feed consumed hereabout is supplied by Mr. Cargill, who is also the leading dealer in lumber and manufacturer of mouldings and house finish. Orders are promptly filled for anything in his line, including grain and its products, hay, straw, spruce, pine and hemlock lumber in the rough or dressed, mouldings, gutters, rails, flooring, clapboards, wood and marble mantels; inside and outside finish, walnut, oak, ash, cherry and other hard woods; brick, lime, cement, plaster, plasterers' hair, etc.

In addition to his other callings Mr. Cargill is an extensive contractor and builder, makes plans and estimates on application, and carries full lines of builders' hardware.

CUTLER & LULL,

Makers of Gold Jewelry—Jay Street, near Elm.

This is one of the comparatively few concerns in this part of the country engaged in the manufacture of strictly genuine gold jewelry on a large scale. Messrs. Frank H. Cutler and Wm. E. Lull formed their present copartnership in 1889, and occupy with a well-equipped factory the second floor of Codding Bros.' building on Jay street near Elm, where they produce beautiful and salable goods, embracing the latest and most attractive styles of brooches, bracelets, bangles, lockets, neck chains, collar buttons, links, scarf, lace, bar, jersey and cuff pins, finger rings, all kinds of earrings — in a word, every description of fine solid gold ornaments except chains. Jobbers and dealers at wholesale all over the United States handle these commodities and find them in steady request.

J. J. & J. M. RICHARDS,

Manufacturing Jewelers—Richards' Building No. 2, Elm Street; New York Office, No. 194 Broadway.

Messrs. James J. and James M. Richards, who occupy the lower floor, 40x80 feet, of the three-story frame Richards building No. 2, on Elm street, are among the old-established and reliable jewelry manufacturers of North Attleboro, where they have been engaged in business for a quarter of a century. Their facilities are first-class in all respects and comprise a complete outfit of modern machinery of the most perfect kind, suited to the rapid and economical production of their specialties, which comprise the best grades and latest novelties in rolled gold plate sleeve buttons and links, studs, bracelets, bangles, etc., sales to jobbers for the domestic and export trade ranging in amount from $25,000 to $30,000 annually, the works giving employment to about twenty hands. The principal office and salesrooms are situated at No. 194 Broadway, New York, where buyers are cordially invited to call, inspect samples and prices, and leave their orders.

JOHN P. BONNETT,

Electroplater and Colorer of Jewelry and Watch Cases — No. 40 Elm Street.

Mr. John P. Bonnett, one of the best known, most largely experienced and most expert electroplaters in this country, was for a number of years in charge of the plating works of the Ames

Company of Chicopee, and subsequently with F. G. Whitney & Co. until 1880, when he went into business on his own account. His premises at No. 40 Elm street comprise two frame buildings—the works proper, one and a-half stories, 25 x 57 feet, and an annex of one story, 20 x 30 feet. His equipment, which is first-class and embraces all modern improved electro-plating apparatus, includes several powerful dynamos driven by a twenty-horse-power steam engine, baths and other appropriate appliances. About twenty skilled hands are employed and kept busy on orders for high-grade electro-plating of all kinds, the specialties covering every description of plating for jewelers, cutlers, tableware manufacturers, arms manufacturers, watch-case makers, etc., throughout the eastern and middle States, the patronage from the trade in this vicinity being expecially liberal. All work done here is of the best quality. Watch-cases are plated by an entirely new process and fully warranted.

YOUNG & STERN,

Manufacturers of Fine Rolled Plated Chains, Necklaces, etc. — Whiting's Building, No. 130 Broad Street.

Young & Bennett, the founders of this house in 1870, built up a widespread fame and a prosperous trade based upon the merit of their productions, not the least notable of which are the celebrated gold filled 14-K. "Pioneer" chains, equal in appearance to solid gold and of the highest order as regards design, workmanship and finish. In January, 1888, Mr. Bennett retired and a new firm was organized, composed of Messrs. Charles P. Young and Lewis Stern. The factory, situated on the ground floor, 35 x 250 feet, of the great three-story brick Whiting building, No. 130 Broad street, is thoroughly equipped in all departments and employs from fifty to sixty hands, the machinery plant being driven by steam. The output, which is very large and valuable, comprises, besides the "Pioneer" chains already mentioned, an endless variety of rolled gold plate chains of fine quality for ladies' and gentlemen's wear, necklaces, charms, etc., which are supplied to jobbers and the wholesale trade at short notice and at favorable prices.

CODDING BROTHERS.

Manufacturers of Jewelry—Jay Street, Near Elm; New York Office and Salesroom, No. 237 Broadway.

The firm of Codding Bros., established 1879, is composed of Messrs. Arthur E., James A., and Edwin A. Codding. The senior member is town treasurer and a trustee of the Attleboro Savings Bank. They erected the Codding building, frame, three stories, 35x80 feet, on Jay street near Elm, and occupy the ground floor for factory purposes. It is provided with a complete modern outfit of rolling, stamping and pressing machinery, steam power and all requisite adjuncts, and, with about twenty-five hands, produces over $20,000 worth of goods per annum, the specialties embracing the latest designs in rolled gold bracelets and bangles. The firm have several energetic salesmen on the road and supply jobbers in all the leading trade centers of the United States and Canada. Their New York office and salesroom are at No. 237 Broadway, where buyers are invited to call and examine goods and prices.

CO-OPERATIVE MANUFACTURING JEWELERS.

Adolph Newhaus, President and Treasurer; James Leary, Secretary; Benjamin Crandall, Salesman—Gold and Silver Plated Jewelry and Novelties—Draper's Building, No. 68 Broad Street.

This is a joint stock association of practical working jewelers, organized in February last with $8,000 capital—ten shares of $800 each, held by Messrs. Adolph Newhaus, James F. Leary, Benjamin Crandall, Stephen Donnell, George Donnell, Fred Franz, Frank Panucker, Charles F. Pardee, Joseph Klebs and John McCann. They have got only fairly started as yet, and are occupying for factory purposes a floor in Draper's building, No. 68 Broad street, but their equipment is entirely new and of the most approved construction; they employ about forty hands under the personal supervision of the stockholders, and there is ample reason to anticipate that the enterprise will prove a very successful one, as they are already filling generous orders from jobbers in the principal trade centers. The association's specialties embrace a general line of novelties in gold, sterling silver and rolled gold and silver plate, including jewelry and fancy articles—chains, brooches, lace, hair and scarf pins, sleeve links and buttons, collar buttons, studs, pocket match safes, hand mirrors, ash trays, napkin rings, etc., in artistic style.

ATTLEBOROUGH FALLS.

Attleborough Falls is situated in the town of North Attleborough, a few miles from the center, with which it is connected by electric railway. It is a bustling village and a prominent seat of the jewelry industry. A branch of the Old Colony railroad extends from Attleboro Center to the Falls.

V. H. BLACKINTON & CO.,

Manufacturers of Society Goods in Metal, Jewelry, Novelties, etc. — Commonwealth Avenue, near Old Colony Railroad Depot.

More than forty years ago Mr. V. H. Blackinton, one of the pioneers of the jewelry industry in this part of the country, established himself at Attleboro Falls and by close attention to business through a long series of years built up a first-class reputation and a trade extending to all sections of the Union. After Mr. Blackinton's death in 1888 the control devolved upon his widow, Mrs. E. W. Blackinton, who formed a copartnership with Mr. E. B. Wilmarth and continued the business under the present style. Mr. Wilmarth, who has had many years' practical experience in this industry, has personal charge of the shops and sales department. The factory is situated on Commonwealth avenue near the Old Colony railroad depot and occupies both floors of a two-story frame building 30 x 80 feet square, fitted up with a complete equipment of special machinery and steam power and employing about twenty-five hands. Sales, principally to the jobbing trade, range from $20,000 to $25,000 per annum. The firm's specialties cover a wide range, embracing every description of society goods in metal, jewelry and novelties, particular attention being given to society goods in metal, jewelry and novelties from standard and original designs, and japanning with the finest and most durable of black japans. Correspondence is solicited andestimates are furnished. Orders promptly filled for G. A. R. wreaths, rank straps and chevrons; S. V. and A. O. H. wreaths; sword, swivels and hooks; shoulder straps and other military goods; fireman, porter and elevator badges to order; metal letters and figures; police breast badges to order; plates with figures, (two sizes), special styles for car drivers and conductors; ribbon badge pins; safety pins, (Salus) patented; society lapel buttons; hat slides and hatters' goods; key rings in brass and tempered steel; plain compasses; hinges and fasteners for plush and leather cases; eye glass hooks; dies and tools furnished.

THE MASON JEWELRY COMPANY.

S. D. Mason, General Manager — Manufacturers of Jewelry — Freeman's Building, Commonwealth Avenue.

Mason, Draper & Co. were the founders of this concern, and were succeeded by the Mason Jewelry Company, of which Mr. S. D. Mason took charge as general manager. The factory, occupying an upper floor of the Freeman building on Commonwealth avenue, is capacious and well appointed in all respects, the facilities embracing steam power and a complete outfit of machinery, and from ten to fifteen operatives being employed. The house makes a general line of handsome and salable jewelry, the specialties comprising the latest novelties in patent spring and coil bracelets from rolled gold plate, sterling silver bangles, bead necklaces, lace and scarf pins, brooches in fine enamel, and many other articles of utility and ornament.

F. MASON & CO.,

Manufacturers of Society Emblems — Freeman's Building, Commonwealth Avenue.

Society and club officials in want of emblematical badges, pins, buttons, etc., will find it profitable in every way to correspond with F. Mason & Co., which firm, established in 1889, occupies one floor of the Freeman building, controls superior facilities, and has the advantage of long experience and unusual skill in the designing department, Mr. Frederick Mason having charge of the business. Ten or twelve men are employed, and a vast deal of fine work in rolled gold plate is turned out for the trade and to order, special commissions receiving the preference.

R. F. SIMMONS & CO.,

Manufacturing Jewelers—Commonwealth Avenue; New York Office and Salesrooms, Nos. 41 and 43 Maiden Lane.

This house, established in 1873 and composed of Messrs. R. F. Simmons, Edgar L. Hixon, and Joseph L. Sweet, ranks with the most extensive manufacturers of rolled gold goods in the United States. The factory occupies the greater portion of Freeman's large three-story 60 x 120-foot frame building on Commonwealth avenue, and is fitted up with a superb equipment of special machinery designed for making chains of every description, tools and appliances of the latest style, steam power, and all facilities for the production of superior goods in large quantities. An idea may be obtained of the volume of business done from the number of hands employed, which is seldom less than 150. The firm confines its attention almost exclusively to the manufacture of gold stock plated chains in endless variety — vest chains, guard chains, fob chains, neck chains, chain bracelets, necklaces, every conceivable kind of chain worn by either sex and all ages—together with a beautiful line of solid gold lockets and seals in an infinitude of styles and designs. A unique feature of this firm's business is that they manufacture every ring, swivel and appendage of whatever nature used on their goods in their own factory, thereby enabling them to guarantee the quality of their goods entire as no competitor can. R. F. Simmons & Co. sell to jobbers generally throughout the country, who are served by traveling salesmen, but in addition they maintain an office and salesrooms at Nos. 41 and 43 Maiden lane, New York, where full lines of their goods are shown, and where the trade are invited to call when in the city and inspect samples and price-lists.

STANLEY BROTHERS,

Manufacturers of Ladies' and Gentlemen's Rolled Plate Chains — High Street, near Commonwealth Avenue.

This house was founded in 1871 by Stanley Brothers & Co. — Stephen and Benjamin Stanley and E. C. Knapp. The latter retired after two years, and the brothers Stanley have since continued business under the present style. Provided with as complete an outfit of chain-making machinery as there is in the vicinty, the firm occupy the lower floor and two Ls of the 30 x 100-foot two-story frame structure on High street near Commonwealth avenue, employ from twenty to forty skilled work people, and obtain steam and water power from the Gold Medal Braid Company, which, by the way, controls the third most extensive water privilege in the State. Messrs. Stanley confine their attention exclusively to the manufacture of rolled gold plate chains for ladies' and gentlemen's wear — goods that for beauty of design and finish and general excellence have few rivals and no superiors. They are handled by the trade all over this continent, and the demand keeps pace with the supply, sales from the factory to jobbers and wholesale dealers ranging from $75,000 to $100,000 per annum. Both members of the firm are practical workmen. They require the services of but one traveler.

W. BARNETT,

Machinist and Tool-Maker — Manufacturer of Jewelers' Tools and Machinery, Shafting, Pulleys, Hangers, etc.—No. 53 Commonwealth Avenue.

About 1860 Wilcox & Mason bought out Oliver Stanley's machine shop in rear of the braid mill. In 1865 Mr. Washington Barnett purchased Mr. Mason's interest and up to 1881 was

junior partner in the firm of Wilcox & Barnett. Then Mr. Wilcox retired, and Mr. Barnett has since continued the business alone. His shop was destroyed by fire in the autumn of 1888, and in March following he fitted up and opened his present establishment in rear of his residence, No. 53 Commonwealth avenue. The building is a one-and-a-half-story frame structure 22 x 32 feet, and equipped with the usual outfit of lathes, etc., driven by a neat three-horse-power steam engine. Mr. Barnett is prepared to fill at short notice and in the very best manner all orders for the construction and repair of jewelers' machinery and tools of every description, shafting, pulleys, hangers, etc. Prices are reasonable and work guaranteed. Mr. Barnett is also agent for the Shipman automatic steam engine of one, two, three, four and five-horse-power, using kerosene oil for fuel, costing little, and specially adapted to the propulsion of small marine craft as well as to the use of printers, farmers, manufacturers, and others.

J. F. STURDY & SONS,

Manufacturers of Gold Stock Plated Chains—No. 8 Mill Street.

Mr. John F. Sturdy founded this well-known house over thirty years ago, and for a long time was sole proprietor. The firm of J. F. Sturdy & Co. was then formed, which survived until 1879, when Messrs. Fred E., Herbert K. and Frank M. Sturdy were admitted and the present style adopted. Messrs. J. F. Sturdy & Sons occupy one entire floor and half of another of the Daggett building, No. 8 Mill street—3,600 square feet of floor space—and employ fifty workmen. Their machinery plant is complete and is driven by either steam or water as desired, the building standing on the bank of Ten-Mile river, with which it is connected by a raceway. The firm manufacture a great variety of gold stock plated chains for all purposes, including men's vest and guard chains, ladies' Victoria and neck chains, eyeglass and children's chains, etc., and are constantly bringing out fresh novelties in that line, besides making a leading specialty of gold tip curbs of elegant design and superior workmanship. They sell to jobbers generally and deal direct with manufacturing jewelers.

W. D. FISHER & CO.,

Manufacturing Jewelers—Daggett Building, No. 8 Mill Street.

The Daggett building, No. 8 Mill street, is a three-story frame structure, 30x80 feet square, and is provided with both steam and water power. One floor is occupied by W. D. Fisher & Co., whose machinery plant is complete and who employ about fifty hands, making specialties of spring swivels, spring rings, and chain trimmings of all kinds, in rolled gold, plate and sterling silver. These goods are supplied to manufacturing jewelers and jobbers generally, and are in high repute with the trade.

The firm is composed of Messrs. Wm. D. Fisher, Wm. A. Fisher and M. A. Mackreth, energetic, progressive and successful business men.

GOLD MEDAL BRAND COMPANY.

H. N. DAGGETT, TREASURER.

GOLD MEDAL BRAID COMPANY.

Handel N. Daggett, Harvey Clap — Manufacturers of Worsted, Silk, Linen and Cotton Braids—High Street, opposite Commonwealth Avenue.

The Gold Medal·Braid Company was incorporated in 1879. In March, 1891, Messrs. Handel N. Daggett and Harvey Clap became sole proprietors of the mill, and are now conducting it as a firm, under the original style. The plant, situated on Ten-mile river, consists of a massive five-story stone building, 60x180 feet in dimensions, fitted up with a comprehensive equipment that includes 1500 braiding machines, driven by combined steam and water power. The working force varies at times from seventy-five to one hundred and fifty, and the output, valued at $150,000 and upward annually, is sold in every city and town in the United States, besides being exported to some extent. It is popularly known under the names "Golden Fleece" and "Atlas," and embraces the choicest grades of worsted, dress and alpaca, silk, linen and cotton star, braided silk and cotton braids of all widths and styles for dress, coat and vest bindings and other purposes.

Mr. Daggett was treasurer and Mr. Clap secretary of the company when operating as a corporation, and are experienced, capable and successful business men. The Willimantic Linen Company of Boston and New York are the selling agents.

B. S. FREEMAN & CO.,

Manufacturing Jewelers—Freeman's Buildings, Commonwealth Avenue; New York Office, No. 194 Broadway.

Freeman's buildings, situated on Commonwealth avenue, may fairly be called the industrial center of Attleboro Falls, since most of the business of the place is carried on in them. They comprise two French-roofed three-story structures, one of brick, 30x50 feet, the other frame, 60 x100 feet.

The firm of B. S. Freeman & Co. occupy all of the smaller and a portion of the larger buildings, both of which are provided with steam power. They have a splendid outfit of modern improved machinery, employ from thirty to forty carefully selected artificers and assistants, and make leading specialties of ladies' and gentlemen's rolled gold plate chains, ladies' chain bracelets and necklaces, in an infinite variety of patterns, including all the latest and most attractive novelties. The output of this house, large in volume and value, is disposed of exclusively to the jobbing trade, by whom dealers all over the country are supplied. The firm, composed of B. Stanley Freeman, senior, and B. Stanley Freeman, junior, was founded forty years ago by the elder Mr. Freeman. The house has an elegant office and salesroom at No. 194 Broadway, New York, where full lines of samples are shown, and where buyers are invited to call.

F. W. WEAVER & CO.,

Manufacturing Jewelers—Robinson Building No. 3, Corner Union Street and Bailey Avenue, Attleboro.

The copartnership between Messrs. F. W. Weaver and Harry P. Kent dates from 1883, when they established themselves in Attleboro and began building up a trade that has made the firm name familiar all over the United States. Their factory, thoroughly equipped in all departments, occupies one floor, 50x90 feet in area, of the big four-story brick Robinson building No. 3, corner of Union street and Bailey avenue, where they employ, as required, from thirty to fifty skilled operatives, and manufacture goods to the value of $50,000 and upward annually. Their specialties include all the latest novelties in high grade rolled gold lace pins, scarf pins, drops, charms, gold plate and sterling silver hair pins, etc., which they supply to the jobbing trade direct from the office here. They have constantly on the road several alert and successful salesmen, and are steadily enlarging the scope and volume of their transactions.

MANSFIELD.

MANSFIELD lies on the northern border of Bristol county, and is bounded on the east by Easton, on the west by North Attleboro, on the south by Norton, and on the north by Foxboro, Norfolk county. Area, 12,913 acres. It was set apart as a separate parish from Norton in 1732, and in April, 1770, made an independent town by act of the General Court. The town has always acquitted herself with credit in time of war or upon other occasions when patriotism and benevolence were appealed to. The present town-house, a spacious and tasty frame structure in the colonial style, was erected in 1882, and contains, besides the usual conveniences, a spacious high-school room. Iron ore was at one time obtained in considerable quantities within the limits of the town, but for some reason mining was abandoned. There is good reason to believe there is plenty of coal of inferior quality beneath the surface, but the vein has never been developed. The Boston & Providence and New Bedford, Taunton & Framingham railroads intersect each other at Mansfield village. The industries comprise the manufacture of jewelry, woolen goods, machine knives, awls and shoe knives, steam windlasses, taps and dies, spindles, monuments, coffin trimmings, castings, baskets, soap, saleratus, etc. The villages are Mansfield Center, West Mansfield and Whiteville. Population, 3,432.

C. D. LYONS & CO.,

Manufacturers of Solid Gold, Sterling Silver and Rolled Gold Plate Jewelry—Spring Street.

The above-named house, composed of Messrs. Charles D. Lyon and Frederick Paine, was established in 1888, employs from thirty to forty skilled jewelers and assistants, and last year made and sold over $30,000 worth of fine goods in all grades, including original novelties in catchy styles and great variety. Their premises comprise the two upper floors of the Kingman & Hodges three-story frame building, 40x80 feet with L, on Spring street, near the Rumford river, from which stream a canal supplies water for a turbine wheel, which, with a steam engine, drives their complete machinery equipment. The firm employs several energetic and successful traveling salesmen, and Mr. Lyons himself is pretty constantly on the road, so that they hardly know what a "dull season" is. The product of the works embraces almost every description of standard jewelry in solid gold, solid silver and rolled gold plate, together with new designs in pins, brooches, etc. They also control the patent and manufacture the famous "Lorimer" bracelet and glove buttoner, in solid gold and silver and rolled gold and silver plate. Orders are promptly filled.

FULLER CARRIAGE COMPANY,

Manufacturers and jobbers of Fine Carriages and Wagons, Harnesses, Robes and Horse Furnishings—Carriage and Sign Painting and General Repairing—School Street.

The carriage making business here was started by Mr. H. D. Fuller in 1884, and he was succeeded in 1887 by his sons, Messrs. H. C. and Edgar W., who prospered to such an extent that early in the present year it was decided to accept the proposition of Mr. W. B. Hodges for admission and organize a company, which, however, has not been incorporated. The shops occupy a two-story frame structure, 30x48 feet in area, and give employment to about a dozen wood workers, blacksmiths, painters and trimmers. Adjoining is the new repository recently erected, frame, two-stories, 32x50 feet, where is shown a large and carefully selected assortment of superior vehicles—coupés, rockaways surreys, buggies, road wagons, phaetons, concords, democrats, sleighs, etc.—from the most reputable Amesbury manufacturers. They are also general dealers in harness, robes, rugs, blankets, whips, brushes, and every description of horse, carriage and stable furnishings.

In their own shops the company build a superior line of light express and delivery wagons, and make repairs of all kinds, skillfully and at short notice. They also make specialties of carriage and sign painting to order. All work done in the best style and warranted. The Messrs. Fuller and Hodges are young, energetic and enterprising, skillful and upright, and deserve the confidence and patronage of the community.

GEORGE A. ROBINSON,

Manufacturer of Cutlery—William Street, West Mansfield.

In the year 1842 Robert McMoran and Robert Fulton, copartners, began the manufacture of knives and shoemakers' awls in a factory on the west side of the thoroughfare now known as Rumford avenue. After nineteen years of reasonable prosperity the firm dissolved in 1861 and a new one was established, composed of Mr. McMoran, George A. Robinson, and Wm. N. McMoran, a grandson of the senior member. A new factory was erected at West Mansfield, and the concern flourished until the death of Mr. McMoran, when the grandson retired and Mr. Robinson became and still remains sole proprietor. He continues to hold the same premises, one story, 40 x 60 feet, equipped with the usual cutlers' machinery and appliances, where he employs eight or ten skilled hands and makes considerable quantities of superior goods, his leading specialties comprising high-grade bread, butchers', cigar-makers', fish, oyster and shoe knives in over 600 different styles, from the best cast steel, neatly finished, fully warranted, and sold by the trade all over the United States.

PLAINVILLE.

THE town of Wrentham is described in its proper place under the head of "Norfolk County." By a mistake the village of Plainville was omitted, and as jewelry manufacturing is its only considerable industry, we insert an account thereof here in connection with the large jewelry centers in Bristol county, with which it is connected by business ties.

Plainville was formerly called Slackville for a family of grain millers of that name. When the name was changed, or for what reason, does not appear, but it is certain that about 1841 Geo. W. Shepardson bought and converted the old stone grist mill into a button factory, which he conducted for two years and then sold out to H. M. Richards, who began the manufacture of gilt jewelry, but sold the plant to Joseph T. Bacon and removed to Providence. Mr. Bacon tore down the old building and erected on its site the main portion of the present Lincoln, Bacon & Co. factory structure. The firm of Bacon, Hodges & Co. engaged in the making of jewelry in 1844, and that firm and its successors have continued the business on the same spot ever since. Others came later, and Plainville has grown into considerable prominence through the enterprise of those who have built up this peculiar interest. It is a neat and prosperous village, provided with churches, schools and the necessary adjuncts of a manufacturing center. An electric railway connects the place with Attleboro and North Attleboro.

ROBINSON BROTHERS,

Manufacturers of Jewelers' Findings—Lincoln, Bacon & Co.'s Building, Cor. South and Bacon Streets.

Messrs. E. Leroy Robinson and L. Eugene Robinson; experienced workers in metals and possessed of a thorough knowledge of trade requirements, formed their present copartnership, fitted up a floor of the Lincoln, Bacon & Co. building, and began the manufacture of jewelers' findings in July, 1890. Their machinery equipment is of the best kind, their facilities extensive and complete; they have in their employ a large force of skilled operatives, and are turning out great quantities of superior goods, which are supplied to jobbers, jewelry manufacturers and the trade generally. While producing almost everything coming under the head of jewelers' findings, the firm make leading specialties of silver and rolled gold swivels, bars, spring rings, etc.

LINCOLN, BACON & CO.,

Manufacturers of Jewelry—Cor. South and Bacon Sts.; New York Office, Nos. 41 and 43 Maiden Lane.

As stated elsewhere, H. M. Richards, the pioneer Plainville jewelry manufacturer, was succeeded in 1844 by Joseph T. Bacon, John H. Hodges and Geo. Mason, who occupied the old Slack mill, Mr. Mason withdrawing a few years later. Messrs. Bacon & Hodges remained in copartnership until 1850, when Mr. Hodges retired. In April of that year the old Slack mill was burned, after which a new factory was erected, the germ of the present establishment. Draper, Tifft & Bacon followed. Mr. John Tifft died in 1851, when the house was reorganized as Draper, Tifft & Co.—Frank S. (a son of Josiah Draper), Frank L. (son of John Tifft), Joseph T. Bacon and James D. Lincoln. Mr. Draper retired in July, 1860, when the style was changed to Lincoln, Tifft & Bacon. The New York office was established about 1853, the factory style being altered to J. T. Bacon & Co. about 1862 and the New York office to Lincoln, Tifft & Co., under which name the firm continued until 1876, when Frank L. Tifft died, after which his interest was purchased by Messrs. Lincoln & Bacon. The business was continued by them under the same name until 1882, when the present copartnership was formed, admitting Harland G., a son of Mr. Bacon, and Daniel C. Schofield of New York, when the style here and in New York was once more changed—this time to Lincoln, Bacon & Co., which firm now owns the commodious buildings occupied by Wade, Davis & Co., the Plainville Stock Company and others. Mr. Bacon, senior, died in 1888. The facilities of the concern are unsurpassed and the products marked by artistic originality and high finish. The factory, one of the largest of the kind, thoroughly equipped in all departments and employing about 100 hands, is situated in the three-story frame Lincoln, Bacon & Co. building at the corner of South and Bacon streets, 100 x 112 feet in area, with two 22 x 75-foot Ls. A sixty horse-power engine drives the machinery. The output, large, attractive and salable, embraces a great variety of standard goods and fresh novelties in ladies' and gentlemen's chains, bracelets, necklaces, brooches, drops, lace pins and dainty ornaments in rolled gold plate. The house deals exclusively with the jobbing and wholesale trade. Joseph T. Bacon was born in Attleboro May 21, 1818, a descendant of an early settler and son of an ex-State senator. At the age of eighteen, having learned button making, he and his brother, Ebenezer, engaged in the manufacture of jewelry on a small scale at Robinsonville. Later the firm became Richards & Bacon, from which Mr. Bacon withdrew in 1838 or 1839 and formed a copartnership with Lewis Holmes in the same business. Mr. Holmes retired in 1841, when the firm of Bacon, Hodges & Mason was organized. His subsequent history is given above. James D. Lincoln was born at Brimfield, Hampden county, March 30, 1823. At seventeen he began work in a Wrentham thread mill; in 1850 engaged as clerk in a New York shoe store, and a year later entered the employ of Draper, Tifft & Bacon, and in June, 1851, took charge of the sales department. A few months later he became and has ever since remained a partner. An honorable business man and public-spirited citizen, courteous and kindly, he is universally respected and enjoys the confidence of all classes.

S. W. OLNEY,

Manufacturer of Jewelers' Findings—No. 44 East Bacon Street.

Mr. S. W. Olney, established 1883, is widely known to and in high repute with jewelry manufacturers all over the United States. His factory, situated at No. 44 Bacon street, is fitted up with the best appliances, a steam engine, etc., and gives employment to a force of operatives that varies in number from five to ten as required. A general line of jewelers' findings is manufactured here, the leading specialties comprising gold, silver and copper shot, imitation screw wire, twist wire, twist wire rings, and seamless balls for jewelers' use—goods of superior quality and in growing demand. Orders are filled direct and at short notice.

PLAINVILLE STOCK COMPANY,

Manufacturing Jewelers—Corner South and Bacon Streets; Office and Salesroom, No. 176 Broadway, New York.

In 1872 the firm of G. Demarest & Co. organized as a copartnership with ten members, and continued under that name for two years, but in July, 1874, dissolved, G. Demarest and Henry Packard retiring, their interests being transferred to the remaining portion of the company, who reorganized as the Plainville Stock company, a copartnership as before. Since that time several members have retired from the business, their interests being bought by the remaining portion of said company, until now four partners with equal interests constitute the company, viz.: D.

H. Corey, W. S. Metcalf, A. W. Burton and E. P. Bennett. Two floors in the commodious three-story frame factory, corner of South and Bacon streets, are occupied by them and fully equipped with all the improved modern machinery, tools, etc., to accommodate the large force they are compelled to employ. They manufacture a standard line of rolled plate, gold front and solid gold jewelry, consisting generally of chains, brooch and lace pins, scarf pins, button sets, bracelets, jersey and stick pins, charms, etc. To designate their goods and protect them from imitations of their styles made from inferior stock by poor workmen, they have adopted and registered the now well-known trade mark "P. S. Co.," which appears on all goods that will admit of being stamped in that manner. Leading as they do in style, workmanship and finish, they are compelled to employ the best designers and workmen, assuring the good will of their ever-increasing patronage. Manufacturing as they do everything they use in their factory —their designs, their stock, tools, dies, etc.—and having had a business experience of twenty years, is a guarantee of reliable goods to all patrons and of fair treatment, Samples can always be seen at the New York office or at the factory. Communications must be addressed to Plainville Stock Co., Plainville, Mass

WADE, DAVIS & CO.,

Manufacturing Jewelers—Corner South and Bacon Streets ; New York Office, Room 4, No. 198 Broadway.

The firm of Wade, Davis & Co. dates from 1876, is composed of Messrs. W. H. Wade, E. P. Davis and C. A. Whiting, and occupies for factory purposes the lower portion of the three-story frame building, 28x100 feet, at the corner of South and Bacon streets. Messrs. Wade and Davis reside here and superintend the mechanical and shipping business, while Mr. Whiting has charge of the New York office, No. 198 Broadway, and looks after the interests of the house in the west and south, supplying jobbers generally. Annual sales vary between $75,000 and $100,000. Of the factory it is only necessary to say that it is quite commodious, is equipped in the most perfect manner, and employs from fifty to seventy-five artisans, besides designers, clerks, etc. The product embraces the freshest and most pleasing novelties in rolled plate jewelry and silver ornaments—bracelets, brooches, hoops, drops, bar, cuff, lace, scarf and jersey pins, etc.—a leading specialty being the originating and making of bracelets in all styles, patent spring, coil, bangle, friendship and success, in plate and silver. The works are reached by telegraph via North Attleboro.

JOHN B. MAINTIEN,

Plain and Fancy Enameler—Lincoln, Bacon & Co.'s Building, Cor. South and Bacon Streets.

The late J. E. Maintien, founder of this concern, was a pioneer enameler, and became one of the most famous in the United States. He first engaged in his vocation at Providence in 1821, removed to Plainville in 1855, subsequently formed a copartnership under the style of J. E. Maintien, and died in 1889, when John B. Maintien succeeded, and is now conducting the business under his own name, with well appointed works on an upper floor of the Lincoln, Bacon & Co. building, corner of South and Bacon streets. From fifteen to twenty hands are employed, and transactions with manufacturing jewelers in this vicinity and throughout the country aggregate nearly $20,000 per annum. Mr. Maintien's facilities are first-class; he carries a large and varied stock of enamels and colors, and does every description of work in his line, making a leading specialty of enameled flowers in artistic styles.

MIDDLESEX COUNTY.

MIDDLESEX was one of the original four counties—Essex, Middlesex, Suffolk and Norfolk—into which the Massachusetts colony was divided by the General Court, May 10, 1643. The towns then in existence were : Charlestown, established June 24, 1629 ; Watertown, Sept. 7, 1630 ; Medford, September 28, 1630 ; Cambridge, September 8, 1633 ; Concord, September 2, 1635 ; Sudbury, September 4, 1639. Woburn was incorporated May 18, 1642, and is the eldest daughter of the county. Reading (now Lynn) was not incorporated until forty-two years afterward. Cambridge is the oldest city, chartered March 17, 1846. Charlestown's incorporation as a city occurred February 22, 1847, but she was annexed to Boston May 14, 1873, and now has no separate existence save in name, and is not even a part of Middlesex county. The following towns, in addition to those already named, have been incorporated within the limits of Middlesex county since 1642. It should be borne in mind that the bounds of the county itself have undergone considerable change and not a little contraction, from which Worcester county was the principal gainer :

Acton,	July 3, 1735.	Lowell,	March 1, 1826.
Arlington,	February 27, 1807.	Malden,	May 2, 1649.
Ashby,	March 5, 1767.	Marlborough,	May 31, 1660.
Ashland,	March 16, 1846.	Maynard,	April 19, 1871.
Ayer,	February 14, 1871.	Melrose,	May 3, 1850.
Bedford,	September 23, 1729.	Natick,	February 10, 1781.
Belmont,	March 18, 1859.	Newton,	January 11, 1688.
Billerica,	May 29, 1655.	North Reading,	March 22, 1853.
Boxborough,	February 25, 1783.	Pepperell,	April 6, 1753.
Brighton,	February 24, 1807.	Sherborn,	May 27, 1764.
Burlington,	February 28, 1799.	Shirley,	January 5, 1753.
Carlisle,	April 28, 1780.	Somerville,	March 3, 1842.
Chelmsford,	May 29, 1655.	South Reading,	February 25, 1812.
Dracut,	February 26, 1701.	Stoneham,	December 17, 1725.
Dunstable,	October 15, 1673.	Stow,	May 16, 1683.
East Sudbury,	April 10, 1780.	Tewksbury,	December 23, 1734.
Everett,	March 9, 1870.	Townsend,	June 29, 1732.
Framingham,	June 25, 1700.	Tyngsborough,	February 23, 1809.
Groton,	May 25, 1655.	Waltham,	January 4, 1737.
Holliston,	December 3, 1724.	Wayland,	April 10, 1780.
Hopkinton,	December 13, 1715.	Westford,	September 23, 1729.
Hudson,	March 19, 1866.	Weston,	January 1, 1712.
Lexington,	March 29, 1712.	Wilmington,	September 25, 1730.
Lincoln,	April 19, 1754.	Winchester,	April 30, 1850.
Littleton,	November 2, 1714.		

Arlington was incorporated as West Cambridge ; name changed April 30, 1867 ; East Sudbury was changed to Wayland March 11, 1835 : South Reading to Wakefield June 30, 1868. Lowell was reincorporated as a city August 5, 1836 ; Malden, March 31, 1881 ; Marlborough, May 23, 1890 ; Newton, June 2, 1873 ; Somerville, April 14, 1871 ; Waltham, June 2, 1884.

Middlesex is bounded on the north by the New Hampshire State line ; on the east by Essex and Suffolk counties ; on the South by Norfolk county, and on the west by Worcester county. The Merrimack (navigable to Lowell), Concord, Nashua and Charles are the principal streams, but numerous lakes and ponds of greater or less magnitude and brooks supply an abundance of water for manufacturing and other purposes. Agriculture is in a rather depressed condition, owing to the inducements offered farmers in the west, but which are steadily growing less, while eastern prospects improve, by reason of denser population and better and more convenient markets. Besides, most western farms are mortgaged to eastern money lenders (savings banks principally), so that as a matter of fact the rich lands nearer the setting sun every year pour their products in greater volume into the coffers of the eastern factory operatives in the form of interest on their deposits. The industries of Middlesex are varied in character and enormous in volume, and are constantly increasing. No country in the world possesses greater advantages for the prosecution of skilled mechanical enterprise on a large scale. The population of the county shows a healthy growth, as follows :

TOWNS.	1880.	1890.	TOWNS.	1880.	1890.
Acton,	1,797	1,897	Marlborough,	10,127	13,805
Arlington,	4,100	5,629	Maynard,	2,291	2,700
Ashby,	914	825	Medford,	7,573	11,079
Ashland,	2,394	2,532	Melrose,	4,560	8,519
Ayer,	1,881	2,148	Natick,	8,479	9,118
Bedford,	931	1,092	Newton,	16,995	24,379
Belmont,	1,615	2,098	North Reading,	900	874
Billerica,	2,000	2,380	Pepperell,	2,348	3,127
Boxborough,	319	325	Reading,	3,181	4,088
Burlington,	711	617	Sherborn,	1,401	1,381
Cambridge,	52,669	70,028	Shirley,	1,365	1,191
Carlisle,	478	481	Somerville,	24,933	40,152
Chelmsford,	2,553	2,695	Stoneham,	4,890	6,155
Concord,	3,922	4,427	Stow,	1,045	903
Dracut,	1,595	1,996	Sudbury,	1,178	1,197
Dunstable,	453	416	Tewksbury,	2,179	2,515
Everett,	4,159	11,068	Townsend,	1,967	1,750
Framingham,	6,235	9,239	Tyngsborough,	631	662
Groton,	1,862	2,057	Wakefield,	5,547	6,982
Holliston,	3,098	2,619	Waltham,	11,712	18,707
Hopkinton,	4,601	4,088	Watertown,	5,426	7,073
Hudson,	3,739	4,670	Wayland,	1,962	2,060
Lexington,	2,460	3,197	Westford,	2,250	2,147
Lincoln,	907	987	Weston,	1,664	1,448
Littleton,	994	1,025	Wilmington,	1,213	933
Lowell,	59,475	77,696	Winchester,	4,861	3,802
Malden,	12,017	23,031	Woburn,	13,499	10,931

Total, 1880, 363,557; 1890, 383,446; gain, 19,889. Property valuation, according to the State census of 1885, $315,911,919. Area of the county, 827 square miles.

FRAMINGHAM.

AS already noted, Framingham was incorporated in 1700; at that time its area was 20,500 acres, but changes in town boundaries have reduced it to about 18,975 acres, bounded on the northeast by Wayland, on the east by Natick, on the southeast by Sherborn, on the southwest by Ashland, on the west by Southborough and Marlborough, and on the north by Sudbury. A portion of Lake Cochituate (described in the article on Natick) lies in the eastern part of Framingham. The early history of the region was not essentially different from that of other towns in this part of the State. In the northerly part of the town are several lofty elevations known as Nobscot, Doeskin hill and Gibbs' mountain; near the southern extremity a cluster of four large ponds, the remainder of the surface being moderately level and the Sudbury river flowing through from southwest to northeast. The villages are Framingham Center, reached by the Old Colony, and South Framingham, midway between Boston and Worcester, reached by the Boston & Albany Railroad, Saxonville, Park's Corner and Brackett's Corner, Hastingsville, Lokerville; Sherbornville, Coburnville, etc. Total population of the town, 9,239, more than half of whom reside at South Framingham. Previous to the building of the Boston & Worcester railroad the center, situated on the great turnpike, was the principal place of business, but with the withdrawal of the stages and the cessation of heavy long distance teaming began the decay of the place and the gradual removal of manufactures and trade to South Framingham and vicinity, so that there is little or nothing but farming doing elsewhere in the town, though the academy, the high school, the State normal school and the Framingham library remain at the center.

The manufactures of the town are quite large and include cotton and woolen fabrics (at Saxonville), carpets and carpet yarns, paper, hats, leather, straw goods, India rubber goods, carriages, shoes, lasts, etc. There are two National, two savings and one co-operative banks. There are also two newspapers—the *Gazette* and the *Tribune.*

FRAMINGHAM SAVINGS BANK.

Franklin E. Gregory, President; Samuel B. Bird, J. Henry Robinson, M. D., Franklin Manson, Vice-Presidents; Luther F. Fuller, Treasurer; Walter Adams, Attorney for Bank—Manson Block, Concord Street.

The Framingham Savings Bank was chartered March 11, 1846, and began business at Framingham center the ensuing May. Colonel Moses Edgell, to whose suggestion and labors its establishment was largely due, was made the first president, a position which he retained and adorned until 1871, when he was succeeded by Mr. George Phipps, who died in 1876. Mr. Charles Upham, who was next chosen for the place, died in 1880, and after him came Mr. Luther Fuller, the present treasurer, who in turn was succeeded by Mr. Adolphus Merriam, who held the position until his death in 1885. The removal to South Framingham occurred in 1882. In 1885 it transpired that the then acting treasurer of the institution had engaged in financial transactions which, while in no way criminal, were calculated to lessen public confidence in the management, and a "run" ensued, a good many of the bank's patrons rushing in mad haste to recover their deposits, which were promptly paid on demand. News of the supposed irregularities spread, however, and the State Savings Bank Commissioner took possession, appointing Mr. Luther F. Fuller, a successful Framingham merchant, to the post of treasurer on August 4th of that year. When it is borne in mind that the depositors numbered thousands, and that the regular 2 1-2 per cent. dividend was placed with the principal in each instance, it must be acknowledged that the conduct of the bank and the demonstration of its solidity form an unique chapter in financing.

The bank was placed under a temporary injunction and a thorough examination of its affairs made by N. P. Lamson, the well-known expert accountant, who rendered a report exonerating the dead treasurer from any personal misappropriation, and, after remaining under the management of the trustees until the removal of the injunction, the bank was reopened for business—paying dollar for dollar, with a dividend of two per cent. on the face value of all deposits.

Franklin E. Gregory, Esq., of Framingham, is now president; Messrs. Samuel B. Bird, of Framingham, J. Henry Robinson, M. D., of Southboro, and Franklin Manson of South Framingham are the vice-presidents; Mr. Fuller remains treasurer; and Mr. Wm. H. Bird, who entered the bank in 1886, is bookkeeper. The board of trustees includes the officers named (with the exception of bookkeeper Bird), Rev. John S. Cullen, and Messrs. Adrian Foote, Walter Adams, Francis C. Stearns, Thomas L. Barber, Edward F. Kendall, Simeon H. Williams and Clifford Folger. The bank occupies commodious and handsomely appointed banking and board rooms in the New Manson block, Concord street. These offices, on the south side of the building, second floor, are commodious, well lighted, fitted up in elegant style, and the large fire-proof vault, constructed with numerous pigeon holes, is built directly over the National bank vault and inclosed by eighteen-inch solid brick walls. Among the notable features and conveniences are large carved oak wardrobes, massive and handsome counters and a long distance telephone. The institution is now in a more flourishing and prosperous condition than ever before, has more than 4000 depositors, embracing all sorts and conditions of men and women—capitalists, merchants, manufacturers, farmers, mechanics, daily laborers, the widows and orphans of well-to-do deceased citizens, working women, high and low, rich and poor, old and young—in Framingham, Holliston, Ashland, Southboro and all neighboring towns. Interest is allowed on all deposits made on or before the first Saturday in each month. Dividend days, first Saturday in May and November. Quarter days, first Saturday of May, August, November and February. Bank open for business from 9 a.m. to 3 p.m., except on Saturday, when the hours are from 9 a. m. to 12 m.

THE AUBURN LAST COMPANY.

E. D. Stone, Treasurer and Superintendent—Manufacturers of Lasts for Leather and Rubber Shoes—Factory, Clark Street.

Mr. Elmer D. Stone, the founder of this company, is a native of Falmouth, Maine, learned last-making in his youth, and has had more than twenty years' experience in the trade. He first established himself at Auburn, Me.—hence the name of the company—in 1876, but in 1882, in order to be within easier reach of his customers, removed to South Framingham, opening a factory on Howard street, which soon proved of too limited a capacity, and in 1884

he secured and occupied his present quarters on Clark street—a two-story frame structure, 30x 50 feet, with basement, attached to which is an engine and boiler-room 24x30 feet, heating pipes and drying-rooms connecting the two buildings. Here, provided with steam power, a complete equipment of lathes and other devices peculiar to the last-making industry, and employing from ten to twenty skilled workmen, the productive capacity being about 300 pairs of lasts per day, he is enabled to fill all orders promptly and satisfactorily. The specialties embrace every description of lasts required by manufacturers of both rubber and leather boots and shoes, and orders are thankfully received and promptly executed in the best style at reasonable prices, all work being of the best material and finish, accurate and faultless.

Mr. Stone began the manufacture of rubber lasts in 1879 and in response to the growing demand has increased his facilities from time to time, until now, with twelve years' experience, he feels entire confidence in his ability to meet the views of patrons as well as the competition of any rival house in the trade. Buying only the choicest rock maple for this class of lasts, he has five drying-rooms of 75,000 to 100,000 blocks capacity, and can never be found short of material of the most desirable kind that will neither warp nor shrink, his heaters being suppled with steam pipes and hot-air blast, thus insuring the best results in drying. The same remarks apply to the facilities for obtaining the best results in ordinary leather boot and shoe lasts. Among the regular patrons of the Auburn Last Company may be named the Para Rubber Company and Gregory & Co., boot and shoe manufacturers, both of this place. Shipping facilities east, west, north and south are first-class, and those sending orders need anticipate no delay in delivery. Mr. Stone is a respected and influential citizen and a prominent Odd Fellow, having passed all the chairs in his lodge and in Waushacum encampment of South Framingham.

NEW ENGLAND RATTAN COMPANY.

William E. Ryan, President and Manager; M. Hollander, Treasurer—Manufacturers of Reed and Rattan Furniture, Sofas, Lounges, Chairs, Tables, Carriages, Stands, etc.—Wellington Ave.

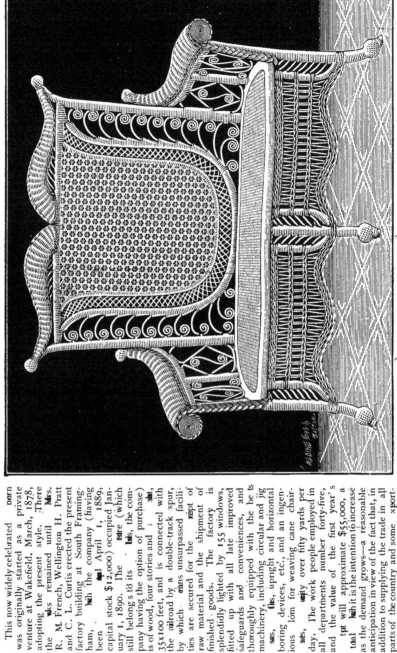

This now widely celebrated concern was originally started as a private venture at Wakefield, March, 1878, adopting the present style. There it was remained until Mrs. R. M. French, Wellington H. Pratt and C. L. Curtis erected the present factory building at South Framingham, with the company (having been incorporated April 1, 1889, capital stock $12,000) occupied January 1, 1890. The store (which still belongs to its house, the company having the option of purchase) is of wood, four stories and is 35x100 feet, and is connected with the railroad by a double-track spur, by which means unsurpassed facilities are secured for the receipt of raw material and the shipment of finished goods. The factory is splendidly lighted by 155 windows, fitted up with all late improved safeguards and conveniences, and thoroughly equipped with the best machinery, including circular and jig saws, the upright and horizontal boring devices, etc., and an ingenious loom for weaving cane chair-seats. The work people employed in all departments number forty-five, over fifty yards per day, and the value of the first year's output will approximate $55,000, a total which it is the intention to increase as the demand grows—a reasonable anticipation in view of the fact that, in addition to supplying the trade in all parts of the country and some exporters, such prominent and extensive dealers as Flint & Co., Cowperthwait & Co., and Bauman Bros. of New York, and the Brooklyn Furniture Company of Brooklyn, are among their regular and heaviest patrons. The goods, which are of the highest order, include every description of rattan and reed chairs, lounges, tables, stands, children's carriages, music racks, parlor and sitting-room suites, together with the freshest and most attractive novelties suited to the trade. Mr. William E. Ryan, the originator, president and general manager of the New England Rattan Company, came to Wakefield, Mass., in

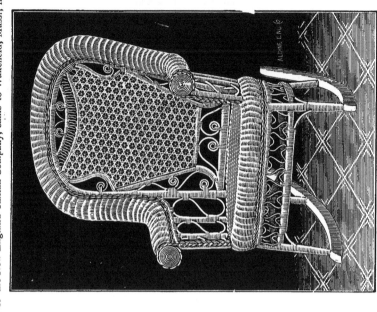

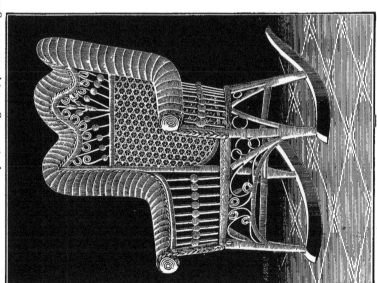

boyhood and learned his trade with the principal rattan manufacturing establishment of that place. His associates are all capable practical business men, and the outlook of the company is most encouraging. All rattan and other foreign material consumed here is imported expressly for the company; the best special skilled labor is employed, and new styles are being constantly designed and given form in the work.

GEORGE H. EAMES,

Manufacturer of Fancy Leather Goods, Violin Strings, Violin Cases, etc.—Rear of No. 49 Union Ave.

It is apparent that any one engaging in the manufacture of goods in which there is such close competition as exists in the fancy leather goods trade must do so with the fixed determination either to place his standard of quality so high as to attract the best class of buyers, or else to sacrifice everything to cheapness in order to force sales. So many have adopted the latter plan that their goods are a drug in the market and can hardly be given away, while those who adhere to legitimate methods find their reward in a moderate degree of prosperity that leaves them at least an approving conscience and a full measure of self-respect. Of this class is Mr. George H. Eames, who, having spent three years of his life in mastering the mechanical part of his vocation, decided, on the retirement of his instructor in 1889, to embark in business on his own account, which he did in September of that year, at first utilizing a room of his parental home for the purpose and doing most of the work himself. In June last he completed and occupied his new factory—a substantial three-story frame structure, 25x38 feet, near his residence. Here, employing eight superior hands and provided with a complete equipment of woodworking, leather-stretching, embossing and violin-string machinery and appliances, he is prepared to respond with the best and tastiest commodities to all demands for standard products and novelties in his line, turning out musical instrument cases—among which is the "Diamond" violin case, double swell, lately invented by Mr. Eames—music rolls, dressing cases, collar and cuff boxes, sample, cases, etc., in endless variety and large quantities and giving special attention to commissions for new designs, fine plush-lined extra finished cases for violins, guitars, cornets, etc. He also manufactures violin and cello strings of the best quality in considerable quantities. He is a young and enterprising scion of an old and respected Framingham family. Upright, courteous and ambitious to excel, he possesses the right elements for a successful business man. His factory is under his constant personal supervision, the utmost care and skill are exercised in all departments, and nothing is left undone to render his goods attractive, substantial and otherwise acceptable. All shells used in the manufacture of musical instrument and other cases are made upon the premises, and his well-constructed, elegantly embossed plush-lined goods cannot be surpassed.

E. E. CRANDALL,

Dealer in Carriages, Wagons, Sleighs, Harnesses, etc.—Carriage Painter and repairer—Irving Street.

Mr. Crandall has been engaged in business here since 1885, and has supplied the people of South Framingham and surrounding country with great numbers of handsome and serviceable vehicles. During the past year he found that his trade had outgrown his facilities, and therefore proceeded to erect a new and commodious three-story and basement carriage repository, 60

x100 feet in area, with 28x35-foot blacksmith and repair shop adjoining—the largest, most complete and convenient establishment of the kind in this part of the State, appropriately fitted up with separate departments for the exhibition of new carriages of all kinds, second-hand vehicles, barges, hacks, wagons, etc., and harnesses; paint shop, packing-room and repair shop. Here

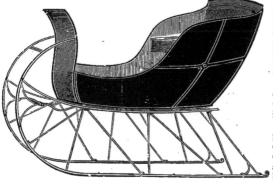

may be seen a line of the finest wheeled vehicles, sleighs and harness ever shown in New England, embracing, among others, samples of choice work from the Biddle & Smart Company of Amesbury, and Moyer's "Banner" wagons, made at Syracuse, N. Y.

Special attention is given to orders for carriage painting and varnishing and repairs. One of ihe best artist carriage painters n America is employed, and premiums were awarded samples of his work at the South Middlesex fair, last fall, and also at the Taunton fair. An exhibit will be made at the Worcester fair this fall. Mr. Crandall came to South Framingham from his native place (Cortland, N. Y.) in 1885, and, though still a young man, has made for himself an enviable

reputation in business and social circles. He is a past grand among Oddfellows, a member of Netus tribe No. 43, I. O. R. M., and a courteous, liberal, popular gentleman.

HOTEL WINTHROP.

J. H. Jordan, Proprietor—Hollis Street.

The Hotel Winthrop is a recent addition to the hotel accommodations of South Framingham, a commodious modern three-story structure erected in 1884, and containing elegant office, reading and dining-rooms, parlors, and twenty-four roomy, cosy, inviting sleeping apartments. The house is lighted by gas throughout, warmed by steam, and fitted with all useful improvements and comforts. The table is first-class, provided with the choicest meats, fish, vegetables, etc., appetizingly prepared and politely served, and rates are remarkably low, accommodations considered. Mr. Jordan is ably assisted by his popular and obliging clerk, Mr. Wm. I. Matthews. Though easy accessible from the railroad stations, the Winthrop is yet far enough away to avoid the noise of passing trains. Mr. James H. Jordan, who last year succeeded Mr. L. A. Bruce in the proprietorship, is a native of Maine, who for many years was a traveling salesman for the Providence Tool Company and the Wardwell Machine Company of Pawtucket. During that time he became widely and favorably known personally, and thoroughly acquainted himself with the wants and wishes of the sample-case fraternity, any representative of which is warmly welcomed, accorded special terms, and attentively served with the best the Winthrop affords, as are the members of theatrical troupes on the road. Mr. Jordan is an active member of Pericles lodge No. 4, K. of P., of South Framingham.

MARLBOROUGH.

WHAT is now Marlborough was formerly a portion of Sudbury, to which was afterward added a grant previously made to the Indians—29,419 acres of the former and 6,000 acres of the latter, making 35,419 acres in all, incorporated May 31, 1660, under the present name. One attack was made upon the settlement during King Philip's war, which resulted in the wounding of one white man, the burning of the meeting-house, thirteen dwellings and eleven barns, the general destruction of fences and fruit-trees, and the killing and wounding of about forty savages. Marlborough sent four companies to Concord, April 19, 1775, and these joined in the pursuit of the British on their retreat to Boston. A portion of the Marlborough contingent subsequently participated in the battle of Bunker Hill, and from that time forward the town contributed liberally of men and means for the prosecution of the war for independence—an example emulated on a large scale by the descendants of the same men in the war for the Union.

The town of Westborough was set apart from Marlborough in 1717, Southborough at a later period, and Northborough afterward from Westborough.

The first Marlborough school-house was built in 1698. In 1790 there were seven school districts. Notwithstanding the setting off of the town of Hudson, mostly from Marlborough territory, in 1866, there are now nearly 2500 enrolled common school pupils in the town limits. Gates Academy was established in 1826, and merged in the high school in 1849.

The Marlborough *Mirror*, anti-slavery and prohibition, was established in October, 1859. The Marlborough *Journal* was started in 1860, and the *Mirror* and *Journal* consolidated the next year. Editor Joy, of the *Journal*, went to the war, and the paper soon stopped. About 1866 the *Mirror* was resuscitated by a Mr. Wood, who sold out in 1871 to Stillman B. Pratt, the original founder, and the name was changed to the *Mirror-Journal*. Later Mr. Pratt started the *Advertiser* and a number of other rural papers, and in 1887 began the *Daily Mirror*, which promptly fell through for lack of patronage—that is, it starved to death in about two years. In 1888 Mr. Pratt founded the *Weekly-American*, a religio-anti-Catholic, anti-trade union, free speech, free press, free school, free shop organ, and in 1889 turned his entire business over to his son. .... Wood Brothers removed the Hudson *Enterprise* to Marlborough and issued the first number of the *Marlborough Weekly Enterprise* September 8, 1888. The venture prospered, and a year later the firm began the publication of a wide-awake daily edition. They have a very fine and costly newspaper and printing establishment: ...... The *Marlborough Times* is an excellent and able weekly, edited and published by Mr. Charles F. Morse ...... The *Marlborough Star* is a neat and sprightly Catholic weekly, devoted to temperance and the interests of the Irish-American element.

There are two National, one savings and one co-operative banks, a fine public library, good water-works, an efficient fire department, and an electric street railway.

The city of Marlborough was incorporated under "An Act to incorporate the City of Marlborough," approved May 23, 1890, which provides for mayor, board of aldermen, common council and school committee. The board of aldermen consists of one member from each of the seven wards, the common council of two from each ward, the school committee of one from each ward, with the mayor as *ex-officio* chairman. The first election under this act was held on the first Tuesday in December, 1890, and S. H. Howe was chosen

Mayor for the term of one year. Four democrats and three republicans were elected aldermen, and nine democrats and five republicans to the common council. The school committee consists of four democrats, two republicans and one independent, the mayor being *ex-officio* chairman. The vote was 1203 for and 1156 against license. The new officers assumed office on the first Monday in January, 1891. Population of city, 13,728. A comprehensive sewerage system is now in course of construction. The leading industry of Marlborough, to which all others are secondary and tributary, is the manufacture of shoes.

THE MARLBORO THEATER.

Francis W. Riley, Owner and Manager—Fairmount Street near Main.

The present Marlboro Theater was originally designed for a skating rink, and was erected in 1883 by Samuel Boyd. The roller skate craze declined soon afterward, and the building was altered and made a public hall in 1885. Three years later (in 1888) it was entirely remodeled and reconstructed under the direction of Mr. F. W. Riley, the owner. It is a large three-story wooden structure, with ornate roof and front, paneled in imitation of gray and brown stone, with gothic windows, 70 feet front, facing Fairmount street, and 135 feet in depth. The entrance is on Fairmount street. The interior is arranged as auditorium, balcony and gallery, handsomely decorated and upholstered, and will comfortably seat 1,060 persons. The stage is 38 by 70 feet, the proscenium 28 feet in height, the drop curtain a work of art, and the establishment provided with nine complete sets of scenery, ample dressing-rooms, gas light, steam heat, and three exits, the stage entrance being on Fairmount street. Traveling dramatic organizations may secure the house on reasonable terms, and it is also rented for concerts, lectures, public meetings, etc. Mr. Riley is a professional musician, organist at the Immaculate Conception Roman Catholic Church, and for several years was professor of music at the State Normal School at Framingham. He is the owner of the city bill boards, employs an efficient corps of bill-posters and distributors, and all bills, circulars, invitations, notices, cards, etc., intrusted to him receive immediate attention and a thorough distribution is guaranteed. It will be for the interest of all advertisers to correspond with Francis W. Riley, Marlboro, Mass.

T. J. BEAUDRY,

Successor to G. J. Hobbs— Manufacturer of Cutting Dies for Leather, Rubber, Paper and Cloth—Florence Street.

Of the many ingenious and useful labor and time-saving appliances required by the modern shoe manufacturer none are more indispensable that a complete assortment of dies for forming the various parts of foot-wear — uppers, counters, soles and heels. The same  remarks hold good as regards manufacturers of thousands of articles in rubber, cloth, paper, sheet metal, etc. We do not know who originated the die-making industry, but that it has flourished in New England for a long time is indisputable. More than thirty years ago Mr. S. K. Taylor began making these devices in Marlboro, and it has been carried on here continuously ever since. Hobbs & Mellen succeeded Mr. Taylor; Mr. Hobbs died, Mr. Mellen retired, and Mr. T. J. Beaudry then purchased the plant, of which he had been the actual manager for a long time, and with improved facilities is enabled to do more and better work than ever before. His equipment is quite comprehensive, his machinery is driven by a 30-horse-power engine, and he employs a full force of skilled workmen—sufficient to prevent delays in the execution of commissions. His specialties embrace every description of dies used by workers in leather, rubber, textiles and paper; his designs are the latest; his materials the choicest, and his workmanship faultless, and he enjoys a large and growing patronage from the New England, middle and western States. Mr. Beaudry was born in Canada, came to the United States in childhood, learned the printing business, "set 'em up" on the Lowell *Times* for some years, then accepted the foremanship of Pratt Bros' Marlboro printing house, and finally abandoned the "art preservative" to enter Mr. George J. Hobbs' employ as manager in 1879. He is as square as an em quad in business matters, a popular citizen, and a respected Odd Fellow and Mason.

ELLIS FILTER COMPANY.

Frank W. Ellis, General Manager—Manufacturers of the Acme Water Filter, Marlboro, Mass.

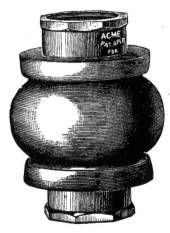

Here is a particular article of extraordinary simplicity that costs but little and is yet of incalculable practical value. All mankind are water drinkers, yet few of them realize how liable they are to swallow with their pellucid beverage the germs of disease and death. It is a fact that the water supply of nearly every city in the world is more or less polluted with organic matter, infusoria, bacilli—call it what you will—which, introduced into the human system, cannot but have a deleterious effect. These can only be advantageously combated in one way—that is, by refusing them admission, and that can only be accomplished by excluding them from the water before it is swallowed. The "Acme" filter performs this office in the most perfect manner, and delivers the water in a state of absolute purity, whether it be obtained from babbling brook, flowing river, stagnant pond, rock-curbed well or family cistern. Years of test and experiment prove that the Acme unfailingly removes all sediment and organic impurities, and is emphatically the most successful of all filters, while it is unsurpassed in elegance of design, simplicity and durability. This wonderful filter is made under letters patent and sold by the Ellis Filter Company, of which Mr. Frank W. Ellis is general manager. The company was organized at Boston in 1885, and removed to Marlboro in 1886. Its trade extends all over the Union, consumers being supplied through traveling or local agents for the most part. Liberal terms are offered agents wherever there are water-works.

NOAH WILLARD.

Livery, Hack and Boarding Stable—Proprietor of "Favorite" Condition Powders, Liniments for Domestic Animals, etc.—Dealer in Grain, Baled Hay and Straw—Nos. 10 and 12 Court Street, near Main.

Mr. Willard, who is a native of Richford, Vt., came to Marlboro in 1867 and purchased of the then proprietor, Joseph Rock, the livery stable established about two months before by the latter. It was not conveniently situated, however, and in 1881 Mr. Willard built the premises Nos. 10 and 12 Court street, to which he removed. The stable is a three-story frame structure, 40x75 feet. On the lower floor are forty comfortable stalls, room for the storage of vehicles, and office; on the second floor are the grain bins, and facilities for compounding medicines for live stock, and on the third floor storage for hay and straw. A number of fine horses and carriages are kept for hire, but in this department a specialty is made of regular and transient board for horses belonging to others, upon which the best care is expended. Mr. Willard carries a large stock of oats, corn, hay and straw, which he delivers to order at lowest market prices. The "Favorite" condition powder prepared by Mr. Willard is in steady request at all seasons, as are the excellent liniments likewise made under his direction for use upon ailing domestic animals.

CITY HOTEL.

N. Willard, Proprietor—No. 117 Main Street, opposite Old Colony Depot.

The City Hotel was built by Mr. Hiram Temple about ten or twelve years ago, and has made for itself a record such as that possessed by but few popular caravansaries in the United States, for, no matter who its proprietor may have been, it turns up year after year standing higher and higher in the popular favor. Much if not all of its continued success is due to its present proprietor, Mr. Noah Willard, who is its mascot, as the record of its proprietorship will show. Mr. Temple was succeeded by Mrs. Celia D. Spring; she by Mr. Willard, who sold to Chas. Andrews, from whom Mr. Willard purchased it again, and after a term was succeeded by E. F. Ellsbree, and he by Hatch & Leighton. After a lengthy term the house was refurnished and refitted and opened by W. F. Brown, who has given way to the ever-popular host,

Mr. Willard, who has lately taken it in charge, and under his management it has resumed its place amongst the popular, fashionable, best-kept and most highly respectable houses of this section. The same success always attends him in his hotel ventures that has marked his efforts in supplying a first-class livery and boarding stable, and grain, feed and hay warehouse to this city, overcoming as he has in the commencement of each, many obstacles, and leaving behind him a pathway strewn with.successes. The building is of brick, four stories, 60 feet front, with a depth of 45 feet, and has a location second to none in the city, being opposite the City hall, the post-office and the Old Colony railroad depot, and in the heart of the business center. The ground floor is occupied by three handsome stores; the office is on the second floor, and is a light, airy and commodious one, containing all of the conveniences which make the soul of the traveler happy as well as being connected with a cosy reading-room. On this floor are situated the parlors, public and private, a suite of very handsome guests' rooms, the dining-hall, kitchen, pantry and living rooms, and on the upper floors are located the sleeping rooms, thirty in number, the whole supplied with steam heat, electric lights, bath-rooms, and everything to be found in a perfectly kept hotel. The cuisine is excellent and the table is always supplied with the choicest viands in the market. The comforts of patrons are looked after by a force of eight assistants under the supervision of Mr. Willard, who is ably assisted by his well-known clerk Mr. William H. Casey, and the $2.00 a day rate makes it the people's price. Special rates are given to commercial travelers, with whom this house is extremely popular. A first-class livery is connected, guaranteeing the best of service in single or double rigs, carriage, party and excursion wagons, etc.

PETER B. DAVEY,

Sanitary Engineer, Steam, Gas and Water Fitter, Plumber, Tin-Plate, Sheet-Iron and Metal Worker—Lawrence Block, No. 107 Main Street.

Mr. Peter B. Davey is an exemplification of what pluck, energy, application to business and personal worth can do for the young man as well as the boy of to-day. About twenty-five years ago he was born in the city of Lawrence, Mass., and very early in life displayed an aptitude for the trade and profession in which he has since made such a brilliant mark. It seems incredible, yet it is an unvarnished fact, that he has had twelve years of the most practical and positive experience, and previous to his establishing himself in business in this city fourteen months ago he had for several years occupied a prominent position with Wm. Forbes & Sons, sanitary engineers and plumbers, of Lawrence, who cannot but miss his acute judgment and mechanical skill. At this particular time in the history of Marlboro it behooves the manufacturer, the property owner and the citizen at large, for the salvation of his pocket-book, to consult a sanitary engineer, a man of vast and varied experience in this particular line, such as is Mr. Davey, before piping his premises, thereby not only having the work done according to the strictest regard for health but also in the most practical and economical manner. Mr. Davey is not only a licensed plumber and sanitary engineer but employs none but the most competent workmen in his service. His store and wareroom, 30x60 feet, Lawrence block, No. 107 Main street, is fitted up in a neat and attractive manner, in which he has on display the newest, best improved and popular styles of heaters, stoves, ranges, furnaces, bath tubs, water closets, wash basins, copper boilers, rubber hose, hose pipe, tin ware and kitchen furnishing goods. His warehouse is stocked with wrought iron, enameled and tarred pipe, tin-lined and lead pipe, and all kinds of pipe fittings. His shop is supplied with new an improved machinery and tools, and with his force of ten skilled workmen is prepared to attend to all orders upon the shortest notice. Roofing and jobbing are made subjects of special attention, and all work is warranted. The immense success made by him since his advent is but the forerunner of the appreciation which will mark his record as the new system of piping gets well under way.

FRANK S. ROCK,

Manufacturer and Bottler of Summer Beverages—Agent for Jones' Ales—Corner Main and South Streets.

Deprived of our sparkling soda or mineral water or other cool and refreshing beverages, this life would be much more sultry for most of us than it is, especially in the summer months. Insomuch as he ministers to the comfort and pleasure of his fellow mortals by supplying them the means of dampening their suffering clay in an agreeable manner, the soda water manufacturer is emphatically a public benefactor and entitled to the unanimous thanks of old and young, big and little, male and female, white, red, yellow and black, who have ever endured the misery of thirst and hot weather at one and the same time. Mr. Frank S. Rock is the leading Marlboro purveyor of bottled joy, has been engaged in that vocation for the past ten years, and

17

has a well appointed establishment at No. 334 Main street, a two-story frame structure 25x40 feet, where, provided with all necessary apparatus, machinery and assistance, he does a large and growing business, preparing the various kinds of birch and root beers, ginger ale, tonic, and soda of all desirable flavors, bottling the same, and delivering in whatever quantity and wherever desired. Orders by mail, telegraph or telephone are given immediate attention. Soda fountains are charged at short notice for druggists and confectioners, his "Puffer" generators being of great capacity. Mr. Rock is also agent for Jones' celebrated Portsmouth ales, and in license years supplies his customers with these as well as with lager beer, wines and liquors in quantities to suit.

JOHN F. DAVEY,

Machinist—Manufacturer of Davey's Pegging Machines, Davey's Patent Ale Faucet, and Ryan's Improved Shingling Bracket — Repairer of Shoe Machinery— No. 15 Florence Street.

The pegging machine seems, next to the lasting machine, to have been the most difficult of all shoe manufacturing appliances to perfect. Several designs worked fairly well, but in each there was some element of incompleteness, some weak point, that kept the operator in constant apprehension of a break-down or failure. The Davey machine, illustrated herewith, is the fruit of seventeen years' continuous study and experiment by a practical machinist and acknowledged expert in this class of machinery, and is constructed upon correct mechanical principles in every part, any of which can be duplicated without delay at small expense. As a whole, the machine is strong, reliable and little likely to get out of order, and with slight attention and adjustment will peg belting in a satisfactory manner. Among those now using this machine with satisfactory results are the Commonwealth Shoe Co., Boyd, Corey & Co., and John A. Frye, Marlboro; A. Coburn & Son, Hopkinton; Gould & Walker, Westboro; Bridges & Co., South Framingham; T. H. Chamberlain, Hudson; the Easton Boot and Shoe Co., Easton, Pa., and C. H. Fargo, No. 116 Market street, Chicago, Ill., to any or all of whom the builder confidently refers. This pegger may also be seen in successful operation at the factories of Houghton & Coolidge, Ashland; J. L. Woodman, Natick; and Isaac Prouty, Spencer. Mr. Davey is also patentee and manufacturer of the Davey ale faucet, now in such general and satisfactory use as to require no description, and of Ryan's improved shingling bracket, made of wrought iron, strong, simple, safe, and indorsed by every one who has seen it in use. Messrs. Beven & Davey started together as machinists in 1878. Mr. Beven retired in 1884. The plant, situated on the ground floor, 30x60 feet, of the building No. 15 Florence street, comprises a fine machine shop equipment, steam power, etc., and six expert workmen are employed under Mr. Davey's personal supervision. His trade is for the most part confined to New England, but orders for new work or repairs are promptly executed and shipped to any part of the United States or Canada, of which latter country Mr. Davey is a native.

J. E. WARREN & CO.,

Carpenters, Contractors and Builders—Shop No. 25 Florence Street, Warehouse No. 259 Main Street.

Mr. J. E. Warren is a successful business man and a skillful mechanic, as is evident from the volume of building operations conducted by him for some years and the continued and increasing demand for his services. He established himself in 1880 at No. 259 Main street—a four-story structure which he still uses for storage purposes, while his new shop, fitted up with appropriate woodworking machinery, is situated on the second floor, 40x80 feet, of No. 25 Florence street, obtaining steam power from below. He employs fifty or sixty men, and contracts for buildings of every description in and around Marlboro. Among the more notable buildings recently erected by him, and which bear witness to his capacity, are Burke's fine modern three-story brick block, 100 feet front; the Franklin block, Nos. 171 to 179 Main street, and the remodeling of the Central Hotel block for the Corey estate. In all of these both work and terms were satisfactory.

FRANK & DUSTON,

Manufacturers of Paper Boxes of All Kinds—No. 9 High Street, corner of Exchange.

The Marlboro Paper Box Company established this factory in 1885, but, for reasons not necessary to recite, retired from business and was succeeded in January, 1889, by Messrs. Alfred R. Frank (for several years manager) and Arthur G. Duston, both young, vigorous, enterprising and capable. The factory building is of four stories, crowned with a mansard roof, very attractive in appearance, and contains 17,000 square feet of flooring, equipped in superb style with the latest improved machinery used in this industry, a 25-horse-power engine and a 40-horse-power tubular boiler, the surplus steam being used for heating and kindred purposes. The firm, who give their undivided personal attention to the various departments, employ regularly 75 expert operatives, and, devoting themselves for the most part to the manufacture of shoe boxes for the local factories, turn out an average of 15,000 per diem, last year's output aggregating in value $50,000, which will probably be exceeded by the figures for 1891. Orders are promptly and carefully filled.

HENRY K. W. ANDREWS & SON,

Contractors and Builders—Shops, Florence Street; Residence, No. 21 Highland St.

Mr. Henry K. W. Andrews has been erecting buildings of wood and brick all over this part of the State for the past nineteen or twenty years, and has succeeded in making for himself a first-class reputation for mechanical skill and business ability, his transactions for several past seasons being very large and requiring the services of many workmen—thirty-five skilled mechanics last year. On April 1, this year, Mr. Andrews' son, Charles H., who is a practical mechanic, designer and builder, was admitted to full partnership, and the style was changed to that of Henry K. W. Andrews & Son, who continue to do business at the old stand, but with a greater force and wider field.

Among the recent contracts awarded to and executed by them may be mentioned the great Commonwealth shoe factory, the Rice & Hutchings shoe factory, John Frye's shoe factory, and the St. Jean Baptiste block, Marlboro; a fine shoe factory at Hudson, and the immense new Stoneham shoe factory, the interior finished in hard pine, and acknowledged one of the best and most tasteful structures of the kind in the State.

The Messrs. Andrews' shop, frame, 50x60 feet, is on Florence street, opposite the box factory, supplied with steam power and all the latest improved machinery—band and circular saws, planing machinery, turning lathes, etc.—where a force of skilled mechanics are constantly employed in getting out material for the thirty men who are engaged in building in this section under the supervision of Mr. Charles H. Andrews. The firm have important contracts at Bristol, Tennessee, where employment is given to thirty assistants, in the erection of several handsome residences, and where they have just been given the contract to build a large and beautiful hotel. The work there is at present under the personal supervision of Mr. Henry K. W. Andrews, who "fit into the war" and is a genial, public-spirited, popular citizen. If you are about to build a residence, a hotel, a factory, or other large buildings, a little care taken in the placing of orders to begin with will save much subsequent trouble, and you will profit by consulting Henry K. W. Andrews & Son, who know their business, make a practice of carrying out their agreements, and have a high reputation for prompt attention to orders in any section of the country. They guarantee first-class work, wood or brick, and give close personal supervision to their business, sparing no pains to maintain the enviable reputation so long enjoyed.

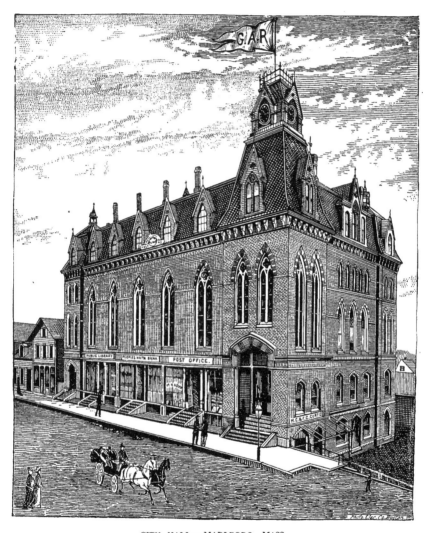

CITY HALL—MARLBORO, MASS.

WOOD & WILLARD,

Established 1860—Manufacturers of Boot and Shoe Machinery and Agents for McKay Parts—Builders of Fire Escapes, Passenger and Freight Elevators—Manufacturers of Shafting, Hangers, Pulleys, Sewing Machine Fixtures, Pipe Fittings and Valves—Repairers of All Kinds of Steam Engines—No. 129 Lincoln Street.

There is a constant and growing demand for shoe machinery of the better kinds, and for improvements upon that already in use—a demand, be it said, which meets with quick response, as witness the rapid increase in patents issued for new devices designed to improve the quality, augment the quantity and reduce the cost of footwear. A house that has achieved distinction in this branch of industry is that named above, established in 1860. The rapid and steady increase of business called for enlarged quarters, better light and extended facilities generally; therefore an entirely new frame building of their own was erected, upon the improved mill system, 50x74 feet, four stories in height, hard pine being used in the construction, the principal timbers 12x15 inches square. The floors are double, four inches thick, and throughout the shops are fitted up with all modern conveniences, including dust blowers, elevators, steam heat, etc., while the equipment of machinery and power is of the first order. Employing twelve or fifteen skilled mechanics, the firm carries a choice stock of materials and turns out large quantities of superior work, their leading specialties embracing the construction and repair of boot and shoe machinery (including the sale of McKay parts, for which they are agents); the supplying and fitting up of shafting, hangers, pulleys, Reeves' wood pulleys, iron pipe, fittings and valves, beside giving prompt and careful attention to the repair of steam engines and the erection of fire escapes, in all of which they excel, as they do in the fitting up of steam piping and automatic sprinkling apparatus. Plans and estimates are furnished at short notice. Orders are also executed for all styles of steel rollers and stitchers for the use of rubber workers, and all who are in need of gilding and embossing machines, power and foot punches, power tip machines and dies, or have sewing and pegging machines to repair, will consult their own interests by sending to this concern. Messrs. Wood & Willard are also manufacturing to order a new elevator which for strength, security, simplicity, compactness, durability and ease of carriage cannot be excelled—the invention of Mr. J. H. Belser, one of the best known patternmakers and mechanics in this part of the State, now in Wood & Willard's employ. Some of the points of advantage possessed by this elevator are thus described: The worm gear and shaft are one solid steel forging. The drum gear is of composition. All bearings and pulleys are self-oiling. The shipping arrangement is entirely different from any other, very simple, and impossible to get out of order. In case the car gets caught in coming down the cable will slacken and the machine will stop; then, if the machine is started through carelessness before the catch is thrown back, it will not injure the machine. It also has a very simple attachment that will stop the machine when the car is at top or bottom of well in case the shipping cable is out of order or broken. They also manufacture a patent automatic gate which is very simple in construction, and a patent automatic stop motion attachment which will stop the car flush with every floor going either way. It is so arranged that it will stop at any floor it is set for without the operator riding with the car. All communications receive immediate and courteous attention. Address Wood & Willard, machinists and manufacturers, Marlboro, Mass.

GLEASON HOUSE.

James M. Gleason & Son, Proprietors—Nos. 71 to 79 Main Street.

The tired and hungry traveler will find a warm welcome and an abundance of creature comforts at the well-known Gleason House, which has the reputation among those who have once enjoyed its hospitality (and always return when visiting Marlboro) of being in all respects one of the best kept and pleasantest hostelries in Massachusetts, outside of Boston. Mr. James M. Gleason, one of the most whole-souled, genial and popular gentlemen with all classes in the State, established this popular caravansary in 1885, where, aided by his amiable and estimable wife and a corps of painstaking and competent assistants eight in number, he has established an enviable reputation, especially among commercial travelers, to whom special rates are made. If ever there was an hotel where the management really strove to make guests feel at home it is the Gleason House. The ground floor of this handsome brick building, Nos. 71 to 79 Main street, is devoted to a commodious office and writing-room; a large, elegantly lighted and cosy reading-room, supplied with newspapers and the current literature of the day; a thoroughly equipped billiard and pool-room, and a neat and tastily arranged barber-shop and bath-rooms, under the supervision of his son, J. Henry Gleason, who became associated with his father in the management about the first of the year under the style J. M. Gleason & Son.

On the second floor are the luxurious parlors, public and private, public and family dining-rooms, kitchen, pantry and living-rooms, while above are the sleeping-rooms, thirty-three in number, beautifully furnished, light, airy, clean and commodious. The house is provided with steam heat, electric lights, fire escapes and everything that can conduce to the ease, enjoyment and safety of guests. The table is famous for abundance, the *cuisine* beyond praise, and the service unexceptionable. To crown all, the house in sufficiently remote from the railroads to avoid noise, and rates are very low, accommodations considered. Mr. James M. Gleason has been known for years in connection with the fire department of Marlboro, having been an active official, and to him is due in a great measure the efficiency it has attained. As musicians he and his cultured family are widely known, and as a caterer for public and private dinners, weddings, receptions, festivals, and at the State militia encampments, none are more favorably or widely known. If you doubt the above facts, just call on Mr. Gleason and be convinced.

E. F. LONGLEY,

Manufacturer of Packing Boxes—Job Planing and Sawing, Knife Grinding, etc.— No. 11 Manning Street.

This is one of the oldest and most extensive box-making plants in Middlesex county, established by Joseph Manning in 1865. The factory has been burned once or twice, and rebuilt, finally passing into the hands of Mr. E. F. Longley in 1885. He has considerably enlarged the building and appurtenances and increased the facilities, and has just completed the paper box factory on an adjoining lot occupied by E. M. Lowe. His own premises comprise a one-story frame mill and shop 50x100 feet, fitted up with an 80-horse-power steam engine and boiler, saws, planers and woodworking appliances generally. Fifteen hands are steadily employed, and besides averaging about 120,000 shoe boxes—valued at $30,000 or $40,000—annually, they do a good deal of other work in the way of job planing and sawing for builders, knife-grinding for leather and paper goods manufacturers, and kindred services.

WINDSOR HOUSE.

Louis Houde, Proprietor—Middleton Block, No. 224 Main Street.

The little city of Marlboro is not only a very busy but very attractive place, and is visited annually by thousands of travelers and tourists, all of whom who go away (for many remain) carry with them agreeable impressions of the people and their institutions, not the least

feature of which is the commodious and delightfully kept Windsor House, occupying the three upper floors of the Middleton block, with entrances at Nos. 224 and 226 Main street. The cordial and cheery reception extended by Mine Host Houde to all who favor him with a sojourn beneath his roof is one of the charms which combine to render the house popular with wayfarers from all parts of the country, however diverse their tastes and occupations. Conveniently arranged, sumptuously furnished, warmed by steam, lighted by electricity, provided with bath-rooms, hot and cold water throughout, fire escapes, electric annunciators, etc., the house contains fifty-two clean and cosy sleeping apartments, a spacious dining-room, two elegant parlors, reading-room and office, bar and barber-shop and all desirable improvements in all departments. The table is first-class, lavishly supplied with the best and choicest food obtainable, including all seasonable dainties, appetizingly prepared by a master cook and politely served by attentive and unobtrusive waiters. Charges are reasonable, and mercantile travelers and theatrical troupes are accorded the usual courtesies. Guests are transferred to and from trains on both roads free of charge. A very handsome and spacious office and billiard and pool hall on the ground floor, with entrance at No. 226 Main Street, have just been added. The office is a very spacious and handsome affair, with large plate glass windows on front and side, giving the most perfect light for reading and writing purposes, and the furnishings and fittings of the newest and latest kinds, making it altogether the most tasty as well as largest in the city. The billiard hall is supplied with new billiard and pool tables of the very latest styles and from the best manufacturers; the appointments are neat and pleasing to the eye, and this department is presided over by a skillful and competent manager with able assistants. The Middleton block was erected in 1882 and the Windsor opened by Mr. Houde the next year, since which time he has continued at its head, with a hiatus of a few months only. A Canadian by birth, Mr. Houde has long been an American citizen and has had much experience as a caterer.

JOHN T. STUART & CO.,

Silver and Nickel Platers—Manufacturers of the Wickersham Patent Quoins for Printers' Use—Lincoln Street.

The firm of John T. Stuart & Co. is a new one, established early in the present year, and occupies the upper floor of a two-story frame building, 30x50 feet, on Mechanics square, where, equipped with the necessary appliances, including baths, dynamos and steam power, and sup-

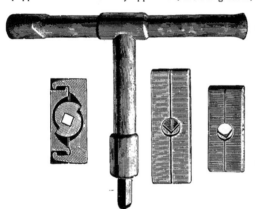

plying sufficient help, they are prepared to execute in the best manner and at short notice all orders for silver and nickel plating of every description. The firm also make a specialty of manufacturing the new and remarkably successful Wickersham patent printers' quoin—an implement which at once strikes the practical job typo as a long step toward if it is not perfection itself. The double wedge and ratchet cast iron quoin long ago superseded the old-style boxwood wedges, mallet and shooting stick in progressive printing houses, and now it seems the time has come for that innovation to make way for a still later and more practical improvement. The Wickersham quoin is composed of two principal pieces, grooved on the inner side and connected at the ends with lugs and dovetail which work freely, while the twin grooves are provided with an eccentric steel disc in the centre of which is a square orifice for the insertion of a wrench, similar to that familiar to all printers. The two halves of the quoin proper are made of homogeneous metal, are about two inches and an eighth long, five-eighths high, and three-quarters of an inch thick, and may be expanded by means of the wrench and disc to a width of a pica and a-half, which is wider than any quoin made, holding its place firmly without the possibility of slipping, preventing the sagging of furniture and consequent "pi." There is no doubt of the general adoption of the new quoin when once introduced. Send for testimonals given by L. Barta & Co., Boston; Peter DeBaun & Co., J. W. Pratt & Son, Willis McDonald & Co., The Williams Printing Co., The Consolidated Printing and Publishing Co., Damon & Peets, James Connor & Sons, New York; The Wenborne Sumner Co., Baffalo, N. Y., and others. Mr. Stuart, who has personal charge of the works, is of English birth, and has resided here for fifteen years. He is about twenty-seven, a practical metal-plater and polisher, and formerly engaged in the leather-staining and blacking business on his own account.

FRANK BILLINGS,

Colorer of Leather, Crimper and Dealer in Leather Remnants—Lincoln Street.

Mr. Frank Billings is a native of Concord and a former resident of Hudson, whence he removed to Marlboro eleven years ago, and was for a long time superintendent of Mr. Elmer Loring's establishment. In September, 1890, he engaged in business for himself, and is rapidly building up a large and prosperous trade. His premises comprise the second floor, 50x75 feet in area, of a two-story building on Lincoln street, fitted up expressly for his occupancy and provided with all needed facilities for handling stock and performing the various operations pertaining to the preparation of leather for the use of manufacturers. He employs six or more men and transacts a business that will aggregate from $15,000 to $20,000 per annum, making leading specialties of the coloring of calf skirting in the best style of the art and the crimping of boot and shoe uppers. He also buys and sells every description of leather, and conducts a regular stock exchange for the convenience of the trade.

MARLBORO DIE COMPANY.

S. F. Draper, F. T. Meagher—Manufacturers of Cutting Dies, Patterns, Bresting Knives, etc., for Cutting Leather, Cloth, Paper, Veneers, etc.—Mechanics Square, Lincoln Street.

This enterprise was started late in the fall of 1890 by Mr. Frank T. Meagher, who in May ast admitted to a copartnership Mr. S. F. Draper, of ·Fayville, who was engaged in the same

business in this city some years ago and has had long experience in this branch of industry. The factory, situated on Lincoln street, is a one-story frame structure 30x60 feet, fitted up with appropriate machinery and steam power, and gives employment to a number of skilled workmen, Messrs. Draper and Meagher personally superintending all operations. The specialties made here embrace every description of cutting dies for the use of boot and shoe, paper collar, cuff, envelope, suspender and leather goods manufacturers, and everything turned out is first-class n point of material, workmanship and finish. They also prepare every varietyof patterns required in any of the above industries, which are accurately drafted from any given standard, and make a superior line of heel bresting knives. All goods made here are fully warranted. Mr. Frank T. Meagher has been known for years as one of the best and most successful die cutters in this section of the country, and his services have been in great demand. As they use no cheap stock their dies are of the very best grade and are warranted for thirty days. Don't be afraid to order new dies, as those made by them can be altered more times than those of any other manufacturers. Scallop and fancy dies a specialty. Orders by mail or express receive prompt and skillful attention.

LOWELL.

ON the 17th of July, 1605, General and Admiral Pierre du Gud, vested by the King of France with the title of Governor of New France (which then consisted of all the eastern and middle States together with Canada), entered the bay upon which Newburyport now stands and discovered the Merrimac, or Merrimack, at its mouth, having previously heard of the beautiful river from Canadian Indians. He called it Gud river, but the Indian name has been retained. The place where the waters of the Concord and Merrimack meet had a greater relative importance 200 years ago than at any time prior to the establishment there of cotton mills. It was the headquarters of one of the five great tribes of Indians found in New England. The sachemship of the Pawtuckets extended to the north and northeast of Massachusetts bay, the tribe numbering over 12,000, and Wamesit, their capital, was here. This spot was dear to the natives on account of the abundant supply of fish, shad, salmon and alewives. Here, in 1653, came Eliot, the apostle to the Indians, and spent many days. Here the English colonial magistrates held court annually in the month of May. The first court in Middlesex was held on the land through which the Boot canal now passes. Tradition says Eliot's log church was on what is now Appleton street. The Indians soon passed away. The bounds of the old Indian capital and those of Lowell singularly coincide. From the first settlement much rafting was done on the Merrimack. The shores, covered with forests, soon became important sources of supply for the Newburyport ship-yards and of timber for transportation elsewhere by water. The passage of the river here is difficult owing to Pawtucket falls, a violent current and sharp pointed rocks, which suggested the first canal. June 27, 1729, the General Court passed an act creating Dudley Atkins Tyng, William Coombs, Joseph Tyler, Nicholas Johnson and Joshua Carter a body politic and corporate forever under the title of the Proprietors of Locks and Canals on the Merrimack River, with the usual powers. A canal

CITY HALL.

one and-a-half miles long, entering the Concord a few rods above its junction with the Merrimack, was constructed. Lowell was taken from the northeastern part of Chelmsford. The territory which now comprises the city was orginally granted to Cambridge, June 2, 1641. June 2, 1793, James Sullivan and others were incorporated as proprietors of the Middlesex canal to improve the navigation of the Merrimack. The canal was opened in 1796. In 1792 the first bridge was built over the Merrimack. In 1801 Moses Hale set up a carding machine in his mill on River Meadow brook. In 1812 John Goulding invented a very curious loom for weaving boot straps, driven by water. Goulding had a factory built for him on the Concord river. His rent was $200 a year, and there he spun cotton yarn in a small way—about 20 yards a day. He also had a carding machine for carding cotton and wool for spinning by hand and making home-spun cloth, and a machine shop for cotton and wool machinery. He made

POST OFFICE BUILDING.

suspender and boot webbings and had a tape loom. The war of 1812 put a stop to English trade, and mills were built wherever water power could be found. Congress increased the duties, and in 1812 Capt. Phineas Whitney and Col. Jonas Fletcher erected a building 50x60 and 40 feet high for a cotton factory, at a cost of $2,500, on the Concord river. This occupied a part of the present site of the Middlesex mills. In 1818 they sold to Thomas Hurd, of Charlestown, and he fitted up the plant for the manufacture of woolen goods, employing twenty hands and producing from sixteen looms 120 yards of satinet per day. The whole process, carding, spinning, weaving and dyeing, was done in the mill. Mr. Hurd subsequently erected a brick edifice and converted both into a woolen factory which ran over fifty looms. Burned in 1826, the mills were rebuilt on a larger scale and sold in 1828 to the Middlesex Company. In 1816 two gain mills were built, one just below the bridge at Pawtucket falls, the other on the canal near the Concord river.

Francis Cabot Lowell, born at Newburyport in 1775, and a graduate of Harvard in 1793, went abroad for the purpose of obtaining information concerning the manufacture of cotton goods, with a view to its introduction into the United States. He investigated the whole process as known in Scotland and England. Wm. Horrocks, of Stockport, England, had patented a *power* loom in 1803 or 1805, and another with improvements in 1813, and, although he kept his secret, Lowell improved his opportunities and constructed one, and with Patrick T. Jackson, of Boston, established a cotton factory at Waltham. They associated themselves with some Boston merchants and obtained a charter, February, 1813,

M. V. M. ARMORY.

under the name of the Boston Manufacturing Company, capital $100,000. Lowell was some time in perfecting his power loom, and, with the aid of a Mr. Moody, made many improvements on Horrocks' machine. They first had one loom in operation and produced cotton cloth that it was found would exceed the demand. Lowell thought the goods would not sell, and was willing to accept twenty-five cents per yard. He was advised by Nathan Appleton to send his product to B. C. Ward & Co., who sold it at auction for something over thirty cents per yard. This was the commencement of the practice of consigning goods on commission. The whole economy of cotton manufacturing was regulated by Lowell, who died in 1817, aged forty-two years.

February 1, 1822, the Merrimack Manufacturing Company was incorporated by Kirk and John W. Boott, Wm. and Ebenezer Appleton ; capital $600,000. In

1822 the dam across the Merrimack at Pawtucket falls was built, and on September 23 of the same year the first mill on the Merrimack was completed, water was let into the canal, the wheel was started, and the first cloth made. The Merrimack print works were started in the autumn of 1824. In February, 1825, the Proprietors of the Locks and Canals on the Merrimack River voted to transfer the water power, locks, lands, machine shops, etc., to a new corporation— the Locks and Canals Company—retaining, however, the print works and sufficient water power for their operation. The Hamilton Manufacturing Company, capital stock $600,000, was incorporated and erected its original mill about this time, and here for the first time the power loom was applied to weaving cotton

MEMORIAL HALL.

drilling and other twilled goods, and with such satisfactory results that in 1831 the same parties, under the style of the Suffolk Company, built additional mills.

March 6, 1826, the first steps were taken for the establishment of a separate town by the appointment of a committee to divide the territory into school and highway districts, the result of which was five school districts and an appropriation of $1,000 for school purposes. The final separation from Chelmsford did not occur, however, until 1830, when an act of incorporation was secured, the name of Lowell adopted (instead of Merrimack as at first intended), and the town government organized—Kirk Boott, moderator; Samuel A. Coburn, clerk; Nathaniel Wright, Oliver M. Whipple and Samuel M. Bachelder, selectmen. Population, 6,477.

A daily stage line to Boston was established in 1826, and in 1827 a. daily mail to and from Boston was added to the business conveniences.

In February, 1828, the Appleton Company—capital stock $600,000—was incorporated, as was the Lowell Manufacturing Company, capital stock $2,000,-000, the latter locating temporarily at Medway until the completion of its mills at this point. The Lowell Bank was incorporated the following October, capital stock $500,000. In 1831 were incorporated the Suffolk Manufacturing Company, capital $600,000 ; the Tremont Mills, capital $600,000, and the Lawrence Manufacturing Company, capital $1,500,000. Then came the Lowell Bleachery in 1832, capital $300,000.

Andrew Jackson, then president of the United States, visited Lowell in 1833.

•ODD FELLOWS BVILDING•
•LOWELL • MASS•
MERRILL & CVTLER ARCHTS
LOWELL MASS

Two years later the populace were treated to a sample of Henry Clay's matchless eloquence.

The Boott Cotton Mills were incorporated in 1835, capital stock $1,500,000.

In November, 1835, the Lowell *Courier* started the agitation for incorporation as a city, and at a town meeting held the ensuing February commissioners were appointed who reported favorably upon the scheme. The Legislature promptly granted a charter, which was approved without delay by the celebrated Edward Everett, then governor of Massachusetts. Elisha Bartlett, a native of Smithfield, R. I., was the first mayor.

Lowell performed a distinguished part in the war for the Union. Four companies of the famous Sixth Massachusetts, mobbed in Baltimore April 16, 1861, were from this city. In all Lowell furnished 5,266 men and officers to the Union armies and one eminent officer—Major-General Robert E. K. Whiting, who was born here—to the Confederates. When it is recalled that at the close of hostilities in 1865 her population was only 30,757, it will be seen that her contribution of fighting material was extremely liberal. Population in 1890, 77,605. Educational facilities are ample and of high order.

The leading industries embrace the manufacture of cotton, woolen, felt, elastic, leather and paper goods, hosiery, bagging, lumber, bolts, nuts, machinery, boilers, engines, proprietary medicines, etc. The city boasts seven National, five savings and one co-operative bank.

The newspaper press of Lowell is creditable in character and sufficiently strong in numbers for a much more populous city. They comprise the Lowell

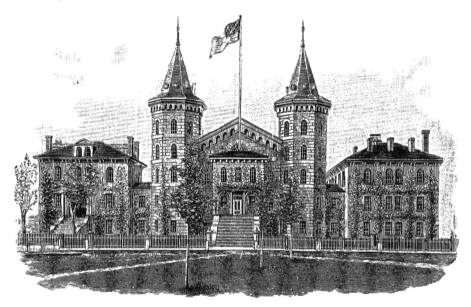

MIDDLESEX COUNTY JAIL.

Daily Courier and its weekly edition, the *Journal*; the latter was started June 25, 1824, as the Chelmsford *Courier*, the named changed a year later to *Phœnix*, to *Merrimack Journal* in 1826, and to *Lowell Journal* in 1827. It was made a daily September 17, 1831, but soon abandoned the attempt and returned to the weekly plan. Publication was suspended in 1834, but resumed as the *Journal and Mercury* in 1835. The latter name was subsequently dropped. The *Courier* was established as a tri-weekly evening paper January 6, 1835. In June, 1836, the time of publication was changed to morning, but resumed as an evening paper in May, 1841, and was made a daily July 1, 1845. Throughout its career the *Courier* has under all circumstances and at all times, in season and out of season, zealously and consistently supported such measures and men as were and are opposed to the democracy.

The *Daily Morning Times*, established August 23, 1872, is the democratic organ, and an intelligent, earnest and influential representative of that great party.

Vox Populi, originally started as an independent paper with the object of correcting public abuses and affording a channel for criticism of local and State administration, is now a republican organ, but still claims the largest circulation of any Lowell paper.

The *Lowell Daily Citizen* is the result of a consolidation, April 28, 1856, of the *Daily Morning News*, the *American Citizen*, and the *Daily Citizen*. It has always been republican in politics.

The *Lowell Morning Mail* was started in July, 1879. From the first it has supported the claims of the republican party. The weekly edition is called the *Saturday Evening Mail.*

The Sun is the most enterprising, wide-awake and prosperous of Lowell's dailies. The first issue was dated August 10, 1878. Democratic, liberal and progressive, *The Sun* deserves and enjoys public confidence and patronage in an exceptional degree.

The *Lowell Daily News* is another successful and influential democratic paper, established may, 1884.

There are two French papers here, *L'Union* and *L'Etoile*, both liberally supported by the Canadian French residents.

As a newspaper graveyard Lowell takes the palm, not less than eighty dailies, tri-weeklies, semi-weeklies, weeklies, semi-monthlies and monthlies having perished here from the same cause—starvation—since the incorporation of the city. *Sic transit gloria mundi!*

SHAW STOCKING COMPANY.

F. J. Dutcher, President; Josiah Butler, Treasurer and Clerk; Geo. L. Hooper, Manager; J. F. Gordon, Superintendent—Manufacturers of the Shawknit Hosiery—Corner of Smith and Shaw Streets.

There are stockings and stockings, and there are besides many imitations that cannot be classified; but the man that has never indulged in Shawknit stockings can hardly establish a  claim to knowledge of luxury in dressing the feet. The writer of this has worn them for several years, and, after an experience of half a century with imported and domestic hosiery, unhesitatingly awards the palm, so far as comfort, neatness and durability are concerned, to the stockings manufactured at Lowell, worn by discriminating people, and recognized by the trade-mark: *Shawknit*

These stockings are made from the best cotton, merino and woolen yarns, hand-finished, and dyed in unfading colors, and if there is a weak spot anywhere in them, we have failed to discover it. The Shaw Stocking Company was incorporated with $30,000 capital stock in October, 1877, for the manufacture of stockings upon the knitting loom invented by Benjamin Franklin Shaw. Eight looms were at once constructed and the company began operations in limited quarters on Broadway. The success of the enterprise was immediate and pronounced; the goods sold on sight wherever shown; the demand very soon outgrew the supply; and an increase of productive capacity became imperative. The capital stock was increased, February, 1879, to $160,000; land was bought, a factory erected, looms were built and set up, and January 1, 1880, the new plant was set in motion. In May following the capital stock was again increased—this time to $240,000—the factory buildings were enlarged, additions were made to the machinery outfit then and subsequently, and this is now, with $360,000 capital stock, one of the largest establishments of its kind in the United States. The mill proper is a two-story-and-basement brick structure, 40 feet front by 240 feet deep, adjacent to which are a dye-house 30x80 feet, a three-story-and-basement building 40x70 feet devoted entirely to dyeing and finishing the Snowblack hosiery, and a two-story warehouse 50x50 feet, the whole heated by steam, lighted by gas, and provided with every useful modern convenience. A forty-horse-power steam engine drives the outfit of machinery, which embraces 257 Shaw stocking-looms and many other machines. The operatives number 500, and the mill, run to its full capacity every working day in the year, produces an average of 800 dozen pairs of stockings daily—240,000 to 250,000 dozens or 2,880,000 pairs yearly. ' Selling direct to the trade east, west, north and south, the company accumulates no stock, but is constantly en. gaged in a hard tussle with advance orders. This prosperous business was managed by Mr. Shaw, the inventor, until he died, in the winter of 1890–91. His patents were unsuccessfully contested in England, where he introduced his loom some years ago.

WOODS, SHERWOOD & CO.,

Manufacturers of Sherwood's Patent White Lustral Wire Ware—No. 150 Bridge St.

Mr. Sherwood was the inventor and patentee of the articles at first made by this house, bu the beautiful, durable and economical as well as extremely useful white lustral wire ware with which the trade and the housekeepers of the country are now familiar was originated by Mr.

Woods, assisted by Mr. Sherwood and others as to particular de. signs and others details. In 1861 the gentlemen named formed a co-partnership under the style of Woods, Sherwood & Co., and began manufacturing—at first, of course, on a limited scale, but in. creasing facilities and output to keep pace with the demand, which has steadily augmented and continues to grow. In 1866 the firm was reinforced by the accession of Mr. C. H. Latham, and since then its great commercial triumphs have been won and markets made in every State of the Union, in Canada, Mexico, South America, Australia and other countries. The works, employing seventy hands, occupy a substantial modern frame three-story build. ing at No. 150 Bridge street, upon which thoroughfare it fronts 45 feet, with a depth of 120 feet. Steam power, steam heat, gas light and all conceivable conveniences are provided, while the equipment of ingenious machinery is complete in every de- partment. The product is extremely large, averaging about 60,000 dozen of neat, strong and salable white lustral twisted wire goods that comprise every article of the kind required in the household, restaurant, office, etc.—holders, handles, rods, easels, stands, baskets, egg beaters, vegetable boil- ers, broilers, casters, toilet boxes, traps, brackets, trays, tongs, chains, racks, cases, drainers, drippers, epergnes, forks, toy furniture, gas heaters, gypsy kettles, picture hang- ers, flower baskets, nut picks, pie racks, plate lifters, potato mashers, toasters, sad iron stands, splasher rods, strainers, table mats, tea and coffee balls, pot stands, vases, watch stands, and many other articles. Medals and diplomas have been awarded Woods, Sherwood & Co. at the following fairs and expositions held in our own and other countries: Mary- land Institute, 1867, *Diploma;* Middlesex Mechanics' Asso- ciation, 1867, *Silver Medal;* New Hampshire Mechanics' and Art Association, 1868, *Gold Medal;* Massachusetts Charitable Mechanic Association, 1869, *Bronze Medal;* New England Agricultural Society, 1871, *First Premium, Silver Medal;* New England Agricultural Society, 1872, *First Premium, Silver Medal;* Cincinnati Industrial Exposition, 1872, *First Premium, Silver Medal;* Cincinnati Industrial ·

Exposition, 1873, *First Premium, Silver Medal;* Massa- chusetts Charitable Mechanic Association, 1874, *Diploma;* International Exhibition of Chili, 1875, *Bronze Medal;* Centennial International Exhibition, Philadelphia, 1876, *Bronze Medal;* Massachusetts Charitable Mechanic Association, 1878, *Bronze Medal;* International Exhibition, Sydney, N. S. W., 1879, *First Premium, Bronze Medal;* World's Industrial and Cotton Centennial Exposition, New Orleans, 1884–5, *Bronze Medal;* North Central and South America Exposition, New Orleans, 1885–6, *Bronze Medal.*

ANDREWS & WHEELER,

Manufacturers of Fine Granite and Marble Monumental and Cemetery Work—
No. 41 Thorndike Street, Adjoining Northern Depot.

Thirty-four years ago—in 1857—Messrs. Andrews & Winter formed a copartnership that lasted for three years, when, in 1860, Mr. Winter retired, and in 1877 Mr. Charles Wheeler accepted an invitation from Mr. Charles H. Andrews and the present firm of Andrews & Wheeler was established. Both are men of taste, culture and practical experience, competent to design and execute with their own hands every description of monumental work, and consequently have made for themselves a high reputation besides securing a very extensive patronage from that large and growing class of people who appreciate what is artistic and appropriate in memorials to departed friends. Examples of their skill are seen in the cemeteries of Lowell and within a radius of twenty-five miles, in addition to which they have filled many orders for shipment to western points, and so far as known they have invariably rendered entire satisfaction in every instance. The firm have well-appointed premises—office, wareroom for the exhibition of sculpture, work-shops, granite sheds, yard, etc.—at No. 41 Thorndike street, adjoining the Northern depot, where they employ about twenty expert assistants and are prepared to execute every description of monumental and cemetery work in the best style and on reasonable terms. A specialty is made of memorials from original designs of their own or others' conception, and drawings and estimates are submitted when required.

LOWELL TRUNK MANUFACTORY.

Patrick F. Devine—Manufacturer of Trunks, Bags, Valises, Extension Cases and Fancy Leather Goods, Wholesale and Retail—No. 32 Middlesex Street.

Among the minor industries that diversify and add to the variety of callings in which the citizens of Lowell are engaged, that of trunk manufacturing is of no little importance, since it tends to keep in circulation at home considerable money that would otherwise go elsewhere. The leading representative of this interest is the Lowell trunk manufactory, established four or five years ago by Devine & Flanagan, to whom Mr. Patrick Devine succeeded on the 13th of August last. The factory, situated at No. 32 Middlesex street, is a one-story frame structure 20 x 50 feet in extent, fitted up with all requisite appliances, and furnishes employment to a number of expert workmen, turning out large quantities of superior alligator and sole-leather, canvas, zinc and paper-covered traveling trunks and sample trunks, sample and traveling cases and bags, and a general line of travelers' goods in handsome styles and of the best material and workmanship. Mr. Devine is an experienced and skillful mechanic, formerly with Josiah Cummings and T. J. Graham of Boston, and personally superintends the factory.

SCRIPTURE'S LAUNDRY,

Frank K. Stearns, Proprietor—No. 116 Lawrence Street.

This laundry was established in 1876 by Isaac F. Scripture, to whom Frank K. Stearns succeeded in 1880. The latter has had long and varied experience in the business, and the work done here gives satisfaction, extraordinary care being exercised to please and to prevent annoyance from the loss or temporary mislaying of goods, while superior work and prompt delivery are characteristic of the establishment under the existing management. Lace curtains and Holland shades receive especial attention, the latter being done up by a process of their own that prevents tearing or other injury and in unequaled style. The building is a two-story frame structure, 90 feet front by 55 feet deep, neat, clean, perfectly lighted and ventilated, provided with all conveniences, including a ten-horse-power steam engine and boiler of ample capacity for all needs, and fitted up with all improved modern laundry machinery and appliances. Thirty-five people are employed, and the capacity is about 18,000 pieces per week. Most of the patronage is from regular city customers, though much is sent in from the surrounding towns. Shirts, fold and cape collars, are ironed entirely by hand.

J. C. AYER CO.

Jacob Rogers, President; Frederick Ayer, Treasurer—Proprietors and Manufacturers of Ayer's Sarsaparilla, Ayer's Cherry Pectoral, Ayer's Hair Vigor, Ayer's Ague Cure, and Ayer's Cathartic Pills—Laboratory, Market Street, Office and Warehouse, No. 98 Middle Street.—See Illustration on Opposite Page.

The aspiration to relieve and remedy human suffering is a noble one, and when that aspiration is seconded by intelligent, well-directed effort, the results attained entitle the laborer to the appellation of philanthropist. This is especially true in the field of medicine—a profession which has contributed to the annals of the race such deathless names as Jenner, Pasteur, Koch and Mackenzie. Equally with these—perhaps in an even greater degree—the name of Ayer is worthy of honor, while there is no question that among the masses of mankind it is far better known and more affectionately regarded that that of either of the illustrious investigators and discoverers first referred to. James Cook Ayer was born at Groton, Conn., May 5, 1818, attended the common school there, and afterward took a course at the Westford (Mass.) academy. From 1838 to 1842 he was clerk and student of pharmacy in the drug-store of Jacob Robbins of Lowell, studied medicine at a later period with Dr. Samuel L. Dana, and was eventually graduated with the degree of M. D. by the University of Pennsylvania. Meanwhile, in April, 1841, he purchased the Robbins drug-store, and developed by investigation and experiment the now world-famous Cherry Pectoral, the success of which as a specific for coughs, colds, lung and throat troubles rendered the subsequent introduction of his later preparations a comparatively easy matter, such is the prestige of an initial triumph fairly won. Dr. Ayer's first removal was from Central street to the present *Mail* building, and in June, 1855, his brother Frederick became associated with him and the style Dr. J. C. Ayer & Co. was adopted by the new firm. Phenomenal prosperity ensued; within three years manufacturing facilities proved inadequate to meet demands, and a second removal became unavoidable, the firm occupying what is now, with numerous additions and extensions and thorough remodeling, the Market street laboratory, an immense four-story brick structure, perfectly arranged and equipped in all departments, with boiler and engine in the cellar, press-room on the ground floor, shipping-room on the second, bindery on the third, and laboratory on the fourth floor, the building containing over 39,200 square feet of floorage. The press, used for printing almanacs in nearly all modern languages, is of special design, constructed on the rotary web perfecting principle, self-inking, self-feeding, with capacity for printing and folding, ready for the binder, 100,000 complete 32-page almanacs daily. If required, the company can make and distribute from this single machine 26,000,000 of almanacs annually—more than enough to supply every family in the United States. Eight hundred tons of paper are consumed by this press annually. The work of the other departments is conducted upon a similar gigantic scale, shipments averaging seventy-five gross of the various preparations per diem. Bottles are received at the rate of a car-load every working day, and the record of 120 days shows arrivals of 1192 tons, or 3,084,624 empty bottles. In 1872 Dr. J. C. Ayer & Co. bought a plot of land in the rear of the laboratory and fronting on Middle street—the site of the old Green schoolhouse—and erected thereon a large office and warehouse structure, bridges spanning the railroad track and connecting the two buildings. The new premises served their purpose very well until a year or two ago, when the J. C. Ayer Company (organized and incorporated October 24, 1877, capital $300,000) added one story and a modern business front to this edifice, making it five stories in height, with a total of over 44,000 square feet in area, and one of the most attractive and commodious, as well as most elegantly fitted and convenient commercial blocks in New England. The office alone affords 7360 square feet of floorage, and is a vast hive of business, no less than sixty male and female clerks, stenographers, type-writers, book-keepers and managers of departments being employed there, under the experienced and watchful eye of Mr. Frederick Ayer, the treasurer, who, though advanced in years, is fully capable of performing the labors and carrying the responsibilities that devolve upon him. We feel that our description of this mammoth concern is inadequate in the matter of details, but plead lack of space as our excuse, for nothing would please us better than to delineate *in extenso* each department and the operations carried on therein. We may add, however, that the J. C. Ayer Company leases the big brick block adjoining the laboratory on Market street, where are stored vast quantities of raw materials, paper, bottles, etc.; that they employ in all over 250 people, and that they are the leading manufacturers of proprietary medicines in the world, their unrivaled Sarsaparilla, Cherry Pectoral, Hair Vigor, Ague Cure and Cathartic Pills being as well known and as popular in the remotest quarters of the globe as in the most enlightened portions of Europe and America.

THE SWAIN TURBINE AND MANUFACTURING COMPANY.

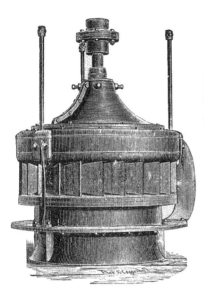

A. F. Nichols, Treasurer and Manager— Manufacturers of Swain Turbine Water Wheels—A. F. Nichols, Iron and Brass Founder—Works: Nashua, N. H., and No. 10 Willie Street, Lowell.

The Swain Turbine is no new and unproved experiment, but an established success of many years' standing, ranking with the best and most generally used water-wheels extant. The invention of A. M. Swain, this wheel has been constructed at Nashua, N. H., by the Swain Turbine Company, and finally by the Swain Turbine and Manufacturing Company, incorporated under the laws of Massachusetts in 1874; capital stock $125,000. For some years past Mr. A. F. Nichols has been treasurer and general manager, making the patterns and castings at his foundry, No. 10 Willie street, Lowell, and shipping the same to Nashua, where the machinists' work is done and the wheels finished and made ready for delivery. They are held in high estimation by water-using mill owners all over the United States, and their popularity in this vicinity and throughout New England is attested by the great number employed by leading manufacturing corporations here and elsewhere, the Merrimack manufacturing Company having one, the Hamilton Manufacturing Company two, the Boott Cotton Mills nine, the Lawrence Manufacturing Company five, the Massachusetts Cotton Mills eight, the Wamesit Power Company one, the Middlesex Company two, while a large number are in constant and satisfactory use at other points, among the owners being the Pacific Mills, the Russell Paper Company and others at Lawrence; Moses T. Stevens & Sons, Haverhill and Andover; the Warren Cotton Mills, West Warren; the Paul Whitin Manufacturing Company, Northbridge; the Washburn & Moen Manufacturing Company, Worcester; the Worthy Paper Company, Mittineague; Byron Weston, Dalton; the Lancaster Mills, Clinton; C. G. Sargent's Sons, Graniteville; S. D. Warren, Boston; Manchester Mills, Manchester, N. H.; the Underhill Edge Tool Company, Nashua, N. H.; the Cumberland Mills, Cumberland, Me.; B. B. & R. Knight, Providence, R. I. (twenty-one); the Pawtucket Hair Cloth Company, Pawtucket, R. I.; Stephen Sanford, Amsterdam, N. Y.; Cohoes Gas Light Company, Cohoes, N. Y.; Republic Iron Company, Marquette, Mich., and the Camperdown Cotton Mills, Greenville, S. C. August 3, 4, 5, 6 and 7, 1874, at the Boott Cotton Mills, James B. Francis, C. E., the well-known Lowell civil engineer, tested a seventy-two-inch Swain turbine, with results thus technically stated: "From 9-inch gate to 13.08-inch gate, or say from about two-thirds gate to full gate, the maximum co-efficient of useful effect varies from 0.828 to 0.839, or about one per cent.; the velocity of the exterior circumference of the wheel relatively to the velocity due the head, corresponding to the maximum coefficient of useful effect, being for 9-inch gate about 0.720, and for full gate about 0.765. At half-gate the maximum coefficient of useful effect is about 0.78, at a relative velocity of about 0.68. At

one-quarter-gate, the maximum coefficient of useful effect is about 0.61 at a relative velocity of about 0.66." Mr. A. F. Nichols, who now owns the majority of the stock and controls the Swain Turbine and Manufacturing Company and its output, has been engaged in the iron and brass foundry business here for nearly thirty-three years. From 1858 to November 1, 1890, he was junior member of the firm of Cole & Nichols, proprietors of the Lowell foundry, of which he is now sole owner. The Lowell foundry plant, situated at No. 10 Willie street, foot of Dutton, comprises a two-story frame building 70x174 feet, connected with which are sheds, yards, etc., the whole covering an area of 100x450 feet. The equipment of both foundry and pattern

shop is complete, including ample steam power ; from forty to fifty hands are employed here, and the output of light and heavy machinery and brass castings is worth from $60,000 to $70,000 per annum. These include driving-wheel lathes, axle and car-wheel lathes, pumps, shafting, hangers, pulleys, and castings for Swain turbines, in the finishing and fitting-up of which from twenty to twenty-five men are employed at Nashua. Considerable of the work done in the two establishments is exported to other countries, Mexico and Australia being the best foreign consumers.

LOWELL STEAM BOILER WORKS.

Richard Dobbins—Manufacturer of Steel and Iron Steam Boilers, Plate Work Generally, and Dobbins' Hollow Steam Press Plates—Tanner Street, near Boston & Lowell R. R.

The Lowell steam boiler works date from 1856, when Mr. William Dobbins embarked in the business of supplying mill-owners and others with boilers and plate iron work of all kinds. The shops have occupied their present location on Tanner street for about fifteen years, and have been under the sole ownership of Mr. Richard Dobbins (a brother of the founder) for a still longer period. The works, burned Aug. 21, 1891, and since re-built on a larger scale, are provided with new and improved machinery that will increace the productive capacity at least one-third, while from fifty to eighty skilled workmen are employed, the number depending upon the state of trade, though transactions average $125,000 per annum, orders being filled not only for shipment to every State in the Union but for export, mostly to the Central and South American republics, Mexico and the West Indies. Every description of steel and iron steam boilers are made from selected materials and in the best style of workmanship, a specialty being made of Corliss upright nest boilers, and another of Dobbins' celebrated hollow steam press plates. Facilities in all departments are, however, first class, and those in want of penstocks, flumes, water, soap and oil tanks, tar and jacket kettles, hydraulic, screw and tallow presses, fire scapes, etc., are invited to correspond with or call upon Mr. Dobbins, as are those who desire to purchase, sell or exchange second-hand boilers of any kind. Attention is also given to repairs of boilers and plate work generally.

ST. CHARLES HOTEL.

Charles M. Dickey, Proprietor—Nos. 171 to 183 Middlesex Street.

The St. Charles, which ranks with the best hotels in the interior of New England, was erected fifteen or sixteen years ago by the late Sam. T. Dresser, who managed it for some years and then started the Dresser House, where he died in 1890. Mr. Charles M. Dickey took charge of the St. Charles in 1888, and by close attention to the wants of the traveling public has made it extremely popular, setting a sumptuous table and in all possible ways ministering to the comfort and pleasure of his guests, both transient and permanent—and of the latter he has many, for no one is more appreciative of the good things of this life than the regular experienced boarder.   In the hard work of popularizing and bringing the house to its present condition of prosperity Mr. Dickey has been and is ably assisted by his courteous and obliging clerk, Mr. Arthur Gordon, a favorite with all who have business or social relations with him, as is also Mr. Dickey himself.   The St. Charles is a large and well-appointed hotel, conveniently situated, brick, four stories in height, with neat office, reading and billiard-rooms, bar, barber shop, etc., on the first floor; sitting-rooms, parlors, dining-room that will accommodate 125 guests at once on the second, and fifty cosy, clean and delightful bed chambers on the third and fourth floors, with baths, hot and cold water, gas and electric lights, and electric bells and fire escapes throughout.   A marble staircase for the use of ladies, children and their protectors forms the private means of access to the upper floors, avoiding the office.   The service is unexceptionable, and those who once partake of the St. Charles' hospitality will be certain to repeat the experience when they again visit Lowell.   Terms are very low, accommodations and facilities considered.

LOWELL SCALE COMPANY,

Manufacturers of Scales and Weighing Machines.—No. 265 Middlesex Street.

The Lowell Scale Company is a new enterprise, established last year by Messrs. True Morton, G. A. Towle and N. E. Annis.   The first and last named are practical scale makers, Mr. Morton having had an experience of nearly thirty-four and Mr. Annis of more than twenty-five years in the business.   The shops occupy floor space 45 x110 feet, and are well equipped with requisite appliances, machinery and steam power, with capacity for manufacturing 2000 scales per annum.   They are now introducing their scales and soliciting inspection, but have already filled many orders and are confident that within a short time they will be shipping to all parts of the world in successful competition with the old established manufacturers, because their scales embrace all modern improvements, are of superior construction, accuracy and durability, and are in all respects the best article of the kind ever offered at the price, provided with all iron and wood center platforms, cast steel and hardened bearings, patent self adjusting platform bearings, brass sliding poise, hardwood pillar and cap, etc.   Messrs. Morton and Towle are natives of Maine, Mr. Annis of Vermont.

JAMES A. READY,

Manufacturer of Steam Boilers, Tanks, Steam Pipe, Steam Press Plates, Fire Escapes, etc.—Fay Street.

Mr. James A. Ready is a native of Lowell and an expert plate steel and iron worker, for a long time foreman of the Lowell steam boiler works, which he resigned in May of last year to establish himself in business on his own account—a venture that has already proved quite successful, while the prospects for the future are very bright indeed.   His works and office on Fay street comprise a one-story frame building 50x60 feet in area, a 20-foot addition being used for boiler and engine-room and for storage purposes.   At present he does not require many assistants, but his working force, though small in numbers, makes up in skill for that deficiency, having been carefully selected by Mr. Ready from his former shopmates, and not a few of them have worked beside him or under his direction for years.   His patronage at this time is principally from local mill owners and manufacturers, with occasional orders from surrounding villages, but is steadily growing both in volume and territory.   Parties in want of anything in his line will consult their own interest by conferring with Mr. Ready, whose specialties embrace every description of steam boilers, tanks, penstocks, steam pipes, steam press plates, turbine wheel plates, draft tubes, tar and jacket kettles, liners for paper engines, etc., together with fire-escapes and plate work of all kinds.   He has devoted much attention to boilers for steam heating, and will construct these in the best style and upon approved principles.   Repairs are promptly made by skilled workmen, and every job turned out is fully warranted.   The works, which are provided with telephone connection, are reached by the Gorham street cars.   Mr. Ready's residence is at No. 118 Walker street.

P. H. HEELON,

Sales, Boarding and Livery Stable—Nos. 247 and 249 Gorham Street.

Mr. Heelon started in business three years ago, when he bought out and assumed the management of a stable on Prescott street. A year later he secured and took possession of the more desirable and commodious premises Nos. 247 and 249 Gorham street—a large three-story

frame structure 57 feet front and 125 feet deep. On the ground floor is the stable, nicely drained and well ventilated, clean and comfortable, containing forty-nine stalls; the carriage-room, filled with handsome vehicles of all kinds, is on the second floor, which is also utilized in part for the storage of hay, straw, grain, mill and chopped feed, etc. A large stock of fine horses is kept for hire, and perhaps as many are boarded for private owners, while numbers of transients are fed and cared for every day, nine or ten hostlers and other help being employed. Horses are also bought and sold when desired, and excellent bargains are frequently offered. Those in want of fine teams, buggies and carriages for pleasure or business driving, or of hacks for weddings, parties, funerals or passenger transfer, will be accommodated at reasonable figures. Special rates are made for commercial travelers. Mr. Heelon is a wide-awake, enterprising, genial man, and personally quite popular with all who know him. He has just put in a new stock of Killam hacks and other fine carriages.

MECHANICS SAVINGS BANK.

Jeremiah Clark, President; Charles C. Hutchinson, Treasurer; Wm. F. Hills, Teller—Mechanics Bank Block, No. 128 Merrimack Street.

The Mechanics Savings Bank, one of the representatives of an unequaled monetary system, was incorporated March 1, 1861. The institution, formerly located on Shattuck street, was removed to the commodious four-story brick structure—the property of the corporation—on Merrimack street, when completed in 1873. The banking-rooms are situate on the second floor. In addition to the officers named above Messrs. Jacob Rogers, Isaac Cooper, Alexander G. Cumnock, Ferdinand Rodliff and Julian V. Keyes are vice-presidents, with a board of trustees made up from the best element of the business public. Number of depositors, 4937. Dividends for 1890, 2 per cent. semi-annually.

SAMUEL G. COOPER,

Manufacturer of Copper Stamps and Stencils—Dealer in Stamping Inks and Supplies—No. 120 Central Street.

Mr. Cooper has been in the same business in this city since 1872—up to 1885 as junior partner in the firm of Corner and Cooper, Mr. Corner retiring at that time. The establishment occupies the entire second floor, 60 x 80 feet, of the brick building No. 120 Central street, and is one of the best appointed and most thoroughly equipped of the kind in the country, giving employment to five or six skillful stamp and stencil designers and cutters. Mr. Cooper is a noted expert, and his work, tasty and perfect in execution, is found all over the United States and Canada, wherever a cotton or woolen mill is running, in addition to which he is beginning to fill orders for shipment beyond seas, having recently made a heavy consignment to China. His annual sales range from $5,000 to $7,000. Mr. Cooper's specialties embrace every description of copper stamps and stencils for cotton and woolen mills, bleacheries and hosieries, head stamps for broadcloths, cassimeres and flannels. He also carries large stocks of and will promptly fill orders for black, blue and red stamping inks, stamping presses, stamping boxes and stamping supplies generally.

It is not necessary to describe the process of roll-covering, as the general reader would take no interest in it and the work is familiar to mill-owners and the trade. Probably the oldest roll-covering establishment in Lowell is that of John Tripp & Co., founded by the late John Tripp in 1852, when he began operations on a small scale in a shop situated in the yard of the Massachusetts Corporation. After his death in 1888 the business was continued by the present firm of John Tripp & Co., composed of Messrs. A. C. Persons and S. C. Wood (both Vermonters and for twenty-five years connected with the concern as employees and partners) and Mrs. E. A. Mansur, a daughter of Mr. Tripp. The works are now situated on the ground floor of the Mechanics' mills, Dutton street, occupying one room 40 x 80 feet, and are completely equipped with Newell Wyllys' machines and other ingenious modern appliances, driven by steam power. From eighteen to twenty experts are employed, and a vast amount of superior work is done, mostly for regular customers in New England, though two Indiana and one South Carolina mills obtain all their new rolls and have all their old ones recovered here. Some idea of the amount of business transacted may be drawn from the materials consumed, which average 18,000 sheepskins, many thousand calfskins and 12,000 yards of woolen goods per annum. The plant is one of the most complete of the kind in the country; only the best workmen are employed, and the reputation of the house for skill and promptitude is of the best. Those who are dissatisfied with their rolls are invited to send in sample orders, which will receive immediate and careful attention. Where it is inconvenient or unadvisable to send rolls, the firm manufactures cotts from selected sheep and calf to fit any kind of rolls, and they can be put on at the mill. All work is guaranteed. The firm refers to its numerous patrons, among whom may be named the Boott Cotton Mills, the Massachusetts and Prescott Cotton Mills, the Tremont and Suffolk Mills, the Lawrence Manufacturing Company, the Appleton Company, the Lowell Machine Shop, of Lowell; Naumkeag Steam Cotton Company, of Salem, Mass.; and many small mills in several States, from Vermont to South Carolina. Address John Tripp & Co., roll coverers, Lowell, Mass.

STURTEVANT & GALER,

Stair and House Finish, Stair Posts, Rails and Balusters, Brackets and Columns— Wood Turning and Job Work—No. 7 Western Avenue.

Mr. F. A. Sturtevant started this establishment alone in 1883, and, after managing it successfully for four years, in 1887 admitted a capable partner in the person of Mr. Emmet E. Galer. The firm occupies two floors and basement (about 3500 square feet) of the large frame building No. 7 Western avenue, where, provided with steam power, saws, planers, moulders, lathes, etc., ample stocks of choice hardwood and other varieties of lumber, and a sufficient force or competent workmen, they are prepared to fill orders in the best style for every description of house finish, giving special attention to plain and artistic stair posts, newels, balusters, brackets and columns, carving and turning in all its branches and general jobbing. For elegance of design and beauty of finish the work done by this firm is unsurpassed. Mr. Sturtevant was born and reared in Lowell, where he is well known to property-owners and the trade. Mr. Galer is a Vermonter, ingenious, enterprising and energetic.

CHAS. H. FROST,

Broker and Dealer in Watches, Jewelry and Diamonds, Musical Instruments and Strings, Fire Arms, Ammunition, etc.—No. 78 Central Street.

For the accommodation of any and all who feel disposed to inspect a splendid assortment of personal ornaments, musical and sporting goods, Mr. Charles H. Frost has for fourteen years past conducted a well appointed store at 78 Central street, where is shown a large and varied stock of fine diamonds and other precious stones, set and unset, imported and American gold and silver watches and jewelry, etc., together with comprehensive lines of optical and fancy goods, musical instruments, violin, guitar and banjo strings, high-grade double and single guns, rifles, pistols and ammunition. He also makes a specialty of repairing fine watches and jewelry. His prices are very low, and all goods and work are warranted as represented. Mr. Frost was for three years engaged in the clothing business at No. 61 Central street, and subsequently acted as salesman in the leading clothing store of T. C. Wilber. He served from May 21, 1861, to August 25, 1865, in the Seventh and Fifteenth Massachusetts batteries, and is a genial, accommodating and popular gentleman.

LOWELL GORING WORKS.

William Frederick Copson—Manufacturer of Elastic Goring and Suspender Braids— Mechanics' Mills Building, Dutton Street.

The usefulness and value of elastic fabrics was long ago demonstrated, and their importance to commerce and trade is universally recognized, while in some branches of surgery they are indispensable. The industry is a growing one, and most of those engaged in it are kept busy filling order from consumers. The Lowell Goring Works, established in 1887 by Mr. Wm. F. Copson, is no exception to the rule, and its products are not permitted to accumulate. They are of the best class and sell at highest prices to manufacturers of shoes, suspenders and shoulder-braces wherever offered, though the greater portion are taken by the Boston and Middletown (Conn.) shoe and suspender trade. The works occupy two rooms, respectively 38 x 50 and 25 x 35 feet, of the Mechanics' Mills building, are equipped with steam power, six looms and thirty braiders, employ ten hands, and make on an average 2000 yards of goring and 250 gross of braid weekly. Mr. Copson was born, reared and learned the art of making elastic fabrics at Leicester, England. Coming to this country, he worked for some time with Hopkins, the Chelsea manufacturer, and then removed to Lowell and set up for himself. He is a blunt, straightforward, industrious, capable and genial son of old Albion, and will doubtless make his way to the front.

THE MIDDLESEX MACHINE COMPANY,

Constructing Engineers—The Economical Arrangement of Power Plants, Warming and Ventilating of Schools, Churches, Residences and Public Buildings—No. 10 Western Avenue.

This firm was organized in 1887 with the purpose in view of manufacturing steam specialties, doing general machine work, and also a general contracting business in their specialty of power plants, heating and ventilation. In 1889, finding that the last branch was increasing to such an extent as to require the greater portion of their time, the machine work and manufacturing was discontinued and their whole attention devoted to this specialty. Mr. John H. Mills of Boston, the author of one of the most comprehensive works published on heat and warming and ventilation of buildings—a thoroughly practical as well as theoretical engineer—was at this time employed as consulting engineer. The firm are located at No. 10 Western avenue, Lowell, occupying on the ground floor a room with power, 40 x 80 feet, with additional storage room adjacent. Here but little of their work is done except the cutting of large pipe and the repairing of tools, most of their work being away from home where plants are being put in. The firm in the busy season employ from thirty to forty men and personally, as far as possible, look after the construction. During the past year they have fitted the New Draper Hall, Abbot Academy, Andover, Mass., with water heat; the Dover City Hall, Dover, N. H.; the Sawyer School at the same place; the Haverhill City Hall, Haverhill, Mass.; the State Insane Asylum, Waterbury, Vt.; two large school-houses, Lowell, Mass.; the Harvard annex building, Cambridge, Mass., besides many large business blocks and private residences. They have also to their credit many examples of the economy of the proper use of steam for power, and control inventions in this line which in practice have proven very satisfactory. In the line of water-heating the firm have made a special study under the direction of Mr. Mills, and have many successful examples of both public buildings and private residences, put in under their direction. The firm are surely now on the road to success, and can point with pride to the successful plants put in by them in the lines of power, heating and ventilation.

MOXIE NERVE FOOD COMPANY.

No. 21 Branch Street.

It is safe to say no article or compound, whether known as a medicine, food, or by any other name, has made the gigantic strides into popularity, and in such an incredibly short space of time, as has the Moxie Nerve Food. The recipe for its compounding had been in the possession of Dr. Augustin Thompson of this city for several years, had been carefully tested by him in his private practice, but not until four years ago, when its efficacy for the cure or prevention of certain diseases had been thoroughly proven to him, did he secure special accommodations for its manufacture. At this time even the doctor, sanguine in temperament though he is, scarce dreamed the phenomenal success so soon to be achieved by it. A company was formed with the doctor at its head, a laboratory was established on Market street near Worthen, and the manufacture was commenced on what at that time was deemed a large scale. Soon, however, the demand had so increased, and its use becoming more and more general as its properties became better known, the Market street quarters were found to be entirely inadequate and the vast building on Branch street formerly used as a skating rink was secured and all its immense floor space, and facilities generally, are devoted to the company's use. In addition, branch factories have been established in different parts of the country, until now there exists scarce a city from Halifax to San Francisco where " Moxie " is unknown or has not been used. Twenty-four men and women and seven horses are kept busily employed by the Branch street factory, and the sales from this factory alone, during the spring months of this year, amounted to nearly 178,800 cases, with the demand still increasing faster than ever before even in its history, as the sale of nearly 22,000 cases during the month of June will attest. All this great business is now handled by the doctor alone, and that all his energy might be devoted to it he has given up one of the largest private practices enjoyed by any physician in our city. The Moxie is claimed to be not a stimulant but a food, a nerve food, artificially digested and made ready for absorption before being taken into the system, and to this pre-digestion is due Moxie's success where other nerve foods have failed. This method of artificial digestion is a secret known only to the doctor, and one which skilled lawyers in court examinations have been unable to make him divulge. Imitation is the sincerest form of flattery, and the success of this company prompted spurious imitations and counterfeits of the genuine Nerve Food, but the doctor has pursued them with so much vigor that of late they have given him a wide berth. The doctor in himself embodies the two things necessary for success—a sound mind in a healthy body. Born in Union, Me., at an early age he moved to Rockland in that State, and there lived until the breaking out of the war, and he is strong and sturdy as the pine tree of his native State. Enlisting in the army as private, the same push and courage distinguished him that has marked his subsequent career. Promotion came rapidly to him, twice on the field being recommended for promotion by General Banks, and after being in seventy-one engagements, among them the assault on Port Hudson, he was mustered out of the service with the rank of Lieutenant Colonel. After the war he practiced medicine in this city about twenty years, and was eminently successful in his large practice. He is well informed, has traveled extensively and always with his eyes open, a man of ideas with the courage to put them in practice, a miniature steam engine in energy and vital force, and one who would succeed in making himself felt in any enterprise in which he might embark. The Moxie company has recently put upon the market two more of Dr. Thompson's preparations, viz: " Moxie Catarrh Cure " and " Safeguard," both in one package. The " Catarrh Cure " is used as a lady does her smelling bottle. It is also a harmless and rich cologne. The " Safeguard "—take five of its tiny pellets on the tongue before retiring and it will do away with the effects from exposure to colds and epidemic diseases during the day. A little dissolved in water, a table-spoonful of same each hour, will break aching and fever from a cold, grippe, pneumonia, fevers, and rheumatism. It is safe to say that the sale of these remedies, for the short time they have been upon the market, has never been equaled in the history of trade. It is a vest-pocket remedy, and everybody has it. This Company is destined to be one of the massive corporations of the country. Moxie is already a household word in two hemispheres.

DAVIS & SARGENT,

Manufacturers of and Dealers in Rough and Dressed Lumber, Clapboards, Lath, Shingles and Packing Boxes—Dimension Timber Sawed to Order—No. 275 Middlesex Street.

This is an old-established and reliable concern, founded by Otis Allen in 1848. Stephen C. Davis succeeded Mr. Allen in 1866, and the present firm was organized upon the admission of Mr. B. F. Sargent in 1872. The plant comprises a one-story-and-basement saw-mill, 50 x 100 feet, on the Pawtucket canal, and a fine two-and-three-story brick planing-mill and factory—

the Davis & Sargent block—fronting on Middlesex street, connected with which is a three-story warehouse and office building, a number of sheds, etc., the yards lying between the saw and planing mills and adjacent to both. The equipment of both mills is first-class and the productive capacity is very large, sixty hands finding steady employment on the premises, while two steam engines of 175 aggregate horse-power drive the machinery. The firm carries large stocks of choice white and yellow pine, spruce, hemlock, whitewood and hardwood lumber, which will be delivered in the rough or dressed to order for the trade. Dimension timbers also are prepared as required, and builders and others supplied with every description of flooring, clapboards, shingles, etc. A specialty is made of packing boxes for corporations and medicine, water closets, tanks, etc., and manufacturers can have their orders filled here to any extent, at short notice and on reasonable terms. The saw-mill on the canal is the only one in Lowell making lumber direct from the log, and turns out over 3,000,000 feet per annum, about 2,500,000 feet of which is worked up in the adjoining shops. The logs come from New Hampshire via the Merrimack river and the canal. Messrs. Davis and Sargent are both natives of New Hampshire, and Mr. Davis was with Mr. Allen from 1852 until he became sole owner in 1866. They own the four-story brick block, 45x180 feet, on Middlesex street, which they rent to small industrial concerns, furnishing steam when needed.

OLD WASHINGTON TAVERN.

W. H. Hawes & Co., Proprietors—Cor. Church and Central Streets.

The Old Washington was built and opened to public patronage in 1826, when Lowell had but 2000 population, and was long the leading hostelry of the place, at which have probably stopped more eminent and notable strangers, American and foreign, than all the newer hotels in the city can boast as guests. The name of the original proprietor is lost, but it has passed  through many hands, among them those of Benj. Thurston, Frank Shaw (now of the American House), and Charlie Duprez, of Duprez and Benedict's minstrels, to whom Mr. C. H. Hanson succeeded in July, 1889, and April 1, 1891, the house was taken by Messrs. William H. Hawes and Walter C. Coburn. The building is a substantial and homelike old-fashioned two-and-a-half-story frame structure, fronting 120 feet on Central and 50 feet on Church streets. On the ground floor are a large, cheery office, bar, barber-shop, two commodious parlors, and a dining-room that will comfortably seat 150 persons, while up stairs are fifty spacious, neat, clean and inviting sleeping apartments, baths, hot and cold water everywhere, and all modern conveniences, including steam heat, gas and electric lights, fire escapes, etc. Recently refitted and refurnished, situated near the Central depot and opera-house, horse cars pass the door every few minutes, affording ready and easy means of reaching any point in the city. At present the specialty is in letting furnished rooms, where guests may live quietly, taking their meals when and where they please. Terms are quite moderate.

TALBOT DYEWOOD AND CHEMICAL COMPANY.

Joseph D. Gould, President; James F. Preston, Treasurer—Manufacturers of Dyewoods and Chemicals and Dealers in Drugs and Dyestuffs—Works at North Billerica; Office and Warehouse, Nos. 24 and 26 Middle St., Lowell.

The Talbot Dyewood and Chemical Company, established in 1840, was incorporated in 1884, with Joseph D. Gould as president, James F. Preston treasurer, and a directory composed of those gentlemen, Charles H. Kohlrausch, jr., Wm. P. Gould and Geo. M. Preston. The old style was C. P. Talbot & Co., and the warerooms were for many years situated in the old city market-house building on Market street, whence they were removed a few years ago to Nos. 24 and 26 Middle street—the Talbot block, built 1877, brick, five stories, 60 x 100 feet—of which they occupy the ground floor and another up stairs. Here are the business offices and salesrooms, where are shown immense stocks of choice prepared dyewoods, dyestuffs, drugs and chemicals for the use of manufacturers and photographers and the convenience of the trade, embracing every preparation employed in making and fixing mordants. An enormous business is transacted. The works at North Billerica cover four and a-half acres and are equipped in a manner commensurate with the character and reputation of the company, whose preparations are famous all over the continent. The history of this concern does not materially differ from that of most other great industries in this country; it is the outgrowth of small beginnings, hard work and tenacity of purpose.

JOEL KNAPP & SON,

Manufacturers of Woodworking and Special Machinery, Loose Pulleys and Builders' Iron—General Jobbers—No. 257 Middlesex Street.

Mr. George L. Richardson started this establishment in 1883, but two years later sold out to Mr. Joel Knapp. Arthur P. Knapp, the son, became a member in 1890. Both are practical iron workers, the elder for twenty years foreman of the Lowell machine shops' bolt and nut department, in which responsible position he was succeeded for five years by his son. Messrs.

Joel Knapp & Son's shops are located on the ground floor of Davis & Sargent's block, No. 257 Middlesex street, occupying two rooms respectively 40 x 40 and 40 x 90 feet, provided with steam power and containing a complete equipment of machinists' tools and appliances. Their working force numbers usually about fifteen, and their output, steadily increasing, aggregated in value for the past year $50,000. This firm manufactures Grosvenor's woodworking machinery and loose pulleys and builds special machinery of every description to order in superior style, but makes leading specialties of general jobbing, repairing and manufacturing, builders' materials, nuts, washers, cap and set screws, studs, etc., in quantities. Grosvenor's swivel saw-bench, illustrated above, is the latest improvement in this class of devices, adapted to and of capacity for large or small woodworking shops, and complete for splitting, squaring, mitreing and grooving. At the same time it is so constructed as to be instantly changed to saw any mitre or bevel required, lengthwise or crosswise of the wood. The operator has only to reach down and turn the lower hand wheel to set the saw to a mitre with the table or any intermediate angle between a mitre and a square, and then by turning the upper hand wheel the saw is adjusted up and down to cut any desired depth required. The small wheel clamps the parts ridgidly while in operation. The splitting rest upon the table is constructed to be used upon either side of the saw and can be rocked either way; or the wide rocking face can be thrown back and the edge of the base of the rest be used for small work. There are two squaring sides, and by setting rest at a mitre to the saw while the saw is set at a mitre with the table, a double mitre is cut. In short, all squaring, mitreing, beveling and grooving is provided for, together with the cutting of shoulders or tenons, etc., without having to make fixtures of any kind. The firm also build to order the Grosvenor variety or irregular moulding machine. They also keep in stock and supply to order all kinds of iron-work for the use of builders, such as cast-iron columns and plates, wrought-iron beams, trusses, ties, anchors, bolts, etc., at short notice and at lowest current prices. They have a large local patronage, but will take pleasure in making estimates and supplying materials, machinery, etc., for shipment to any railroad point.

F. G. CUMMINGS,

Manufacturer of Plain and Fancy Wood Boxes—Wamesit Mills, Dutton Street.

Mr. Frank G. Cummings began manufacturing fancy wood boxes twelve years ago, and by close attention to business and the exercise of ingenuity and good taste has built up a flourishing trade, most of his output being taken by Boston and New York manufacturers of fine confectionery, chocolate, perfumes, liquid glue, etc., though he executes special orders for high-grade packing cases, nearly all of his work, however, being dovetailed at the corners, with sliding lids. His factory, employing seven hands, occupies one floor, 40x45 feet, of the Wamesit steam mills building, fitted up with steam power, saws, planers, dovetailing (or locking) machines, grooving machines, squeezers, etc., and can turn out 1000 boxes per diem. These are of the best quality, neat, strong, and comparatively cheap. Mr. Cummings was born at Tyngsboro, seven miles from Lowell, has lived in this city since boyhood, is a thorough practical mechanic, and superintends his own factory.

JONATHAN HOLT & CO.,

Manufacturers of Glue for All Purposes—Tanner Street; P. O. Address, Box 513, Ayer City.

The manufacture of glue is a unique industry which has been brought to great perfection by the above-named firm, established in 1880 and composed of Messrs. Jonathan Holt and Frank J. Sherwood. Their plant, situated on Tanner street, comprises the factory building proper, frame, two stories, 30x80 feet, and two sheds respectively 25x50 and 25x100 feet. The equipment includes an eighteen-horse-power steam engine and all requisite improved appliances; six hand are employed, and the output averages about 100 tons annually of superior glue and from 25 to 30 tons of grease, most of which is disposed of in this market and consumed by Lowell wood-workers, emery wheel manufacturers, woolen weavers, bookbinders, printers, paper box makers, kalsominers and others. They are also manufacturers of a composition for roll coverers and belt makers, which is meeting with a large sale.

SAMUEL M. CHASE,

(Successor to Chase Brothers)—Book, Job and Commercial Printer—Room 5, Bank Building, Shattuck Street.

Mr. Samuel M. Chase, a practical and experienced printer, has a very neat, compact and thoroughly appointed establishment on the same floor with the Institution for Savings, Bank building, Shattuck street, where, provided with the latest styles of type, materials and machinery, he will be pleased to receive and execute, at short notice, and in a superior manner, every description of plain and fancy job, commercial, office and society printing, at reasonable prices. He has a liberal patronage from the business men of Lowell and vicinity, and never fails to render satisfaction in any kind of work he undertakes. Mr. Chase is a native of Andover, and learned his trade in Lowell, where most of his life has been spent. He was connected with the *Vox Populi* when issued from the corner of Central and Middle streets; was for twelve years junior member of the firm of Brown & Chase, job printers; was subsequently a reporter for and editorial writer on the *Mail* and other Lowell papers; served as city clerk during 1885-86, and once more took up the mallet and shooting stick—that is, the patent quoin and wrench—two or three years ago, and will probably continue during the remaining years of his life to devote his best efforts to the elevation of the art of printing.

WARE BROTHERS,

Merchant Tailors—No. 521-2 Merrimack Street, Up Stairs.

Messrs. Thomas C. and Alfred D. Ware formed the existing copartnership about six years ago and established themselves in business at No. 52½ Merrimack street, occupying the second floor for display of goods, cutting department, etc., the workshops, employing from fourteen to eighteen hands, being situated above. This house devotes exclusive attention to fine merchant tailoring, and, carrying a choice and varied stock of the best imported and domestic woolens, offers superior inducements to those who appreciate high-grade materials. Both brothers are practical and experienced cutters; all work is done on honor, and patrons may depend upon unsurpassed materials, trimmings, fit, style and workmanship at lowest living prices. In this instance at least merit wins, and Ware Brothers command a large and steadily increasing trade from the most desirable class of city and country patrons.

W. A. DICKINSON,

Manufacturer of Scouring, Fulling and Powdered Soaps and Prime Tallow—Cor. Howard and Tanner Streets.

Mr. W. A. Dickinson, who is a native of Bristol, N. H., and was formerly a Boston clothing merchant, began the manufacture of detergents in this city about ten years ago, and three years later located permanently at his present stand at the corner of Harvard and Tanner streets.

His works consist of a two-story-and-basement frame building, 40 x 100 feet, fitted up with the necessary equipment of cauldrons, presses, grinders, etc., driven by a fifteen-horse-power steam engine. Five experienced hands are employed, and the output of scouring, fulling and powdered soaps, laundry and domestic soaps is very large and of high grade, as is attested by the heavy demand for home consumption—by mill-owners and housekeepers—though considerable shipments are made to distant points south and west. He also deals extensively in toilet soaps. Mr. Dickinson's "Banner" and "Extra Family" brands are unexcelled for the laundry and for general household use.

AMERICAN BOLT COMPANY,

Manufacturers of Bolts, Nuts, Coach or Lag Screws, Building Bolts and Irons, Forgings, Bolt and Nut Machinery, Truss Rods, Turnbuckles, etc.—Miles. F. Brennan, President and General Manager; Percy Parker, Treasurer—No. 270 Lawrence Street.

The American Bolt Company, as the successor in direct line of the founders, is the oldest and one of the most extensive representatives of its particular industry in this country. Previous to 1847 all bolts and nuts were made laboriously at the forge and bench by the consumer, and the wholesale manufacture of these devices for the trade was unheard of. In that

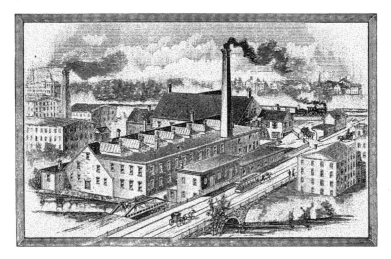

year Messrs. James Meadowcraft and George C. Smith formed a copartnership, rented a shop in the Wamesit yard, set up several forges, employed a few skilled blacksmiths, and thus laid the foundation of an interest that has since had a powerful influence upon all manufacturing industries. Their methods were at first of a primitive character, but improvement after improvement, invention after invention succeeded each other, until a stage of development has now been reached beyond which further advance seems impossible. It were unprofitable to follow in detail the history of the firm, who were bought out by Hope & Butcher in 1863. James Winter, the inventor of a bolt-heading machine, was admitted in 1865. Mr. Hope retired in 1879, and in 1881 the present company was incorporated, capital stock $200,000. Further improvements and enlargements of plant and buildings ensued, and the latter now comprise two great stone and brick structures of two and three stories, constituting the works proper, surrounded by warehouses, tenements for help, etc. The machinery is driven by two turbines of 150 and 75 horse-power respectively, a 150-horse-power steam engine being held in reserve. Two hundred operatives earn a livelihood in the various departments; over 1500 tons of iron are consumed annually, and the output, which embraces every description of commercial bolt and nut, from the tiniest to the largest, aggregated in value for the past year about $200,000. These goods are handled by the trade all over this country and exported in considerable quantities to Canada, Mexico, the West Indies and South America, being used for every conceivable purpose to which this class of mechanical devices can be applied. A detailed description of the processes employed in their production would only weary the reader without any compensating advantage. President Brennan has been connected with this concern for more than twenty-three years, having entered as an apprentice in 1867. He has filled, well and acceptably—with signal ability—every intervening position, is a thorough practical business man of rare capacity and sound judgment as well as competent mechanic and able financier, and it is not too much to say that to his energy, industry and enterprise, combined with his excellent management, is due the fact that the company has for some years been enabled to maintain its leading position in this particular field of effort.

W. E. HATCH,

Manufacturer of Brackets, Stair Posts, Newels, Balusters, Window Frames and House Finish—Scroll Sawyer and Wood Turner—Cushing Street, Wamesit Mills.

Mr. Hatch, who set himself up in business at the Wamesit mills on Dutton street about seven years ago, removing subsequently to Cushing street, is an enterprising, energetic and tactful mechanic and manufacturer who is steadily making for himself a high reputation and building up a large and flourishing trade. His premises consist of a two-story frame building 40x40 feet, with the necessary appurtenances, equipped with a fine complement of wood-working machinery—saws of all kinds, planers, lathes, etc.—driven by steam power; he employs a sufficient force of skilled workmen, and is well prepared to execute all orders for superior work in his line, making specialties of art brackets, stair posts and newels from standard and original designs, while his facilities for making door and window frames, balusters and house-finish, scroll sawing and wood-turning, are unsurpassed. His work is of the highest order and moderate prices rule.

JOHN F. ROGERS,

Undertaker, Embalmer and General Funeral Director—No. 350 Central Street, Nolan Block ; Residence, No. 21 Cedar Street.

Mr. Rogers has but recently established himself here as a funeral director, occupying the commodious and convenient rooms No. 350 Central street, fitted up expressly for the purpose

and provided with all modern appliances required for the successful prosecution of his calling in all its branches, his facilities embracing the latest improved embalming apparatus, full lines of elegant metal and wood caskets, several fine hearses in black and white for adults and children, handsome horses and carriages, careful drivers, and, in a word, everything necessary and of the very best. His office, open night and day, has telephone connection, and an ample force of skilled assistants are employed. His hearses alone, of the latest and most beautiful design, cost $3,500 cash. His stock of robes, gloves, crape, and funeral decorations is the largest and best selected in the city, and nothing is wanting for the stylish and decorous management of funerals upon any desired scale of economy or magnificence, while terms are quite reasonable. Mr. Rogers is a native of Merrimack, N. H., born thirty-two years ago. Lowell has been his home for thirty years, thirteen of which were passed in the service of the Lowell Manufacturing Company. He attended the New York College, corner of Ninety-third street and Second avenue, for one term for the purpose of learning embalming, and was subsequently for one year in the employ of Mr. E. T. Wilson, New Bedford's leading funeral director, with whom he learned all the practical details of the profession. He is a popular citizen and was a member of the city council in 1888. Promptitude, good taste and courtesy characterize all of his business transactions.

PARSONS & MEALEY,

Manufacturers of Copper Stamps and Stencils for Cotton and Woolen Mills, Bleacheries, Hosieries, etc.—Block Cutters and Dealers in Inks, Presses, Boxes and Stamping Supplies—No. 9 Fletcher Street.

It is pretty safe to conclude that a concern established for forty-five years, and doing a more prosperous business at last than ever before in its career, is worthy of confidence and has won

its position upon merit alone. Such an one is the noted stamp and stencil house of Parsons &
Mealey, originally founded in 1845 by R. J. Dewhurst, the style subsequently changing to
Dewhurst & Parsons, to whom Parsons & Mealey succeeded in 1880. Mr. Parsons died in
1881, since which time Mr. John J. Mealey has continued in sole control under the former
name, Parsons & Mealey. The works occupy two floors 30 x 40 feet up stairs at No. 9
Fletcher street, one of which is divided by partitions into four rooms, used for office, designers'
room, storage, etc., while that above is utilized for factory purposes exclusively, giving
employment to four experts and fitted up and provided with the best improved tools and appliances. Here are made to order every description of copper stamps and stencils required by
manufacturers of cotton and woolen fabrics and hosiery, bleachers and others. Block cutting
from original designs is also made a leading specialty, and inks, presses, boxes and stamping
supplies of all kinds are furnished as required. First-class materials and workmanship,
promptitude in the execution and delivery of work and goods, courtesy, liberality and moderate
prices combined constitute the secret of long-continued and growing prosperity. Orders are
received almost daily by mail from all parts of the United States, and the house controls a large
Canadian trade. Correspondence is solicited, and no pains are spared to render satisfaction.

DARIUS WHITHED,

Manufacturer of Soaps and Candles and Dealer in Hides, Tallow and Calf Skins— No. 64 School Street, near Middlesex.

This concern was founded nearly fifty years ago by the late Samuel Horn, the style subsequently changing to Samuel Horn & Co. and so remaining until about five years ago, when Mr.
Darius Whithed purchased the plant and business and continued under his own name. The
works, quite extensive, are situated in Tewksbury, the office and warehouse occupying a two-
story frame building, 30 x 50 feet, on School street, near Middlesex, this city. In all nine or
ten hands are employed, and Mr. Whithed controls a good trade in Massachusetts and adjoining States, making specialties of hard and soft soaps for mill and laundry purposes, candles,
tallow and grease, of all of which he carries heavy stocks to fill orders. He also buys and sells
green hides and calf skins. He is a native of New Hampshire, and an upright and liberal
man and good citizen.

D. H. WILSON & CO.,

Coppersmiths, Plumbers, Steam and Gas Fitters—Manufacturers of Slasher Cylin- ders, Silk and Dresser Cylinders, Color and Dye Kettles, and All Kinds of Mill Copper Work—Nos. 64 and 65 Dutton Street.

This house was established in 1873 by Mr. D. H. Wilson and a brother since retired, and
up to two years ago occupied the Connors building, No. 179 Central street, when the firm re-

moved to their own handsome three-
story-and-basement brick building, 30
x 78 feet, Nos. 64 and 65 Dutton street.
Mr. Wilson employs twenty-four or
more expert workmen, and also has
with him as assistants his sons Henry
D. and Arthur C., who are acquiring a
practical business and mechanical training. The elder Mr. Wilson is famous
as the originator of valuable improvements in slasher cylinders, color and
dye kettles. His copper slasher cylinder, economical of steam and adapted
to all classes of work, is a ring cylinder,
constructed in the most workmanlike
manner from carefully selected materials, and with proper usage cannot
give out. The cavity cylinder is heavier,
stronger, and more particularly designed
for heavy work. These cylinders are
made with double shells of copper, the
spiders, shafts, rings, etc., being of iron as usual, but differing somewhat from the old style.
When desired the inner works of old cylinders are removed, put in order, and the cylinders

reconstructed with copper shells, the effectiveness of the machine being vastly increased. Old cylinders may also be rebuilt with all improvements, using the old spiders, rings, shafts and valves and substituting inside and outside copper shells, heads and buckets, for less than a complete new cylinder would cost. Cavity or hollow cylinders of copper, superior in all respects to the iron cylinder, are made new for less money than the old-style cylinder. These are constructed with outside copper shell and iron heads, 60-inch face, four, five, six and seven feet steam space. Mr. Wilson also makes dyeing and dressing machine cylinders of copper, dye kettles and copper-work generally, in any desired size or kind at low prices. He also gives prompt attention to calls for repairs, sends experienced workmen when required, and allows fair prices for old cylinders for which new are substituted. Among the mills now using Mr. Wilson's cylinders—some as many as six sets, and all with satisfactory results—are the Boott, Massachusetts, Prescott, Hamilton, Tremont and Suffolk, of Lowell; the Dwight, Chicopee and Naumkeag, of Salem; the Upper Pacific, of Lawrence; the Mechanics, of Fall River; the Androscoggin, of Lewiston, Me.; the Harmony, of Cohoes, N. Y., and others.

B. F. STEVENS,

F. C. Stevens, Foreman—Machinist—Manufacturer of Pulley Lathes and Lock Corner Box Machines—Nos. 16, 18 and 20 Arch Street.

For more than forty years Mr. B. F. Stevens has been engaged in the construction in this city of high-grade machinery in various forms, making leading specialties of the pulley lathe illustrated herewith in its latest improved form and the world-renowned James' power feeding

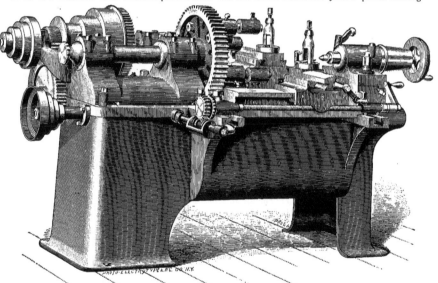

lock-corner box machine—the latter entirely remodeled and perfected and covered by patents of which Mr. Stevens has entire control. As now built this machine is unrivaled for box-makers' use, and, though it works satisfactorily in lumber of any ordinary thickness, is more especially designed for preparing ⅝ to inch stuff. Of Mr. Stevens' own machine little need be said. Our engraving conveys a good idea of its general appearance, and the machine itself, in its old or new form, is familiar to most mechanics who employ appliances of this kind. Its superiority in its own particular department is undisputed and apparent to any one competent to compare and judge intelligently in such matters. Mr. Stevens' shops, under the careful and experienced supervision of his son, F. C., occupy the two-story stone and frame building 40 x 75 feet, with L, Nos, 16, 18 and 20 Arch street, near the Northern depot. Here are employed from fifteen to twenty first-class workmen and a complete outfit of machinery driven by steam, and lathes and dovetailers to the value of about $18,000 are made annually to the order of New England, western and southern customers. The elder Mr. Stevens, born in Dracut, across the Merrimack from Lowell, is the fifth B. F. in direct descent, a fine mechanic and an estimable old citizen. His son and foreman, trained to machine building from boyhood, is familiar with all the details of the business, manufacturing and commercial.

20

THE KNOWLES SCALE WORKS.

Wm. H. Thompson, Proprietor—Manufacturers of Platform and Counter Scales—
Fletcher Street.

The importance of using absolutely correct scales for weighing commodities c a n hardly be overestimated, both buyer and seller being equally interested—the former in obtaining all that he pays for and the latter in maintaining his reputation for fair and honest dealing. Great mechanical skill and long experience are requisite to success in the manufacture of an appliance upon which so much depends, and for that reason the purchaser of scales should make sure that the device offered him is the product of an old-established concern of known standing, or at least of skilled experts. Among the most widely and most favorably known scale making concerns of New England is the Knowles Scale Works, founded in 1837 by Woods & Nute, to whom John A. Knowles, jr., succeeded, Mr. Wm. H. Thompson, a resident of Salem, becoming proprietor in 1884. The fame of the establishment was greatly extended under Mr. Knowles' administration, and for that reason and as a compliment to his able predecessor, Mr. Thompson has retained the style. The works on Fletcher street comprise a substantial and commodious three-story brick building 40 feet front by 120 feet deep, fitted up with a comprehensive plant of machinery and appliances, including a 10-horse-power electric motor of approved style. A considerable number of superior mechanics are employed, some of whom have been here for many years. The output comprises a variety of platform and counter scales, the leading specialties including the widely known "Bedford" and "Star" scales, "Lowell Standard" platform—illustrated herewith—all iron platform, stout axles and wheels, hardened steel pivots, accurate and durable; the "New England Union" single and double-beam scoop scale, capacity half an ounce to 240 pounds; the "Lowell" counter scale, capacity half an ounce to 25 pounds, and the "Even Balances," capacity four-pound and eight-pound, with and without side beam. Every scale is fully warranted, and they are thoroughly reliable, while the prices are remarkably low. These scales are made to conform to all foreign standards, are in use all over the United States, and are being exported largely to the West Indies, Mexico, Central and South America, Australia, Africa and other countries. The works, operated to their full capacity, can turn out 6000 scales of all classes annually, and it is Mr. Thompson's ambition to reach that point very soon.

MERRIMACK CROQUET COMPANY.

B. F. Colby—Manufacturer of Croquet, Ten Pins, Ring Toss, Dumb Bells, Indian
Clubs and Christmas Toys, and Castor Wheels—St. Hyacinth Street, Ayer City.

The Merrimack Croquet Companys' works, now the largest and most complete of the kind
in existence, were established a good many years ago. Mr. B. F. Colby succeeded parties who
had been in control from 1872, and was himself sole proprietor for several years, Mr. S. P.
Griffin joining him in 1888, but retiring later. A copy of the company's latest catalogue has
come under our notice, and we unhesitatingly pronounce it a gem, so far as design, engraving,
composition, colors, presswork and paper in their most skillful combinations, regardless of expense, can be made to represent art, the various implements illustrated being shown in the

natural colors of the wood, and even the red and blue stripes, pedestals, etc., being faithfully
imitated by the printer. The goods produced by this company are of original design, made
from the choicest hard-woods—in part of Turkish box, lignum vitæ, and other foreign woods—
and are of the highest grade, finished by a new method that greatly improves their appearance,
and decorated in fadeless colors that water will not effect—a desideratum long sought but never
found until Mr. Colby's experiments were crowned with success. The company confidently
challenges competition in quality, finish and prices. Their products comprise full lines of
lawn croquet in great variety of handsome styles; parlor floor and parlor table croquet; new
model ten pins, ring toss, dumb bells, Indian clubs; Moore's patent new flexible hammocks in
which wood slats are substituted for and make a swinging couch far more comfortable, convenient and durable than the old-style shapeless bag hammock; the flexible swinging easy
chair, safest, coolest and easiest ever devised, adjustable to long or short occupants, and recommended by physicians for invalids and convalescents; and Moore's patent tree chair, at-
tachable to trees or other upright objects—just the thing for picnics, out-door intertainments and
sketching. This company are also the most extensive American manufactures of lignum vitæ
castor wheels, and sole manufacturers of hub castor wheels, made by special patented machinery, of which they own the patents, besides turning out great quantities of camp chairs,
steamer chairs, lignum vitæ carpenter's mallets, bowling alley balls, oak dowels, small lock-
cornered wooden boxes, general fancy wood-work, and lathe turning to order. The factory,
situated on St. Hyacinth street, Ayer City, is a commodious and convenient three-story-and-
basement brick structure, 50 x 150 feet, lighted by gas, heated by steam, and containing an
equipment so perfect and comprehensive that no attempted description could do it justice.
Much of the machinery is of special design and construction, invented or remodeled by Mr.
Colby, and without duplicates elsewhere—all driven by a 100-horse-power steam engine.
Seventy-five competent workmen are employed, and the output is enormous. The goods are
supplied to the trade all over our own country and exported to British America, Canada, England, France, Germany, Australia and other distant lands.

LOWELL FELTING MILLS,

H. M. Thompson, Proprietor—Manufacturer of Hair Felt in All Widths and Thicknesses—Pawtucket Street.

It has long been a demonstrated and conceded fact that hair felt is unequaled by any other known material as a non-conductor of heat, and therefore unrivaled for jacketing boilers and steam pipes, preventing radiation and consequent condensation. For the same reason, and because of its flexibility and the ease with which it is cut and fitted, hair felt is largely employed for lining and packing purposes by engineers and machinists. Among the largest manufacturers of this commodity in America are the Lowell Felting Mills, situated on Pawtucket street, Proprietor H. M. Thompson having his office on the premises. This enterprise owes its inception to Moses A. Johnson and Isaac Schofield, who in 1860 began the manufacture of felt from American and Russian cow hair at the foot of Howe street, Belvidere. Mr. Schofield retired in 1866, whereupon Messrs. Joseph S. Wiggins and George Brierton of Boston joined with Mr. Johnson in the purchase of a steam saw-mill on Pawtucket street, which was demolished and the present mill erected on the site, the firm adopting the existing style, Lowell Felting Mills, which has since been purchased by and is now owned by Mr. Thompson. The buildings consist of a commodious stone and wood mill, roomy warehouses and extensive yards, and the equipment is complete, embracing all modern improvements, the machinery being driven by a 60-horse-power steam engine. From fifteen to twenty hands are employed, and the output of superior jacketing, lining and packing felts from one-eighth to two inches thick and one to two yards wide is very heavy, the annual consumption of imported and domestic cow-hair averaging 1,200,000 pounds. These felts are sold in wholesale or retail lots to suit, and orders promptly executed.

SAMUEL G. COOPER,

Manufacturer of Copper Stamps and Stencils—Dealer in Stamping Inks and Supplies—No. 120 Central Street.

Mr. Cooper has been in the same business in this city since 1872—up to 1885 as junior partner in the firm of Corner and Cooper, Mr. Corner retiring at that time. The establishment occupies the entire second floor, 60 x 80 feet, of the brick building No. 120 Central street, and is one of the best appointed and most thoroughly equipped of the kind in the country, giving employment to five or six skillful stamp and stencil designers and cutters. Mr. Cooper is a noted expert, and his work, tasty and perfect in execution, is found all over the United States and Canada, wherever a cotton or woolen mill is running, in addition to which he is beginning to fill orders for shipment beyond seas, having recently made a heavy consignment to China. His annual sales range from $5,000 to $7,000. Mr. Cooper's specialties embrace every description of copper stamps and stencils for cotton and woolen mills, bleacheries and hosieries, head stamps for broadcloths, cassimeres and flannels. He also carries large stocks of and will promptly fill orders for black, blue and red stamping inks, stamping presses, stamping boxes and stamping supplies generally.

DOHERTY BROS.,

Iron Founders—Manufacturers of Machinery and Tool Castings—Paine Street,
near B. & M. R. R.

Messrs. John F. and James F. Doherty where born at Ayer, while William C. is a native of Bedford, Mass. All are practical foundrymen, brought up to the business and familiar with all its details. About four years ago an opportunity presented to purchase the foundry established at Ayer Junction by Briggs & Kelley (both deceased), which the brothers availed themselves of, and there remained, doing an excellent business, until the beginning of the present year, when, having completed their new works on Payne street, they took possession, making their first casting here on the 21st of January. The building is a handsome frame structure 50 x 200 feet in area, three stories in height at the front and one story in rear, equipped with a 20-horse-power electric motor and all newly improved foundry appliances. At the start twenty-five men —skilled molders and assistants—are employed, but the force will be increased as required. The firm has hitherto made little effort to extend its trade beyond Lowell and this vicinity, but having made a long stride toward a commanding place in the iron foundry industry, they will not stop until they have secured a good share of the business of the country, more especially in the department of machinery and tool castings, for the correct making of which they have excellent facilities and an established reputation.

JEREMIAH CLARK,

Machinery Agency for the Purchase, Sale and Exchange of Cotton, Woolen and Other Machinery, New and Second-Hand Card Clothing, Belting, etc.—Shops and Warehouses, Perrin Street; Office, No. 63 Dutton Street.

Mr. Clark, a native of Vermont and for thirty years connected with the great Lowell Machine Shop corporation, established in February, 1867, a modest machinery agency which he has gradually developed to its present proportions. His office, show and salesrooms are

situated on the ground floor of the large three-story brick building No. 63 Dutton street, with an immense stock stored in the big warehouses seen in our cut, containing over two acres of floor space, where is shown an endless variety of new and second-hand cotton and woolen machinery, card clothing, belting, etc. A well-equipped machine-shop adjoins the warehouses, where a competent force of workmen are kept constantly employed on repairs, alterations and improvements. Parties in want of anything required in the manufacture of cotton or woolen fabrics, whether new or second-hand, will be safe in placing their orders with Mr. Clark. Be the purpose for which it is needed what it may—the making of textiles, sewing, wood, iron sheet metal or leather working—he either has on hand or will procure the machine. He also carries a large and varied stock of card clothing, leather belting, steam engines and boilers, etc., old and new and of every conceivable kind and style. Mr. C.'s territory embraces every manufacturing city and village in the United States and Canada, east of the Rocky Mountains. Catalogues are sent to anyone on request.

ALLEN HOWARD,

Manufacturer of Caskets and Coffins—Corner Dutton and Fletcher Streets.

This well-known and largely patronized concern was established in 1878 by J. M. Torsey, and passed into the hands of Mr. Allen Howard, a native of Waldoboro, Maine, for some years  a foreman in the employ of the Boston Bridge Company, and a resident of Lowell since 1865. Mr. Howard's premises, situated in the large frame building corner of Dutton and Fletcher streets, comprise two handsomely appointed storage and salesrooms on the ground floor and workshop and finishing room up stairs. He carries a large and varied assortment of wood and metal caskets and coffins, of his own manufacture, besides a general line of samples from leading makers, and is prepared to supply anything of the kind required by undertakers, from the cost-liest to the cheapest grade. He has in his service a number of tasteful skilled workmen and sells largely to the trade in Lowell, Lawrence, Manchester, Salem, Haverhill and surrounding villages, principally at wholesale.

S. C. & G. H. SMITH,

Manufacturers of Cap and Set Screws—No. 277 Broadway.

Machinery builders generally are perfectly aware of the difficulty of making accurate and reliable cap and set screws, and the majority of them wisely refrain from attempting a kind of work to succeed in which they must not only command the services of specially trained workmen

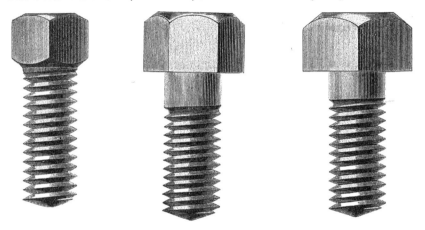

but must also devise and construct special machinery, that in use being covered by patents and not built for sale. Among the oldest and most successful manufacturers of this particular class of requisites is the firm of S. C. & G. H. Smith, founded twenty-five years ago by the senior member, Mr. Samuel C. Smith, with whom his brother George H. became associated later. They occupy one floor 40 x 128 feet in area, with entrance at No. 277 Broadway, and have at hand every convenience for the production of cap and set screws in large quantities—ingenious and unique machinery of their own invention and construction, a complete plant of accessories, electric power, and the services of twelve expert screw-makers. The products of this establishment are held in high repute by machinists everywhere, and are in general demand not only at home but abroad, the firm shipping to nearly every State of the Union besides exporting to Canada, Australia and other countries. The demand is steadily growing, sales for 1890 footing up about $16,000.

WHITTIER COTTON MILLS.

E. M. Tucke, President; Helen A. Whittier, Treasurer; Nelson Whittier, General Manager; Walter R. B. Whittier, Superintendent—Manufacturers of Yarns, Twines, Cord, Rope and Banding—Fire Hose Cords, both Warp and Weft, a Specialty—Goods Sold Directly from the Mills—Stackpole Street.

The Whittier cotton mills comprise an old-established plant, formerly conducted by Whittier & Sons, but incorporated in 1887, capital stock $75,000. The mill building is of brick, three stories in height, about 125x300 feet in area, and contains an elaborate equipment that includes a 275-horse-power steam engine, 5000 spindles, and cards, twisting and rope-making machinery to match. Seventy-five hands is the usual complement of employes, and the mills are never idle save on Sunday and holidays or in case of accident, as there is constant demand for all the yarns, twines, cords, rope and banding that can be produced, the value of the output ranging from $150,000 to $200,000 per annum. It is distributed throughout the country, but principally in New England.

LOWELL TOOL AND ENGINE COMPANY.

McNab Brothers—Builders of Automatic, Throttling and Compound Engines of All Kinds—Mill Work, Repairs, etc.—Main Street, Ayer City.

Messrs. Duncan and Donald McNab (the former president, the latter secretary of the Lowell Tool and Engine Company) established themselves in business on their own account about nine years ago. They have devoted themselves industriously to the improvement of the steam engine and its adaptation to special purposes with most encouraging results, making specialties of automatic cut-off engines, horizontal automatic engines, high-speed engines, engines for driving electric generators, wood-working and iron-working machinery, etc., together with dynamos and electric motors of simple yet effectual form. An engine exhibited by them at the Middlesex fair attracted much attention and was referred to by the *Citizen* in the following terms: "The engine is forty-horse-power, horizontal, and has an automatic cut-off, simplicity itself in its working and capable of the closest regulation, which adapts it particularly for electric lighting purposes. This automatic arrangement affects the throw-off eccentric, and consequently the point of cut-off, according to the load the engine is driving. A mechanical arrangement also secures the key and strap on the connecting rod, which does away with the old and troublesome attachment. This is done by means of an ear on the end of a key, secured by two checked nuts in place of the set screw on the side, which closes up and swells the key. The slide bars, also, are a new feature, the bearing surfaces being of a most substantial character. On the bottom slide bar there is a projection on each side which retains the oil, keeps the engine clean, and is quite economical. The slide block has the advantage of a clean and oily surface to move in all the time. A patent piston is inside the cylinder, and the McNabs pride themselves on the automatic cut-off." The Lowell Tool and Engine Company's shops, situated at the intersection of Brook and Lincoln streets, Ayer City, comprise two one-story frame buildings respectively 40 x 65 and 30 x 40 feet, well equipped with steam power and all requisite tools for constructing machinery. The company employs from fifteen to twenty men, gives attention to calls for mill work, shafting, the reboring of cylinders and general repairs, and transacts a business amounting to about $35,000 per annum.

TAYLOR ROOF SHINGLING COMPANY.

F. A. Taylor, Proprietor—No. 92 Bartlett Street.

Mr. F. A. Taylor, born at Carlisle, has passed the greater part of his life in Lowell, but was for three years in California and the far west. Returning, he in 1876 established the Taylor Roof Shingling Company, and by the exercise of tact, energy and industry, united with skill and reliability both in responding to calls and the character of his workmanship, has made a success of his venture—a department of industry of which, so far as we are informed, no one else ever thought as a specialty, the general presumption being that any competent carpenter can make a satisfactory shingle roof. Mr. Taylor's facilities are first-class in all respects; he' employs from eight to ten expert workmen; all shingles used by him are sawn expressly for his trade and bear the brand "Taylor Roof Shingling Co.;" and the utmost care is taken to make every job wind and water-proof, strong and enduring. As an indication of the extent of his business it may be stated here that his consumption of materials averages 2,000,000 shingles, twenty tons of zinc, six tons of sheet lead and twenty tons best steel nails annually. Roofing of all kinds—shingle, tin, sheet iron, felt, gravel, slate, etc.—is done to order, and special attention given to repairing and re-roofing houses, mills, factories, etc., for non-resident property-owners. He warrants all his work.

OLD COLONY TRUST COMPANY.

T. Jefferson Coolidge, Jr,, President; C. S. Tuckerman, Secretary and Treasurer; Joseph G. Stearns, Superintendent Safe Deposit Vaults—Ames Building, cor. Washington and Court Sts.

This institution, incorporated May 8, 1890, capital stock $1,000,000, paid-up surplus $500,-000, sprang into instant and tremendous popularity with the business public, not only because of the immense usefulness it promised but of the absolute security presented by the board of directors, which embraces many of the best and most responsible names in New England, or the country, to wit: T. Jefferson Coolidge, jr., president, Frederick L. Ames, John F. Anderson, John L. Bremer, Martin Brimmer, T. Jefferson Coolidge, George F. Fabyan, George P. Gardner, Francis L. Higginson, Henry 'S. Howe, Walter Hunnewell, W. Powell Mason, George Von L. Meyer, Laurence Minot, Richard Olney, Henry R. Reed, Lucius M. Sargent, Nathaniel Thayer, John I. Waterbury, Stephen M. Weld and Henry C. Weston. The first offices occupied were at No. 50 State street, and the doors were opened for business June 14, 1890. It soon became manifest that the accommodations were entirely inadequate, so the ground floor of the new Ames building at the corner of Washington and Court streets was leased, and when that magnificent fourteen-story granite-and-sandstone fire-proof edifice was completed early in the present year, the Trust Company removed to what is unquestionably the most perfect and elaborate banking-house east of New York if not on the continent. The business of the company continuing to increase, it has been necessary to provide additional space, and the fine banking rooms over the present quarters have been leased from January 1st, 1892. The offices are superbly fitted up in mahogany, plate glass and marble, with rich and costly brass and bronze railings, frescoed ceilings and every evidence of wealth and power. In the basement are the safe deposit vaults, of the latest improved construction, impregnable alike to thieves and fire, and further provided with every safeguard that ingenuity can devise or integrity supply. Boxes here are rented at reasonable figures, ranging from $10 to $100 per annum, according to size, and depositors carry their own keys, not even the officials having access to the compartments or their contents, while special coupon rooms are supplied to ladies. Mr. Joseph G. Stearns is superintendent of the deposit vaults, which offer the best possible storage for stocks, bonds, securities, title deeds, mortgages, diamonds and other valuables of a portable character. The company transacts a general and very extensive banking business, allows interest on daily balances subject to check, and solicits personal accounts, of which a leading specialty is made, cashing coupons and collecting dividends for depositors free of charge. It also acts as agent in financial transactions, and as agent for transfers, registrar and trustee under mortgages. In a word, every description of monetary transactions, the custody of funds of all kinds and the conduct of a general fiduciary trust is assured by this corporation, which offers the best possible guarantees of good faith, reliability and responsibility. The subjoined statement of August 1, 1891, will perhaps convey some idea of the high estimation in which the Old Colony Trust Company is held.

ASSETS.		LIABILITIES.	
Loans,	$3,529,399 47	Capital Stock,	$1,000,000 00
City and other Bonds at or under par,	389.295 19	Surplus,	500,000 00
Deposit Vaults,	62.714 35	Undivided Profits and Interest,	112,588 70
Expenses Paid,	11,918 93	State Tax,	11,000 00
Cash on hand,	210,419 97	Deposits,	3,542,576 52
Cash in Bank,	962,417 31		
Total,	$5,166,165 22	Total,	$5,166,165 22

E. HAPGOOD & SON,

Manufacturers of Wool, Cotton, Hair, Fibre, Husk, Tow, Wool-top and Cotton-top Mattresses—Dealers in Bedding, Wool and Spring Beds—No. 17 High Street.

This is the most extensive mattress manufacturing concern in Lowell, if not in New England, and was founded eighteen or twenty years ago by the late Ephraim Hapgood, after whose death his widow and son Edgar succeeded to the management. The office is at No. 79 High street, and connected therewith is factory No. 1, frame, three stories, 25 x 80 feet; No. 2, situated on Lawrence street, also a three-story frame structure, is 30 x 110 feet, with picker and boiler-houses attached. From thirty-five to forty hands are employed at both places, and the combined capacity is one hundred and twenty-five finished mattresses of all kinds daily. Their trade extends to all parts of the Union, and is mostly with furniture dealers, house furnishers, etc., though orders are executed for hotel men and others in quantities. Every description of mattresses are made here in superior style and at reasonable prices, from any desired materials —wool, cotton, hair, fibre, husk, excelsior, wool and cotton-top.

NEW ENGLAND BUNTING COMPANY.

E. S. Hylan, Treasurer and Manager—Manufacturers of Bunting, Fancy Worsteds, Cotton Carriage Robes, Turkey Red Awning Stripes, Flags, etc.—Davidson St.

The plant now occupied by this company was established about thirty-five years ago by John Holt, who employed it for the manufacture of flannels up to the time of his death. Mr. E. S. Hylan purchased the property and founded the New England Bunting Company in 1881, though it was not incorporated until 1888; capital stock $25,000; treasurer and manager, E. S. Hylan; selling agents, N. Boynton & Co., Nos. 87 and 89 Commercial street, Boston. The mill proper is a sturdy-looking three-story stone building 30 x 80 feet, with frame addition, and is well equipped with appropriate machinery, including three warpers, twenty broad and fifty-two narrow looms and all other requisites, driven by a 60-horse-power steam engine. From thirty to forty operatives are employed, and the output, of the best quality, is quite large—from 2800 to 3000 yards of bunting daily, 10000 cotton carriage robes weekly, besides considerable quantities of Turkey red awning stripes, flags, etc. Orders should be sent to the selling agents at Boston, Messrs. N. Boynton & Co., Nos. 87 and 89 Commercial street.

GEO. L. CADY,

Manufacturer of Engine and Hand Lathes, Jackson's Patent Electric Engines, Semple's Book-Trimming Machines, Loom Harness Hooks and Eyes, Belt Hooks, etc.—Dealer in Machinists' and Mill Supplies—Corner Western Avenue and Fletcher Street.

Mr. Cady, formerly located on Middlesex street, was at one time a very extensive manufacturer of engine and foot lathes, but, finding the business rather overdone in this city, removed to Western avenue and Fletcher street, where, occupying two commodious floors and basement, he devotes his attention more especially to orders for experimental machinery, though he still builds and repairs the devices upon which his prosperity was founded and executes commissions for loom harness hooks and eyes, belt hooks, and machinists' and mill supplies. In the palmy days of the trade he kept forty men at work on foot lathes alone; now he employs a comparatively small force, yet turns out considerable fine work of other kinds, having contracts for the construction of the famous Semple book-trimmer and the Jackson patent electric motor. He has two young sons, and it is his desire that they may succeed him in the business of machine-building, in which event he designs erecting great shops and giving them a grand start in life. Personally Mr. Cady is now and for some years has been largely interested in real estate transactions. He was Captain of Company G, of the celebrated Sixth Massachusetts volunteers, of Baltimore riot memory, and is a prominent member of the G. A. R.

LOWELL WORSTED MILLS.

James Dugdale, Proprietor—Commission Spinner of Worsted, Mohair, Camel's Hair and Mixed Yarns—No. 72 Willie Street.

Mr. James Dugdale is a native of Lancashire, England. At a tender age he was set at work in the worsted mills at Dolphinholme, changing at a later day to the worsted mills at Bradford in Yorkshire. Forty-four years ago he came to this country, and, having lived in Lowell during most of the time since, is pretty thoroughly Americanized. His first business venture was made in a small mill on the Whipple's mills premises, but, having purchased the stone mill and grounds at No. 72 Willie street, he refitted and occupied the building in 1868. It is a remarkably substantial stone structure of three stories and attic, 40 x 100 feet, and adorned with a quaint stone chimney—a survivor of a dead-and-gone age, apparently designed to out-rival in endurance the eternal hills, and the only remaining example of the primitive smoke-stack in this vicinity. The Lowell worsted mills are remarkably well equipped with the best modern machinery for the manufacture of worsted, mohair, camel's hair and mixed yarns for cassimeres, coatings and knit goods, improved patent knot-preventing doublers for two to six-ply yarns, combs, cards, 2000 spindles, etc., while ninety operatives find steady work in the various departments, denoting a large aggregate output, though, as all the spinning is done on commission, the precise figures are difficult to obtain. Mr. D. also keeps in stock, for the convenience of customers, a general assortment of skeins, tubes, dresser spools, shuttle bobbins, five-inch spools, etc. A 150-horse-power steam engine drives the machinery of this mill and of several other shops and factories operated by tenants of Mr. Dugdale.

HARRIMAN BROS.,

Manufacturers of Elastic and Non-Elastic Webs, Web Straps, Braids and Suspenders—No. 123 Hale Street.

Messrs. Joseph and John Harriman have long been residents of Lowell. Industrious and enterprising, they some years ago began the manufacture on a small scale of webs, suspenders, etc., putting into their work extraordinary taste and skill and finding ready sale for their goods, steadily increasing their facilities and output as the demand grew. They first enlarged their plant in 1885 and again in 1886, and now occupy the two-story frame building No. 123 Hale street, 40 x 40 feet, with L 32 x 35 feet, fitted up with steam power, special looms, sewing machines, etc., and giving employment to about thirty-five hands. The leading specialties made here include a superior line of elastic and non-elastic webs, web straps, braids and suspenders. Every article is of the very best quality, only the choicest materials and most expert workmanship being employed, consequently there is no accumulation of stock. Some of the goods— notably a line of fine suspenders—are made up on the premises, but for the most .part the braids and webs are shipped direct to the New York selling agent, by whom they are disposed of to the shoe, suspender, dressmaking and surgical appliance trades and others requiring this class of materials.

SAM'L E. & T. STOTT,

Manufacturers of Card Clothing for Jute, Flax and Other Fibres, Gills, Circles, Fallers, Gill, Card and Comb Pins, etc.—Meadowcroft Street.

Here is one card-clothing house which is not entangled in the meshes of the trust and is content to do business on business principles and on actual merit, in open competition with all legitimate rivals. The firm, established in 1876, consists of Messrs. Samuel E. and T. Stoty (brothers), practical workmen and competent business men. The works occupy a two-story frame building, 45 x 80 feet, on Meadowcroft street, and are thoroughly equipped in all departments with the latest improved machinery for stretching and cutting wire, for cutting off "peris," for drilling lags and gills, for grinding and finishing, and for all required purposes, the whole driven by a 20-horse-power steam engine, while about thirty expert workmen are kept busily engaged in those operations wherein manual labor is indispensable. The products comprise superior lines of needle and diamond pointed wood and leather card clothing for use in preparing vegetable fibres, machine wool combs, shoddy and waste pickers, rag dusters, circles, gills, fallers, hackles, gill, card and comb pins, etc., and the output is large and of great value, being supplied direct to manufacturers all over New England, the demand from other parts of the country growing at a gratifying rate.

LEWIS D. GUMB,

Granite and Marble Cutter—Contractor for Monumental, Cemetery and Building Work—Corner Gorham Street and Carter Place.

Mr. L. D. Gumb is a native of Nova Scotia and a practical designer and sculptor of monumental and architectural granite and marble. He removed to Westerly, R. I., in 1870. In 1872 he began business in Sterling, Conn., but remained there only a year, when he removed to Lowell, where his genius, skill and industry have made him a fine reputation and enabled him to achieve marked business success. His excellent taste and artistic and mechanical ability are attested by the numerous difficult and exacting contracts he has executed here, among the most notable of which may be mentioned the Shedd memorial tomb in the Lowell cemetery and the granite work of the Faulkner residence on Belmont avenue. Mr. Gumb's office and show rooms are situated at the corner of Gorham street and Carter place, where he occupies his own three-story frame building, 25 x 50 feet. Here are exhibited many specimens of his work, mostly monuments, gravestones, etc., together with drawings for others. His yards, fitted up with steam power, polishing machines, etc., and employing twenty expert workmen, are situated at the corner of Gorham and Maple streets, covering between two and three acres. He has a complete plant and enjoys a large local patronage besides shipping some to the west. His leading specialties comprise monuments and fronts for buildings in granite from architects' designs. Mr. Gumb is ably assisted by his brothers Richard and Harry, respectively foreman and salesman, which enables him to give immediate and skillful attention to all orders for finished work and requests for drawings.

THE NORTON DOOR CHECK AND SPRING COMPANY.

James P. Flynn, President; Charles S. Penhallow, Treasurer—Office, 505 Sears
Building.

The door check and spring shown in the accompanying cut is really a triumph of mechanical genius and the most perfect practical appliance for the purpose ever devised. The numbers denote the names of the parts. and are for the guidance of the purchaser when ordering.

Briefly, the apparatus consists of a cylinder, piston, spring, and self-adjusting valve, the whole provided with suitable brackets and adapted to be attached to the top part of a door and the frame over the door. In it are combined two opposing powers—the spring, for closing the door (drawing with greatest power when nearest closed), and the check, or cushioning of the piston on air, which brings the door to a momentary pause near the jamb, then quietly and surely closing and latching it by the operation of the spring, the operation being regulated by the automatic valve, which permits the air to enter the cylinder while opening the door, and while closing exhausts the air more or less as the force exerted on the door to close it is greater or less. The parts of the device are so arranged together that the greater the force exerted to close the door the greater the resistance offered; consequently no slam or jar can occur. Of all the appliances ever designed for this purpose the Norton door check and spring is the only one that has actually succeeded. Nothing equals it for the noiseless closing of doors and the prevention of glass-breaking, and every hotel, car, steamboat, business house, residence, church, theater, hospital, public building and office door should be equipped with it. The Norton Door Check and Spring Company was incorporated in 1881, capital stock $200,000; board of directors—James P. Flynn, president; Col. Charles R. Codman, Frank Wood, Russell Gray and Charles S. Penhallow, treasurer, all of Boston. The office is situated in the Sears building, and the corporation does a large and growing business, selling in all parts of the world. London, England, is the great distributing point for European countries, and sends out about $2,000 worth of the door checks weekly to France, Spain, Italy, Russia, Egypt, Norway, Australia, etc., while the Boston office is kept busy supplying the United States, Mexican and South American orders. The vast fourteen-story Ames building is fitted throughout with this time-saving, noise-preventing device. Send for circular.

CLINTON L. BRUCE,

Manufacturer of Medicinal and Surgical Plasters—Porus, Blister, Mustard, Corn, Bunion, Court, Surgeons' Adhesive, Insinglass and Dressing Plasters of Every Description—Proprietor of Bruce's Liquid Glue and Bruce's Salve.

Twelve years ago Mr. Bruce commenced the manufacture of plasters, and his business has steadily increased.   He has never soliclted business outside of the New England States, but has received orders from all parts of the United States and British provinces.   Mr. Bruce has

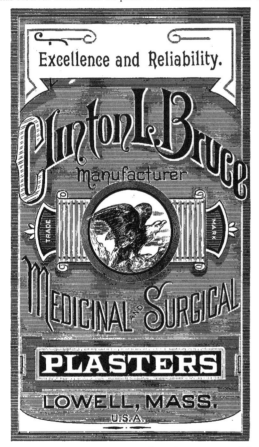

customers who have used his goods since he commenced bus. iness, and never during his whole experience has he had any goods manufactured by him returned as not good or unsala. able. ' Mr. Bruce makes a specialty of surgeons' adhesive, isinglass and dressing plasters, court plasters of every description, corn, bunion, mustard, spice and blister plasters. The goods, carefully and skillfully made, are of the finest quality ever manufactured. He has the experience and the "know how," and attends personally to the manufacturing, and it is his constant aim not. only to equal but to excel in all products peculiar to his trade, thereby gaining a reputation as the manufacturer of the finest goods of the kind in the world. His motto is "EXCELLENCE AND RELIABILITY."   Bruce's adhesive plaster is made of three different thicknesses of cloth— a light, called "Bruce's Surgeons' adhesive, a medium called Bruce's Surgeons' .corsalet, and a heavy extension plaster, Bruce's Swan's down. For the varied operations of the surgeon, in private and hospital practice, this plaster deserves special recognition. It can be applied almost instantly; the application of moisture conveyed in any form (the most convenient being that of a wetted sponge) causes it to adhere quickly. Mr. Bruce says: "I have frequently come in contact with leading surgeons of the country, and have been solicited from time to time to make adhesive plaster that could be relied upon. I believe I have now the most perfect adhesive plaster ever produced. It is antiseptic, very susceptible to the slightest wetting, very adhesive, quickly applied, and a plaster that will remain firm and will neither slide nor stretch, nor irritate the parts to which it is applied; being waterproof, wounds can be cleansed without redressing, whilst the mild, antiseptic action prevents putrefaction. It remains servicable in any climate, is not affected by age, heat or cold, and cannot spoil. Such an adhesive plaster has long been sought for by the busy surgeon, and such a plaster I am now pleased to present to the medical fraternity, where it has been fully tested and indorsed as the best Adhesive Plaster in the market." Bruce's Swan's down plaster—the original and only reliable extension plaster, the only plaster of the kind—is as near perfection as can be. It has made a reputation for the manufacturer, Clinton L. Bruce, a country wide, as the plaster that was needed, the best ever produced.

What home surgeons say of Bruce's adhesive plasters:

MR. CLINTON L. BRUCE: *Sir*—I have no hesitation in saying that the adhesive plaster manufactured by you is decidedly the best article of the kind I have ever seen.
Lowell, Mass.   GILMAN KIMBALL, M. D.

CLINTON L. BRUCE: *Dear Sir*—I have used your "Swansdown" plaster during the past year and have found it superior to the English moleskin or any other plaster I have seen. The advantages of the plaster over others consist mainly in its greater adhesive properties and its imperviousness to water. It is not injuriously affected by heat or cold. In several cases I have maintained extensions upon a fractured thigh for six weeks with this plaster without any reapplication.
Lowell, Mass.   J. C. IRISH, M. D.

CLINTON L. BRUCE: *Dear Sir*—I have used Bruce's adhesive plasters for the past year and a-half, and consider them superior to any I have ever used.
Lowell, Mass.   L. S. FOX, M. D,

MR. CLINTON L. BRUCE: *Sir*—I have used the Surgeons' adhesive plaster manufactured by you for some time with satisfactory results, and can recommend it to the profession as being scientifically made and thoroughly reliable.
Lowell, Mass.   JOHN H. GILMAN, M. D.

MR. C. L. BRUCE: *Dear Sir*—In my opinion your Surgeons' adhesive plaster has no superior. An oily dressing will not affect the plaster.
Lowell, Mass.   C. W. TAYLOR, M. D.

CLINTON L. BRUCE: *Dear Sir*—Having used the plasters manufactured by you in all kinds of surgical dressings, I would say I think they far excel any plaster that I have ever used.
Concord, N. H., May 22, 1886.   A. H. CROSBY, M D.

I have used your isinglass plasters the past year with great satisfaction.
Concord, N. H., May 22, 1886.   CHAS. R. WALKER, M. D,

CLINTON L. BRUCE: *Dear Sir*—Your plasters seem to me superior to anything of the kind I have ever used or seen.
Concord, N. H., May 21, 1886,   S. C. MORRILL, M. D.

CLINTON L. BRUCE: *Dear Sir*—I have used the plasters manufactured by you for several years and have found them satisfactory and reliable every time.
Suncook, N. H.   GEO. H. LARABEE, M. D.

CLINTON L. BRUCE: *Dear Sir*—I have used all kinds of Surgeon's adhesive plasters made by you in my practice for the past five years, and have always found them reliable ; prefer them to any other make.
Nashua, N. H.   GEO. H. WILBUR, M. D.

The preference, confidence and recommendations with which practioners and pharmacists continually favor Mr. Bruce are indeed gratifying and are fully appreciated, and they can be assured that his best efforts and energies will be vigilantly directed toward sustaining the reputation of his plasters.

NORTHERN INVESTMENT COMPANY.

George Leonard, President and General Agent; Alden A. Howe, Treasurer—Offices, Rooms 7 to 11 Advertiser Building, No. 246 Washington Street, Boston.

Investments in real estate, wisely made, make surer and better returns, on the whole, than any other, while those in choice city business sites, carefully selected, may be fairly pronounced the very cream of all investments. Certain prosperous eastern and western cities present magnificent opportunities of this kind, and it is to this class of investments that the Northern Investment Company confines its attention, eschewing mortgages with all their train of evils to both borrower and lender, and purchasing outright for cash at low prices, improving the property, and relying upon a regular income from rents than upon any other source for dividends, thus eliminating speculation (save in so far as that term may apply to natural increase of values—"unearned increment" as our single tax friends call it), law-suits, foreclosure proceedings and other expensive annoyances. This company was incorporated in 1890, authorized capital stock $20,000,000. The president is Mr. George Leonard, a practical real estate man of more than thirty-five years' experience, general agent of the Boston Investment Company and the Massachusetts Real Estate Company, and an expert whose integrity and sound judgment are recognized and conceded on all hands. Thomas Weston, the noted Boston counsellor, speaks of Mr. Leonard as a gentleman of great enterprise, energy and high personal character, "who has had large dealings in the purchase and sale of real estate, and upon whose judgment my clients and myself have been in the habit of relying, and I know of no man upon whose judgment I should place more confidence in matters pertaining to the value of real estate." Treasurer Alden A. Howe is a trained financier, with fifteen years' experience as cashier of the Quinsigamond National Bank of Worcester and the First National Bank of Grafton. The board of directors embraces, besides the gentlemen named, Messrs. W. A. Faulkner, president Traders' National Bank, Boston ; Charles W. Perkins, cashier Massachusetts National Bank, Boston ; George L. Joy, president Union Loan and Trust Company, Sioux City, Iowa, and A. L. Stetson of Sioux City, a man of large experience in real estate. Auditors — Lafayette Burr, treasurer National Dock and Warehouse

Company, Boston; John F. Howell, auditor of City of Worcester.   Clerk, John R. Allen; assistant clerk, Wm. Chaffee.   Attorney, Arthur M. Alger, ex-mayor of Taunton, Mass.   The company owns improved and unimproved real estate in Sioux City to the value (cash cost price) of one million eight hundred thousand dollars.   Regular dividends of six and one-half per cent. per annum are payable quarterly in February, May, August and November, at the Traders' National Bank, Boston.   Stockholders of the Boston Investment Company and the Massachusetts Real Estate Company are taking this stock with avidity.   They extend to the general public the opportunity to invest, and to them stock will be issued on receipt of their orders, accompanied by the cash, at the offices of the company, rooms 7, 8, 9, 10 and 11 Advertiser building, No. 246 Washington street, Boston, Mass., where intending investors and others interested are invited to call or address their communications.

RIDGWAY FURNACE COMPANY.

Manufacturers of the Ridgway Revolving Open Fire-Pot Furnace — No. 76 Union Street, Boston, Mass.

The Ridgway furnace has now been before the public for a number of years, subjected to the severest practical tests, and has proved itself the equal in all respects and in many the unapproached superior of any furnace ever designed

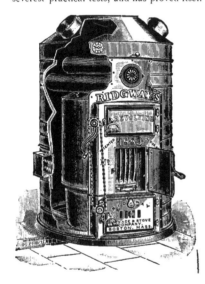

for similar purposes—the thorough, healthful and economical heating of residences, small factories, office buildings, etc. In open competition with the furnaces of other noted makers the Ridgway received the highest and only special award of the Massachusetts Charitable Mechanics' Association in 1884, and again in 1887 a special diploma from the same association for continued excellence. The drawbacks of the ordinary solid cast-iron fire-pot and of the brick-lined fire-pot are obvious and well known. In the case of the first it is difficult to maintain slow combustion without quenching the fire; the second is deficient in heating power, because the bricks, being nonconductors, impede the transmission of heat to the radiators, are easily broken and require frequent renewal, and the fire-pot, becoming covered with clinkers to a depth of several inches, is occasionally so reduced in interior dimensions as to render a satisfactory fire impossible. The revolving open fire-pot of the Ridgway furnace completely does away with these objections, and presents the following points of advantage: The fire-pot, being made in sections, allows of expansion and contraction without warping or cracking, as is the result where they are made in one solid piece. There is no sifting of ashes, as the combustion of the fuel is complete. The construction of the open fire-pot insures a naturally perfect combustion, which is impossible to obtain in a solid pot. The combustion is so perfect that neither clinkers nor gas result. The gases are burned on the sides of the pot near the radiator, as well as on the top. By revolving the fire-pot the ashes are shaken out without packing the coal, as is the case with the old method of shaking the grate, which necessitates the use of the poker through the grate to loosen it so the air can pass through to support combustion. In running a continuous low fire it is superior to all others. The putting on of fresh coal does not smother or retard the fire, as it burns out through the sides of the pot, gradually igniting the fresh coal, and consuming the gases as fast as generated, thereby saving a great waste of gas and the cooling of the furnace. There is no fire brick between the fire and the radiator to obstruct the passage of heat. The fire-pot being open (on the sides), the condition of the fire can be seen at a glance, and access had to every part of it. The grate can be dumped the same as in the ordinary furnace. In the portable furnaces the casing has a tin lining. An automatic regulator is furnished with every furnace, so sensitive that closing the registers will check the draft. Eight years' use with no visible wear proves its durability. The Ridgway Furnace Company is in possession of numberless testimonials from owners of these furnaces in eastern and central Massachusetts, all of which express unbounded satisfaction with the furnace and its workings, An illustrated descriptive pamphlet is mailed to any address upon application, and the furnace is exhibited and fully explained to those interested who will call at the company's office and salesrooms, No. 76 Union street, Boston, Mass.

INDEX TO
REPRESENTATIVE. HOUSES.

PAGE.

AMUSEMENTS.
Bates' Opera House, Attleboro, . 207
Marlboro (The) Theater, Marlboro, . 239
New Worcester Theater, Worcester, . 60

Architects.
Kingston, John P., Worcester, . . . 116
Patston & Lincoln, Worcester, . . . 52

Awl Manufacturers.
American Awl Co., Worcester, . . . 82

BADGE & CHARM MANUFACTURERS.
Streeter, C. E. & Co., Attleboro, . 206

Band Saw Machine Manufacturers.
Burgess, W. F. & Co., Worcester, . . 111

Banks—National.
Bristol County National, Taunton, . . 194
Central National, Worcester, . . . 78
Citizens' National, Worcester, . . . 56
City National, Worcester, ... 65
First National, Attleboro, ... 209
Franklin National, Franklin, . . . 161
North Attleboro National, N. Attleboro, 216
Worcester National, ... 41

Banks—Savings.
Attleboro Savings Bank, N. Attleboro, 218
Bristol County Savings Bank, Taunton, 184
Framingham Savings Bank, South
Framingham, ... 232
Mechanics Savings Bank, Lowell, . . 263
People's Savings Bank, Worcester, . 107
Worcester County Institution for Sav-
ings, Worcester, ... 54

Bicycles.
Holland & Havener, Worcester, . . 66

Boat Builders.
Coburn, A. A., Worcester, ... 98
Webb, Geo. E., Worcester, . . . 91

Boiler Works.
Allen, Wm. & Sons, Worcester, . 102
Flynn Boiler Works, Fall River, . . 174
Stewart Boiler Works, Worcester, . . 57

Bolt and Nut Manufacturers.
American Bolt Co., Lowell, . . 270–271

Boot and Shoe Machinery Manufacturers.
Adams, John J., Worcester, ... 84
Dustin & Clark, Spencer, ... 120

Boot and Shoe Manufacturers.
Athol Shoe Co., Athol, ... 159
Bacon & Sibley, Spencer, . . . 117
Bacon, Young & Co., Spencer, . . . 119
Hewitt, Chas. & Co., Taunton, . . 189
Green, J. & Co., Spencer, ... 117
Hill & Greene, Athol, ... 159
Jones, E. & Co., Spencer, . . . 119
Prouty, Isaac & Co., Spencer, . . 118
Smith, H. E. & Co., Worcester, . . 81
Valpey & Anthony Shoe Co., Leomin-
ster, ... 154

Bottlers.
Rock, Frank S., Marlboro, . . . 241

Box Manufacturer.
Cummings, F. G., Lowell, ... 268
Sproat, J. C., Taunton, ... 185

PAGE.

Braid Manufacturers.
Gold Medal Braid Co., Attleboro Falls, 225

Brass Founders.
Shaw, L. & Son, Worcester, . . . 88
Trefethen, D. A., Taunton, ... 292
Union Brass Foundry, Lowell, . . . 285

Builders' Supplies.
Metcalf, O. F. & Sons, Franklin, . . 165

Bunting Manufacturers.
New England Bunting Co., Lowell, . 281

Button Manufacturers.
Cushman, H. L. & Co., Taunton, . . 186

CARBONATED BEVERAGE MFR.
Hagar, Wm. S., Worcester, . . 110

Cap and Set Screw Manufacturers.
Smith, S. C. & G. H., Lowell, . . . 278

Card Clothing Manufacturers.
Stott, S. E. & T., Lowell, ... 282

Carpet Manufacturers.
Bigelow Carpet Co., Clinton, . . . 137
Worcester Carpet Co., Worcester, . . 55

Carriage Manufacturers.
Crandall, E. E., South Framing-
ham, ... 236–237
Fuller Carriage Co., Mansfield, . . . 226

Casket and Coffin Manufacturer.
Howard, Allen, Lowell, ... 277

Cassimere Manufacturers.
Ray's Woolen Co., Franklin, . . . 164

Chemists and Dye Works.
Talbot Dyewood and Chemical Co.,
Lowell, ... 267

Cigar Manufacturers.
Bristol Cigar Co., North Attleboro, . 216
Shattuck, M. E. & Co., Worcester, . 112
Shattuck, O. P., Worcester, ... 114

Civil Engineers and Surveyors.
Shedd & Sarle, Worcester, ... 96

Clothiers.
Bell Clothing Co., Worcester, . . . 47
Boston Clothing Co., Worcester, . . 93
Eames, D. H. & Co., Worcester, . . 113
Macullar & Son, Worcester, ... 50
McElroy & Cushman, Taunton, . . 184
Ware-Pratt Co., Worcester, . . . 68

Clothing Manufacturers.
Dighton Rock Pants Co., Taunton, . . 184
Ware-Pratt Co., Worcester, . . . 68
Worcester Pants Mfg. Co., ... 64

Conservatory of Music.
N. E. Conservatory of Music, Boston, 292

Coffin Plates, etc.
Eldridge & Co., Taunton, ... 185

Contractors and Builders.
Andrews, Henry K. W. & Son, Marl-
boro, ... 243
Darling Bros., Worcester, ... 52
Kingston, Geo., Worcester, ... 116
Norcross Brothers, Worcester, . . . 87
Pellett Bros., Worcester, ... 99
Warren, J. E. & Co., Marlboro, . . 242

PAGE.

Copper Manufacturers.
Taunton Copper Mfg. Co., Taunton, . 189
Copper and Sheet Iron Works.
Vanier & Slaterly, Attleboro, . . . 212
Wilson, D. H. & Co., Lowell, . 272–273
Corset Manufacturers.
Worcester Corset Co., ... 51
Cotton Mills.
Elizabeth Poole Mills, Taunton, . . 182
Laurel Lake Mills, Fall River, . . . 175
Narragansett Mills, Fall River, . . . 173
Osborn Mills, Fall River, ... 177
Whittier Cotton Mills, Lowell, . . . 278
Cotton Mill Machinery.
Draper, George & Sons, Hopedale, . 145
Cotton Yarn Manufacturers.
Canoe River Mills, Taunton, . . . 197
Orswell Mills, Fitchburg, ... 135
Cotton Warp and Twine Manufacturers.
Fitchburg Cotton Mill, Fitchburg, . . 127
Wyoming Mills, Fall River, ... 178
Croquet Manufacturers.
Merrimack Croquet Co., Lowell, . . 275
Crucible Manufacturers.
Phœnix Mfg. Co., Taunton, ... 186
Cutlery Manufacturers.
Robinson, G. A., W. Mansfield, . . 227
Mason, H. H., Worcester, ... 96
DENTIST.
Kendrick, F. H., Worcester, . . 113
Desk Manufacturers.
Union Desk Co., Leominster, . . . 152
Dies—Manufacturers.
Beaudry, T. J., Marlboro, ... 239
Marlboro Die Co., ... 248
Door Check and Spring.
Norton Door Check and Spring Co., Boston,
Dress Goods Manufacturers. [283
Parkhill Mfg. Co., Fitchburg, . . . 125
Drill Manufacturers.
Burnham, Geo. & Co., Worcester, . . 58
Snyder, J. E., Worcester, ... 103
Drop Forgings Manufacturers.
Speirs, J. C. & Co. Worcester, . . . 86
Drugs and Chemicals.
Borden & Remington, Fall River, . . 178
Dry Goods.
Denholm & McKay Co., Worcester, . 106
Duck Manufacturers.
Fitchburg Duck Mills, Fitchburg, . . 131
Dyers.
Attleboro Dye Works, Attleboro, . . 201
Whitney & Molt, Millbury, ... 156
ELASTIC WEB MANUFACTURERS.
Harriman Bros., Lowell, ... 282
Electricians—Manufacturers.
Clemons, M. E., Attleboro, ... 209
Smith Electric Co., Attleboro, . . . 204
Electro-platers.
Bonnett, John P., North Attleboro, . 220
Smith, C. E. & Bro., Attleboro, . . 208
Enamelers.
Maintien, John B., Plainville, . . . 229
Endowment Order.
Non-Secret Endowment Order, Worcester, ... 100
Engine Builders.
Burgess, W. F. & Co., Worcester, . . 111

PAGE.

FELT GOODS MANUFACTURERS.
City Mills Co., Franklin, ... 163
Felt Manufacturers.
Lowell Felting Mills, Lowell, . . . 276
Fertilizer Manufacturers.
Jefferds, John G., Worcester, . . . 50
File Manufacturers.
Fitchburg File Works, Fitchburg, . . 135
Webster File Works, Taunton, . . . 198
Filters—Manufacturers.
Ellis Filter Co., Marlboro, ... 240
Fire Appliances.
Worcester Fire Appliance Co., (The)
Worcester, ... 105
Fire Arms Manufacturers.
Johnson, Iver & Co., Worcester, . . 72
Fire Brick and Stove Lining Mfrs.
Dighton Stove Lining Co., Dighton, . 199
French & Winslow, Taunton, . . . 192
Presbrey Stove Lining Co., Taunton, . 191
Taunton Stove Lining Co., Taunton, . 192
Union Stove Lining Co., Taunton, . . 182
Williams Stove Lining Co., Taunton, 192
Flavoring Extracts, etc.
Lyon, N. U., Fall River, ... 178
Sargeant, S. M., Oakham, ... 157
Flour, Hay, Grain, etc.
Hancock, T. E. & Co., North Attleboro, 215
Metcalf, O. F. & Sons, Franklin, . . 165
Funeral Directors and Embalmers.
Rogers, John F., Lowell, ... 271
Furniture, Carpets, etc.
Hancock, T. E. & Co., North Attleboro, 215
GINGHAM MANUFACTURERS.
Fitchburg Mfg. Co., Fitchburg, . 135
Lancaster (The) Mills, Clinton, . . 139
Parkhill Mfg. Co., Fitchburg, . . . 125
Whittenton Mfg. Co., Taunton, . . 188
Furnace Manufacturers.
Ridgway Furnace Co., Boston, . . . 286
Glue Manufacturers.
Jonathan Holt & Co., Lowell, . . . 269
Gold and Silver Refiners.
Slade & Whipple, Attleboro, . . . 203
Goring Manufacturers.
Lowell Goring Works, Lowell, . . 265
Grain Bags, Twine, etc.
Franklin Cotton Co., Franklin, . . . 164
Granite and Marble Cutters.
Gumb, Lewis D., Lowell, ... 282
Granite Quarries.
Milford Pink Granite Co., Milford, . . 140
Sherman, T. N. & Co., Milford, . . 143
Grist and Planing Mills.
Cargill, E. S., North Attleboro, . . . 219
Groceries—Wholesale.
Hancock, T. E. & Co., North Attleboro, 215
Harness Manufacturers.
Newhall, Geo. N. & Co., Worcester, . 40
HATTERS, TAILORS, ETC.
McElroy & Cushman, Taunton, . 184
Horse Blankets, etc.
Ray Fabric Co., Franklin, ... 164
Horse Clippers.
Coates' Clipper Mfg. Co., Worcester, . 97
Hotels.
American House, Fitchburg, . . . 127
Bay State House, Worcester, . . . 82

PAGE.

Briggs House, Attleboro, ... 207
Brunswick, (The) Worcester,   .   .   . 111
Central House, Ashland, ... 286
City Hotel, Marlboro, ... 240–241
City Hotel, Taunton.   193
Fitchburg Hotel, Fitchburg, ... 125
Gleason House, ... 245–246
Hotel Parker, Worcester, ... 72
Hotel William, Milford, ... 142
Hotel Winthrop, South Framingham, 237
International House, North Attleboro, 215
Lake View House, Worcester,   .   .   . 91
Leominster Hotel, Leominster,   .   . 153
Lincoln House, Worcester, ... 61
Mansion House, Milford, ... 143
Massasoit House, Spencer,   .   .   . 120
Mellen House, Fall River, ... 175
Old Washington Tavern, Lowell,   .   . 267
Opera-house Hotel and Café, Attleboro, 208
Park Hotel, Attleboro, ... 211
St. Charles Hotel, Lowell,   .   . 261–262
Waldo House, Worcester, ... 64
Whitney House, Westborough,   .   .   . 154
Windsor House, Marlboro,   .   . 246–247
Hot Water Heaters, etc.
Foxboro Foundry and Machine Co.,
    Foxboro, ... 166

INSIDE WOODWORK, ETC.
    Hatch, W. E., Lowell, ... 271
    Jones, Irving E., Milford,   .   .   . 143
    Sturtevant & Galer, Lowell,   .   .   . 264
Insurance—Life.
State Mutual Assurance Company of
    Worcester, ... 42
Investment Company.
    Northern Investment Co., Boston,   . 285
Iron and Steel.
    Blake, Boutwell & Co., Worcester,   . 73
    Congdon, Carpenter & Co., Fall River, 177
    Pratt & Inman, Worcester,   .   .   . 90
Iron Foundries.
    Doherty Bros., Lowell, ... 280
Iron Planers.
    Wheeler, J. S. & Co., Worcester,   . 46

JERSEY CLOTH, ETC.
    Franklin Knitting Co., Franklin,   . 165
    Pero Prespey, Worcester,   .   .   . 99
Jewelers.
    Davis, Nelson H., Worcester,   .   . 59
    Frost, Chas. H., Lowell,   .   .   . 265
Jewelers' Findings—Manufacturers.
    Copeland, J. O. & Co., North Attleboro, 213
    Olney, S. W., Plainville, ... 228
    Robinson Brothers, Plainville,   .   . 227
Jewelers' Machinery Manufacturers.
    Walcott (The) Mfg. Co., North Attle-
    boro, ... 214
Jewelry Manufacturers.
    Anthony, John, Attleboro,   .   .   . 208
    Barrows, H. F. & Co., North Attleboro, 216
    Bates & Bacon, Attleboro,   :   .   . 210
    Bates Button Co., Attleboro,   .   . 208
    Blackinton, R. & Co., North Attleboro, 218
    Blackinton, V. H. & Co., Attleboro
    Falls, ... 221
    Blackinton, W. & S., Attleboro,   . 206
    Bliss, A. H. & Co., North Attleboro,   . 217
    Briggs, D. F. Co. (The), Attleboro,   . 212
    Bugbee & Niles, North Attleboro,   . 217

PAGE.

Bushee, A. & Co., Attleboro,   .   .   . 204
Cheever, J. G. & Co., North Attleboro, 214
Codding Bros., North Attleboro,   .   . 221
Co-operative Mfg. Jewelers, N. Attle-
    boro, ... 221
Cutler & Lull, North Attleboro,   .   . 219
Dean, G. A. & Co., Attleboro,   .   .   . 202
Demarest & Brady, North Attleboro,   . 218
Draper, O. M., North Attleboro,   .   . 215
Ellis, Livsey & Co., Attleboro,   .   . 211
Fisher, W. D. & Co., Attleboro Falls, 223
Freeman, B. S. & Co., Attleboro Falls, 225
Healey Bros., North Attleboro,   .   . 213
Horton, Angell & Co., Attleboro,   .   . 204
Inman, J. T. & Co., Attleboro,   .   . 203
Jenney, E. V., North Attleboro,   .   . 213
Lincoln, Bacon & Co., Plainville,   .   . 228
Lyons, C. D. & Co., Mansfield,   .   . 226
MacDonald, R. B., Attleboro,   .   .   . 207
Mason Jewelry Co., Attleboro Falls,   . 222
Pennington, L. W., Worcester,   .   . 94
Plainville Stock Co., Plainville,   .   . 228
Richards, J. J. & J. M., N. Attleboro, 222
Richards' Mfg. Co., Attleboro,   .   .   . 205
Sadler, F. H., Attleboro, ... 210
Sandland, Capron & Co., N. Attleboro, 213
Sandland, E. C. & Co., N. Attleboro, 217
Schilling, August, North Attleboro,   . 214
Shepardson, F. L. & Co., N. Attleboro, 214
Short, Nerney & Co., Attleboro,   .   . 206
Simmons, R. F. & Co., Attleboro Falls, 222
Sadler, F. H. & Co., Attleboro,   .   . 210
Stanley Bros., Attleboro Falls,   .   . 222
Streeter Bros., Attleboro, ... 203
Sturdy, J. F. & Sons, Attleboro Falls, 223
Wade, Davis & Co., Plainville,   .   . 229
Weaver, F. W. & Co., Attleboro,   .   . 225
Wetherell, C. A. & Co., Attleboro,   . 211
Wilmarth, Holmes & Co., Attleboro,   . 210
Wilmarth, W. H. & Co., Attleboro,   . 202
Witherell, P. E., Attleboro,   .   .   . 205
Young & Stern, North Attleboro,   .   . 220

KNITTING MILLS.
    Excelsior Knitting Mills, Lowell,   . 280
    Shaw Stocking Co., Lowell,   . 255–256
LADIES' UNDERWEAR MFRS.
    Burns, Wm. H. & Co., Worcester, 86
Last Manufacturers.
    Auburn (The) Last Co., South Fram-
    ingham, ... 233
    Marlboro Last Co., Marlboro,   .   . 292
    Porter & Gardiner, Worcester,   .   . 71
Lathe Manufacturers.
    Waymoth, A. D. & Co., Fitchburg,   . 134
Laundries.
    Bay State Laundry, Worcester,   .   . 115
    Cook, C. B., Laundry Co., Worcester, 71
    Scripture's Laundry, Lowell,   .   . 257
Leather Colorers and Dealers.
    Billings, Frank, Marlboro,   .   . 247–248
Leather Specialties.
    Eames, George H., South Framingham, 236
    Warren, J. J. Co., Worcester,   .   . 44
Linen Manufacturers.
    Stevens (The) Linen Co., Webster,   . 158
Lithographers.
    Forbes Lith. Mfg. Co., Boston,   .   .
    2d and 4th pages cover.

PAGE.

Livery Stables.
Bennett, F. A., Fitchburg, ... 126
Draper, C. H., Worcester, ... 45
Harrub Stable, Taunton, ... 187
Haskill, John F., Milford, ... 142
Heelon, P. H., Lowell, ... 263
Hildreth, C. H., 2d, Worcester, . . 75
Kendrick, Geo. P. & Co., Worcester, . 116
Kirby, Chas. & Co., Fall River, . . 176
Narragansett Stable, Fall River, . . 178
Willard, Noah, Marlboro, ... 240
Loom Builders.
Crompton Loom Works, Worcester, . 62
Knowles' Loom Works, Worcester, . 48
Steel, Albert H., (narrow fabrics) Wor-
cester, ... 60
Lumber Dealers.
Cargill, E. S., North Attleboro, . . 219
Davis & Sargent, Lowell, . . 266-267
Priest (Chas. A.) Lumber Co., Fitch-
burg, ... 133
Sanders & Buffington, Taunton, . . 195
Stone, E. E. & Co., Spencer, . . . 168
Williams, A. G. & Co., Taunton, . . 194
MACHINE KNIVES—MFRS.
Hardy, L. & Co., Worcester, . . 108
Coes, L. & Co., Worcester, ... 93
Machinery Agent.
Clark, Jeremiah, Lowell, ... 277
Machinery Manufacturers.
Johnson & Bassett, Worcester, . . . 77
Knapp, Joel & Son, Lowell, . . . 268
Machine Screw Manufacturers.
Winslow & Curtis Machine Screw Co.,
Worcester, ... 54
Machinists.
Barnett, W., Attleboro Falls, . . . 223
Brown, Wm. H., Worcester, . . . 78
Cady, Geo. L., Lowell, ... 281
Doherty Bros., Lowell, ... 280
Kilburn, Lincoln & Co., Fall River, . 177
Knight, E. O., Worcester, ... 90
Mann, F. W., Milford, ... 144
Putnam Machine Co., Fitchburg, . . 131
Sawyer, Ezra, Worcester, ... 104
Sawyer, Jos. A. & Son, Worcester, . 101
Stevens, B. F., Lowell, ... 273
Strange's Machine Works, Taunton, . 187
Young, W. C. & Co., Worcester, . . 92
Magazine Air Rifles—Manufacturers.
Warren, J. J. Co., Worcester, . . . 45
Malleable Iron Works.
Arcade Malleable Iron Works, Worces-
ter, ... 3d page cover.
Worcester Malleable Iron Works, Wor-
cester, ... 3d page cover.
Marble and Granite Works.
Andrews & Wheeler, Lowell, . . . 257
Boston Marble and Granite Co., Wor-
cester, ... 56
Burt, D. Arthur & Co., Taunton, . . 197
Evans & Co., Worcester, . . . 85
Mattress Manufacturer.
Hapgood, E. & Son, Lowell, . . . 280
Ware, M. B., Worcester, ... 81
Mechanical Engineers.
Middlesex Machine Co., Lowell, . . 265
Medicinal and Surgical Plaster Mfr.
Bruce, Clinton L., Lowell, . . 284-285

PAGE.

Mill Spools.
Murdock, William, Winchendon, ,. . 151
Mill Supplles.
Sumner Pratt & Co., Worcester, . . 76
Moulding Manufacturers.
Clark Moulding Works, Worcester, . 95
NEATSFOOT OIL MFRS.
Hargraves Mfg. Co., Fall River, . 176
Nickel Platers.
Taunton Nickel Plating Co., Taunton, 190
Nuts and Screws.
McCloud, Crane & Minter, Worcester, 105
OIL EXTRACTOR.
Sawin, J. J., Worcester, ... 65
Oils.
Borden & Remington, Fall River, . . 178
Howe, G. S. & A. J., Worcester, . . 104
Worcester Oil Works, Worcester, . . 112
Organ Manufacturers.
Ingalls, G. W. & Co., Worcester, . . 97
Mason & Risch, Worcester, ... 73
PACKING BOX MFRS.
Greenwood, S. A., Careyville, . . 167
Longley, E. F., Marlboro, ... 246
Pads, Polishing Felts and Rubber Linings.
Waite's Felting Mills, Franklin, . . 165
Pails and Packages.
Brown's (Wm.) Sons, Winchendon, . 152
Painters' and Masons' Supplies.
Borden & Remington, Fall River, . . 178
Paper Box Manufacturers.
Babcock, A. H., Attleboro, ... 210
Frank & Duston, Marlboro, ... 243
Humphrey, C. W., Worcester, . . . 76
Paper Manufacturers.
Lincoln, L. & Co., Dighton, . . . 199
Paper Mill Appliances.
Davis, Ezekiel, Fitchburg, ... 136
Photographers.
Blair, C. L., Worcester, ... 108
Physicians.
Solomon, W. B. (Dr.), Fall River, . 174
Pleasure Resorts.
Eyrie (The), Worcester, ... 114
Plow Manufacturers.
Ames Plow Co., Worcester, ... 108
Plumbers and Gas Fitters.
Vanier & Slaterly, Attleboro, . . . 212
Wilson, D. H. & Co., Lowell, . 272-273
Pork Packers.
White, Pevey & Dexter Co., Worcester, 57
Pump Manufacturers.
Burgess, W. F. & Co., Worcester, . . 111
Printers.
Chase, Samuel M., Lowell, ... 269
Felt, W. E. W., Worcester, . . . 70
Glidden, H. F., Lowell, ... 292
Kirschner, J. & Sons, Worcester, . . 103
Private Sanitarium.
Highlands (The), Winchendon, . . 149
Proprietary Medicines.
Ayer, J. C. Co., Lowell, ... 259
Moxie Nerve Food Co., Lowell, . . 266
REED FURNITURE, ETC.,
Converse, M. E. & Co., Winchendon, 148
New England Rattan Co., South Fram-
ingham, ... 234-235
Refrigerators—Manufacturers.
Atherton, F. A., Worcester, ... 67

PAGE.

Rock Drill Manufacturers.
  Burleigh Rock Drill Co., Fitchburg, . 129
Roll Coverers, etc.
  Tripp, John & Co., Lowell, ... 264
SADDLERY HARDWARE.
  Newhall, Geo. N. & Co., Worcester, 40
Safe Deposit Companies.
  State Safe Deposit Co., Worcester, . 43
Sanitary Engineer.
  Davey, Peter B., Marlboro, ... 241
Sash Rod Fixtures—Manufacturers.
  Fowler & Company, Worcester, . . 84
Saw Manufacturers.
  Simonds Mfg. Co., Fitchburg, . . . 126
Saw Mill Manufacturers.
  Lovell (F. S.) Machine Co., Fitchburg, 132
Scale Manufacturers.
  Knowles Scale Works, Lowell, . . 274
  Lowell Scale Co., Lowell, ... 262
Sewer and Drain Pipe.
  Borden & Remington, Fall River, . . 178
Shear Manufacturers.
  New England Shear Mf'y, Worcester, 110
Shinglers.
  Taylor Roof Shingling Co., Lowell, . 279
Shirt Manufacturers.
  D'Allaird, Geo. J., Fitchburg, . . . 134
Shoddy Manufacturers.
  Ray's Woolen Co., Franklin, . . . 164
Shoe Machinery, etc.
  Davey, John F., Marlboro, ... 242
  Wood & Willard, Marlboro, . . 245
Shoe Racks, Boot Trees, etc.
  Sumner, C. A., Milford, ... 141
Shuttles and Shuttle Irons.
  Dudley, D. T. & Son, Wilkinsonville, 156
Silver Platers.
  Stuart, John T. & Co., Marlboro, . . 247
Silverware Manufacturers.
  Reed & Barton, Taunton, ... 181
  Reed, Barton & Co., Taunton, . . . 191
  West Silver Co., Taunton, ... 183
Skate Manufacturers.
  Winslow Skate Mfg. Co., Worcester, . 53
Soap Manufacturers.
  Dickinson, W. A., Lowell, . . 269–270
  Whithed, Darius, Lowell, ... 272
Society Goods Manufacturers.
  Blackinton, V.H. & Co., Attleboro Falls, 221
  Mason, F. & Co., Attleboro Falls, . . 222
Spindles, Shuttle Irons, etc.
  Westcott, A. A. & Sons, Hopedale, . 147
Stamps, Stencils, etc.
  Cooper, S. G., Lowell, ... 263
  Parsons & Mealey, Lowell, ... 271
Starch—Wholesale.
  Borden & Remington, Fall River, . . 178
Steam Boiler Manufacturers.
  Lowell Steam Boiler Works, . . . 261
  Ready, James, Lowell, ... 262
Steam Engine Builders.
  Brown, C. H. & Co., Fitchburg, . . 128
  Fitchburg Steam Engine Co., Fitchburg, 124
  Lowell Tool and Engine Co., . . . 279
Steam, Gas and Water Fitters, etc.
  Davey, Peter B., Marlboro, ... 241
  Sweet & Tucker, Taunton, ... 189
Stocking Manufacturers.
  Shaw Stocking Co., Lowell, . . 255–256

PAGE.

Stone Ware Manufacturers.
  Wright, F. T. & Son, Taunton, . . . 193
Stove Lining Manufacturers.
  Dighton Stove Lining Co., Dighton, . 199
Stove, Range, etc., mfrs.
  Co-operative Stove Co., North Dighton, 200
  New England Stove Co., Taunton, . 182
  Taunton Iron Works, Taunton, - . . 195
  Thomas, Oscar G., Taunton, . . . 195
Suspender Manufacturers.
  Harriman Bros., Lowell, ... 282
TACK MANUFACTRERS.
  Somers, E. J., Worcester, . . . 66
  Somers, P. E., Worcester, ... 104
Tailors—Merchant.
  Ware Bros., Lowell, ... 269
Textile Machinery.
  Parker (J. B.) Machine Co., Clinton, 137
Tinware Manufacturers.
  Wilde, S. A. Mfg. Co., Taunton, . . 188
Tool Manufacturers.
  Piper & Bosworth, Winchendon, . . 149
Tool and Engine Manufacturers.
  Lowell Tool and Engine Co., Lowell, 279
Trunk Manufacturers.
  Lowell Trunk Manufactory, Lowell, . 257
Trust Company.
  Old Colony Trust Company, Boston, . 280
Turbine Wheel Manufacturers.
  Swain Turbine and Manufacturing Co.,
    Lowell, ... 260–261
Twist Drill Manufacturers.
  New Process Twist Drill Co., Taunton, 190
WALL PAPER AND SHADES.
  Hancock & Co., N. Attleboro, 215
Watch Case Manufacturers.
  Bates & Bacon, Attleboro, ... 210
White Lustral Wire Ware Manufacturers.
  Woods, Sherwood & Co., Lowell, . . 256
Wire Cloth Manufacturers.
  Clinton Wire Cloth Co., Clinton, . . 139
  Wright & Colton Wire Cloth Co., Wor. 83
Wire Goods Manufacturers.
  Dean, Henry E. & Co., Worcester, . 79
  Wire Goods Co. (The), Worcester, . 115
Wire Manufacturers.
  Spencer Wire Co., Spencer, ... 168
  Washburn & Moen Mfg. Co., Wor. 27
Woodworking Machinery.
  Goodspeed, G. N., Winchendon, . . 151
  Strange's Machine Works, Taunton, . 187
  Streeter, Alvin, Winchendon, . . . 150
Woolen Machinery.
  Harwood & Quincy Machine Co., Wor. 109
Woolen Waste.
  Chase, John & Sons, Webster, . . . 157
Woolen Yarn Manufacturers.
  Bradford Yarn Mill, East Brookfield, . 200
  Capron, Chas. C., Medway, ... 167
  Crook Brothers, South Wrentham, . . 167
  Monoosnock Mill, Leominster, . . . 153
Worsted Machinery Supplies.
  Gee, Chas. E., Lowell, ... 283
Worsted Manufacturers.
  Beoli Mills, Fitchburg, ... 136
  Leominster Worsted Co., Leominster, 153
  Lowell Worsted Mills, Lowell, . . . 281
Wrench Manufacturers.
  Coes Wrench Co., Worcester, . . . 80

ONE OF NEW ENGLAND'S MOST WIDELY KNOWN EDUCATIONAL INSTITUTIONS.

The Oldest of its Kind in America—The Largest in the World.

FOUNDED BY DR. EBEN TOURJEE.   CARL FAELTEN, DIRECTOR.

The Institution is conducted by a board of fifty trustees, and solely for the public good. It is commended no less highly by the extent and importance of its past achievements than by the following factors of its present estate, to wit:—

An Enviable Location in Boston, America's Great Art Center — A Thorough Organization and Most Complete General Equipment—A Large and Eminent Corps of Teachers—Splendid Facilities for Imparting Instruction—Systematic and Comprehensive Courses of Study—Many and Valuable Free Collateral Advantages—A Safe and Inviting Home for Lady Pupils—The Assurance of an Ever Increasing Success.

Over 40,000 of its pupils have already gone out to multiply its influences for good, and **the demand for its graduates is far in excess of the supply.**

SYSTEMATIC INSTRUCTION is given in all departments of Music, Elocution, the Fine Arts, General Literature and Languages, and Piano and Organ Tuning, by the ablest American and European artists and teachers, and in **Class or Private Lessons** as desired.

The *"HOME"* supplies every needed comfort and safeguard, being under the immediate supervision of the Director, Preceptress, Resident Physician and Lady Assistants. The entire building is heated by steam and lighted by electricity.

Terms reasonable. Tuition, $5 to $30 per term of ten weeks. Living expense, including board and room, $5 to $8.50 per week.

Full information may be secured by calling at the Institution, or through its **ILLUSTRAT-ED CALENDER, S**ent Free on application to

FRANK W. HALE, General Manager,

Franklin Square, Boston, Mass.

CENTRAL EDITION.

Inland
MASSACHUSETTS

HOOSAC.

THE Elstner Pub. Co. Publishers, Worcester, Mass.

ILLUSTRATED.

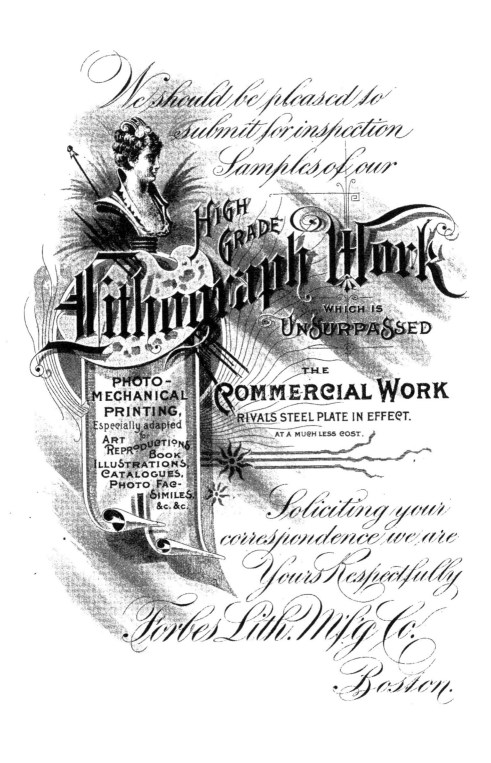

WORCESTER MALLEABLE IRON WORKS,

GEO. B. BUCKINGHAM, Proprietor,

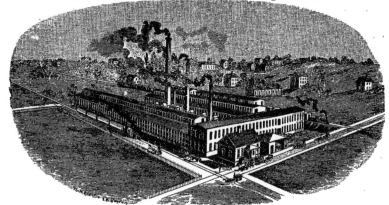

MANUFACTURER OF

Refined Malleable Iron and Steel Castings

OF THE FINEST QUALITY, TO ORDER.

WORCESTER, MASS.

ESTABLISHED 1850.

ARCADE MALLEABLE IRON CO.,

WARREN McFARLAND & CO.

MALLEABLE IRON AND STEEL CASTINGS,

CHILLED ROLLS, RETORTS, &c.

63, 65 & 67 Washington Square, opposite Union Passenger Station,

GEO. B. BUCKINGHAM, Proprietor.

WORCESTER, MASS.

Forbes Lithograph Mfg. Co.

FINE COLOR AND COMMERCIAL WORK.

Reproductions by the Albertype Process.

Home Office: BOSTON, 181 Devonshire St.

Works at CHELSEA

Branch Offices:

NEW YORK, { 1 West 25th St. / 280 Broadway.

PHILADELPHIA, 529 Arch St.

BALTIMORE, 16 Post Office Ave.

CHICAGO, 21 Wabash Ave.

SAN FRANCISCO, 109 California St.

PROVIDENCE, R.I. 55 Westminster St.

Lightning Source UK Ltd.
Milton Keynes UK
UKHW010008090219

336872UK00005B/159/P